COMMANDO
DESPATCH RIDER

By the same author

Marine Commando, Sicily and Salerno 1943
with 41 Royal Marines Commando, Robert Hale Ltd 1988,
re-issued in paperback 1994.

They Did What Was Asked of Them,
41 (Royal Marines) Commando 1942–1946
Firebird Books, reprinted 1996.

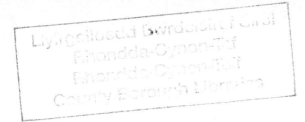
COMMANDO DESPATCH RIDER

WITH 41 ROYAL MARINES COMMANDO IN NORTH-WEST EUROPE 1944–1945

by

RAYMOND MITCHELL

WITH A FOREWORD BY
MAJOR GENERAL JULIAN THOMPSON
CB, OBE

LEO COOPER

First published in Great Britain 2001 by
LEO COOPER
an imprint of Pen & Sword Books
47 Church Street
Barnsley
South Yorkshire S70 2AS

Copyright © 2001 by Raymond Mitchell
ISBN 0 85052 797 X

A CIP catalogue record for this book is
available from the British Library.

Typeset in 11/13pt Sabon by
Phoenix Typesetting, Ilkley, West Yorkshire.
Printed and bound by
CPI UK

Dedicated to the memory of

Ply/X 111113 Marine H.T.W.B. (Bill) SWINDALE
No. 41 (Royal Marines) Commando

Killed in Action, 6 June 1944
Lion-sur-Mer, Normandy

a fellow 'Geordie' and good friend

CONTENTS

FOREWORD

by
MAJOR GENERAL JULIAN THOMPSON
CB OBE

Before Ray Mitchell reached the age of 24 he had taken part in four of the major Allied amphibious assaults of the Second World War: Sicily, Salerno, Normandy and Walcheren, all with 41 (Royal Marines) Commando. This book is about the latter two; his experiences in the first two operations are the subject of an earlier book, *Marine Commando: Sicily and Salerno 1943 with 41 Royal Marines Commando*. His latest book is more than just an account of the great events of June and November 1944, it is also a marine's eye view of the campaign in North-West Europe.

Ray Mitchell kept a diary, which, for security reasons, was forbidden. This, now lodged in the Imperial War Museum, is the basis for his new book. As an author who has spent much time researching in the archives of the Imperial War Museum, I can vouch for the value of books based on diaries written at the time. Time can play tricks with even the sharpest of memories and Ray Mitchell's book is all the more valuable as a testimony to one Royal Marine's experiences because he can refer to his diaries as a back-up to his recall of events.

Anyone not familiar with commando soldiering might regard being a despatch rider (DR – or Dog Roger in the phonetic alphabet of the time) as a 'cushy number'. Starting with landing on Sword Beach on D-Day carrying a 75 lb Welbike (folding motorcycle) in his arms, down the see-sawing wooden landing plank of one of the infamous Landing Craft Infantry (Small), Ray Mitchell's experiences as a DR varied from 'hairy' to 'hilarious', mostly the former.

ix

A DR's life was both lonely and dangerous. Carrying despatches necessitates knowing exactly where you are going and how to get there, including avoiding any route that will lead you straight into enemy hands, all of which requires good map-reading. Road and tracks were usually pinpointed on the enemy's map and treated to frequent doses of artillery and mortar fire. If that was not enough, 'friendly' traffic was an added hazard. DRs were, of course, also required to take their place as riflemen from time to time.

Churchill wrote about the Westkapelle operations at Walcheren, 'The extreme gallantry of the Royal Marines stands forth'. Ray Mitchell was one of the Commando DRs selected to land with his comrades of the 4th Special Service Brigade to capture the five great batteries of coastal guns guarding the entrance to the River Scheldt. He recalls that, in contrast to Normandy five months earlier, 'The task force had been put ashore, and all craft still seaworthy had been withdrawn. There would be no streams of supplies, no back-up, no reinforcements: the Brigade was on its own'. The only way off the saucer-shaped island, whose centre had been deliberately flooded, was by silencing the batteries sited on its sand-dune rim, a costly and hazardous operation.

In 'normal' circumstances 'man proposes, God disposes'. In battle it is the other way around, 'God', in the form of the higher command, may propose the strategy, but the outcome will ulti- mately depend upon what someone called the most exclusive club in the world: the relatively small number of those who do the actual fighting. The Royal Marines Commandos occupy a special corner of that club. This is a fascinating account of the second part of one marine's very busy war in that company.

GLOSSARY

Ack-ack	*Anti-aircraft*, from early signaller's spelling code for radio or telephone – e.g. 'A' for *Ack*, 'B' for *Beer*, 'C' for *Charlie*, etc., and was applied to both the guns and to the bursting shells.
ADS	Advanced Dressing Station – the next stop for a casualty after he had been 'patched up' at his Unit's RAP (qv).
AMGOT	Allied Military Government of Occupied Territories
AVRE	Armoured Vehicle, Royal Engineers, basically a Churchill heavy tank but specifically adapted for attacking reinforced concrete fortifications. Its primary armament was a 290mm spigot mortar which hurled a 40-pound missile, known as a 'flying dustbin', a distance of some 80 yards.
AWOL	Absent Without Official Leave.
Bangalore Torpedo	A six-foot length of 2½ inch diameter steel tubing packed with explosive, used for blowing a gap in barbed wire and detonating mines. Two or more could be fixed together and pushed forward to deal with broad defences.
Benghazi Cooker	Metal container, such as a biscuit tin, partially filled with sand which would be doused with petrol and set alight to heat water for a 'brew up' (qv).
Blighty one	A wound that was severe enough to get a serviceman sent back to the UK – or *Blighty*,

	a corruption of the Hindi word *bilayati*, meaning *foreign*.
Bren (Gun)	A Light Machine Gun (LMG) named from the first two letters of the Czechoslovakian town *Brno* where it originated and *Enfield* where it was later manufactured – 0.303 inch/7.65mm calibre.
Brew-up	1. Make a brew of tea. 2. A tank bursting into flames after being hit by a shell.
Buffalo	Common name for a *Landing Vehicle Tracked*, (*LVT*) qv.
Burton (Gone for a . . .)	Been killed. Originating in the RAF, as the medical centre for new intakes in Blackpool was set up in the former premises of *Burton the Tailor*.
Buzz	Naval term for 'rumour', hence *buzzmonger*, one who spreads them.
CCS	Casualty Clearing Station – the primary function of which was to ensure that all casualties were fully documented.
Compo	'Composite'. The standard Field Rations of WWII. All the creature needs for fourteen Service Personnel for one day – tinned food, cigarettes (seven per person per day), confectionery and toilet paper – were packed in stout hardboard boxes and labelled 'A' to 'E', according to the food content.
CS	Continuous Service. The usual name for a 'regular' Royal Marine as opposed to an HO (qv).
D-Day	The day on which any planned military operation was to be initiated, now synonymous with 6 June 1944 – the biggest one of WWII.
Dead ground	Any area which lay below the line of enemy small arms fire (qv) and was therefore safe from that form of attack.
Dhobying	Washing clothes – in the Indian Army a *dhobi* was a washerwoman.

Dog Tags	Identity discs, two in number and of different shapes, stamped with the bearer's Name, Regimental Number and Religion. All Service personnel were required to wear them around their necks and, if killed, one was snipped off for the records, while the other would identify the dead man.
Dripping	Naval term for grumbling, hence *Dripper*.
DUKW (Duck)	Amphibious wheeled vehicle, being the factory coding of the manufacturer, General Motors, D=1942, U=Amphibious, K=all-wheel drive, W=dual rear axles; naturally, they were known as 'ducks'.
Eighty-eight	German gun of 88mm calibre, originally designed as an anti-aircraft weapon but quickly to become their most effective general artillery piece – most especially as an SP (qv).
Erk	Slang term for an aircraftman, possibly derived from 'erg' the unit of work or energy in physics (i.e. a force of one dyne acting through a distance of one centimetre).
False Beach	A submerged sandbank on which a landing craft could ground, forcing the attacking troops to wade or swim ashore.
FDL	Forward Defended Locality – the 'Front Line', when there isn't a continuous line of trenches, as there was in WWI, denoting the boundary of territory held by a military formation.
Flak	Anti-aircraft fire, arising from the initial letters of 'anti-aircraft gun' in German – *Flieger Abwehr Kanone*.
FOB	Forward Officer Bombardment. A Royal Navy Officer who landed with a Military Unit to call for, and direct, naval gunfire when required.
FOO	Forward Observation Officer. A Royal Artillery Officer who was the Army equivalent of an FOB. The arrival of FOB and FOO

	personnel was a clear indication that a Unit would soon be going into action.
Gunga Din	The name of Rudyard Kipling's fictitious water carrier, which was applied to the Unit water truck, and also to its driver.
Head or Heads	The naval term for toilet, going back to the days of sail when the only facilities were lavatory seats fitted outboard near the bows or *head* of the vessel.
H-Hour	The precise time when any military operation was to be initiated.
HO	Hostilities Only. Term applied to a Royal Marine who had enlisted, 'For the duration of the present emergency' as opposed to a CS (qv).
Jeep	American General Purpose (i.e. 'Gee P') vehicle.
Jerrican	German-designed petrol can holding 20 litres (4½ gallons), the design was unashamedly filched from the Jerries.
LCA	Landing Craft Assault, 41ft 6 long, 10ft beam, draft 2ft 3in, carried 35 fully armed and equipped troops.
LCF	Landing Craft Flak, an LCT MkIII (qv) with crew of twelve and fifty Royal Marines to man the twelve 2-pdr pom-poms or 20mm Oerlikons.
LCG (L)	Landing Craft Gun (Large). Basic particulars as LCT with crew of forty-eight, including Royal Marine gunners, main armament two 4.7 inch naval guns.
LCG (M)	Landing Craft Gun (Medium) vessel with a displacement of 380 tons, crew of thirty-one (including RM gunners), main armament two 17- or 25-pounders.
LCI (L)	Landing Craft Infantry (Large), 387 tons displacement, crew of twenty-eight, load nine Officers and 196 Other Ranks.
LCI (S)	Landing Craft Infantry (Small), 110 tons

	displacement, crew of seventeen, load six Officers and ninety-six Other Ranks.
LCS (L)	Landing Craft Support (Large), of 116 tons displacement with a crew of twenty-five including RM gunners, armament one 6-pdr in Valentine tank turret, twin 20 mm Oerlikons and twin 0.5-inch machine-guns.
LCT	Landing Craft Tank, the Mark III had a displacement of 640 tons and the Mark IV 586 tons; carrying capacities of 300 and 350 tons respectively.
LCT (R)	Landing Craft Tank (Rocket), basically an LCT Mark III but fitted with 1080 (Mark 1) or 936 (Mark 2) rocket launchers; all these missiles being electrically fired in a succession of 24-bomb salvoes.
Lee Enfield	The standard service rifle of WWII, 0.303 inch calibre, weight 9 pounds.
LMG	Light machine-gun, see *Bren*.
LVT	Landing Vehicle Tracked, the Mark II, the *Buffalo*, was 26 feet long overall, stood eight feet high on its tracks and could carry twenty-four fully equipped men or three tons of cargo at 25 mph on land, 5.4 knots in water.
Mae West	Inflatable rubber life jacket, worn around the chest, named after a female film star of the time who was well-endowed in that area.
Matelot (Matlo)	The French word for 'sailor' but 'Royals' (qv) apply it to all naval personnel.
MMG	Medium machine-gun, usually the 0.303 calibre, belt-fed water-cooled Vickers gun.
MOA	Marine Officer's Attendant or batman.
Monitor	A shallow-draught naval vessel designed to get close inshore in order to bombard enemy positions with its two large-calibre guns.
Mortar	An infantry weapon which is, basically, a steel tube to direct bombs on to the enemy. Unlike an artillery piece, the bore is not rifled and there is, generally, a fixed firing-pin at its

	base, so the only 'firing' that is required is to slide a bomb down the barrel.
Nutty	The matelot's (qv) name for chocolate, with or without nuts.
Oerlikon	20mm magazine-fed gun developed in Switzerland. It fired explosive shells at 450 rounds a minute and was used primarily as an anti-aircraft weapon, in either a single or twin mounting.
O-Group	Order Group, when the commander calls appropriate personnel together to issue his orders for a coming operation.
Oppo	Close friend, the 'opposite number' of a two-man team.
Out pipes	Stop smoking, even cigarettes.
PIAT	Projector, Infantry, Anti-tank. A very effective infantryman's answer to tanks. Weighing 34 pounds, it fired a 2¾lb bomb capable of penetrating 4" of armour at a range of 120 yards.
Pom-pom	A 40mm calibre quick-firing anti-aircraft weapon, which could project an explosive shell weighing 1.684 lb (but generally referred to as a '2 pounder') to a height of 13,000 feet. Used in a single barrel mounting but more often in a quadruple mounting, making it a *multiple pop-pom*.
Pusser/Pusser's	Anything which is of indisputable official origin (*pusser issue*) or anyone who acts strictly 'in accordance with the book', (*a pusser officer*) but used in many lighthearted ways such as *pusser's dust* for instant coffee, while *a drop of pusser's* means real naval rum. The word is a corruption of Purser, the RN name for the Paymaster and Supplies Officer in days gone by.
RAP	Regimental Aid Post, the first stop for anyone wounded in action, manned by RAMC Medical Orderlies or RN SBAs (qv).

Rear Echelon	That part of a Military Unit which remains in the rear areas when the fighting element goes 'Up Front'.
Royal	In addition to its use as an adjective – e.g. when referring to the House of Windsor – it is also used as a noun by naval personnel, who generally refer to a Royal Marine as a 'Royal'.
SBA	Sick Berth Attendant – the naval equivalent of a Medical Orderly.
Sin Bo'sun	A naval Padre, also known as a Sky Pilot.
Small Arms	Small calibre weapons, automatic or otherwise, which fire bullets, as opposed to bombs or shells.
SP	Self-propelled, referring to guns, and particularly to the German 88 (qv).
TCV	Troop-carrying Vehicle. Standard American 2½ ton six-wheeler truck fitted with fore-and-aft slatted seats.
10 (I-A)	No. 10 (Inter-Allied) Commando – formed from foreign nationals, including Germans, who had volunteered to fight as Commandos for the Allies. The Troops (of 60–70 men) were organized by country of origin, e.g. there were Belgian, Dutch, French and Norwegian Troops.
Tiddley	Smart, of neat appearance, not to be confused with *tiddly*, which is tipsy.
2 i/c	Second-in-Command.
TSMG	Thompson, sub-machine-gun – the 'Tommy Gun' of Chicago gangsters in the 1920s. During WWII the military version had a 'straight down' 20-round magazine instead of the gangsters' circular 50-round version.
Weasel	Small 'jeep-sized' amphibious tracked vehicle capable of carrying half a ton of crew and equipment at 25 mph on land, or 5 knots in water.
Winger	Same as 'oppo'.

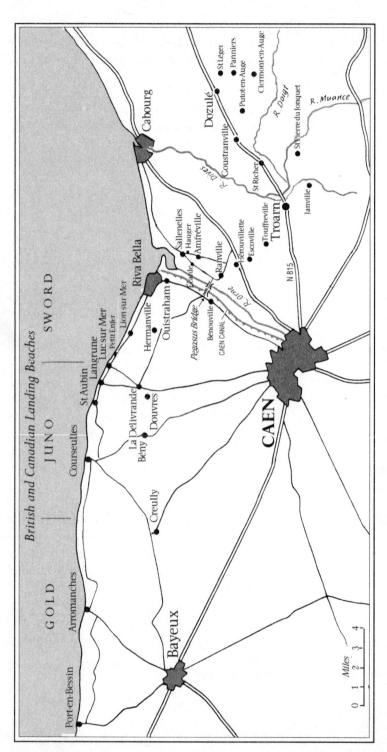

The Normandy Beachhead and the 'Breakout'

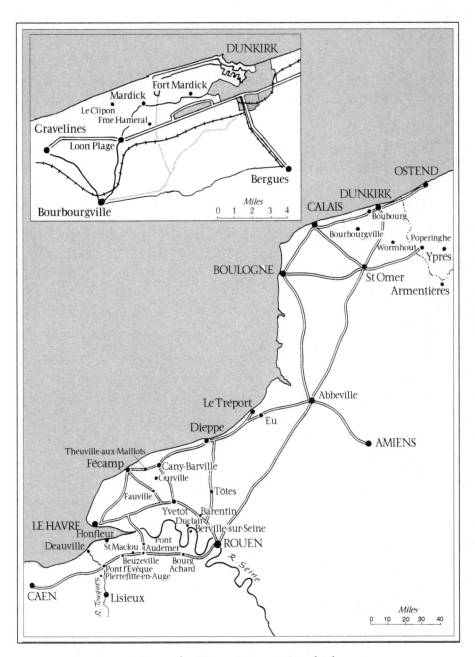

From the River Seine to Dunkirk

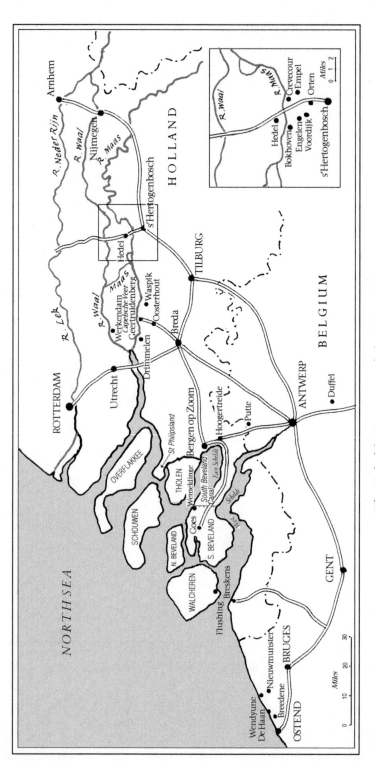

The Scheldt Estuary and the River Maas

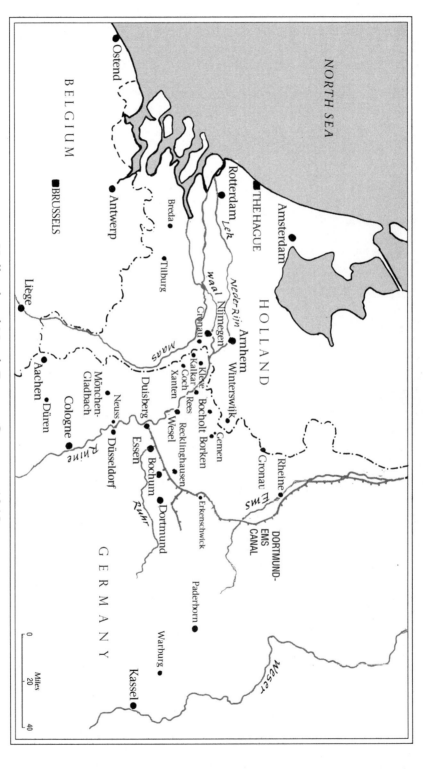

Holland and North Eastern Germany, 1945

AUTHOR'S PREFACE

On 3 September 1939, when Britain declared war on Germany, I was just two months short of my nineteenth birthday and keen to 'get into it'. My eldest brother Rex, six years my senior, was a Sergeant-Pilot in No. 220 (General Reconnaissance) Squadron of the RAF and, wishing to follow in his footsteps, I applied to an RAF Recruiting Office. Very quickly, however, an eyesight test confirmed that my colour vision made me unfit for full flying duties. Suspecting that this defect would also go against me if I tried for the Royal Navy, I opted for the Army and, deciding to go for an élite regiment, wrote to the Coldstream Guards. The reply stated that their age limits for recruitment were 20 to 38 years, so there was no possibility of enlisting there.

Two weeks later my brother was killed. He had been second pilot of a Lockheed Hudson aircraft which, on returning to Thornaby-on-Tees RAF Station from a patrol over the North Sea, crashed on to a house in Darlington. All on board died, but no civilians were harmed. As my other elder brother, Lawrence, was a deck officer in the Merchant Navy, I felt it would be too much for my parents if I were to volunteer for the Services at that time, so I made no more attempts to join up until late February 1940. I then wrote to the Royal Engineers, but the reply was, 'It is regretted that your age, which is considerably under the required standard, prevents your enlistment into the Army at present.'

This seemed to be the end of the line for me, until I learned that the Royal Marines were accepting younger men. On 26 June I

1

applied to the same Recruiting Centre which had written the above letter and was issued with an Identity Card certifying that I had applied to serve in the Royal Marines and would receive instructions later. A week or so afterwards I was called to present myself for medical examination and, barely three weeks after my original application, received a communication stating – 'If you are still willing . . .'! to report for instructions on 3 August and that I would be required to join my Depot four days after that.

In consequence, on 7 August 1940 I was one of a batch of recruits 'collected' at Woodbury Road halt, on the railway line from Exeter to Exmouth, and a Sergeant 'marched' us to the nearby Royal Marines Reserve Depot, Exton. Since the war this depot has been completely redeveloped and renamed as The Commando Training Centre Royal Marines, Lympstone.

After six weeks' initial training, followed by three weeks in the Records Office at Chatham Barracks, I was back at Exton, where the 103rd Royal Marines Brigade was being formed and I was posted to the 8th Battalion as Orderly Room Clerk. More and more recruit squads were allocated to create the Battalion, but, within a matter of weeks, the reverse process was being put in train, as drafts left the embryo Battalion, posted to other Royal Marines formations more urgently in need of men.

By the end of January 1941 the Battalion had been reduced to a nucleus of the Commanding Officer, Second-in-Command, Adjutant, other chosen Officers, most of the Senior NCOs, plus a few score selected Junior NCOs and men. On 8 February this 'hard core' of a Battalion took over the empty Thurlestone Hotel in South Devon to create and operate the Royal Marines Officer Cadet Training Unit. After six months of being engaged in this task, by which time NCOs were also being trained at Thurlestone and the establishment had been renamed the Royal Marines Military School, the original staff was released to re-form the 8th Battalion as a fighting unit. On 24 August the unit moved to Dalditch Camp, on Woodbury Common, only a few miles from the Exton Depot. On completion of their initial training at the Depot, squad after squad of men were marched up to Dalditch Camp and allocated to either the 7th or the 8th Battalion, both of which were being brought up to operational strength at the camp. In addition to military training, the men would also spend a few periods each week on 'Camp Construction', helping civilian contractors to replace the Bell tents and marquees with Nissen huts.

At Dalditch my long-standing request to 'escape' from the Orderly Room and return to General Duties was finally granted and I was posted to the Mortar Platoon. A few weeks later, however, the Battalion received its allocation of Bren Gun Carriers and there was a call for volunteers to form the Motorcycle Section of the Carrier Platoon, so I put my name down. My experience as a motorcyclist extended to no more than 'once around the block on my brother's Rudge', but I was accepted. My job in the Section was anti-tank rifleman and I remained as such throughout the following twelve months or so of Battalion and Brigade training in Devon, and in South Wales, until October 1942. The 8th Battalion, then stationed in Llanion Barracks, Pembroke Dock, was chosen to form the second Royal Marines Commando. The first, known as 'A' Commando, had been formed early in the year and had taken part in the ill-conceived Dieppe Raid; our Battalion was to create 'B' Commando.

As the strength of a battalion was something over 800 men, and a Commando comprised only about 450, there would have to be a major slimming down in numbers. Most tradesmen would be automatically excluded – there would be no place for cooks, for example, as the Commando would be living in civilian homes, nor for transport drivers, as the new unit would 'carry it all on their backs'. Older men, and those less fit, could be expected to be passed over and the reshuffle no doubt presented an ideal opportunity to shed 'undesirables'. Nevertheless, for two days everyone was on tenterhooks as to whether they would be 'in' or 'out'. At a parade of the entire Battalion on the Saturday morning the composition of the new Troops was announced and it was a great relief to learn that the Carrier Platoon was being transformed into 'Q' Troop of the new Commando and that I had become a rifleman in No. 7 Section of that Troop.

Two days later 'Q' was one of the Troops which moved to Weymouth to begin living in civilian homes and to becoming accustomed to getting themselves to the specified place of parade at the required time of day, which could equally well be ten o'clock at night as eight o'clock in the morning. During the next few weeks, all seven Troops – six Rifle Troops, 'A', 'B', 'P', 'Q', 'X' and 'Y', and Headquarters Troops – were located on the Isle of Wight and the unit was restyled 'No. 41 (Royal Marines) Commando'.

Commando training proceeded on the Isle of Wight and in Scotland until mid-June 1943, when the Commando, along with the original Royal Marine Commando, now styled No. 40, boarded two Infantry Landing ships, already well-packed with untold hundreds of Canadian troops, which were part of a large convoy lying in the Clyde Estuary, off Greenock. That convoy was to carry the entire Canadian First Division, together with all of its arms, munitions, transport, stores and supporting units, to join General Montgomery's Eighth Army for the invasion of Sicily. The two Commandos spearheaded the Canadians' landing, near the town of Pachino in the south-east corner of the island. An account of this, and the Commando's part in the US Fifth Army's landings on the Italian mainland two months later, are covered in my book *Marine Commando, Sicily and Salerno 1943 with 41 Royal Marines Commando*, published in hardback by Robert Hale, London 1988, now reissued in paperback.

The present book takes up the story from the time of the unit's return to the UK early in January 1944 and covers the next two years until my release from the Royal Marines in 1946. Soon after arrival in England in 1944 my role changed from Rifleman to that of Despatch Rider and in that capacity I participated in the D-day landing, spent the ensuing weeks in the Normandy beachhead, followed by the pursuit through northern France; the Walcheren landing to open the Port of Antwerp on 1 November; winter months on the Maas River Front in Holland and, finally, occupation duties in Germany until November 1945.

During the war it was, technically, an offence to keep a diary, lest it should fall into enemy hands and divulge military information. However, I began jotting things down as soon as I joined up at Exton before knowing that I was committing an offence. Later, I felt that the ban surely couldn't apply to anyone as lowly as myself so far away from the enemy. My 'diary' entries were, in general, simply a matter of recording something as and when I felt in the mood, so there were gaps in the narrative which had to be filled by other means. Fortuitously, the crucial year of 1944 was recorded by me on a day-to-day basis, thanks to a 'Gentleman's Diary', which gave much information about shooting seasons, etc.! It was inscribed 'From Mother, Christmas 1943'. I passed that Christmas Day in Algeria, so didn't receive the diary until January 1944, on disembarkation leave following the Commando's return to the UK.

When released in 1946 I had a motley collection of six books/diaries, which are now lodged in the Imperial War Museum, and the inner conviction that some day I would string the contents together to give a cohesive account of my five and a half years in uniform, if only for my family's sake. Those years in uniform, however, had persuaded me that I should aspire to something more than the clerking position I had left behind, so I applied to the City Engineer of Newcastle upon Tyne to become an 'Engineering Learner' and, on being accepted, began to study, at nights and weekends, to become qualified as a Civil Engineer.

In consequence of this, then getting married and raising a family, the work of setting down my wartime experiences proceeded slowly, 'by fits and starts', over the years, which eventually lengthened into decades. When I had eventually linked together my own records of the period from August 1940 to March 1946, I obtained a copy of the Unit War Diary, to ensure accurate correlation with official records. Then, considering the possibility of publication, I decided to concentrate in the first instance on the Mediterranean period, which I finalized and this was subsequently accepted for publication by Robert Hale.

In 1992 the Veterans of the WWII 41 RM Commando felt that a History of the wartime unit should be written and I undertook the task. Thanks to the efforts of a small Publication Committee, which invited financial support from former members of the unit, publication of the resulting book, *They Did What Was Asked of Them, 41 (Royal Marines) Commando 1942–46*, was achieved in 1996. This was on the basis that, when all costs of publication had been met, and such advance financial support repaid, all subsequent proceeds would be donated to the Royal Marines Museum Heritage Appeal Fund, and this situation was achieved within twelve months of publication. My deep involvement in the Unit History, which extended to supporting the Committee in advertising, sales and distribution matters, further delayed the completion of the present work, but it did ensure that the overall facts of the campaign in North-West Europe were refreshed and that their presentation is correct.

I couldn't end this Preface without acknowledging the immeasurable assistance, in gaining information and sorting out facts, which I have received from a number of official organizations. Firstly, my deep appreciation and thanks go to the Director and Staff of the Royal Marines Museum for their long-standing help in clarifying doubtful episodes. Then, grateful thanks must also go to the staffs of the various departments of the Imperial War Museum which I have consulted over the years for their courteous help. This has ranged from supplying details of WWII weapons and military vehicles, cartographical information and copies of official war photographs. I also appreciate the help given by the Air and Naval Historical Branches of the Ministry of Defence, the Public Record Office, the Army Museum and the Royal Air Force Museum.

In conclusion, I would, once again, like to acknowledge my deep appreciation of the continuing support I have received from my wife, Joan. Over many years she has typed and retyped drafts of this work, giving useful comments upon the 'flow', 'understandability' and punctuation in the process, then undertook a final 'proof read' to check that I had complied with her suggestions!

Chapter 1

FROM RIFLEMAN TO DESPATCH RIDER

At 0600 hrs on Tuesday 4 January 1944 the docks at Gourock, on the Firth of Clyde, were wet with drizzle, cold and misty. For the hundreds of men lining the rails of the recently-berthed troopship, SS *Otranto*, their first sight of Britain after months of absence was bleak and unattractive. There were no fluttering flags, no military bands, no cheering crowds – none of the 'Welcome Home!' trappings which the cinema screen generally accords to troops returning from a successful campaign. Just a glistening quayside bustling with khaki-clad figures humping loads of military equipment and being bawled at by their NCOs to 'Come on! Get fell in!' More long files of men in full marching order, each burdened with his personal weapon and kitbag, many shivering involuntarily in the unaccustomed winter chill, were gingerly picking their way down slippery gangplanks to swell the throng below.

For the British at least, Gourock meant 'Blighty', 'the UK', 'Home', so for them it was sufficient just to be back there all in one piece, with the uninviting weather no more than a minor irritation. Not so fortunate were the hundreds of Commonwealth troops who had travelled on the same ship. They were still thousands of miles from their own countries and couldn't even hazard a guess as to how many more months or years it would be before *they* saw their homes again. Some other passengers must have had even more doubts in their minds, a few score German prisoners of war, unshaven and still dressed in crumpled Afrika Korps desert uniforms with, here and there, an Iron Cross dangling from a ribbon around the neck, who were yet to be put ashore. Nevertheless, for the whole heterogeneous mass of service personnel, women as well as men, that seemingly inhospitable corner of Britain at War did at least mean the end of a cramped ten-day sea voyage from Algiers.

Amongst those going ashore were the four hundred or so officers and men of 41 (Royal Marines) Commando and a rifleman in 'Q', one of the six Rifle or 'Fighting' Troops, was CH/X 100977 Marine Raymond Mitchell, author of these memoirs. The Commando had returned to the same Scottish port from which it had embarked for overseas service six months previously.

On 28 June 1943, a hot and brilliantly sunny summer's day, the Unit had sailed from the Clyde on board the SS *Durban Castle*, a 35,000-ton luxury liner of the Union Castle Line, then doing its war service as an Infantry Landing Ship, with rows of LCAs (Landing Craft Assault) lining her tall sides. She had been one of a large convoy carrying the entire Canadian First Division, some 18,000 men, with all its artillery, tanks, transport and stores, to join General Montgomery's Eighth Army in the invasion of Sicily. 41 Commando, together with her sister Unit, No. 40 Royal Marines Commando, had been given the task of neutralizing Italian coastal strong points which could threaten the Canadian landings. These two units were the first British sea-borne troops to go ashore – at 0246 hours on Thursday 9 July 1943 – and by spearheading the return of Allied Armies, absent from the continent since the débâcle of the fall of France in 1940, they initiated the liberation of Europe.

Two months later, on 10 September 1943, then as part of US General Mark Clark's Fifth Army, 41 Royal Marines and No. 2 Army Commandos, had made a night assault across the beach at Vietri sul Mare, as part of the Allied landings near Salerno aimed at the capture of Naples. Both Commandos suffered heavy casualties during the nine days of touch-and-go fighting before the Fifth Army had established itself securely on the Italian mainland.

When withdrawn back to Sicily, less than two weeks after it had sailed from there, 41 could muster little more than half of its original strength. The Unit had lost most of its commissioned officers and was without a Commanding Officer as Lieutenant Colonel B.J.D. 'Bertie' Lumsden RM had been seriously wounded on the second day ashore. During the last minutes of the Commando's action at Salerno, I myself received a leg wound from a German hand-grenade and was evacuated to a Canadian hospital in North Africa.

After first returning to Aci Castello, its starting point for the Salerno operation, the Commando later moved into 'winter quarters' in Catania. With replacements arriving from the UK and wounded re-joining from hospital, the Unit was being re-formed. In mid-November we sailed for Algiers, to be shipped back to the UK, but were disembarked at Bizerta in Tunisia, supposedly to complete the journey by train. However, after three days in World War One '40 men or 8 horses' wagons, during which only 120 miles were covered, the Unit reached Bône (now Annaba) and marched to a tented camp on desert sand.

There the Commando languished for six weeks, while the 'Top Brass' debated whether it should be sent back to the UK to take part in the Second Front, the invasion of France, or be employed in Jugoslavia. In November Lieutenant Colonel T.W. Gray arrived to take over as Commanding Officer, but the Commando was kept waiting until, like a bolt from the blue, two days before Christmas, he announced that a ship was lying in Algiers harbour, ready to take us home.

Early next morning, Christmas Eve 1943, 41 Commando left No. 4 Transit Camp in a convoy of American TCVs (Troop Carrying Vehicles) and flurries of dust. Forty hours later, after alternate roasting under the African sun and freezing in the near-zero night temperatures, very late on Christmas Day the Unit climbed laboriously up a steep ladder on to the deck of the SS *Otranto*. Ours must have been her last intake of passengers; in the very early hours of Boxing Day the engines throbbed into life at the start of what turned out to be an uneventful voyage to the Clyde.

At Gourock, after assembling on the dockside and being 'mustered', Troop by Troop, the Commando marched off. Minds became occupied with the possibility of a customs or military police examination before clearing the docks area – a number of men had picked up 'souvenirs' such as binoculars, cameras, German Lügers or Italian Beretta automatics, which it would have been very galling to have had to surrender. Another concern was to get home while the oranges, lemons and tangerines bought in Bône were still edible. At that stage of the war citrus fruit was unobtainable in the UK and

9

a supply of vitamin C would be almost as welcome as ourselves. One minor personal concern was whether our Padre, the Rev John Wallis DSC, would go ashore still wearing the 'full set' of moustache and beard he had grown overseas. I had wagered a day's pay that he wouldn't, but he did.

In the event no Customs Officers nor MPs (military policemen) were encountered, but, after a short march to a docks railway platform, it was found that a reception committee was indeed awaiting our arrival. Despite the early hour and the miserable wintry weather, a dozen or more ladies of the WVS (Women's Voluntary Service) stood at the ready beside a line of trestle tables piled high with either packets of sandwiches or morning papers. Every man, as he filed past, was handed one of each. Then, like excited children off on a Sunday school outing, we clambered on board the waiting LMS (London Midland and Scottish Railway) train.

As soon as kitbags and rifles had been stacked in the corridor and weighty webbing equipment heaved up on to the racks, everyone was in holiday mood. As well as the fillip of being newly back from a war zone, that journey would be the first in a 'real' train since travelling to that same station, for embarkation, the previous June. In comparison with the '8 chevaux ou 40 hommes' wagons from Bizerta to Bône, British Third Class railway coaches would be the height of luxury.

When the train chuffed off every openable window was crammed with as many heads as could be poked out and it left to the accompaniment of whoops of delight and rounds of hurrahs. So it continued throughout the day; everyone encountered en route, standing at level crossings, passed at a distance in the fields, or waiting on the platforms of the many stations we speeded through was greeted with gales of spontaneous cheers and wildly waving arms. Every girl in sight, within earshot or not, pretty, plain or downright ugly, was bombarded with salvoes of wolf whistles.

The journey continued in a general mood of high hilarity, although there were a few minor grumbles from time to time. These started early with our Scottish comrades from Clydeside, passing within a few miles of their homes, bemoaning the fact that in a few days' time they would have to travel all the way back to those very stations on disembarkation leave. Then the men from the Borders became vociferous about the nearness of their firesides, followed

10

by the Northern English and by afternoon it was the Midlanders.

As was commonplace during the war, stops were frequent, often long and invariably unexplained. The railway authorities must have considered that the then current admonitory warning, 'Careless Talk Costs Lives' applied to their operations, so the train moved, stopped then started away again, all without explanation. The exuberance continued until the early darkness of a winter's evening required the black-out blinds to be pulled down. The carriages quietened as men turned to reading newspapers or became involved in card schools of pontoon, solo or brag. Eventually these too gave way to an untidy sprawl of sleeping Marines draped over any convenient surface of seat or floor, while the train continued to rumble fitfully on.

With daylight it fell to the Londoners to point out their own particular neighbourhoods of 'The Smoke' as the train kept rolling ever southwards. At about half past nine a final squeal of brakes heralded the Commando's arrival at its destination – Deal. Commands to detrain, get rigged and get fell in rang out along the line of carriages and, to the hiss of escaping steam, stiff men tumbled out to form up on the station platform.

The weather, in marked contrast to the previous morning, was Spring-like and bright with sunshine. Kit bags were stacked for collection by a fatigue party and, when reported 'All present and correct', the Commando marched out of the station. The initial euphoria of returning to the UK had evaporated, the six months' sojourn in the Mediterranean area was over and here was just another march. Minds became occupied with the prospect of food, a wash and shave, and wondering what the billets would be like.

It was pleasant enough to march through quiet residential streets, find ourselves entering the Royal Marines Barrack and then to be led on to the wide expanse of the parade ground. The Commando was halted Troop by Troop, turned into line and given the usual orders of 'Stand at – ease!' and 'Stand easy!' On the far side of the parade ground a few squads of immaculately uniformed recruits were being put through their paces at close-order drill under the critical eye of an officer, resplendent in 'blues' uniform, peaked cap and gleaming brasswork, obviously the Depot Adjutant.

Then our presence on *his* parade ground impinged upon his

11

consciousness and he suffered what could only be described as an instantaneous attack of mobile apoplexy. Pivoting on his heel, he steamed across the vast expanse of concrete towards 41's officer group and it was patently obvious that our grubby, dishevelled and unshaven presence was desecrating his holy of holies. Six months' active service, terminating in a ten-days' troopship voyage, followed immediately by twenty-seven non-stop hours on a troop train, were as nothing compared with the niceties of protocol attaching to the parade ground of a Royal Marines' Barracks! The Commando was called to attention and marched off.

After dispersal to mess halls for a belated breakfast, there came the allocation of barrack-rooms, a wash and shave, and the issue of new battledress uniforms to ensure that, in future, we would conform to the sartorial requirements of the barracks. The remainder of the day was given over to cleaning weapons and equipment in preparation for an inspection, scheduled for the following morning, by General Sturges, Royal Marines, Officer Commanding the Special Service Group. In May 1942 he had been in command of all the land forces involved in taking Diego Suarez, Madagascar, from the Vichy French to ensure that the naval base didn't fall into Japanese hands.

While preparing for his inspection, I went time and again to the depot Post Office hoping to send a telegram home, but it was always swamped with scores of others with the same idea in mind so I never managed it. That night most of the unit luxuriated in real beds for the first time since leaving Troon some six months previously.

On parade next morning it was abruptly announced that the General's inspection had been cancelled and the Commando would go on leave instead. Then followed a mad 'flap' of queueing-up for the issue of leave passes, travel warrants and ration cards, and a pay parade. Transport got us to the railway station just in time to catch the early afternoon train to London.

My travelling companion was Bill 'Geordie' Swindale, the fellow Tynesider to whom I have dedicated this book; he lived in Gateshead. We just managed to squeeze on board the crowded 20.20 out of Kings Cross, but got no further than the corridor, as all compartments were packed to overflowing. That was where we passed the journey, and it was 05.10 next morning before we stumbled from the fuggy train on to the chilly No. 8 platform of Newcastle Central Station. Nine hours to cover two hundred and eighty miles wasn't at all bad for rail travel in wartime Britain.

I arrived home to find that my mother was in Oxford, where sister Evelyn was daily expecting to give birth to her second child. My eldest brother Rex, a Sergeant-Pilot in the RAF, had been killed in November 1939, and the next eldest, Lawrence, was at sea as a Deck Officer in the Merchant Navy. With my father at work all day, and my younger sister and brother, Marjorie and Douglas, both at school, there was no alternative for me but to take over as cook. It was, therefore, something of a relief to be able to escape to Oxford for the last few days of leave, to see my mother and inspect baby nephew Peter Charles. His sister, Pauline Ann, four years old at the time, still retains a vivid memory of that visit, in the form of a pair of 'enormous boots', as she describes them, pushed close to her nose as she crouched shyly under the bed.

The normal time for the expiry of a period of Service leave was '2359 hrs' – one minute before midnight – but on Friday 21 January 1944 train timetables dictated that, to avoid being AWOL (absent without official leave), I had to arrive in Deal at 1700 hours. The town was under a 'shell warning' – like Dover and other nearby coastal towns, Deal was within range of the heavy German cross-Channel guns – but it proved to be a quiet night.

Next morning we received General Sturges' delayed 'Jolly good show, chaps!' address, but his inspection had been cancelled and later in the day came the welcome news of an early move into 'civvy billets' in the Margate/Ramsgate area. Living with civilian families was an integral part of the commando training system, designed to inculcate a degree of independence and self-reliance in the men. Everyone was individually responsible for getting himself to the next place of parade on time, whether it was at 8 o'clock in the morning for a 'pusser' parade and weapons inspection, or 10 o'clock at night with blackened faces and rubber-soled boots for a 'night stunt'.

To the 60-odd men of 'Q', however, the day also brought the bad news that the Troop was to be disbanded. The 'Raiding Party, carry it all on your backs' concept of Commando Units had been abandoned and in future they would be provided with transport. The overall structure of Units had also been changed by reducing the

13

number of Rifle Troops from six to five and upgrading the Heavy Weapons Section of HQ Troop (Vickers medium machine-guns and 3-inch mortars) to full 'Support Troop' status.

The prime factor in choosing 'Q' as the Troop to go was undoubtedly because it had ceased to exist as an entity on 11 September 1943, on Dragonea Hill above Vietri sul Mare, near Salerno. Heavy casualties had been suffered that day, which included all three commissioned officers – Troop Commander Captain R.M. Stott and Lieutenant D.C. Lloyd killed, and Lieutenant P.H. Haydon seriously wounded. Lieutenant Haydon was awarded the Distinguished Service Order for his action that day and, at barely twenty years of age, was the youngest Royal Marines Officer in World War Two to receive that high award. Many months later, promoted to Captain, he re-joined the Commando as a Troop Commander, but was killed in action on the island of Walcheren, Holland, in November 1944.

Another consideration in the choice of Troop for disbandment was likely to have been that, when 41 Commando was created from the fully-trained 8th Battalion Royal Marines, 'Q' had been formed largely from the Carrier Platoon. Bren Gun Carrier drivers and men of the Motorcycle Section possessed skills which would be useful in the motorization of the Unit. Corporal George 'Jan' Maley, for example, was appointed Transport Sergeant and Bill Smith, Bren gunner in the Motorcycle Section, became a Despatch Rider. The rest of the Troop was 'shared out' amongst the other Rifle Troops and I went to 'P'.

On Monday morning, 24 January, 'Q' Troop paraded for a final period of drill and a valedictory address by Captain Grant. He had been with us in the Carrier Platoon, then was a Lieutenant Section Commander in 'Q', before transferring to 'Heavy Weapons', and was at that time Troop Commander of 'S', the newly formed Support Troop.

On Tuesday 25 January the Commando assembled for a 'pep talk' by its new Commanding Officer, Tim Gray, and next day marched out of Deal barracks – 'B' 'S' 'X' and 'Y' Troops heading for Margate, 'A' 'P' and HQ going to Ramsgate. Much of the route lay along the coast road with the seawards view obstructed by broad barbed wire entanglements, anti-tank obstacles and gun emplacements. In Ramsgate itself there were more evidences of being in a 'front line' position on the south coast – numerous plots of grass-covered empty space where once there had been buildings.

I was billeted with Harry Weiss in Moss Rose Cottage, fronting the main street, where our host family was very welcoming, as we found everyone in Ramsgate. Nevertheless we weren't too happy about having to remove a dog or a cat from any comfortable chair in the house before sitting down, so we decided upon a move and began looking for new digs. We soon found another billet, with the Sayer family in Hardres Road and, not wishing to hurt anyone's feelings, said that we were to move closer to our Troop Office, which was true, if only by about two minutes' walk. 'P' Troop Commander, Captain Bill Sloley, nothing if not unconventional, had located his HQ in a back room of the North Pole public house on the Margate Road. Commando Daily Orders were pinned up behind the bar of 'the public', so there was always a good reason for being outside the Troop Office with a drink in your hand. Also behind the bar was a small blackboard on which the landlord kept a tally of air raid and shell warnings and, at 2230 hrs on Friday 28 January 1944, as I was reading Daily Orders, he amended the total to '2409'.

Earlier that day our previous CO, Lieutenant Colonel Lumsden, badly wounded at Salerno some four months earlier, came to welcome his old Unit back to the UK. The Colonel was accompanied by Sergeant 'Nigger' Branchett, who had been a Marine clerk with me in the Orderly Room of the 8th Battalion in 1940/41, who offered me a 'square number' (cushy) job. He needed a clerk at Brigade Rear Echelon, which would remain in Canterbury no matter where the rest of the Brigade went, but I wasn't tempted.

Nevertheless, despite refusing that offer, I was soon to get a change of occupation and, as had been the case when first getting into clerking with Nigger, without really wanting it. I had, fleetingly, encountered Jan Maley in his new role of Transport Sergeant and he, being fully aware of my motorcycling background, had called out, 'Hey, Mitch! – I'm getting nine motorbikes tomorrow'. My automatic, and unthinking, response had been to reply, 'You'll be wanting some DRs then,' but thought no more of it.

On the Sunday afternoon Harry and I were occupied in moving to our new billet and, in consequence, missed the first showing at the local cinema (Sunday cinemas were a wartime innovation) and were queueing-up for the second house when the first one came streaming out. Amongst the flood of people emerging was Jan Maley and, on catching sight of me, his invariably cheerful face widened into a broad grin. Too far away to talk, he extended both arms in line with his shoulders and, while nodding his head vigorously, went through the motions of operating a motor cycle twist grip with his right hand.

The meaning of Jan's pantomime was unmistakable to me and next morning it was conveyed to the rest of the Commando. Part II of Daily Orders, which dealt with pay, promotions and appointments, carried the item: Transferred from 'P' Troop to HQ Troop as Despatch Rider – CH/X 100977 Mne Mitchell, R.

Chapter 2

UK TRIPS AND CONCENTRATION CAMPS

That my transfer from 'P' Troop to HQ had appeared in Daily Orders made it a *fait accompli*. The only way to alter the situation would have been to put in a formal request to return to General Duties, which would have put Jan in an awkward position as he had clearly thought that I was seeking the transfer. At the same time, with the break-up of 'Q' Troop, I was back with friends of long standing because, in addition to Bill Smith, two other former motorcyclists of the Carrier Platoon, Jackie Horsfield and 'Killer' Barker, had become DRs, while the two former Despatch Riders of the 8th Battalion, who had not previously been in the Commando, now came back. Despatch Riding carried no extra 'tradesman's' pay but there was no doubt that it would be a much less strenuous occupation than being a rifleman in a Fighting Troop, so I decided to bide my time.

My Lee-Enfield rifle and bayonet were returned to store in exchange for a Colt 45 automatic pistol and I was issued with riding gear – breeches, riding boots, crash helmet, jerkin, mackintosh coat, gloves and goggles. The motorcycles were 350cc overhead valve Ariels, nippier machines than the heavier side-valve Norton 500s we had used in the Carrier Platoon, but all were well past their first flush of youth.

The Unit's complement of six despatch riders, with a Corporal-in-charge, came under the command of the Signals Officer who was responsible for maintaining round-the-clock communication links within the Commando, with Brigade Headquarters and with such

17

other units as was necessary. The nerve centre was the Signals Despatch Office (SDO), where telephone exchange, radio links and Despatch Riders were based. In Ramsgate the SDO was set up in an empty semi-detached house in a steeply-sloping street leading down to the wired-in seafront near the western edge of town.

In the UK Despatch Riders delivered everything that couldn't be transmitted by telephone, including officers on occasions, while in the field they carried all written messages and were the 'last resort' when neither field telephone nor radio contact could be made. Two were 'Duty' at any time, for a 24-hour tour starting at 0800 hours, and slept fully clothed on the SDO floor, ready to depart at a moment's notice. Two more acted as 'Stand-by' during the day to carry out any trips needed when both Duty men were out. They returned to their billets at night and, next day, took over from the Duty DRs, who went 'Off Duty' to carry out maintenance and repairs, and undertake any special trips which might be required.

Most trips were in the Ramsgate/Margate area, but others could be of fifty miles or more, and every day there would be at least two runs to Brigade Headquarters in Canterbury, which involved a round trip of some 40 miles. As it was mid-winter not all journeys by motorbike were pleasant affairs, but the life-style of a DR was remarkably unfettered compared with that of men in the Fighting Troops. Nevertheless, my mind continued to be niggled with thoughts of transferring back to 'P' Troop, although, as more Carrier Platoon personnel gravitated to transport roles, the urge tended to become less strong.

On the whole, life as a DR proceeded smoothly, but some days were packed with incident. One such included three round trips to Brigade, two mechanical breakdowns, running out of petrol and being booked for speeding. To crown everything, that evening I was ordered to Canterbury again, with instructions to take the Brigade Duty Officer, with an important message, to Brigadier 'Jumbo' Leicester, out on a training exercise 'somewhere in Kent'. Surprisingly, my instructions were to report to the officer at a hotel in town, where he gave me a shilling for a drink and instructions to report back nearer closing time!

On my return he climbed on to the luggage rack – our bikes had no pillion seats – and off we went into the obscurity of a blacked-out wartime winter's night. The masked headlamp illuminated little more than the front wheel, so intense concentration plus a measure of good luck were needed simply to keep us out of the roadside ditches. The officer was supposed to know where we were going, but it seemed to be entirely a matter of trial and error, and it was midnight before the Brigadier's HQ had been tracked down to an isolated farmhouse. By the time the officer had conducted his business, had been returned to Canterbury and I had found my way back to Ramsgate the early hours were well advanced before I was able to curl up on the SDO floor.

Some daylight journeys could be equally demanding. One such was a fifty-mile round trip to Folkestone in near-Arctic conditions, riding over ice-covered roads through driving hail, with the left forearm shielding my face and only the right hand to control the bike. As some small recompense, on the return journey I made a five-mile detour to RAF Hawkinge, where I knew a hometown friend, Doug Blair, was stationed with a Servicing Commando which always had a cup of tea handy.

Living with the Sayer family in Hardres Road was pleasant and comfortable. He was a civilian employee at the nearby Manston RAF station and Harry and I would occasionally join him and Mrs S at their local, Hennekens. Their daughter, Betty, serving in the Women's Land Army, came home from time to time and I suspected that Mrs Sayer thought of me as a likely lad in that direction.

Duty evenings in the SDO were generally quiet and, having an urge to learn how to drive, the presence of some of the Commando's vehicles parked overnight on the roadway outside the office proved an irresistible temptation. The smallest, and so the most appropriate for my purpose, was the water truck, invariably known as the Gunga Din after Rudyard Kipling's fictitious Indian water carrier. Therefore, after spending some time familiarizing myself with the controls, I took a deep breath, switched on and pressed the starter. The engine blurrrped into life and, after a few starts and stops, getting accustomed to the response of the accelerator, I decided that that was enough for a beginning.

On a subsequent evening the water truck was parked last in line offering an easy return to base, so I decided to have a go. The engine started easily and, without putting it in gear, releasing the hand-brake allowed the gradient of the road to get us moving. After steering away from the kerb, then making sure that the footbrake was working, I engaged bottom gear and we were off! The streets were completely empty and, without changing gear, I managed to negotiate four right-hand turns to bring us back to the starting position, feeling rather weak and sticky. On future occasions I ventured into higher gears, but it was always a touch-and-go business, and too risky – both the actual driving and the possibility of being caught at it – to do more than crawl around the nearby streets.

The Gunga Din was fitted with slatted walkways along the top of the tank, to give access to the filling manhole, and these were often used as repositories for tools, etc, when carrying out vehicle maintenance. On the morning after one of my driving jaunts, everyone within earshot was subjected to a tirade of accusations from the Signals Sergeant, demanding to know who had 'swiped' an oil can he had left on the water truck the previous evening. I slunk away, wondering vaguely at which street corner it had fallen off.

As it turned out, that was my last driving session in Ramsgate as, on returning from seven days' leave on Good Friday 7 April 1944, I learned that I was to leave next day with an Advance Party going to Hastings to arrange billets for the Commando. When the Main Body arrived a week later, I was put with Harry Weiss and Bill Marshall, both jeep drivers by that time, in St Anne's Hotel, a private guest-house in Grosvenor Gardens, where some elderly ladies were still in residence. Brigade Headquarters had remained in Canterbury, so every Brigade trip – and there were still at least two every day – now meant a hundred miles in the saddle.

Since sailing from Algiers the previous December it had been common knowledge that the Commando was earmarked for the Second Front invasion of Europe and now, as the first months of 1944 were passing, it was clear that it couldn't long be delayed. An indication that things were beginning to move came towards the end of April with rumours of an imminent large-scale exercise, codenamed Fabius. By all accounts it was to be more logistic than military, designed to gather together some tens of thousands of the men who would be involved on 'the Day' and rehearse the arrangements for their transportation, accommodation, feeding and embarkation.

Fabius remained no more than a rumour until Friday 28 April, when Killer Barker and I were abruptly detailed-off to join the Commando contingent leaving next day, our dress to be 'fighting order' and without motorbikes. I welcomed it as a chance to test the few residual feelings I had about returning to General Duties, but just the minor chores of cleaning and assembling the webbing equipment, then parading for inspection, foreign to us for more than three months, gave a slight jolt to the nervous system. The march to the railway station raised more question marks about the wisdom of any such change.

The Unit detrained at Botley, near Southampton, where a string of TCVs was waiting to take us on a circuitous journey through rural Hampshire which ended up at an immense tented town labelled simply 'C8'. It was a 'concentration camp', in the original Boer War sense of 'bringing together', and was as security-conscious as those notorious ones in German-occupied Europe. Its eight-feet-high perimeter fence, topped-off with barbed wire, was patrolled by armed guards rehearsing the role they would carry out when it would be necessary to ensure that no one who might let slip military information could leave. C8 was already bursting at the seams with many hundreds of troops and the fact that they were mainly Canadians probably accounted for the good food and the wide choice of film shows which we enjoyed in the evenings.

The first stage of Fabius was simply to exercise the camp staff in housing and feeding immense numbers of men; all we had to do was collect and eat our meals at specified times. Food was issued on a slick production line basis with long files of men continuously moving in front of lines of trestle tables laden with steaming dixies of food and drink. Behind the tables stood cooks with ladles at the ready and, as each man reached a dixie, the two parts of his mess tin in one hand and enamel mug in the other, he received a splodge of 'meat' in one and a splodge of 'sweet' in the other, while his mug caught a splosh of liquid – tea for us, coffee for the Canadians.

The processes of eating and the washing of mess tins and mugs afterwards were equally expeditious. A brief sojourn on a wooden bench alongside one of the scores of long tables in huge marquee mess-tents sufficed to dispose of the food, then out again. First to scrape any uneaten remnants into a bin as pig swill, then to a row of three forty-gallon petrol drums of water, kept on the boil over wood fires, for a quick swish of utensils in each one in turn, then everything was ready to be packed away again.

Sunday was a repeat performance, but on Monday, May Day, TCVs transferred us to another camp which looked precisely the same but was labelled 'C3' this time. The staff there must have needed practice in dealing with officers, because each man was issued with a camp bed before joining the food queue.

Next morning a more active phase of Fabius began when TCVs transported the Commando to a backwater of the Solent, in readiness to board LCI(S)s Landing Craft Infantry (Small), the type of craft we would soon be using 'for real'. These vessels could carry ninety fully armed men in three small 'holds', but, having wooden hulls covered with steel 'scales', they were poor 'sea boats'. The sea was judged too rough for them, so, after hanging around all day vainly hoping that conditions would improve, we were returned to camp.

Wednesday started off similarly when, like a few hundred pawns in a mammoth game of chess, we were transported to a different Southampton backwater and again settled down to wait throughout the morning. A sister unit, No. 45 (Royal Marines) Commando, was nearby doing just the same until a football was produced and an inter-Commando match was quickly organized. The powers that be must have waited prudently until the game had gone to full time because the final whistle was also the signal for NCOs to start shouting, 'All right lads! Get rigged and get fell in!' and almost a thousand men trooped on board the waiting craft.

When the ten LCIs carrying the two Commandos had been eased out of the small creek into the wide expanse of Southampton Water they became only one small part of a vast assemblage of shipping. In every direction lay untold numbers of ships and landing craft of all types, shapes and sizes. We steamed out into the fairway, moored to buoys until dusk when, together with a large part of the armada, the LCIs cast off and sailed off into the night.

Early next morning 41 Commando's LCIs were moving in line

abreast towards the shore to carry out mock attacks on objectives in and around Littlehampton. The craft were rammed on to the beach, the ramps splashed down into about three feet of water and everyone sprinted, rather wetly, ashore. With no specific role in the attacks, we DRs simply tagged along behind, to be told in due course that the Commando had 'achieved its primary objectives' by 0830 hours. The unit's part in the exercise was over by noon, but it was evening before a train arrived to return us to Hastings.

On the following Monday four DRs were detailed off to accompany the Commando for more landing exercises, again without motorcycles. In the early evening civilian coaches took the Commando to Newhaven where, after putting weapons and equipment aboard the allocated landing craft, we were given the 'freedom of the dockyard' until 2200hrs, when the flotilla sailed out. By next morning the craft were once again moving in line abreast towards the beach at Littlehampton. Crewmen launched the ramps and everyone doubled ashore, only to be called back to get on board again. The ramps were retracted, the LCIs pulled off, circled out into deeper water, re-formed into line and came in again. This procedure was repeated time and again, seeming to indicate it was for the Navy's benefit rather than ours. After a few hours of this occupation the LCIs returned the Commando to Newhaven and trucks delivered us back to Hastings.

The increasing frequency of exercises made it clear that the day for the invasion of Europe, D-Day, was drawing near. All military operations were planned to begin at 'H-Hour' on 'D-Day' and these two reference points enabled the entire sequence of events, before and after the initial assault, to be planned in advance of any starting date having been fixed. All phases of preparation – moving troops, tanks, supplies, aircraft, ships, etc – would be 'D minus 30, 20, 10 etc', while reinforcements, supplies, etc, would be fixed for 'D plus 1, 2, 3, etc.' There were a multitude of 'D-Days' during the war and no one could have foreseen that the term was to become synonymous with 6 June 1944.

Shortly after the Newhaven exercise it was revealed that the four DRs who had been chosen to take part were the ones who would go ashore with the Fighting Troops on D-Day. By that time I had come to accept that I would remain as a Despatch Rider and was pleased to know that I was 'in' for the invasion of France.

During the second week of May we received the motorcycles to be used during the first days in France – 125cc, two-stroke Famous James. They were primitive and slow in comparison with our 350cc Ariels and their small, squeaky, bulb horns would have better suited a child's kiddicar. As the bikes had no speedometers the actual speed of travel wasn't known but, for the fifty-mile journey to Canterbury, it was simply a matter of twisting the throttle wide open then sitting patiently until you arrived there about one and a half hours later. We soon convinced the Signals Officer that they weren't fast enough to cope with the greatly increased flow of signals traffic in the lead-up to D-Day, so we reverted to the Ariels.

By this time all the unit's transport, apart from motorcycles, had been waterproofed by encasing the electrics in a waterproof, plasticine-like material and extending exhaust pipes and air intakes up to the top of the cab. In addition, every vehicle had been allocated the precise load of men, guns, ammunition, tools, spares, rations, Famous James etc, it was to carry ashore, with a detailed loading plan specifying precisely where each item was to be placed. The exact order of loading and unloading was practised by drivers and others involved until they could do both blindfold.

41 Commando's move towards D-Day was initiated on 17 May when a batch of fully-loaded jeeps, accompanied by the DRs who would not be going ashore on D-Day, left for an unknown destination. Later that same day the four 'D-Day DRs' were each issued with a third machine, a 98cc Excelsior Welbike or 'parascooter' to be carried ashore.

The Welbike had been designed to fit into a standard parachute container and, with handlebars, seat and footrests folded, the overall dimensions were no more than 4'3" × 1'3" × 12". It had a wheelbase of little more than 3 feet, with wheels fitted with 12" × 2" tyres and weighed 75 lbs. It was good fun to tootle around the streets of Hastings on such miniature motorbikes, occasioning turned heads, raised eyebrows and questioning stares, but we were very quickly and curtly told to 'KEEP THEM FOR THE DAY!'

During the following days more and more vehicles rolled away to unknown destinations. On May 23 the last of our operational transport left and with them went Bill and Harry. Our landlady, 'Ma' Sheldrake, shed a few tears as she kissed them goodbye, but had to quickly dry her eyes as the door had barely closed behind them before she was opening it again to admit three Army Commandos, arriving to take over the billet. I was moved down to the basement for what turned out to be my last night in St Anne's Hotel.

Next day, 24 May, Empire Day in 1944, I was suddenly relieved as Duty DR, with orders to pack all kit and equipment and report to HQ by 1730 hours. At the appointed time the 'D-Day element' of the Commando paraded outside their various Troop offices all ready to go, but were told that departure wouldn't be until early the following morning. Arms and equipment were stacked in the offices and shore leave was granted until 1030, when all returned to bed down on the floor beside their gear. By that time a goodly proportion of our number, officers as well as men, were exhibiting the effects of a real humdinger of a 'last night ashore', to the obvious disgust of our Commanding Officer.

By six o'clock next morning the Unit, sore heads and all, was on its way by train, and TCVs completed the journey to another of those huge canvas concentration camps, where once again we found ourselves incarcerated with many hundreds of troops, mostly Canadians. For a change, this one was near 'civilization', on West Common, Southampton; it was soon dubbed 'Stalag C19'.

That evening, although all others were allowed to spend the evening in town, 41 was confined to camp by our CO as a punishment for the previous evening's over-indulgence by a minority. That had in fact been the last opportunity for a night ashore; the camp was 'sealed' next day and thereafter no one was allowed out except in a supervised party. It was galling to see civilians going about their normal business on the other side of the fence, close enough to touch, but it was forbidden even to speak to them. We were as effectively cut off as if already overseas.

For my part, after months of living almost like a civilian with the comparatively light duties of a Despatch Rider, it wasn't a pleasant change to have to sleep on the bare ground, to spend an hour fire-watching most nights and be unceremoniously roused by 0630 reveille. As this was followed by morning parade and weapons inspection, perhaps followed by a route march, I was glad to be able to console myself that my real job was still that of a Despatch Rider.

On our second day in camp we were allocated to the specific craft that would carry us ashore on D-Day. Each craft had been given a serial number and thereafter all instructions given over the Tannoy public address system were by those serial numbers, rather than Units or Troops. To ensure that the loss of a single landing craft would not result in losing the entire command structure, Headquarters Troop had been distributed between the five landing craft allocated to the Unit and I had to respond to 'Serial Number two-five-six . . .'. Also distributed between the serials were the dozen or so German-speaking men from No. 10 Inter-Allied Commando who would accompany patrols and act as interpreters when the Commando was in contact with the enemy.

In Stalag C19 a previously-made suggestion by Captain Peter Howes-Dufton, CO of 'Y' Troop, that the Unit should be allowed to grow beards for the invasion was given the go-ahead by Colonel Gray and a 'Best Beard by D-Day' competition was instigated. As naval personnel, Royal Marines were required to 'put in a chit' (i.e. submit a written request) for 'permission to grow', and removal too was subject to 'permission to shave off'. A period of grace was allowed before having to make a beard 'official' and in my case the results after a few days – tufts of hair sprouting out here and there, with wide expanses of nothing in between – decided me to shave off. All except the moustache, that is, which has been retained as a 'souvenir de la guerre'.

The weather, which had been hot and sunny on our arrival in C 19, grew hotter over the next few days and by Sunday 29th, Whit Sunday, the country was under heatwave conditions. In the afternoon the Commando paraded in 'shirt sleeve order without arms or equipment' to be led out of camp on a training-cum-keep-the-mind-occupied march. With three days' growth of beard, we undoubtedly looked a pretty scruffy lot and, dressed in khaki shirts without collars, sleeves rolled up and trouser braces exposed, no one could possibly have guessed that those nondescript marchers were normally spick and span Royal Marines. On that hot holiday Sunday afternoon, there were few civilians in the city streets, hardly any girls for the wolf whistle treatment and little of interest.

Beyond the city limits, however, things were more interesting, as the shady country roads, completely devoid of people and of traffic, were virtually a never-ending Quartermaster's Store. Along the grass verges edging every carriageway, hidden from the air beneath the canopies of hedgerow trees, were continuous lines of military vehicles of all descriptions, parked nose to tail with hardly any room for a playing card between them. Where there weren't vehicles there were incredibly long stacks of munitions and other military stores. Some stretches were protected from the weather by low arches of corrugated iron, while others were completely shrouded in tarpaulin sheets, stoutly roped to prevent ingress. On each batch, painted white and large, were reference letters and numbers which told the RASC personnel precisely what lay concealed there. Untold quantities of military supplies were waiting in readiness alongside good roads and needing only to be loaded into trucks for transportation to the nearby docks for shipment to France.

The Mediterranean weather continued into Whit Monday when we spent much of the day in a closely guarded, swelteringly hot 'Operations Marquee', as briefing for the forthcoming invasion started. We were given the overall picture of the operation, code-named, as is now well known, OVERLORD, and learned the major specific units that would be taking part. As details of the airborne, infantry and armoured divisions, and other units to be involved, the air and naval support to be provided, radar diversions to mislead the enemy etc, etc, etc, were unfolded, we were overawed by the unbelievable immensity of the scheme.

By reference to large-scale topographical maps of the area to be attacked, with all actual place names replaced by code-words such as 'Ganges', 'Vienna' and 'Poland', a detailed exposition of the invasion plans was given. It was learned at first hand all those things which are now common knowledge – the five main landing beaches, two code-named UTAH and OMAHA for the American First Army under General Bradley at the western end of the invasion coast, and three, GOLD, JUNO and SWORD for General Dempsey's British Second Army, with its substantial proportion of Canadian troops, to the east.

On each flank of the fifty-mile invasion front airborne troops – American west of UTAH and British east of SWORD – were to secure river crossings ready for the breakout from the beachhead. On the British eastern flank troops of the Sixth Airborne Division would land, by parachute and glider, some hours before the seaborne assault began. They had three tasks: to seize the bridges

27

spanning the river and canal linking a town code-named 'Poland' with the Channel coast, to neutralize a German coast defence battery which commanded the landing beaches and to hold a bridgehead on the enemy side of the river 'Ganges', for the eventual breakout from the beachhead of the British Army.

It was crucial for the reinforcement and supply of the Airborne troops that the bridges, lying some four miles from the sea, should be taken intact. The plan therefore was to set down gliders on the narrow strip of land between river bridge and canal bridge, and close enough to the abutments, to enable the troops to get out, reach the bridges and overcome the German guards before they had time to detonate explosive charges thought to be already in place.

The D-Day objectives of the various units were divulged and we were particularly interested in the tasks of the two British Special Service Brigades which were to be involved. These Brigades were No. 1, comprising 3, 4 and 6 Army and 45 Royal Marines Commandos, and No. 4 made up of 41, 46, 47 and 48 Royal Marines Commandos, the strength of each Commando being of the order of 450 men. No. 1 Brigade, which would form the extreme left flank of the entire Allied seaborne landing force, had the task of pushing rapidly inland in order to link up with the Airborne troops at the bridges. Of No. 4 Brigade, 41 and 48 Commandos would land straddling the junction of SWORD and JUNO beaches, to clear the coastal towns in the area, while 46 was to be held in reserve to go ashore next day, D+1, as reinforcement. 47 was given an independent D-Day role on the western flank of the British forces, the capture of Port-en-Bessin, and would land on GOLD beach.

On this occasion the employment of the Commando forces was to be different from usual. Instead of spearheading the attack, they were to land through 'holes' punched in the strong German beach defences by the tanks and guns of more heavily equipped infantry divisions. The Commandos' job would be to widen the point of attack by neutralizing enemy positions remaining along the coast.

The infantry brigades were to concentrate all their efforts upon pushing inland, without concerning themselves about what they might be leaving behind, which meant that none of their tanks, artillery or mortars would be available to support the Commandos in their tasks. 41 Commando was to land behind the leading elements of the 3rd British Infantry Division (3 Div) on SWORD beach, while 48 would follow the 3rd Canadian Infantry Division (3 Can Div) on to JUNO. The two Commandos would then move east and west respectively to clear the coastline between the two points of attack.

Once ashore, 41 Commando was to strike westwards to attack Lion-sur-Mer, a small coastal resort defended by two German positions, a strongpoint at a crossroads near the town and a nearby fortified château. To deal with these, the unit was organized into 'Force I', led by the Commanding Officer, and 'Force II', under the Second-in-Command, Major Barclay. After that the Commando was to attack another town further along the coast and there link-up with 48. The primary D-Day task of the entire British and Canadian attacking force was to be the capture of the town, some eight miles inland, codenamed 'Poland' on the briefing maps.

At the conclusion of that first briefing session each man was handed a small booklet entitled *France*, similar in format to the one called *Italy* we had received before the Sicily landing almost twelve months earlier. It gave sketchy information about the country, its people and language, plus the usual instructions on how troops were expected to behave towards the civilian population, but, more than that, it negated the entire rigmarole of false names on the maps! Its frontispiece is a small map of France, with all the real place names, so it required no more than a glance to recognize the shape of the invasion coastline. This, as is now well-known, extended from the Cherbourg peninsula to the River Orne; it was the Orne bridges that were to be secured by the Sixth Airborne Division, and 'Poland', the 2nd Army's D-Day objective, was the city of Caen.

That evening the DRs, riding their parascooters, were escorted to a nearby petrol filling station where RASC men topped up the tanks. We enjoyed a pleasant if brief outing, but it did occur to us that, as the Welbike's fuel tank held little more than 6 pints, the whole operation could have been accomplished by one man with a jerrican of petrol and a quart of oil!

Over the next few days more details were given of the part the Commando was to play in the landing, without us having to admit that we already knew the general location of the area of disembarkation. We also studied aerial photographs of the SWORD beach area, to visualize the Commando's route to its objectives and to learn more details of the German defences in the area.

H-hour on SWORD beach was set for 0720 hours, but, in the hours of darkness before that, detachments of Royal Engineer and Royal Marine divers would be at work in the shallow inshore waters, rendering harmless German defences planted there to impede landing craft. The action proper would be initiated by a massive naval bombardment of the coast defences; then, prior to the infantry going in to assault, 'swimming tanks', launched from landing craft a few miles offshore, would touch down on the selected beaches. From a hull-down position in the sea, with only their gun turrets exposed above water, the tanks would engage any remaining German defences at close range.

These tanks had flotation girdles – six feet high canvas 'walls' – fitted to the hull which, when erected by compressed air, completely surrounded that part of the tank above the tracks, enabling it to float. On beaching, the walls would be collapsed at the touch of a lever to lie like a skirt about the hull and the tank could go into action immediately. They were fitted with twin propellers turned by the main driving shaft, which gave them a speed of five knots in water and also their technical name of 'Duplex Drive', or simply 'DD', tanks.

After the DDs, it would then be the turn of the Crabs or flail tanks, to explode mines buried in the sand. These were modified Shermans fitted with two massive arms supporting a steel drum, to which lengths of heavy chain were attached. As the Crabs trundled up the beach, with drum rotating, the chains flailed the beach ahead, exploding any mines in their path, leaving a safe route for the infantry to follow. 41 Commando was scheduled to go ashore at 0840, by which time things could be expected to be hotting up, both weather- and other-wise.

At a pay parade later that day we received the equivalent of ten shillings (four days' pay) in 'invasion money' – 200 francs of the French currency issued by AMGOT (Allied Military Government of Occupied Territories) which enabled those who had run out of English money to get back into the card schools; it took the bankers very little time to adjust to handling pounds, shillings – and francs.

The heatwave continued until Wednesday 31 May when part of HQ Troop unexpectedly departed for an unrevealed destination.

June began with appreciably cooler weather and a day of talks. First the Padre, then the Medical Officer, gave us counsel in their respective fields, after which it was the turn of the Commanding Officer. The CO's basic job was to convey General Montgomery's Message to the Troops: 'If things go as planned, and every man does his job to the best of his ability, Germany will be out of the war by October or November – and Japan six months later.' In the event, things didn't turn out that way, so perhaps there was someone who didn't do his job quite to the best of his ability. Such dates, however, didn't impinge upon us very greatly because at the time we firmly believed that, once the invasion forces had been securely established ashore, all Commandos would return to the UK, to be held in readiness for any further landings that might be required.

Every evening in C19 the mess tents doubled up as cinemas and the camp was well provided with films. By wandering around the vast canvas town you could find a different show every night. Many were recent releases, including *Yankee Doodle Dandy* and *And the Angels Sing*. We also felt chuffed at seeing Bing Crosby playing the Roman Catholic father in *Going My Way* some time before the film's general release in the UK.

Cinema shows were the only form of organized entertainment available to the rank and file, as the camp was completely 'dry'. To partially redress this last fact, immediately after the trio of talks on hopes, health and the hereafter, there was a second pay parade when each man received another ten shillings of due pay, in English money this time, to enable us to visit a public house.

This sounded great and engendered gleeful anticipation of another 'Glorious First of June' – it just happened to be the 150th anniversary of Admiral Howe's victory over the French off Ushant in 1794 in which Royal Marines had played such a useful part. In the event it turned out to be rather a low-key affair, far removed from any normal 'few pints at the local'.

After the evening meal all volunteers for 'Operation Pub' were fallen in and marched out of camp. The rendezvous had obviously been reconnoitred in advance and any thoughts of resting an elbow on the bar whilst chatting-up a barmaid, or even passing the time of day with mine host, were quickly dispelled. We found ourselves crammed, shoulder to shoulder, into a small garden area behind the hotel and told to stay there. Orders were taken by officers and senior NCOs, who brought out the drinks, to be consumed where standing. Two pints per man was the ration, after which it was: 'All right lads, that's your lot – Get fell in outside', followed by a brisk march back to camp. The British tend to take their pleasures rather seriously.

The weather continued cool, as more briefings and final preparations went ahead. On Friday 2 June we were issued with a few items of 'Commando' equipment, designed to help us escape in the event of being taken prisoner, to be secreted about our persons. These included maps printed on very fine silk which could be folded into amazingly small dimensions, small files and a variety of compasses, for sewing into pocket flaps or uniform linings. To a casual observer my compass was no more than a pair of standard brass trouser buttons, but one was fitted with a needle-point fulcrum and the other had tiny steel inserts which caused it to behave as a magnetic needle. I also opened up one of the seams of the trousers to conceal a three-inch-long file.

On the morning of Saturday 3 June it was announced that we would be leaving C19 next day; D-Day was scheduled for Monday morning, 5 June. Personal ammunition and enough food to feed ourselves for the first two days ashore was issued, then came an unexpected packing problem. Each man received a free issue of a hundred cigarettes which had somehow been wangled by our Padre, the Rev Caradoc Hughes, but whether or not by divine intervention wasn't revealed.

During the last few days in C19 the stream of military traffic passing the camp had increased to flood proportions. By day and night guns, tanks, trucks and jeeps had clanked and rumbled past, no doubt some of the build-up forces moving into marshalling areas vacated by the D-Day vehicles already loaded on board their craft.

At 0820 hrs on Sunday morning a Communion Service was held for those who wanted it and this was followed at 1000 hrs by a regular Church of England Parade. We had kitted-up ready to move off when given the bombshell news that the invasion had been postponed! Maybe for only twenty-four hours, but. . . . We returned to waiting and playing cards, and, to my great astonishment, I won 250 francs at pontoon – maybe a good omen.

Rain began to fall during the evening and by lights-out the

weather was cool, wet and definitely dicey. We turned in, with our minds full of conjecture. Would we move off next morning or would the whole complicated business have to be gone through again in time for the next 'propitious' day for tides which wouldn't be for another month?

Chapter 3

D-DAY, SIXTH OF JUNE 1944

Monday dawned bright and clear and, even as we awoke, the message was in the air – OVERLORD was ON! D-Day would be one day later than originally planned but the long-awaited Allied invasion of France was all set to go ahead next day, Tuesday, Sixth of June.

Blankets were returned to store at 0900 hours and, after a meal at noon, we boarded TCVs for the short, dusty ride to the embarkation point which we had used previously, at Warsash on the River Hamble. After the inevitable, unexplained wait, the Commando filed on board the five LCI(S)s which were to carry it to France. Late in the afternoon the craft eased away from their berths, steamed a short distance and moored to buoys anchored in the fairway. These indicated our allotted position in the vast armada being gathered together in Southampton Water and spilling out into the Solent.

Those who had been involved in the Commando's two previous landings in the Mediterranean had already experienced similar vast build-ups of the almost unbelievable numbers of ships and invasion craft needed for an assault upon an enemy-held coast and this one re-awakened our amazement and wonder. Everywhere we looked there were more and yet more vessels of all sizes, shapes and types, and this, we knew, was only one of goodness knows how many other such marshalling areas along the south coast of England. Other convoys from more distant locations were already at sea. We had been slotted into our own little niche in the overall scheme of things and could at least draw comfort from the fact that, what-ever the morrow might bring, there would certainly be a lot of our own people over there with us.

1:50,000 maps of our stretch of the Normandy coast were produced and we began to learn the names of the towns and villages soon to be seen at first hand. The Commando would go ashore on the beach of Hermanville-sur-Mer, a small town lying a mile or so inland, and would move on to clear Lion-sur-Mer, then press on to Luc-sur-Mer and link up with 48.

Familiarizing myself with our area of operations, I noticed the name of a small place lying between Lion and Luc – Petit Enfer, and thought that, next morning, 'Little Hell' could very well live up to its name. I also learned that the gun battery on the far side of the River Orne, said to threaten the landing beaches, was at Merville.

The armada assembling off Southampton continued to grow ever larger throughout the afternoon and evening until, at around 2130 hours, our craft were unhitched from the buoys. We took our place in the seemingly unending stream of vessels moving down the Solent, passing the Isle of Wight and into the English Channel. There was nothing for us to do but await the passage of time, putting our trust in God and the Royal Navy to get us unscathed to the right place at the right time next morning.

Most remained on deck, marvelling at the unbelievable sight of the innumerable black shapes sailing with us, until they became lost in the overall darkness. Then we moved down to the messdecks, three small 'boxes' each accommodating about thirty men with only an army blanket to wrap around oneself before settling down on the deck. We were accustomed to bedding down just where and when directed, so slept reasonably well throughout what turned out to be an uneventful night.

We awoke next morning to feel the landing craft being tossed about by a very disturbed sea and the sound of heavy guns engaging enemy shore installations coming down to us. Called out on deck, we stretched legs and cleared lungs of the fuggy fumes of the cramped messdeck, finding the early morning sea air, even in 'Glorious June', to be breathtakingly cold. The coastline of France was no more than a dark smudge on our port bow and all around were the silhouettes of the multitude of other vessels moving with us relentlessly towards the shore; some of our number were being sick over the side.

It would be more than an hour before we could expect to touch down and it was breakfast time. As we carried our own rations, we had the choice of menu, so I opted for the self-heating soup. The can was fitted with a chemical element running down the centre which, activated by a ring pull, had the contents piping hot within a few seconds. Mine appeared to be tomato and it tasted marvellous on the way down, but the rolling and pitching of the LCI suddenly persuaded my insides that they would feel very much better without anything like tomato soup to contend with. I joined the others at the ship's rail.

Ahead, along the coast to the west, we could see the rippling flashes of gunfire from sea and shore. The rumble of the Naval bombardment, pouring salvo after salvo on to the German defences, and the enemy's reply, grew louder by the minute. We were enjoying a ringside seat for such a momentous occasion, but weren't allowed to watch for long. 'All right! (it was always "all right", even when we knew that things were anything but right) Back to your messdecks and wait to be called up'. No reason was given for cooping us up, certainly no one had any thoughts of jumping overboard and swimming home.

The messdeck, although still slightly fuggy, was warm and cosy after our chilly sojourn on deck. We kitted up, checked weapons and equipment yet again, then sat around smoking and wondering. I was still somewhat apprehensive about humping the parascooter ashore. I had extended the seat, handlebars and footrests ready to wheel it along the deck when the time came, but realized that the tricky part would be heaving that 75 lbs of metal on to my shoulder and getting down the ramp, with goodness knows what kind of 'muck' flying around.

For the next half-hour or more it was frightening and frustrating to be confined below decks. Moving into calmer water closer inshore, the rolling and pitching became much less pronounced, but, as we came within range of the German guns, the landing craft's movements became violent and spasmodic. The shriek of incoming shells came to us quite clearly, but all we could do was to hunch our shoulders and exchange wry looks at each uncontrolled bounce and sway resulting from nearby explosions.

The cacophony of noise coming down to us increased in intensity; there was no way of sorting out the causes and meanings of all the whines explosions and thumps, but they told us that we were getting very close to the beach. By then we were not so much concerned about what was going on ashore as just getting our feet on dry land before the craft caught a packet.

The urgent notice of our release came at last, bawled down from the deck, 'All right, lads! We're touching down – on deck quick!' We crowded out into the daylight to be immediately assailed by an incredible medley of sights, sounds and smells. There were momentary glimpses of an untidy, straggling line of craft nosed up onto a crowded beach littered with tanks and other vehicles, many of them burning, scurrying figures and bodies in the water. Then there were the smells of cordite and of smoke drifting from burning ships and tanks. Everything taking place, the swaying of our landing craft, the crackling small arms fire, the whines of shells and their crashing detonations, were absorbed by impressions; there was no conscious looking about, the overriding concern was to get ashore in the shortest space of time.

I was on the port side, crouching low against the midships deckhouse, grasping the handles of my parascooter, ready to start pushing, when the urgent shriek of an incoming shell terminated in a shattering explosion on the starboard side of our craft. There was no time to assess whether it had been an actual hit or a near miss, nor even to wonder who, if anyone, had been hit; the voice of authority was urging us to, 'Keep moving! Get the hell out of it!! Get ashore!!!' I began to push the bike along the deck, closely following the man in front and being chivvied to move faster by the one behind.

At the bows there was a bottle-neck. Our LCI was wallowing skew-on to the beach; the bottom of the port ramp had floated away and was leading down into deep water in the general direction of England. Only the starboard ramp was usable and that was on the skew, both with the LCI and with the shore; men were queueing to get on to it. With only its bows in contact with terra firma, the craft was rolling helplessly in the sloshing motions of the sea. The only dry way down to France was via a narrow strip of timber gangway which was bucking and swaying like a cakewalk at a fair.

From my eye-level view, some fifteen feet above the beach, it was obvious that shouldering the Welbike and attempting to run down the ramp would probably have resulted in one very wet Marine and a waterlogged and useless piece of machinery. When my turn came to descend, therefore, I cradled the machine in my arms, stepped on to the ramp and sat down! Then, like a small child making its way downstairs nursing a teddy bear, I executed a rapid boots-and-bottom descent until I could swing my legs into shallow water and hop off. I splashed through a few yards of sea and kept on running over the deep soft sand, following a string of men disappearing into a large crater some twenty yards from the water's edge. I dropped the bike on the edge and rolled in beside them.

That temporary refuge, blasted out of the sand by an aerial bomb or large-calibre shell, was perhaps twenty-five feet across and five deep, and already occupied by a score of men. Some were lining the inland edge, firing rifles and a Bren in the direction of a wire fence, looking more like chain link than barbed wire, only a few dozen yards away. A fleeting impression of field-grey uniforms on the other side of the wire was cut off a split second later when a Churchill tank trundled to a halt between shell-hole and fence. The hatch was flung open, two crew members rapidly emerged and, standing exposed on the turret, reached down to drag out one of their comrades, who dangled limp and bloody from their hands. They were lowering him gently to the sand when our officer gave the order to follow him and doubled off along the beach to our right.

Even as I was humping the bike on to my shoulder the others were moving away and I was soon falling further and further behind. After only a dozen yards of stumbling through the soft sand, the weight became too much, so I dropped the machine and began to push it. The small wheels sank down to their axles and, instead of turning, simply gouged a furrow in the sand. For several minutes I alternated between trying to push the bike and heaving it up for another carry, until I was sweating like a stuck pig and my muscles could take no more. The others were out of sight, having disappeared through a gap in the tall hedge bounding the beach a few hundred yards ahead of me; it was obvious that my only hope of catching up would be to abandon the machine. I was then along-side a knocked-out Churchill tank, three of her crew crouching on the sand alongside. I dropped the Welbike in front of the first one and gasped, 'Here, Jack! Want a motorbike?' Without waiting for any response, I flexed aching muscles and ran on.

Relieved of the strain of concentrating everything upon coping with the parascooter, even as I ran my eyes and mind absorbed a little more of the turmoil about me. The landing had been timed for high tide, to enable craft to pass over obstacles in the water, so the action was concentrated on a narrow strip of dry sand. Tanks and other vehicles were burning on the beach, shattered craft were on fire at the water's edge and shells were falling here, there and anywhere. Amongst the floating debris being lapped against the shore, dead men, still supported by their Mae West life jackets, were bobbing about like corks. Other bodies lay scattered haphazardly over the sand.

Running past one of those dead men, I heard the urgent swishing of an incoming salvo which was obviously going to land very close and he seemed to offer an improved chance of survival. Without hesitation, I flung myself down alongside the body hoping, as proved to be the case, that the shells would land on the other side of him. I'm sure he would have understood. Fortunately, in soft ground, missiles go deep before exploding and their effect is directed upwards rather than outwards, so that their killing range is more confined.

No sooner had the shells burst than I was up and running, quickly reaching the gap through which the others had disappeared, where I was amazed to find two infantrymen digging a slit trench right there in the sand. They must have been new to the invasion game as the first rule of any landing was GET OFF THE BEACH! – to some place for which the enemy didn't have the map coordinates displayed in front of every artillery piece within range.

I ran through the gap to find myself on the narrow, unmetalled coastal road made familiar by maps and aerial photographs. The simple act of stepping on to it effected an instantaneous transition from the chaos and death of a crowded invasion beach to the deserted, if still noisy, seclusion of a residential area. There were some evidences of destruction, the road was strewn with rubble and draped with a tangle of wires from shattered telegraph poles, but the far side was lined with towering, three- or four-storeyed, half-timbered houses with steeply sloping roofs and pointed gables over their upper windows.

I had turned right and was running westwards in the direction of Lion-sur-Mer. From our briefings I knew that, a hundred yards or so ahead, this coastal track formed a junction with a road leading inland towards Caen. A short distance further on would be a Y-junction, both arms of which led to Lion, but the actual one to be used by the Commando had been left to be decided by 'prevailing circumstances' after the landing.

Just before reaching the junction I came upon a wounded infantryman, slumped against a wall bounding the right-hand side of the track. He had suffered a pretty bad leg wound, which I knew I couldn't do much about. 'Anything I can do for you, mate?' I asked. 'I'm OK,' he answered, 'but I wouldn't mind a fag.' I lit a cigarette and placed it between his lips. 'I'm OK,' he repeated, 'better push off and catch up with your pals.'

I left him with a 'Best of luck, chum!' and, on reaching the junction, came upon two stragglers of the Commando, crouching low in a ditch as an assortment of missiles passed over. They were debating which of the two roads to Lion to take and we all moved forward to have a closer look at the alternatives. At that moment an angry multiple whine heralded the imminent approach of another salvo of shells which weren't going to pass over. Instinctively we dived to the nearest cover, the shop premises forming the apex of the angle between the two roads to Lion, which was already devoid of a door and had no glass in its windows.

After the shells had exploded unpleasantly close we raised our heads to find that our refuge had been in the local Post Office-cum-Stationers. Amongst the debris littering the floor were scores of picture postcards, two of which caught my eye, one of Hermanville Plage where we had just landed, deserted apart from a solitary rowing boat, while the other was of the shop we were in. I pushed them inside my battledress blouse.

Of the two routes to Lion the left fork skirted open country, being built up along the right-hand side only, while the other, lying nearer the sea, was narrow, overhung with trees and high walls ran along both sides. That one looked safer, so we started off at the double, but, almost instantaneously, another batch of shells shrieked in to impact on the carriageway only a few score yards ahead. We hesitated momentarily, but guessed that shells, like lightning, probably wouldn't strike in the same place twice. We ran on, over the shell craters, very shallow ones as the shells had fallen on a hard, paved surface, passing through the last vestiges of smoke and the lingering smell of burnt explosive. A few minutes later, reaching the edge of a more built-up part of Lion we came upon the tail end of HQ Troop, crouching on the pavement against the walls of buildings on the left hand side of the road.

They were awaiting orders to move forward into the centre of town and weren't slow in giving us a ribbing for having fallen behind. Hardly had our trio flopped to the ground for a breather, however, than everyone was ordered to their feet and we were running at full pelt along the narrow pavement, making very little noise in our rubber-soled 'brothel creeper' boots.

We were passing within a few feet of the abutting houses and, framed in a number of the ground-floor windows could be seen the faces of curious, apprehensive, inhabitants of Lion-sur-Mer. The presence of British troops in their small French town would have made it abundantly clear to them that the Second Front in Europe had indeed started and that they were right in the middle of it. For a fleeting moment I gained the impression of an open view to our right in the direction of the English Channel, then once again there were buildings lining both sides of the street. We were halted and told to 'Wait Here!'

Sweating profusely from the combination of the now hot June sunshine and our exertions, we dropped to the pavement and sat with backs against the wall of the buildings sucking in lungsful of air. Given permission to 'Carry on smoking', green berets were removed to wipe streaming brows and also to get at the cigarettes and matches stashed there, to better their chances of a dry landing. Our group of HQ Marines had landed on the forecourt of a small shop and, surprisingly, its door was standing open for business. One of our number, who had left his matches in a trousers pocket and found them damp and useless, called across, 'Hey, Mitch! This is a paper shop. They probably sell matches. Go and buy us some will yer?' My few words of schoolboy French had put me on the spot, but it was a case of *noblesse oblige*, so I searched the depths of memory for the right words, took his five franc AMGOT note and went inside.

41

There was a young girl and an elderly lady behind the counter and when I said, '*Avez-vous des allumettes, s'il vous plait?*' Matches were produced, the note I proffered was accepted and they gave me change. Looking back, I have puzzled over how they had treated my request so phlegmatically, as though it was an everyday occurrence to sell matches in the middle of an invasion and to accept a previously unseen currency in payment. Nevertheless that, undoubtedly, must have been the very first 'invasion money' spent in the OVERLORD operation.

There is no doubt that the situation of our group of HQ personnel at that time was rather incongruous. Barely a mile away the beach of death and destruction on which we had landed was still receiving a pounding of artillery fire, yet here we were, sitting on the pavement in the sunshine. The morning air all about was filled with the sounds of whining projectiles and crumping explosions, but nothing was coming our way so we had time to reflect upon our great good fortune at having survived the greatest seaborne landing of all time. Similar but more distant sounds of gun-fire were coming to us from the direction of other landing beaches further along the coast beyond Lion-sur-Mer.

Then we began to hear the sounds of lighter explosions, probably mortar fire, coming from only a few hundred yards away, which indicated that forward elements of the Commando hadn't progressed very far. Whether the fire was 'ours' or 'theirs' was a matter of conjecture, but it was quite close and slightly disconcerting. However, there was obviously nothing that our particular little batch of HQ Troop was required to do for the time being, so we just sat in the sunshine, smoked and chatted.

We hadn't been there for long when an agitated French lady approached from the direction of the town centre. She clearly had something of import to impart so, as the only Britisher around with even a smattering of French, I went across to help. After asking her to speak more slowly, I gathered that there was a wounded soldier in her house and, with one of our Sick Berth Attendants, accompanied her through narrow alleyways then upstairs into her front bedroom. Sure enough, lying fully clothed on the bed was an Army private who had oozed a sticky mess of blood onto her snowy sheets and pillow from a jagged gash in his shoulder.

The SBA removed the soldier's battledress blouse, tore open his shirt, cleaned the wound and applied a field dressing. We talked about moving him, but the lady intimated that she didn't mind him staying for the time being. With his wound neatly dressed, the pongo's main concern became the fact that he had lost the fighting order pack containing his food, so we left him some of our own to be going on with.

Hardly had we returned to the paper shop than someone called out, 'Hey, Mitch, what does, "*blessay*" mean?' Another lady had come to report that she too had a wounded soldier. I persuaded a different Sick Bay Tiffie to go with her by himself. I couldn't afford to give away too much of my food ration.

We had been waiting for orders for perhaps an hour when a pronounced build-up of mortar/artillery fire in the immediate vicinity confirmed the fact that the forward Troops of the Commando were having problems. It was clearly unsafe to be hanging around in the open streets, so we were quickly moved into the grounds of a church and set to work digging slit trenches.

I was assigned to a position alongside a tarmacadam path near where a trench for the Headquarters Signaller was being excavated. As we were digging, driblets of information filtered through and we learned the names of some of the numerous men of the Unit who had become casualties. The dead included my oppo, 'Geordie' Swindale from Gateshead, killed by a shell burst; the RSM 'Horace' Belcher, who had trodden on a mine, and our Second-in-Command, Major Barclay who, not many weeks earlier, had docked me three days' pay for speeding.

In view of the loss of his 2 i/c and some Troop Commanders, Colonel Gray had taken over command of Force II as well as Force I and attempted to proceed with the Unit's tasks as planned. Heavy casualties on the beach, however, had delayed assembly and greatly reduced the number of men available to him for the attacks on the Commando's two objectives. On top of this, all the Navy's bombardment signallers, assigned to the Commando for the first wave, had been wounded on the beach and their radio sets rendered useless, so it was impossible to call for any supporting gunfire. In addition, the attached Centaur tanks had been knocked out early in the day and, in consequence, the Fighting Troops had no close-up artillery support when moving in towards their objectives.

In view of heavy losses on the beach, tanks of any description had been at a premium, but, after the Centaurs had been knocked out, three AVREs (Armoured Vehicles, Royal Engineers) had been made available to support 'P' and 'Y' Troops as they moved forward with the South Lancs to attack the Lion-sur-Mer strongpoint. Those vehicles were based on Churchill tank chassis, but their function was to attack reinforced concrete fortifications at close range, not to provide infantry support. Their single artillery piece was a huge 290mm spigot mortar, designed to hurl 40lb 'flying dustbin' missiles at concrete blockhouses. Their range, however, was no more than 80 yards and they had a maximum rate of fire of only three rounds per minute.

The AVREs, nevertheless, led the Commando's advance upon the strongpoint, firing their Besa machine guns, primarily providing an armoured shield for our men. Unfortunately, at a range of about 100 yards, a well-sited German anti-tank gun (later identified as a 50mm PAK 38) opened up on them and, one after another, all three were knocked out. 'Y' Troop Commander, Captain Peter Howes-Dufton was killed and the Troop suffered other casualties before they could take up positions in houses on both sides of the road from which to engage the enemy.

The arrangements for these operations, and putting them into effect, occupied most of the morning. Then 'B' Troop, pushing forward towards the château, had come under heavy fire from German mortars and a field gun. By that time 41 Commando's own mortar section had expended all of its immediately available ammunition, so couldn't retaliate. Being without any artillery or mortar support, 'B' Troop was unable to move forward and was ordered to hold fast where they were.

As this was going on, Headquarters Troop, as well as excavating some protection for itself, had been operating the overall command functions. All Signals, Intelligence, Medical and general co-ordinating requirements had been carried out from holes in the churchyard. At an early stage a push bike was produced and I had been given signals to deliver in the vicinity. As the morning advanced the mortar fire became heavier and closer. Men were having to distinguish between the urgent, short, sharp 'SWISH! SWISSH!, SWISSSH!'es, which meant, 'heads down quick', as a batch of missiles was going to land very close, and the more leisurely, 'SSSWWWIIIISSSSHHH'es of those bombs which were on a flatter trajectory, and so would fall at a safe distance, so far as they were concerned.

It was probably around noon when an officer called me across to the Signals trench to say that some of the Commando's jeeps, together with a Famous James motorbike, would soon be coming ashore at Hermanville Plage, and sent me off to bring them up. Once clear of the churchyard, cycling back to the beach, conditions were appreciably quieter until nearing the Post Office again, as that area was still receiving attention from German artillery. During the few short hours since diving for cover in the shop, the deserted coastal road had been transformed. A continuous flow of military vehicles of all descriptions was now streaming from the beach area, while an impeccably turned-out military police sergeant was on point duty at the road junction. Wearing white belt, anklets and gauntlet gloves, his arms were in continuous motion, chivvying drivers to keep moving and directing them to make the left turn towards Caen. As I neared the junction a flurry of incoming shells prompted another dive for cover, but the MP on point duty carried on imperturbably.

Beyond him the secluded residential road I had to myself that morning had also changed beyond all recognition. The hedge had been bulldozed out of existence, the road lay open to the beach and was choc-a-bloc with a one-way, nose-to-tail stream of military vehicles with many many more seeking an opportunity to join in.

The beach too, still littered with burnt-out tanks and other debris, had also changed remarkably. The tide had ebbed, so there was now very much more of it and, except for those sunk and disabled still lying in the shallows, the LCIs had gone. In their place were dozens of LCTs (Landing Craft, Tank) disgorging guns, trucks, jeeps, ambulances, staff cars, mobile workshops and every other item of military mechanization. Strip after strip of steel Somerfield tracking funnelled them across the soft sand, to continually feed the flood of vehicles heading towards the MP on point duty.

I had been given the serial number of the LCT to find, but guessed that it would be simpler just to look for the Commando's own identification number, '93', painted on the front and rear of every vehicle. I had to ride the push-bike along a much greater length of road than I ran along earlier in the day, but, suddenly, 'Bingo!'

– there was an LCT which had obviously just dropped its ramp and a bunch of 93s was clearly visible. They had a short, splashy trip ashore, but the waterproofing of the engines proved effective and there were no problems. On the back of one of the jeeps reclined a Famous James motorbike. When it was lifted off I swung my leg over the saddle, depressed the kick-start and the engine burst into life. A triumphant squeeze of its pathetic little bulb horn, however, produced no more than a gurgling squirt of seawater.

Leading the string of jeeps back along the track, I had to convince the MP that my little convoy was indeed the exception and that our route lay not inland towards Caen but along the coast to Lion. After moving past him, the road was deserted once more and in a matter of minutes we were back with Commando HQ at the church. The shell/mortar fire was much worse than when I had left and everyone was preparing to move out.

It appeared that 'A' and 'B' Troops had been heavily attacked as they neared the château and Colonel Gray, anticipating a general enemy counter-attack and still being without any artillery support, had decided to pull back a short distance to hold a more defensible line. The jeeps I had led forward were immediately put to good use in moving Commando HQ and evacuating casualties.

HQ travelled about half a mile down the road, through a gateway in the hedge on the left-hand side and up a track on the other side of the hedge leading to the apple orchard chosen by Colonel Gray for his HQ area. To the right of this track open fields stretched away towards the coast and about three hundred yards away, half-left from the gateway on a slight rise in the land, stood a large modern bungalow. It was reasonably intact, but had obviously been badly damaged by a shell or bomb and was deserted.

With Commando Headquarters being in the orchard, some two hundred yards from the gate, the jeeps, on their return from ambulance service, were parked alongside the hedge, hidden from the air by the overhanging trees and camouflage netting. We all set-to digging slit trenches in the narrow verge between track and hedge, a slow and laborious business with the one-piece entrenching tool comprising no more than a 6" long 'pick' at one end, and a 6" × 5" 'shovel' at the other. Work was halted from time to time by the arrival of shells or mortar bombs, so the afternoon had advanced into evening before sufficient earth had been removed to create holes large enough to enable us to curl up below ground level and sleep with a reasonable degree of safety.

Whilst engaged with this digging, although the rank and file didn't know it at the time, the Commando had come under the command of the 9th British Infantry Brigade (9 Bde), which hadn't come ashore until H + 6, i.e. around 1330 hours. Two of their battalions, the 5th Lincolnshires and the Royal Ulster Rifles, had been sent to assist 41 in the coastal sector, where the Brigade Commander had deployed them to extend the perimeter begun by Colonel Gray earlier in the day. Fortunately, one of the jeeps brought forward had been that of the RN Forward Officer Bombardment (FOB) who finally made radio contact with destroyers lying off-shore and called for a prolonged shoot onto both the château and strongpoint. It lasted from 1700 hours to 1800 hours and, whilst in progress, Lieutenant Stevens reported back with half of 'A' Troop which had been cut off when the unit had pulled back earlier in the day.

As the shadows lengthened there seemed little doubt that HQ would spend the night in that position and, as no other transport had reached us, there wouldn't be any blankets for bedding down. The only coverings in our equipment were waterproof sheets and anti-gas capes, so Bill Smith and I decided to reconnoitre the bombed bungalow. The interior was a shambles of demolished walls, wrecked furniture and shattered household goods, but amongst the rubble we came across a dusty red quilt, which we decided to 'liberate' and returned to our hole with it in some glee. The quilt performed yeoman service that night and for many more nights thereafter, but we never did get the opportunity of returning it to its owner.

By dusk all was quiet in our vicinity. The sky to the north-west, beyond the open fields abutting our narrow track, glowed bright orange in the setting sun and was streaked with long, grey clouds. The Isle of Wight lay barely a hundred miles away in that general direction, but we might have been at the other side of the world.

Then the calm of late evening was disturbed by the drone of many aircraft engines and men tensed themselves ready to dive for cover. However, when long strings of aircraft could be distinguished, as silhouettes against the colourful sky, it was obvious that they were coming from England. As they came nearer it could be seen that each one was towing a glider; it was the Sixth Air Landing Brigade, going in to reinforce the Sixth Airborne Division and No. 1 Special Service Brigade, holding a bridgehead on the far side of the River Orne.

As the aerial armada drew near a few shells burst amongst the aircraft, showing that there were still a few enemy anti-aircraft guns within range, but the planes didn't falter. They had appeared from about half-left, looking towards the coast and, as they flew across our front, spontaneous bursts of cheering came from the men on the ground. When the leading planes disappeared from sight below the trees a few miles away to the right, however, a build-up of crackling anti-aircraft fire subdued all jollity. Barely five miles away, beyond the Orne bridges, the gliders were swooping down to a hot reception. All we could do was to wish the troops in them a silent 'Good luck, chaps'.

Within a matter of minutes the leading planes, having released their gliders, were heading back the way they had come. Altogether our unexpected session of evening entertainment lasted little more than twenty minutes from the first rumble of approaching engines to the last planes disappearing northwards. As they were leaving there was the inevitable wag within earshot whose thoughts had perhaps been in other minds. 'Just think,' he said, 'those bloody RAF pilots'll be back swilling beer in their canteens in about an hour's time,' but most of us would much rather not have been reminded of that sort of thing.

With darkness came the enemy bombers, but they weren't after us. Their target was the mass of shipping lying off the invasion beaches and it was clear that they were directing their attention not towards nearby SWORD beach, but further west in the direction of GOLD and JUNO. Anyhow, that gave us something else to watch – tracers arching skyward, exploding ack-ack shells and the flashing explosions of bombs silhouetting the skyline of the inter-vening landscape. It was all happening some miles away, so we were no more than interested spectators. Bill and I eventually settled down for our first night in French soil and, thanks to the borrowed red quilt, it was warm enough. Apart from taking our normal turns on guard duty, the hours of darkness and the inevitable dawn stand-to passed without incident.

Not until long after the war did I learn more about the action our Commando had been involved in that day. At the time it was happening there was no opportunity to ask questions, it was largely a case of just being thankful that 'Number One' was still in one piece and concentrating your other thoughts upon such things as food and rest. It seems, however, that the German defenders in the Lion- and Luc-sur-Mer area, which lay between the 41 and 48 Commando beaches, had managed to maintain their positions after the first assaults and that a battalion of Panzer Grenadiers, supported by tanks, had, later in the day, attacked from the direction of Caen to link up with them.

By evening six tanks and a Company of infantry had in fact reached the coast where they managed to contact Germans still in position there. This had created the possibility of developing a wedge between the British and Canadian forces. The arrival of the 6th Air Landing Brigade, which we witnessed without knowing just who they were, had, perhaps, persuaded them to pull back.

The Official War Diary of 41 Royal Marines Commando for D-Day records that the unit suffered 140 casualties, including four Officers and twenty-two Other Ranks killed, out of a total landing strength of 437 officers and men.

Chapter 4

IN THE NORMANDY BEACHHEAD

Like every day in the forward areas, Wednesday 7 June, D + 1, on the outskirts of Lion-sur-Mer, began with a dawn stand-to. Attacks were sometimes initiated when there was just sufficient daylight to enable attacking troops to maintain contact in the hope of catching the enemy before he was fully organized. All ranks were, therefore, wide-awake and in defensive positions well before sunrise just in case. Not until full daylight had been well established, there having been no attack, were we stood down to flex cramped muscles and think of breakfast.

With stand down, however, the unit was alerted for an 'immediate' move off, so it was a case of getting something into one's inside as quickly as possible. The tin of hot soup which had ended up in the English Channel twenty-four hours previously would have been ideal, but I had to make do with dehydrated porridge. The individual block of porridge oats, dried milk and sugar was intended to be crumbled into a mess tin of boiling water, but I ate mine like a bar of chocolate and achieved the porridge effect by drinking hot tea.

Then, kitted up ready to go, we awaited the order to start engines, and waited, and waited. Intermittent salvoes of shells and mortar bombs were being exchanged in our general neighbourhood and sporadic outbursts of small-arms fire could be heard from the direction of the strongpoint and château. Although some elements of the German army were still active in our area, the main forces of both sides were now some eight or nine miles inland, in the vicinity of Caen, the D-Day objective which had not been achieved.

The waiting had continued for about two hours when sounds of approaching air activity drew all eyes skyward, to see Spitfires in hot pursuit of three German Heinkel bombers flying low in our direction. Attention concentrated on one of the latter with some puzzlement when a large cylindrical object was seen to fall from its belly, but when it opened to disgorge a tumbling cascade of small silvery objects, the truth clicked home. Urgent yells of 'Anti-personnel . . . !! sent us scattering for cover and there was barely time to dive into the narrow gap between jeep and hedge before scores of small bombs were bursting like vicious fire crackers all around.

Hundreds of the bombs had been scattered over a wide area and, although the men who had been by the jeeps were unscathed, in the Headquarters orchard a few score yards away four had been killed and nine wounded. Two of those killed were attached personnel, the Royal Artillery Forward Observation Officer and the Corporal-in-charge of the Brigade Headquarters Signals Link. The wounded included our Commanding Officer, Colonel Gray, and the Chaplain, the Rev Caradoc Hughes RNVR. One HQ Signaller who had dived into his foxhole was unhurt but found his steel helmet, left on the soil outside, had been lacerated by bomb splinters.

With the Colonel evacuated and Major Barclay having been killed the previous day, (ten out of twenty-two officers of the Commando had become casualties in 24 hours), command of the unit devolved upon the Adjutant, Major John Taplin. He was then aged only 23, having joined us as a Second Lieutenant fresh from Cadet School almost three years earlier.

Shortly after the casualties had been evacuated the Commando received its orders. The bulk of the unit was to support 5 Lincs in an attack on the château, while HQ and one Fighting Troop would move around the German positions to make a sweep further inland towards Luc-sur-Mer. Bill Smith was the Despatch Rider chosen to accompany the Lincolnshires, so I was obliged to hand over the Famous James and proceed on foot.

The out-flanking party moved off inland – long, snaking files of men spaced out along each side of the road, weapons at the ready, eyes scouring the countryside. It was empty apart from a few groups of tank men removing flotation girdles and transport drivers 'de-waterproofing' their engines. After about a mile the straggling column turned on to a minor road lined with 'bocage'-type dykes, which ran roughly parallel to the coast in the direction of Luc. Two château-like estates were encountered en route and we made searches of the buildings and grounds; the occupants, interrogated by officers, appeared reluctant to seem too friendly, perhaps thinking that the Germans might return and consider them collaborators.

There was no hint of any urgency in the progress, the column just meandered along through a hot summer's afternoon. News came that the attack on the château had been successful, with very few casualties but not much effect upon the Germans, as most had managed to escape. 5 Lincs and 41 Commando had then moved on towards the other German position, the strongpoint.

By late afternoon the marching column was passing small farms and groups of cottages where the people were obviously delighted to see us. Women and young girls stood by the roadside clutching bunches of roses and, as we trudged past, blooms were pushed into battledress pockets, behind ammunition pouches or under the shoulder straps of webbing equipment. Old men sitting in the sunshine were not so demonstrative, but most held up two fingers in the V sign; there were shouts of 'Vive les Anglais!' All in all it engendered the feeling of being a hot and sticky conquering hero!

In the early evening the column was halted where it would spend the night and Commando HQ set about organizing itself in a farm at a crossroads on high ground giving a view of the sea about a mile away. With the Signallers, the DRs were assigned to a straw-covered, smelly but cosy corner of the farmyard, where it was a great relief to shed arms and equipment. Soon we were able to enjoy the civilizing luxury of the first wash and shave since leaving Stalag C19 at Southampton. Was that only two days ago? It seemed like half a lifetime!

News filtered through that the attack on the Lion strongpoint had been successful, although no details were forthcoming. 41 had not been involved as 9 Brigade had detached the unit from 5 Lincs and sent it forward independently to Luc-sur-Mer, which they had occupied without opposition earlier that evening. 46 (RM) Commando, after landing that morning, had cleared Petit Enfer against some determined opposition, but all was now quiet there too.

Spruced-up but hungry, we finished off the last of the individual 48-hour rations we had carried ashore and, as darkness fell, our 'evening entertainment' began. From our high vantage point we watched a succession of German bombing attacks on the ships lying off the beaches and the impressive ack-ack barrage blasted into the sky to counter them. In the farmyard, much removed from all that, we passed a pleasantly quiet night, interrupted only by a two-hour stint of sentry duty.

By next morning, 8 June (D + 2), it was abundantly clear that the tide of battle had left us far behind. There was no dawn stand-to; we were allowed to sleep in the straw until 0600 hrs. The initial Allied push towards Caen had been contained by the Germans throwing reinforcements into the line piecemeal, just as and when they arrived in the battle area, ignoring losses. The British and Canadians had only been able to counter this by rushing more and more men and materials from the beaches until conditions were stabilized. It would be many weeks before Caen was eventually taken, but, so far as we were concerned, the main German forces were at least eight miles away, it was a pleasant summer's morning and there was time for a leisurely breakfast.

Our individual supplies of food were finished, but the '14 men for one day' boxes of composite ('Compo') rations had reached us. This meant breakfasting on tinned bacon or tinned sausage (depending upon the box received by the group), bulked out with hard tack biscuits. Someone, hoping to better this, called out, 'Hey, Mitch! Go 'n see if you can buy us some eggs.' My French was successful and the asking price of 5 francs each (about 2½ pence then, 1p in decimal currency) was reasonable. At first the farmer's wife was sceptical about accepting the 'invasion money' proferred, but was finally persuaded and our little group enjoyed two fried eggs each to supplement our basic issue.

After breakfast we quitted the farm for the short march down to Luc-sur-Mer, where a vacant house near the centre of town had been taken over for Commando Headquarters. By the time we arrived signallers were stringing out field telephone lines to link HQ with the other troops. With the radio jeeps parked in a small garden at the rear of the premises, and the drivers busy with their daily maintenance, it was very much like being on a 'stunt' in the UK.

46 RM Commando had moved out of Luc that morning, heading for La Délivrande, a small town some two and a half miles away, near which some Germans were holding out in two fortified radar stations. 41 RM Commando had become responsible for the area around Luc-sur-Mer and Petit Enfer, so most of the men were positioned for local defence, although some, aided by French Resistance men, were engaged in rounding up collaborators and searching the countryside for German snipers.

In Luc-sur-Mer a cheerful, bubbling holiday atmosphere prevailed and the streets, bright with sunshine were thronged with people. Café doors stood open and, when a passing Frenchman invited me to join him for an apéritif, I was happy to accept. Unfortunately his choice was Pernod, a liquor for which I never acquired a taste, so I politely declined a second. Later in the day, Claudie, a boy of about four, spent some time with *les Anglais*, providing French conversational practice nearer my own level of expertise.

On that day, too, I first encountered Abdul, a swarthy hook-nosed individual of undoubted Arab origin, who was standing stiffly and proudly to attention facing the HQ doorway. He wore a crumpled lightweight blue uniform with brass buttons, right hand grasping the sling of an antiquated but well-cleaned rifle slung over the shoulder, left hand resting on a battered bugle dangling from a tasselled golden cord across his chest and on his head he sported a French steel helmet. As I looked in his direction, the cheeky, self-laudatory smile on his face widened into a jubilant ear-to-ear grin of large white teeth.

I passed him with a nod, to ask the Orderly Room clerk, 'What the heck . . . ?' The Arab, apparently, had been discovered on D-Day in one of the houses in which 'Y' Troop had sought cover when it came under fire, moving forward with the AVREs, firing his rifle at the German position. A slave-worker with the German Todt Organization working on the coast defences, he had decamped when the invasion started and now wanted to stay with the Commando! The idea of anyone, particularly a non-European, seeking to join up with Royal Marines in the middle of a war seemed too absurd for words.

The Unit's sojourn in Luc-sur-Mer was short-lived. The very next day, 9 June, 41 followed 46 to La Délivrande, where 4 Special Service Brigade was to form a perimeter around the radar stations. These were understood to be occupied by some 200 men housed in deep reinforced concrete bunkers, proof against all but the very heaviest artillery shell, and with substantial artillery and mortar capability. The original garrison had been augmented by Panzer Grenadiers who had escaped from the château and strongpoint.

Next day 41 Commando moved forward to take over positions occupied by a battalion of the Black Watch of the 51st Highland Division (51 Div), but were kept waiting for almost two hours before being able to occupy the prepared positions. As usual, the Germans were aware that a change-over was in progress and peppered the area with artillery and mortar fire in the hope of catching men in the open. The weather was unfriendly too, having changed to cool and overcast.

When the Germans appreciated that their fresh adversaries were in position they ceased firing and the unit passed a relatively quiet night. For much of it the advanced elements were sending out patrols, probing forward towards the German blockhouses to get acquainted with the lie of the land. On the other side of the perimeter 48 Commando were making similar sorties from their positions near Douvres.

That situation lasted a bare twenty-four hours because, on the evening of 11 June, 4 SS Brigade was temporarily split up. 47 and 48 Commandos, together with Brigade HQ, were placed under the command of 6th Airborne Division and moved off to join them in the bridgehead on the other side of the River Orne; 46 Commando was transferred to Canadian Command, so moved into their sector. This left 41 to look after the radar stations on its own, but without 'S' Troop, temporarily placed under command of 48 Commando.

The depleted Commando, with no more close-up support than two Centaur tanks, was spread out to form a loosely-held perimeter around the entire German position. HQ moved out of holes in the ground to a hutted complex in a wooded area nearer Bény-sur-Mer, which had been the radar stations' control base. Two of the Fighting Troops were positioned along the forward edge of the woods facing the German barbed wire and other Troops of the Commando took over the positions on the far side of the German pocket vacated by 48.

The military situation at the radar stations was complicated by the fact that the flat farmland between them and Bény was being rapidly transformed into an advanced airstrip for the RAF. Less than half a mile from Commando HQ part of the Bény wood was being bulldozed out of existence to provide the required length of runway. By this time a batch of the Commando's transport, including the Ariel motorcycles, had caught up with the unit and the DRs were trying to settle down to a 'normal' routine. However, with the Troops of the Commando strung out around an indeterminate enemy position a mile or more in diameter and an airfield being constructed on the doorstep, it proved to be a rather hairy business, far removed from carefree riding along quiet roads in rural England.

The initial, crucial problem was to pinpoint where the Headquarters of the five Fighting Troops had been set up, because, during the first hours in every new location, even Commando HQ didn't know precisely where they were. On my very first trip at the radar stations, an Officer handed me a signal for 'P' Troop on the other side of the German position. Then, describing a circle on the map with his index finger, said, 'You'll find their HQ somewhere in that area, make a note of where it is and let me know when you get back.'

From my map I determined the appropriate roads to get me around to the other side of the German position and the one leading towards the roughly-indicated HQ position, and off I went. I knew that the most I could hope to find, by way of identification, would be a cryptic 'P HQ' chalked on a gatepost, on a chunk of stone in the verge, or on a plank of wood propped against the hedge. So, when heading down the last leg of the trip, I was travelling very slowly, eyes searching both sides of the road. Nevertheless, I was suddenly assailed by an urgent shout coming from behind me, 'Come back, you silly bastard!!' I stopped in a hurry and turned my head to look down the muzzle of the Bren gun of one of the Troop's forward positions, well-camouflaged in a ditch.

The gun's crew weren't at all happy about the possibility of my having given away their position to a German OP, which might direct mortar fire upon them. My suggestion that they should put up some bloody signs to let people know where the hell they were wasn't received with any gratitude. I was rapidly given directions to Troop HQ and shoo-ed away, but at least I was able to ensure that the next DR going to 'P' knew when to stop.

That was a foretaste of life as an operational DR. Invariably the job involved periods of scary loneliness, riding between the SDO and the forward Troop, wondering if you really were on the right road and with no great confidence of actually finding their HQ even if you were. Then, after you had done the almost impossible and found what you were looking for, it was an odds-on bet that they would be in no way pleased to see you. The first confirmation of having achieved your goal could very well be a shadowy figure lunging out of the darkness of the night to grab you by the shoulders and hiss in your ear, 'For Christ's sake, shut that bloody thing off! The whole fricking German army can hear you.'

The day after 41's take-over of the radar stations I was handed a despatch for 6th Airborne Division on the other side of the River Orne. With it came the usual imprecise directions, 'You'll easily find their HQ – it's in Ranville'. I traced out the route on the map – three miles to Luc, then six more along the coast road to Ouistreham, to turn right and follow the river inland. It was another three miles to Bénouville, where a sharp left-hand bend would take me towards the canal and river bridges; Ranville lay about one and a half miles away on the other side. Almost as an afterthought I was advised, 'Don't dawdle on the bridges. They are under enemy observation.'

I left Commando HQ with mixed feelings of curiosity and trepidation. The journey would be a fourteen-mile sortie into unknown territory and was undoubtedly 'up front'. I knew that the 6th Airborne's bridgehead on the other side of the River Orne and Caen canal was still very much as it had been immediately after the initial assault. It had been reinforced by No. 1 Special Service Brigade linking-up with them on D-Day and, two days ago, by 47 and 48 Commandos, but this meant only that the original slim perimeter on the far side of the Orne bridges had been strengthened, not extended, and every part of it was well within the range of German artillery.

After three quiet country miles I reached the coast road which took me past the bustling beach areas of Riva Bella and Ouistreham. There un-ending streams of trucks carrying arms, ammunition and stores were pouring ashore, to augment huge stockpiles being built up along the front, and all to the intense interest of crowds of French civilians in holiday mood. Turning inland at the mouth of the Orne, however, those scenes of comforting activity were immediately replaced by the belt of 'nothingness' which invariably lay between the 'rear' and 'forward' areas. An empty, meandering road took me through a completely deserted countryside. There was no traffic, no sign of human beings, no animals in the fields, and even the birds seemed absent. I was the only moving thing in that dead landscape and the unmistakable crumps of exploding shells in the middle distance ahead grew louder by the minute.

At Bénouville a sharp left turn revealed an empty ribbon of road leading down to the two bridges, only five hundred yards apart, which span the Caen canal and the River Orne. Beyond the bridges the road climbed towards high ground where spurts of billowing smoke around a belt of trees on the skyline indicated a multiplicty of bursting shells. I paused briefly for reflection and decided that the best chance of getting across before any guns could be brought to bear would be to twist the throttle wide open and – 'GO!'

The Ariel swept down the hill just as fast as it would go, skimmed over the bridges, then, roaring up the hill on the far side, I eased back on the throttle. Shells were falling uncomfortably close and, not being entirely sure of the route, I was contemplating ditching the bike and taking cover to consult the map. At that point, however, a head followed by an arm making urgent 'Stop!' signals materialized from the grass verge on the left-hand side of the road. Rapidly braking to a halt revealed a Military Policeman who, amazingly, wasn't crouching low in his slit trench, but standing upright in one so deep that his chin was at ground level!

'Airborne HQ?' I queried, mentally wondering just how he would get out of that hole in a hurry should the occasion arise. The arm waved up the hill, while the head said, 'The right fork and straight on to the village', then both disappeared again. I opened the throttle and pulled away. His directions were adequate; 6th Airborne HQ was located in the basement of a shell-shattered house and ten minutes later I was back on the road with a reply. Speeding down towards the bridges again, there was no sign of the MP, so either he was way down in his hole or I was travelling too fast to see him.

The bridge over the Caen canal has gone into the history books and on to the maps of Normandy as 'Pegasus Bridge', named after the winged-horse symbol of the 6th Airborne Division. Ranville too has its place in history, being the first village in France to be liberated, and a plaque on the wall of Place du 6 Juin 1944 records that it 'was wrested from the Germans at 2.30 a.m. on June 6th, 1944, by the 13th (Lancashire) Battalion, Parachute Regiment'.

At the radar stations life for the Fighting Troops had settled down to a cat-and-mouse situation of exchanging shells. Should either side consider it necessary to fire off a few rounds, the other felt obliged to send some back in return. The Corps Commander, Lieutenant-General Crocker, had directed that no unnecessary casualties were to be suffered in trying to take the radar stations: the operational requirement was simply to ensure that the Germans stayed where they were and created no problems for the Allied forces.

From time to time the Royal Artillery would have a go with their '7-point-2s' (7.2" howitzers), but even their hefty 200-pound shells weren't heavy enough to do more than chip the massive concrete bunkers emblazoned, as I saw later, with the names of earlier German military leaders such as HINDENBURG and LUDENDORFF. Nevertheless such loads of explosive would probably have disturbed the inmates and perhaps prompted them to wonder just what they were achieving by remaining there. To augment the close-up artillery support provided by the two Centaur tanks, 'P' Troop had found a German anti-tank gun with a supply of ammunition and were delighted to blast it off at the slightest pretext.

In the early hours of 13 June the senior of our German-speaking 10 I-A Commando men, CSM O' Neill (Czechoslovakian by birth but with a wartime British name), led a party with bangalore torpedoes to blow a gap in the outer German wire and minefield defence to enable AVRES to get in close enough to hurl 'Flying Dustbins' carrying 26-pound demolition charges against the German bunkers. The AVREs completed their shoot without attracting any return fire and two men of 'A' Troop, led by Lieutenant Stevens, passed through and blew a gap in the inner wire. This provoked the Germans into opening up rapid fire with machine guns and machine carbines from four separate positions. But they were shooting wildly in the darkness, not knowing where the Marines were and, after a fifteen-minute fire fight, the 'A' Troop men withdrew without casualties. For a protracted period thereafter the Germans vented their spleen with mortar and shellfire.

Later that same day I had a second trip across the River Orne to our own Brigade Headquarters, which I would find 'Somewhere along the road to Sallenelles'. It was another lonely ride beyond Ouistreham, a similar brief pause at Bénouville to survéy the bridges and another 'belt' down into the valley and up the other side. There was no sign of the MP this time as I swept up the hill to take the left fork leading down river towards the sea and Sallenelles, instead of going right to Ranville.

Once around the bend I was in 'glider country', where the Sixth Air Landing Brigade, seen flying in on D-Day, had come to earth. The fields abutting the road were littered with gliders, lying so close together that it seemed as though they had been lowered in by crane. Some had wings torn off by colliding with trees or other gliders, many had split open on landing and a pitiable few were no more than heaps of shattered timber and perspex. How so many had managed to get down, at night, without engines and without killing everyone on board, was little short of miraculous. There are worse ways of going to war than landing from the sea.

Brigade HQ was found without trouble. After a couple of miles along the road a good '4 SS HQ' sign in the verge directed me up a narrow track to a farm. On the return trip I had passed the glider fields and was rounding the bend towards the Orne bridges when a shell exploded in the field directly ahead, barely fifty yards away, quickly followed by another and another and another. Instinctively I 'rode to ground' – a technique learned for precisely any such self-preservation situation – and landed in a shallow depression against the hedge, with my bike lying alongside.

Lying there, hugging Mother Earth, I realized that here was another 'minus' of a Despatch Rider's life – the noise of a motorcycle engine drowns the whine of approaching shells. With the engine silenced, I could follow it all – German shells coming in towards Ranville and the bridges area, and our guns opening up in retaliation. After a while there was a lull, as if both sides were pausing for breath, so I hauled the bike upright and raced off down the hill, kicking the engine into life on the move. Bike and I shot back over the bridges to the relative peace of the beachhead as if the bats of hell were close behind.

In marked contrast, there were trips 'back' to British landing beaches, which stretched from the mouth of the Orne in the east to St Aubin and Courseulles in the west. On such trips, once clear of any 'hate session' which might be in progress around the Douvres/La Délivrande position, it was no more than taking a spin in glorious weather along empty roads winding through pleasant countryside. Then it wasn't unknown for me to attract the curious stares and shrugs of locals as a mad Englishman rode past carolling his own version of Maurice Chevalier's song, 'Auprès de ma blonde, il fait bon, fait bon, fait bon . . .'!

Many buildings in that coastal strip of Normandy had been damaged by bombs or shell-fire and one unusual example lay on the route to Courseulles. Nearing Langrune the top of a slender church steeple could be seen poking above the trees and roofs, but not until rounding a bend in the road could it be seen that there was a neatly-drilled hole about half-way up. Clearly, a shell had passed through without exploding, leaving the main supporting timbers and most of the tiling still intact.

At Courseulles the quiet countryside of rural Normandy had been transformed into an unbelievably vast military stores complex, a noisy world of trucks, bustle and dust. Behind the beaches of Sicily there had been huge stockpiles of war *matériel*, growing larger by the minute, as DUKWS ferried load after load ashore from supply ships anchored close inshore. Then, more recently, prior to D-Day, we had marched past mile after camouflaged mile of vehicles, stores and munitions lining the country roads around Southampton, but at Courseulles it looked as though the entire countryside was being submerged beneath never-ending supply dumps. Whole fields had become open air warehouses, containing row after row after row of towering stacks of boxes, crates, cans and drums of food, petrol, oil, arms and ammunition – everything, it would appear, from chinagraph pencils to Churchill tanks. Between the interminable lines there was just sufficient width for trucks to enter and be loaded for the Front.

The extent of the supply dumps was so great that it had apparently been considered futile to make any attempt at camouflage and to rely solely upon the RAF keeping the Luftwaffe away. In any case, much of the area must have been partially hidden by the continuous clouds of dust raised by never-ending lines of trucks trundling from beach to stockpiles and from stockpiles to the forward areas.

My first trip to Courseulles was at the instigation of the Adjutant, on the off-chance that there was an Army Post Office there which might be sitting on some mail for the Unit, because none had reached us. After much riding around and many enquiries, I eventually located the APO and, sure enough, there was a bag of mail for 41 RM Commando awaiting delivery or collection. It was a relief to be able to escape from the turmoil around Courseulles and head back to the relative quiet of Bény woods, and with a sense of great achievement – a bag of mail draped over the luggage rack! That was probably the only occasion on which my arrival anywhere was greeted with general jubilation, but there was nothing in the bag for me.

Most days included at least one plastering of the radar stations by the RA's 7.2s and most nights Commando patrols would go out, perhaps to blow additional gaps in the enemy barbed wire or just to clear away a few more mines. On some nights, however, they would quietly worm their way right up to the gun slits of the blockhouses, so that our 10 I-A men could eavesdrop on German small talk and learn something about enemy intentions and morale. On one such occasion Sergeant Hazelhurst of 'A', before leading the patrol back, felt incensed enough to bang on the steel door of one of the blockhouses with his Tommy-gun butt, bawling at the occupants to stop being such bloody fools and come out! There were undoubtedly some inmates who understood what he said but there was no response.

From time to time a German would sneak out to surrender and one of them volunteered the information that they were getting short of food and water. The next night the Luftwaffe did make a parachute drop but 'P' Troop got to the container first. Instead of food and water, however, the drop comprised small arms ammunition, replacement breech blocks for anti-tank guns and booby traps.

One evening an Allied aircraft was seen to be in trouble, almost directly overhead, and we guessed that the pilot had been making for the almost completed airstrip nearby when he found that he couldn't make it. Seven crew members baled out and all parachutes opened. As they floated safely earthwards the parachutes drifted out of our sight below the treetops and bursts of machine-gun fire were heard coming from the radar stations, although nothing was learned of the outcome.

The Bény airstrip became operational on 14 June when a squadron of 'Tiffies', rocket-firing Typhoon aircraft, started flying from there. Their flight paths for take-off and landing took them close to the radar stations and it must have been disconcerting for the pilots to have German machine gunners greet them with streams of bullets. On one occasion the Commando HQ area too was disconcerted when a Tiffy was being 'bombed up' and a rocket launched itself from the aircraft's wing and tore its fiery way through our wood.

It was undoubtedly the complications of having a pocket of active enemy and their 'containing' troops living cheek by jowl with an operational RAF airstrip that persuaded the Corps Commander that enough was enough. On 16 June, therefore, Lieutenant Colonel E.C.E. Palmer RM, who had arrived to take over command of the unit only two days previously, received orders to terminate the German occupation of the Douvres/La Délivrande radar stations. He was allocated the support of the tanks of the 22nd Dragoons and the AVREs of 5 Assault Squadron RE – forty-four armoured fighting vehicles in all – to help the Commando do it.

The plan was that, after a 30-minute barrage by 7.2s, three teams of Crabs (flail tanks) would make gaps in the German wire and minefields, then would provide covering fire for the AVREs to go forward to loose off their flying dustbins. Some Royal Engineers would dismount from their vehicles under smoke cover to place charges against those blockouses the AVREs could not reach. The finale would be tanks acting as an armoured shield for the Royal Marines of 41 Commando: 'B' 'P' and 'X' Troops, with 'Y' in reserve, would advance through the gaps to 'winkle out' the Germans in the larger southern radar station, while 'A' would take care of the small northern one.

At 1630 hours on Saturday, 17 June (D+11), an intense barrage of 7.2s opened up and half an hour later, right on schedule, the Crabs started on the minefield. At 1720 the AVREs moved in to bombard the blockhouses for twenty minutes. Then, at 1740, the Commando moved in and, as the Unit War Diary records: 'the enemy had been dazed, shocked or frightened into surrender and came out in large numbers with their hands up.' By 1830 it was all over, the 'bag' of prisoners being five officers and 222 other ranks. The Commando suffered only one man wounded; there were two RE casualties and one Crab was knocked out. 41's total casualties around the radar stations had been three killed and three wounded.

In a BBC radio broadcast on 18 June 1944 Frank Gillard reported that some of the Douvres bunkers extended to four stories below ground, although I didn't get to see inside any of them until fifty years later when some were reopened as a tourist attraction.

My role in the assault had been no more than being one of those 'who only stand and wait', at the Signals Despatch Office, ready to deliver any messages that might be required. There weren't any, so it was merely a case of listening to the 'noises off'. In consequence, I saw none of the wrist watches, bayonets, Leica cameras, Zeiss binoculars, Lüger pistols and Nazi officers' ceremonial swords which invariably changed sides on such occasions. The only 'souvenir' that fell into my hands I found in one of the small peripheral pillboxes when poking about afterwards. It was a German/French phrase book entitled, *Wie heisst auf Französisch . . . ?* and clearly its previous owner, a German soldier destined for a British prisoner of war camp, had realized that he would have no further need to know what things were called in French. The book wasn't much use to me either.

On the evening of that same day, riding back to HQ, I took an unaccustomed 'exploratory' route and came upon a small, roughly-painted sign set in the roadside verge which read, simply, '3210 SC'. Cryptic as it was, it told me a lot – I had stumbled across Doug Blair, the fellow Novocastrian and boyhood friend whom I had visited at snowbound RAF Hawkinge some months previously. I turned into the gateway and was soon being accorded the welcome of an honoured guest – a cup of tea and a place in their pontoon school.

Doug's unit was one of the RAF's Servicing Commandos whose job was to closely follow-up invasion forces to get captured enemy airfields (or, as at Bény, newly constructed advanced airstrips) operational as quickly as possible and keep the squadrons flying until their own ground crews arrived. 3210 SC had come ashore on D + 1 and, without either of us knowing it, Doug and I had been next-door neighbours for more than a week.

Return to Commando HQ that evening was to a 'hot buzz' that, with the radar station episode finalized, 41 was on the top line for return to the UK. We were lulled to sleep by the ever-held belief that, once the beachhead had been secured, we would be sent home. A more immediate result of the removal of the Germans from our neighbourhood, however, was the absence of any stand-to procedure next morning. Dawn passed unnoticed and, as it just happened to be a Sunday, we were permitted a 'lie-in' until 0600.

The day continued to be unusually quiet. The Commando had been absorbed into the peaceful conditions of a well-behind-the-lines coastal area and, being off-duty, it was possible for me to pay another visit to 3210 SC. I found that, with the arrival of the Tiffy squadron's own ground crew, their duties at Bény were at an end and they were under orders to move on the morrow, to an airfield near Bayeux. In the meantime, pontoon continued to be the order of the day and the Erks were only too pleased to make room once more for a Bootneck with a few francs in his pocket. That was our last game at Bény and arrival back at HQ was to learn that 41 too would be moving out next day.

Not entirely unexpected, the Commando's move would *not* be the rumoured return to the UK, nor even a comfortable transfer 'back' like 3210 SC. The Unit was destined to join the other two Commandos of 4 SS Brigade on the other side of the River Orne, to add our 300-plus men to the forces holding the bridgehead.

Chapter 5

FIRST WEEKS EAST OF THE ORNE

If you are destined to live in a hole in the ground few things make life more unpleasant than bad weather and Monday 19 June 1944, when 41 Commando moved from the radar stations into the Orne Bridgehead, was wet and very windy.

The Unit followed the same general route I had taken on my previous trips there, but the journey was much more protracted as the men had to march because the bulk of the Unit's transport was still in the UK awaiting slots in the shipping programme. The few vehicles that had arrived kept to the slow progress by leap-frogging ahead, then waiting by the roadside while the long column of well-spaced-out men marched past. Naturally, drivers and DRs alike became the butts of much verbal banter from the passing foot-sloggers, but it did help to divert their minds from the drudgery.

The Germans were aware that reinforcements were on the way and, when the column was approaching Bénouville, their artillery opened up, sending much less light-hearted diversions in our direction. However, with well-tuned ears picking out those shells which demanded a rapid dive into the nearest ditch and the ground having been softened by rain, it is remarkable how men can pass through intermittent shellfire without injury. Conditions became particularly unpleasant as we neared the bridges, but, by making rapid progress during periods of lull, all got across unscathed.

After crossing the river and canal, the Commando came under command of the 51st (Highland) Division and the Fighting Troops

66

relieved a battalion of the Argyll and Sutherland Highlanders positioned around the bridges. Headquarters Troop carried on to take the left-hand curve towards the glider fields, Brigade Headquarters and Sallenelles. With rain dripping from the trees, it was ironic for wet, marching men to pass warning signs designed to curb speeding transport drivers, which carried words such as, 'Slow Down – Dust Brings Shells!'

HQ marched on for about a mile beyond the road junction, then halted in a shallow gravel pit, some 6–7 feet deep extending for many hundreds of yards in all directions. This was to be our resting place for the night and, by then, the wet and rather miserable day was well-advanced so it was time to dig slit trenches. The usual artillery exchange 'hate session' sparked off by our arrival in the bridgehead provided an accompaniment to the work, which was made frustrating by the gravel walls continually falling in. The weather stayed reasonably dry until time to bed down, then the rain started again. It continued for much of the night and most of us found it preferable to remain 'on watch', huddled together for warmth, rather than trying to sleep in wet, gravelly holes.

The bridgehead extended along the east bank of the Orne for little more than six miles, from the Channel coast to the outskirts of Caen, with the bridges over the river and canal lying roughly at the half-way point. It enclosed a narrow envelope of territory which, at maximum, where a salient bulged out towards Troarn, was no more than six miles deep, so the whole area was within the range of enemy artillery and mortars.

Tuesday brought an improvement in the weather. Although still very windy, the rain had stopped and a warming sun began to dry wet uniforms. After breakfast HQ moved a mile or so further up the road, then turned off into an area of flat open fields stretching towards the Orne near Écarde, a handful of farm buildings and cottages. During the afternoon the rest of the unit joined us, having been relieved by the Derbyshire Yeomanry, and the Commando was now under the command of 6 Airborne Div. It would be some days before the fighting troops moved into the forward positions, which were little more than a mile away near Sallenelles; the fields around Écarde would be the 'Rear Echelon' and rest area. The immediate task, in order to get any rest at night, was to start digging; the DRs were directed to one end of a large field and instinctively all selected spots close to a hedge, where it seemed safer.

Frank Barker and I agreed to share a hole and, as it was to be semi-permanent, decided that it should be about double-bed size, say five feet wide by 6–7 feet long, and set to work with our puny entrenching tools. Despite the recent rain, the ground was hard and stony, and hour followed hour as we hacked our way down, only to hit solid bedrock at a depth of less than two feet. Others, digging near different hedgerows, were finding a greater depth of topsoil, but we decided to make do with the hole we had rather than start digging all over again.

Some form of top protection would be essential against air-bursting shrapnel shells, falling splinters from our own ack-ack fire and small calibre missiles, so we set about roofing it over. Branches torn from trees served as roof timbers which were covered with brushwood to support the excavated earth heaped on top. The work extended into the following day, but even on completion we had no illusions about the protection probably being more psychological than real.

In use, the dug-out was claustrophobic as there was barely sufficient headroom to squirm inside with a blanket for covering and a fighting order pack to serve as a pillow. Nevertheless it wasn't long before we had the luxury of being able to read in bed. Lamps were fashioned from the cylindrical '50s' cigarette tins in the Compo rations by punching a hole in the lid for a strip of 'four by two' (the 4" × 2" strips of flannel pulled through a rifle barrel to clean the bore) as a wick and paraffin from the QM's store as fuel. There were drawbacks; the lamp had to be within inches of the reading material to be of any use at all, while oily black products of combustion settled on both page and person, and the confined air space became a pocket of unsavoury fug.

By Thursday 22 June the wind had eased considerably and the day grew very hot. The rough weather during the previous few days, however, had put the entire OVERLORD operation in jeopardy. Gale force winds, the strongest for forty years, and blowing onshore, the worst possible direction, had caused a calamitous amount of damage to the two prefabricated 'Mulberry' harbours being assembled to supply the invasion forces. The one intended for American use at Port-en-Bessin had been damaged beyond repair and had to be abandoned. Parts of it were salvaged to help repair the British/Canadian harbour at Arromanches, but completion was delayed for some weeks.

One immediate consequence of the improved weather was that the RAF bounced back into business and ground troops were treated to the sight of a huge force of heavy bombers passing overhead en route for another attack on Caen. The massed aircraft attracted much German anti-aircraft fire, the sky becoming peppered with puffs of smoke from exploding shells, but all planes passed safely over. Later that day it was learned that 41 would leave Écarde next morning to relieve 48 Commando in the forward positions near Sallenelles, and three despatch riders were to go with Advance Headquarters – 'Dripper', 'Heg' and me. Dripper Thompson was a small, hair-receding, angular sort of chap never without something to grumble or 'drip' about, hence his nickname, whereas Frank Heggarty, a Scouser, was too full of *joie de vivre* to think about grumbling.

The short move forward wasn't accomplished without incident. Naval vessels lying offshore were carrying out a shoot on the German positions, to keep their heads down while the change-over was taking place, but a few of their 'wides' fell near our column, wounding two Marines.

48 had set up their Commando and Troop Headquarters in houses and farm buildings close behind the forward positions held by their Fighting Troops. With no continuous 'Front Line', as had been the case in WWI, small groups of men, armed with Vickers machine guns, Brens or rifles, occupied a string of small, separate slit trenches to form a 'Forward Defended Locality' (FDL).

The 'Headquarters Building', which housed the Signallers and DRs, was a detached two-storey house near the brow of a hill, beyond which the road continued down into Sallenelles. The village was only a few hundred yards away, but completely screened from view by intervening trees. An offshoot of garage and outhouse abutting the carriageway was used as cook-house and George Fradley, a massively-built placid young West Countryman, one of the attached 'Brigade Link' Signallers, acted as cook. To the rear of the house a large orchard fell away to the river, giving a wide panoramic view towards Riva Bella, Ouistreham and the landing beaches beyond. To the right could be seen the estuary of the Orne linking up with the English Channel and, further right, a mile or so of enemy occupied coastline beyond Sallenelles was visible.

The sector taken over from 48 had the distinction of being the extreme left flank of the entire invasion front, which stretched fifty miles to the west, as far as the Cherbourg Peninsula. Sallenelles lay in a no-man's-land between the opposing armies, being untenable by either side because of its low-lying situation. Some of the villagers had steadfastly refused to leave their homes, so it stood like a ghost town with inhabitants.

Also taken over from 48 Commando was Les Aigles, a long, rambling two-storeyed building which they had dubbed 'The Patrol House'. A standing patrol of about thirty men was stationed there, to keep the village under constant surveillance, and it served as a base for reconnaissance (recce) patrols. It also provided a useful vantage point for snipers, watching the German positions some 400 yards away. In 41's first two days there they reported one certain and two probable hits.

On occasions the patrol house came to be patronized by authorized 'sightseers'. A history of 48 Commando, by their Heavy Weapons Officer Captain T.G. Linnell, records a *Daily Telegraph* war correspondent describing his trip there as 'A visit to General Eisenhower's Left-hand Man'. The reporter also made great play of having been able to take a glass of cider in a café in no-man's-land!

That first evening at Sallenelles personnel at Advanced HQ had a grandstand view of a massive parachute supply drop over the landing beaches. Scores of transport planes streamed in to drop stick after stick of containers until the entire sky over the coast was polka-dotted with brightly coloured parachutes. This additional support to the invasion forces had obviously been witnessed by the Germans and, probably frustrated at being unable to do anything about it, vented their spleen upon us, with a prolonged plastering of the Commando positions. This included the Rear Echelon at Écarde and it was widely rumoured that farmers in the area had removed cattle from the fields and taken cover shortly before it started!

The house we were occupying hadn't been strengthened or protected in any way, so, whenever conditions became too hot for comfort, all non-essential personnel would adjourn to their off-duty sleeping quarters, dug-outs in the orchard. The hole allocated to Heg and myself was a first-class effort, with a good three feet of headroom, was about the same in width and had a thick covering of earth on top. It even had a blast wall of two sheets of corrugated iron sheeting packed with earth across the entrance and neatly cut steps for easy access. We always felt reasonably safe down there, even during the heaviest of the many bombardments which came our way, but we rarely had a decent night's sleep as the accommodation was invariably shared with mosquitoes. The French variety were ten times worse than anything experienced in Sicily and there were no mosquito nets. No matter how many of the little horrors we incinerated on the dug-out ceiling with our paraffin lamps, there were always scores more to carry on the attack. It was no consolation to know that there was no danger of contracting malaria.

The role of the troops in the Orne Bridgehead, cut off as they were by river and canal, was entirely different from that of the rest of the British and Canadian forces. In the main beachhead all efforts were being directed towards pushing forward to capture Caen, whereas in the bridgehead the prime requirement was merely to stay put and keep the Germans fully occupied. It was therefore a static war of mortaring, machine-gunning and patrol activity, with the Royal Artillery and Royal Navy indulging in frequent artillery shoots.

By day and night there would be 'standing' patrols in or near Sallenelles, when men would lie up in concealed positions to monitor the movements of the enemy. Most days, too, reconnaissance patrols would probe forward to test out the strength and alertness of the German positions and from time to time fighting patrols would go forward to create alarm and confusion in the enemy lines, inflict casualties and, if possible, bring back a prisoner for interrogation.

Most of these patrols would include one or more German speakers of 10 I-A Commando to interpret any conversations that might be overheard, and it soon became apparent that a large proportion of the enemy facing 41 were not native Germans but less-than-enthusiastic soldiers of the Third Reich, conscripted from Poland, Czechoslovakia and other Central European countries. From time to time some would come across to our lines, extremely happy to have finished with fighting for Hitler. One such deserter volunteered the information that, in two weeks, his ninety-strong company had suffered forty-three casualties.

On the second night after our arrival a fighting patrol from 46 Commando, which was holding the sector to our immediate right, caused considerable havoc in the German lines and Jerry demonstrated his annoyance by directing a prolonged session of machine-gun and mortar fire onto all positions in the sector. A number of bombs fell within the Headquarters orchard, some landing as close as twenty yards from our hole. 'P' Troop's galley received a direct hit, but it was unoccupied at that time of night and the only casualties were a few tins of Compo biscuits.

A sealed tin of these 'hard tack' biscuits provided the bulk and roughage of the '14 men for one day' boxes of Compo rations. Boxes were lettered 'A' to 'G' to indicate the contents, with main meals ranging from steak and kidney pudding followed by mixed fruit pudding, down to corned beef and rice pudding. There was no choice in the matter and, by the time supplies had travelled down from the DID (Divisional Issuing Depot) to a small group in the forward positions, most of the preferred boxes had been filtered out.

With Compo rations the job of cook involved little more than boiling water, some to heat the cans of food and some to make 'Compo tea'. The latter simply meant sprinkling a pre-mix of tea, dried milk and sugar into a dixie of boiling water and stirring, which could result in a reasonable drink but might equally well end up as a dust-covered, curdled, undrinkable concoction. However, the job of cook in the forward areas was not without its own particular hazards.

Close proximity to the enemy ruled out the use of standard field cooking equipment, the hydro burner (a large primus cylinder which shot a roaring tongue of flame between two steel firebars), as the noise would have pin-pointed every HQ in the area. Some quieter means of boiling water had to be adopted and recourse was made to a legacy of the Eighth Army's campaign in North Africa, the Benghazi Cooker or Benghazi Burner. This was simply a metal container (empty biscuit tins were fine) partially filled with sand and dowsed with petrol, two commodities widely available to Desert Rats. When set alight the cookers were very effective in providing heat, but there were two drawbacks – they deposited greasy black soot upon everything within range and the burning time was unpredictable. It was frustrating for a cook to see the flames of his cooker starting to plop out just as the water for making tea was coming to the boil and this sometimes goaded him into acting rashly.

The prudent thing was to wait patiently until the sand had cooled down or at least drag the hot stove outside before refuelling, but some cooks poured petrol on the hot sand. The inevitable result was a grey mist of petrol vapour flowing over the galley floor (we were surprised to learn that it was heavier than air) and, with other stoves burning nearby, there would be a panic evacuation until a massive WHOOOOMP signalled that the freshly-fuelled stove had been rekindled by a neighbour. Few cooks in the forward areas had any eyebrows.

Days at Advanced HQ began very early in the morning with dawn stand-to, were rarely dull and invariably included sessions of mortar and artillery activity. Two days after our arrival a morning barrage from the Royal Artillery lasted for about three hours, then, in the afternoon, the Royal Navy had a shoot of their own; the German response was widespread and prolonged. This was still in progress when Bill Marshall was instructed to put his jeep at the disposal of CSM Morgan, (acting-RSM since Horace Belcher had been killed) and CSM O'Neill of 10 I-A Commando, who, with Corporal Dick Harman of HQ Troop, had a mission 'back to the beaches'. CSM O'Neill elected to drive, so, with CSM Morgan in the front passenger seat and Bill and Dick in the back, off they went. When the jeep returned some hours later, with Bill driving, there were jagged gashes in its side and the only passenger was Dick Harman, in some pain from a badly bruised back. It appeared that, as they were nearing the beach area, a shell had landed close by, wounding both Sergeant Majors, and Dick was struck by a chunk of brick. Bill was unscathed and completed the journey with two casualties for evacuation. One of the CSMs and Dick Harman have given conflicting versions of the purpose of that trip. One was to obtain German anti-tank gun breech blocks from the radar stations and the other to use Royal Marines connections on naval vessels lying offshore to obtain some bread. Take your pick!

Next morning the DRs at Advanced HQ were relieved and

73

moved back to the holes previously excavated at Écarde. Despite the short distance involved, it was like moving into a different world, conditions were so very much quieter. Also, after carrying out maintenance on our machines, and if no extra duty had been allocated, there was time for other pursuits. Having learned that another of our jeep drivers, Dickie Deeks, had been authorized to make a trip that afternoon to contact an uncle in the RAF somewhere near Bayeux, I was granted permission to accompany him.

Off we went in holiday mood, passing 'our' beach area, smothered with war material and military transport, then via Bény, which was still as quiet as ever. Only a few miles further on, and well short of Bayeux, we located his uncle at an RAF station near Creully. As I had hoped, there was also a sign reading '3210 SC' so, while Dickie was with his uncle, I was with Doug Blair's crowd in another game of pontoon. That night at Écarde a German patrol managed to work its way through the FDLs and we were kept awake much of the time, wondering about the implications of the long bursts of small arms fire we heard from time to time.

At Rear Echelon I learned that 'Abdul', the Arab Todt worker who wanted to fight the Germans, had actually been allowed to stay with the Commando. Dressed in British battledress, only his obvious North African features distinguished him from the rest of us. He had been given some non-combatant occupation in HQ Troop and, despite an almost total lack of English, was popular and happy to be there. I doubt if Abdul recognized me from that first meeting in Luc-sur-Mer, but we got into conversation and it was obvious that he understood my French much better than anybody else's English. Even to my ears, his pronunciation was atrocious, but we struck up a friendly rapport and thereafter looked out for each other on my returns from Advanced HQ. Each time he saw me again his face would light up into a broad grin as he hurried forward calling out, 'Meesh! Meesh!' He never did manage to get his tongue around 'Mitch'.

Rumours of an imminent return to the UK had flared up again – this time to take part in a parade through London on Sunday, 2 July, no less! – but the actuality, was rather different. We moved back up to Sallenelles on Saturday, 1 July, and our arrival there coincided with a heavy plastering of the Commando area. A number of shells fell around the headquarters house, one being close enough to crash a large chunk of casing into a wall near the galley. The evening was relatively peaceful, but when darkness fell things became too noisy for sleep. At 0130 hours everyone was roused to stand-to and a particularly prolonged pasting around 0500 seemed to be the prelude to a concerted attack, but things eventually quietened down again. Maybe the Germans had realized that it was Sunday and a day of rest, so wanted to catch up with the sleep they had lost whilst depriving us of ours.

That Sunday turned out to be a quiet one for Commando HQ and, as a bonus, from our hilltop position overlooking the Orne valley, we became spectators of a neat demonstration of German artillery expertise. Interest was aroused by the 'Crummmmps' of shells exploding at a safe distance. Then the white puffs of their explosions were seen popping up some distance short of a group of farm buildings on the other side of the river about a mile away. After that first salvo there was a short pause and we could visualize the artillery commander giving the order 'Up two hundred' to instruct the gunners to increase the range by two hundred yards, or metres in their case. The next salvo fell at about the same distance beyond the farm as the first had been in front – a perfect straddle. Again we imagined the next order 'Down one hundred' and the third salvo burst neatly amongst the farm buildings. After a few more flurries of shells, with no signs of other activity, it must have been acknowledged that the farm was deserted and the firing ceased.

At Sallenelles the amount of time Despatch Riders spent in riding motorcycles was very small, much of our time being occupied with guard duties and taking cover. In such a compact, static situation, the bulk of the signals traffic was passed by field telephone. With a good earth connection at each end, a single cable, strung out along the hedgerows and between trees, connected the 'subscribers' to the headquarters switchboard. Radio links weren't used as they would be in mobile situations, although the one to Brigade Headquarters was invariably kept open to back up the telephone. On occasions, however, a shell or bomb burst would sever a telephone line and the duty DR, the 'third line of defence', would take the message in writing. A signalman would also have to go out to find the fault by following the line of the wire, tracing it hand by hand in the darkness if need be, until the break was found and could be repaired. One night at Sallenelles a Signalman was doing just that when he trod on a mine and was killed.

Most of the DRs' trips were of short duration – to the headquarters of the other Commandos, 46 was at Hauger and 45 at Amfréville, or back to Rear Echelon at Écarde. The three-mile run to 6 Airborne Div at Ranville was one of the longest. On 6 July I was seconded to 46 Commando for a few days and reported to their HQ at Hauger, a château in extensive grounds, where I was allocated a hole near the entrance gates. Apart from sleeping in a different hole and having different faces about me, conditions there were pretty much the same as at Sallenelles.

Next morning, Friday 7 July, the sky was overcast, with sufficient cloud cover to tempt the Luftwaffe to send over some of their fighter-bomb 'sneakers' on strafing sorties. I had a trip to 6 Airborne at Ranville and, returning along the Amfrévile–Hauger road, came upon four ammunition trucks near le Plein, which had obviously been shot-up a short time before. Three were no more than smoking heaps of hot metal, but the fourth was still burning furiously and making unpleasant explosive noises as I opened the throttle and scooted past.

During the afternoon the clouds cleared and by evening visibility was perfect when the first drone of many approaching aircraft swivelled all eyes skyward. There was no doubt that they were 'ours', a huge straggling air armada of Lancaster and Halifax bombers coming in from the north. Squadron after squadron, widely spaced out like untidy gaggles of geese, were moving unhurriedly towards us. As they passed close by, German ack-ack guns opened fire, sending crackling smoke-puffs of bursting shells spattering the sky amongst the aircraft, and soon there was no doubt as to the planes' target.

Hauger stands on high ground overlooking the flat lowlands which stretch towards Caen, some seven miles away. The city itself was hidden from us by intervening trees, but puffs of smoke, ranging in colour from white to black, were seen rising above them. For perhaps half a minute, as the smoke from the multitude of bomb bursts merged into one continuous curtain, only the steady drone of aircraft engines and the crumps and crackling of anti-aircraft fire could be heard. Then the first thumping detonations of heavy bombs arrived, which soon coalesced into a continuous, awesome rumble as plane after plane after plane released its bomb load.

Minutes after the first puffs had appeared over Caen aircraft, with their mission accomplished, were streaming back, still in formation at the same altitude and at the same unhurried pace. As scores of bombers continued to pass us in two streams, one heading towards and the other returning from a pall of rumbling smoke, the spectacle assumed an unreal quality. The bombers had become an incredible aerial conveyor belt, picking up deadly explosives in England and depositing them on the city of Caen. From time to time an aircraft would issue a trail of black smoke, turn slowly out of line and glide to earth. A few suddenly plummeted out of the sky in vertical dives, to be followed down by a handful of billowing parachutes.

The spectacle lasted for over an hour and, as the dusk deepened, the vast pall of smoke changed into a dull red glow. Then darkness fell, the German ground forces in the area unleashed a mortar and artillery barrage upon everything within range. It continued for most of the night, during which a salvo of nebelwerfer bombs removed all the remaining glass from the windows of our HQ building. Although the literal translation of 'nebelwerfer' is 'smoke thrower', the name was applied to a range of large-calibre multiple-barrelled mortars. The packages of explosives flung into the air announced their approach with a fearsome, unstable, multiple swisssshing sound which was quite different from that of any other incoming projectiles.

The air attack on Caen, on 7 July 1944, was one of the heaviest aerial bombardments in support of ground troops ever mounted. 460 bombers were involved and 2300 tons of explosives had been dropped. Next morning the British and Canadians put in a three-pronged attack and by the following day, Sunday the 9th, all of the city on the north bank of the river had been taken. That evening orders were received to be in our holes by 2200 hrs as all units along the bridgehead front were to supplement the Royal Artillery in a 'harassing task' by engaging the enemy with every available machine gun and mortar, to which the Germans would inevitably reply.

Down in our hole Heg and I were lulled to sleep by the continuous rumble of British gun and mortar fire – 41 Commando's

3" mortars alone loosed off over 350 bombs – but it wasn't until shortly after stand-to next morning that we began to be bothered by salvoes of German bombs in return. As this was followed by prolonged periods of heavy and light automatic fire, we waited tensely for the anticipated infantry attack, but were eventually stood-down for a belated breakfast.

Later in the day it was learned that the 2nd Army had put in a further attack that morning in the River Odon sector and the previous night's activity had been laid on to divert the enemy's attention.

Chapter 6

LIFE IN THE ORNE BRIDGEHEAD

During the next few weeks life east of the Orne settled down into the pattern of four- or five-day stints at Advanced HQ, interspersed with shorter periods at Écarde. Neither place was particularly safe and on occasion both could be dangerous, but we seemed to develop a sixth sense about the imminent arrival of missiles. Having stretched out for an afternoon snooze in the warm sunshine at Rear Echelon, you would suddenly find yourself in your hole as a batch of shells burst nearby.

Rumours about an early return to the UK continued unabated and, even after every successive one had proved unfounded, many would still swallow the next. Naturally, everyone would have preferred to be sleeping in real beds in England, drawing six shillings and eight pence per day rather than bedding-down in the soil of France, receiving only three shillings a day, which included six pence per day Field Service Allowance. However, what niggled most was a feeling that, despite specialized Commando training, the unit appeared to have slipped into the role of the PBI – Poor Bloody Infantry.

For a Despatch Rider with a unit 'stuck in the line', however, life had some pluses to help offset the minuses. These pluses included having the men of the fighting troops between you and the enemy and not being required to risk your neck on patrols. Then there was the mobility which occasioned journeys into more normal areas where there were such things as civilians and cafés. The minuses included having to get on your bike and go when all sorts of 'muck' might be flying about and others were safe in their holes; riding at night without lights along roads you could barely see and with no certainty about where you were supposed to be going.

At Advanced HQ there was never much time to spare between eating, sleeping, delivering signals, being on watch and taking cover, but at Rear Echelon, interspersed between duty requirements, there would be time to call one's own. 'Trips ashore' were non-existent, so letter-writing and reading the few books available were the main pursuits, although some tried their hands at sketching, while others engaged in carving perspex. The windscreens and windows of the scores of crashed gliders littering the fields were soon being fashioned by rear area troops into rings, pendants and, most popular of all, paper knives.

On most days these individual pastimes would be supplemented by some form of aerial activity which varied according to the weather. Whenever the sky was overcast the Luftwaffe would send over 'sneakers', which would swoop in low, inflict as much damage as possible with bombs and cannon fire, then zoom up again to lose themselves in the clouds before RAF fighters arrived. Conditions for sneakers were particularly good during the second week of July when there would be two or three sorties over our area every day each one involving up to a dozen aircraft. As they streaked overhead, flying low through a sky peppered with bursting anti-aircraft shells, we would watch expectantly for signs of any being hit and most days one or two would 'make smoke' and turn away, to our whoops of delight. The loudest cheers came when a plane took a sudden vertical dive and ended up as a funeral pyre of black smoke. On only one occasion was a crippled British aeroplane seen in our air space – a Lightning began falling from the sky, but that too raised a cheer when the crew floated down by parachute.

During fine weather the skies above Normandy were the sole preserve of the Allied air forces and our aerial entertainment would be provided by the bomber wings. One such spectacle, we realized later, had been prefaced by two days of military build-up which had begun on Sunday 16 July. Then all non-vital traffic had been ordered off the roads around Écarde, which were then taken over by an unending stream of every type of vehicle – guns and personnel carriers, tanks on transporters, supply and ammunition trucks, Troop Carrying Vehicles, field kitchens, jeeps, staff cars, mobile workshops, field ambulances, etc, etc, etc, and the flow continued by day and night.

On 16 July too, I learned later, General Montgomery held an investiture in the bridgehead at which two of our Commando were decorated – recently promoted Captain Stevens received the Military Cross and Sergeant Wither the Military Medal. It was also given out that our previous CO, Lieutenant Colonel Gray, wounded in the air attack on D+1, had also been awarded the Military Cross.

At dawn on Tuesday 18 July the entire countryside erupted into multitudinous lightning flashes and thundering explosions as the artillery of the British Second Army opened fire. The uproar was escalated a short while later by the multiple drones and throbbing of many aircraft engines, soon to be followed by the dull rumbling thumps of heavy bomb bursts not many miles away. When the sun rose squadron after squadron of loaded bombers were seen passing overhead and minutes later were returning empty. For hour after hour the medley of noises – the droning of aircraft engines, the crackling and thumps of ack-ack and field artillery fire and the explosions of innumerable shells and bombs – continued as a background to our bridgehead duties.

While it was happening we had no idea what it was all about, but that massive artillery and aerial bombardment had been the softening-up process for Operation GOODWOOD, the attack by British and Canadians to gain control of the high ground commanding the road from Caen to Falaise. Targeted on the German Panzer Group West in the area south-east of Caen, the aerial bombardment had involved 2000 planes which delivered 7700 tons of bombs and was, in the words of Air Chief Marshal Leigh Mallory, 'the heaviest and most concentrated air attack in support of ground forces ever attempted'.

That night the Rear Echelon area was subjected to a vicious German backlash, a prolonged series of air raids aimed at halting the forward movement of supplies to sustain the attack. In our shallow, lightly protected hole, Killer and I passed some hairy hours, with all the sound effects coming through only too clearly. Out of a background cacophony of crackling ack-ack shells and the tumult of aircraft engines would come the high-pitched screams of individual dive bombers as, one after another, they plummeted down to attack some nearby target. We lay helpless and bemused as time and again the whistling bombs were followed by the blasting crashes of nearby explosions. All we could do was to curl up as small as possible and hope for the best. Nearby, two supply trucks were hit and burned well into the night, providing a useful beacon for further attacks.

The GOODWOOD push succeeded in breaking the German lines and on Wednesday 19 July the capture of Caen was completed by the occupation of that part of the city lying south of the river. Despite the colossal land and air bombardments, however, the Germans had been able to put up strong resistance and the 11th Armoured Division alone had lost over 100 tanks. Next day the weather broke and heavy rain poured down for two days, changing the dust of Normandy into the equivalent of Flanders mud; GOODWOOD became, literally, bogged down.

The rain played havoc with the rear areas too, where most of the dug-outs were rendered uninhabitable, forcing men to risk sleeping in the backs of trucks. With inches of mud in the fields, wheeled transport which had previously been using numerous tracks of sun-baked earth, couldn't move off the metalled roads. Riding motorcycles was impossible and the DRs were allocated a jeep. I was very pleased that my limited driving experience wasn't put to the test under such conditions. Early on Saturday 22 July the rain stopped; hot sunshine was soon drying out the soggy countryside and the Second Army resumed its attack.

Next morning, Sunday 23rd, I began another spell of duty at Advanced HQ and, by chance, was given the opportunity of seeing at first hand some of the effects of the bombing of Caen. One of our Troop Sergeant Majors – the lean and lanky, much-tattooed extrovert TSM Crookes of 'A' Troop – had been given permission to seek out his brother, a tank commander with the 2nd Battalion Grenadier Guards, who had been involved in GOODWOOD. They were out of the line somewhere to the south of Caen and I was detailed off to take TSM Crookes there on the back of my motor-cycle. As the Ariel had no pillion seat he had to sit on the tubular steel luggage rack, using the rear wheel hub nuts as footrests.

The trip started off towards the bridges, but we didn't cross over, as our route lay through Hérouvillette. There the bike was sucked into a continuous stream of military vehicles, all heading for the southern part of Caen. Being struck in a meandering stream of nose-to-tail traffic was no place for a self-respecting DR, so I began to struggle to make headway. We overtook vehicle after vehicle, through clouds of choking dust, hardly seeing, let alone having time to avoid, the innumerable potholes which seemed to continually increase in number. It was a rough ride for me, with a saddle to reduce the effects, but my pillion passenger must have had a much worse time, having to take it all without any padding.

After a while we entered the industrial suburb of Colombelles which only a few days previously had been the German front line. Two months of almost continuous shelling and unprecedented aerial bombardment had turned it into a moonscape of complete devastation. There wasn't a single undamaged building to be seen; the entire area had been reduced to a series of unbelievable hillocks of shattered bricks and masonry from which protruded roof timbers and the twisted steel skeletons of industrial buildings.

The carriageway was only as wide as bulldozers had been able to clear a route through the ruins and every few yards was pock-marked with roughly-filled bomb and shell craters. Where 12-ton Tallboy ('Blockbuster' or 'Factory Remover') bombs had fallen on the road, the Royal Engineers hadn't attempted to fill the monster craters – some thirty feet in diameter and six or more deep – but had simply bulldozed a new route through the ruins of abutting buildings. Despite the recent rain, everything was covered with a thick coating of dust, being continually stirred up by the long caterpillar of lumbering vehicles. In some places it had settled so thickly that backfilled craters were completely camouflaged and revealed themselves only when the motorcycle began to buck and bounce with bone-jarring jolts.

On reaching the Faubourg de Vaucelles, the inner city area, we were relieved to get a smoother ride. Much of the original road surface was still intact, although greatly reduced in width where buildings had collapsed on to the carriageway. Many tall blocks were still standing and at first glance appeared only superficially damaged, but closer inspection showed that they were no more than bomb-scarred masonry facades, cloaking gutted, rubbish-filled interiors. Over everything, everywhere, hung the unmistakable stench of decaying human flesh.

Leaving the dead city, we entered an equally dead countryside with very different evidences of war – the military wreckage of the fighting that had taken place there only a few days earlier. The roadside was lined, and adjacent fields dotted, with shot-up and burned-out vehicles – tanks, trucks and half-tracks. All the knocked-out tanks we passed were British. Many were no more than blackened shells, having burst into flames ('brewed up' was the current term) on being hit. Some had been blasted on to their sides and lay like monstrous dead beetles; others appeared undamaged until a closer look revealed that one of the tracks had been blown off. At one point, on the left-hand side of the road, a group of four Shermans stood near the top of a grassy knoll in almost precise line abreast and perhaps sixty feet apart. There could be no doubt that German gunners, ready and waiting for them, had picked each one off in turn as it crested the brow of the hill. Just what was in TSM Crookes' mind as we passed through that mile or two of dead tanks would be difficult to imagine.

In addition to the knocked-out vehicles, the entire countryside was littered with the pathetic minutiae of a recent battle. There were heaps of spent shell cases, empty ammunition boxes and mortar bomb carriers, abandoned pieces of webbing equipment, steel helmets, water bottles, entrenching tools – and the dead. Low mounds of earth showed where they lay in their shallow graves. Some were alone – perhaps an infantryman killed as he moved forward – while others lay in small groups, probably the crew of a field gun or tank. Each grave was marked with a rough cross or simply by a rifle thrust muzzle first into the ground and topped with a steel helmet to indicate 'ours' or 'theirs'.

We enquired of the very few British troops we came across as to the whereabouts of the Grenadier Guards and were eventually directed down a narrow lane. There, parked nose-to-tail on a wide grass verge, hidden from the air by the overhang of mature trees, was a line of Shermans. A few tank men were standing beside the first one and, when TSM Crookes asked about his brother, there was an immediate nodding of heads and a shout of 'Crooksey!' went down the line. A face, bearing a marked resemblance to the one on the back of my bike, popped out from behind one of the tanks. Mission accomplished! The tanks were moving up that evening, so TSM Crookes decided to go back to Sallenelles and request permission to return later in the day to bid his brother adieu. We completed another round trip in the afternoon.

That wasn't the end of a busy day and the evening episode was rather more scary. Jan Maley, our Transport Sergeant, required some spare parts, a jeep had to take him back to collect them and, as Duty DR, it was my job to drive. I broke into a cold sweat and my brain raced into top gear. Should I admit that the total extent of my driving experience was no more than a few unofficial trips in the water truck at Ramsgate and so brand myself as a delinquent as well as a non-driver, or . . . ?

'Right-o sarge!' I said and, taking it all very gently, thinking out every move well in advance, we set off. Thankfully there was nothing else on the road that Sunday evening and, on our safe return, there was a great feeling of satisfaction at having accomplished another mission that day. Jan will never know into what suspect hands he had entrusted himself that evening – unless he happens to read this!

Two days after that first 'official' drive of mine the whole Commando was cheered by another 'first' – the first issue of bread since leaving England! It is difficult to comprehend why troops so close to their homeland should have been required to eat dog biscuits for seven weeks, but that's how it was. The first ration was no more than half a slice per man and it was almost two weeks before bread became a regular part of our diet.

By then, too, the basic compo rations were being supplemented by issues of rice and those two wartime innovations designed to save shipping space, dried eggs and dehydrated potatoes. In retrospect, it seems strange that eggs were never 'dehydrated', nor were potatoes ever 'dried'. Then, with water added for cooking, dried eggs were invariably said to have been 're-constituted' – but no one ever talked about 're-constituted' potatoes.

At Rear Echelon there wasn't the same concern about preparing meals as George Fradley bestowed upon those he prepared at Advanced HQ. Without the need for silent cooking, and with more mouths to feed, all finesse had disappeared. The cans could have come from different boxes of Compo and, on occasions, they hadn't been punctured. In consequence, the scalding hot can plopped into your mess tin would not only be devoid of any identifying label but both ends could be domed-out under internal steam pressure. Then, with a handkerchief or green beret, the can would be held firmly on the ground, pointing away from fellow diners, and stabbed with a jack-knife. The resulting spray of steam and scalding liquid undoubtedly lost a few proteins, but the bomb had been rendered safe and could be cut open to discover what was on the menu.

Abdul had soon absorbed an impressive string of English swear words, which he enunciated with relish, if little understanding, but when I was at Rear Echelon we had sessions of exchanging languages. We began with counting and, raising fingers, I would say, 'One, Two, Three, Four, Five . . .', which Abdul would imitate and write down phonetically. Then he would do the same in Arabic and I wrote down the sounds – 'Wahed, Zhooge, Claytah, Rhemah, Rhumsah . . .', etc. We then progressed to the days of the week, 'Kuneen, Claytah, Lairvah . . .' and objects around us, like 'rifle' – umkahlah, 'pistol' – verdeen, 'socks' – treshe . . . etc. etc. His spidery squiggles of written Arabic were no more than worm tracks to me, as, no doubt, were my English words to him.

The most productive outcome of these language sessions was to be able to put him in touch with his family. From his identity card as a slave labourer, we had discovered earlier that his full name was Adelasis ben Assouet, so thereafter we called him 'Ben', rather than having outsiders hear some of His Majesty's Royal Marines referring to one of their number as 'Abdul'. I learned from Ben that he came from Fez in Morocco, and that a brother, Semohammed, who worked for the Post Office there, understood English and French. I decided to try to let his folks know that Ben was safe and well.

As a letter written in Arabic would undoubtedly have confused the military censors, I wrote a brief note in English, saying that Ben was in good health and friendly hands, translated it into French and got Ben to sign it with his worm tracks. The unit's BLA (British Liberation Army) address was given for any possible reply and I put the letter in an Active Service envelope, addressed to 'Semohammed ben Assouet, Bureau de Postes, Fez, Morocco', and Ben addressed it in Arabic. It was a long shot, but it came off! Some weeks later Ben, with an even wider grin than usual and an arm around my shoulder, told me that he had had a reply from his brother.

Throughout July a series of actions in other sectors of the beach-head, of which we were largely unaware, was developing the American 'right hook' through northern France. Concurrently the British and Canadians were keeping up a continual pressure to engage as many German troops as possible, to ease the task of the Americans, and also suggest that the main thrust towards Paris would come from that sector. In consequence of the Allied efforts, on a front of only fifty miles, the Germans were compelled to deploy no less than eleven panzer divisions, precisely half the number on the entire Russian front of eight hundred miles.

With all this activity going on in other parts of Normandy, the continuing 'marking time' in the Orne bridgehead wasn't popular with many of the troops being kept in restraint there. So much so that, towards the end of July, General Montgomery felt it necessary to issue an Order of the Day stressing how vital it was for him to be absolutely certain of the security of his left flank whilst carrying out the various preliminary manoeuvres of the battle plan. The Orne bridgehead, it said, 'was the hinge-pin for the eventual break-out of all the Allied forces'.

Towards the end of July I returned to Rear Echelon to find that we had no dug-out. The field had been taken over by the REs for the construction of a new road to link up with the two pontoon bridges built to supplement the existing road crossing of river and canal. The Germans knew what was happening and, on the 27th, took advantage of cloudy weather to make an unsuccessful attempt to bomb the bridges. On the 30th a thousand-bomber raid was carried out as 'softening-up' for another Second Army attack south of Caen, timed to coincide with the American thrust towards Avranches, which started their wide sweep towards Paris.

During the first week of August the DRs, alternating between Rear Echelon and Advanced HQ, seemed to get 'plastered' in both places. At Écarde German artillery was trying to undo the RE's work on the new road and at Sallenelles the artillery and mortar exchanges had been stepped up in line with increased activity all along the front. On Friday 4 August the Commando suffered eleven casualties and next day we began to hear 'buzzes' about an imminent move into the 'Troarn Bulge'.

All we knew about that sector, some six miles to the west of us, was that there was a salient protruding into the German lines towards the town of Troarn and, from all accounts, it was 'hot'. On Sunday the rumour was confirmed; the operational strength of the Commando was to move into the bulge next day, leaving Rear Echelon where it was. That night the Germans appeared to give the

Commando a prolonged farewell barrage and on the Monday morning, just before moving off, a batch of shells scored direct hits on the row of farm cottages which had just been vacated by the Commando Sick Bay.

That day, August 7, was August Bank Holiday Monday in the UK, but it was no holiday for 41 Commando. Jackie Horsfield and I had been detailed off to shepherd the transport column carrying the Commando to its new location and to remain there with Advanced HQ. The convoy had first to go back towards the Orne bridges, then our route lay via Ranville and Hérouvillette, both badly damaged, then through the ruins of Éscoville, which had been shelled and bombed virtually out of existence. Then we passed into the empty 'nothingness' of the countryside between 'rear' and 'forward' areas. A gloomy, overcast sky matched a rather sombre occasion.

Slow progress was mandatory. Every few hundred yards, nailed to trees or set up in the grass verge, were 'up front' injunctions not to attract shells by raising dust. These ranged from the cautionary 'SLOW! – dust means shells', through more precise 'MAXIMUM speed – 5 mph', to blatantly threatening 'Slow Down! – YOU HAVE BEEN WARNED!!' Despite strict adherence to all such admonitions, our progress into the Troarn Bulge was accompanied by outbursts of shellfire. The screaming approach of shells and their blasting explosions seemed ever more personal the further we travelled. Even without the convoy making dust, the Germans were undoubtedly aware that a change-over was taking place, knew which roads were being used and were hoping to catch some of us in the open.

Nearing the forward area, sections of the convoy were detached to proceed to their own specific locations and the vehicles carrying Advanced HQ and two of the Fighting Troops were halted at a level crossing on the edge of a wood with the order 'No mechanized vehicles beyond this point'. The Unit being relieved, a battalion of the Hallamshire Regiment, had learned the hard way that the Germans in that sector reacted to noise as well as dust. Jack and I propped our bikes against the railway embankment and joined the rest to complete the journey on foot.

The Headquarters area being taken over was about half a mile into the wood and every DR trip had to begin and end with that walk. The two Fighting Troops carried on some hundreds of yards further to occupy forward positions at the edge of the wood, which was the limit of the FDLs of the British salient. The unit had inherited some very good Army holes – large, deep and solidly roofed with heavy baulks of timber and a good thickness of earth. An exception was the Signals Despatch Office, which had been constructed at ground level by digging into a steep bank-side, enclosing the front of the excavation with a thick wall of sandbags and roofing over with stout timbers and a few feet of earth. A narrow entrance was protected by a blast wall of sandbags and a rolled-up tarpaulin sheet was anchored in the earth cover, ready to be dropped at night. From the top of the doorway a spider's web of field telephone wires radiated through the trees. The dugout was just large enough to accommodate a rickety wooden table for the Commando telephone exchange, a chair for the duty signaller and an area of beaten earth behind him for the duty DR.

One unexpected asset of the HQ area was a 'recreation room'! – a hole about ten feet square, with almost six feet of headroom, well roofed-over and protected. Throughout our stay there, at almost any hour of the day or night, no matter how much 'muck' was flying around outside, it would be filled with cigarette smoke and off-watch Marines engrossed in one or more serious games of pontoon, nap or brag.

The 'welcoming bombardment', hoping to inflict casualties before men reached the prepared positions, had had some success, including Lieutenant Robinson and Sergeant Murray of 'X' Troop, both killed, and it kept on coming. For three days and nights, with only occasional let-ups, shells or mortar bombs were falling somewhere in the neighbourhood and, during the whole ten days of the Unit's tenure of that position, most periods of 'quiet' could be measured in minutes rather than hours.

This almost continuous enemy activity made the life of a DR, moving around in the open, far from a snug hole, particularly hairy. In daylight the drawback of the approach of shells being masked by the motorbike's engine was disturbing enough, but rides after dark added other problems. Being on duty at night meant remaining fully clothed, ready to go at a moment's notice. Curled up in a blanket behind the duty signaller, ears were always attuned to the cranking of the call-up handle. A few turns meant that all was well, but when it went on and on, it was time to steel yourself for the Signaller's, 'Sorry sir, I can't raise them, the line must be cut'. The inevitable consequence would be, 'Better send the DR then,' and you would squirm into your riding coat. Then, shoulders hunched against the cold, a half-mile stumble through the trees, kick the engine into life and off on a lonely ride.

If the night was 'noisy', and most of them were, the mind would be too fully occupied in trying to sort out what was happening around you to think of much else. If things were quiet, however, it was easy to imagine that every German for miles around was listening to your approach and getting ready to do something unpleasant about it. When it became necessary to stop and switch off the engine to consult the map or search for a gap in the hedge on foot the complete silence was even worse and there was an immediate itching to start up again, just to hear a friendly noise. Either way, day or night, quiet or noisy, without fail, the first comforting words to greet you at your destination would be 'For Christ's sake, shut that bloody thing off!'

Being in a salient added a further complication because, when travelling laterally across it, 'the front' was both ahead and behind you. In the gathering dusk of one evening, riding slowly along an unfamiliar lane, eyes straining to pick out anything that might direct me to my destination, I was brought to a halt by a shadowy figure, rifle at the ready, materializing from the hedgeline. ''Ere myte!', it said, 'I woon't gow no furvver dahn there – unless yer message is fer the Jerries.' I thanked my Cockney saviour and beat a hasty retreat.

'S' Troop was positioned in the ruins of a well-shelled brick-works, about a mile east of Touffreville. It was less than half a mile from Commando HQ as the crow flies, but to get there circum-spectly by road meant a ride of about three miles, and every trip was guaranteed to be eventful, as 'S' undoubtedly attracted more attention than any of the other Troops. This could have been because the Germans knew that our mortars were based there, or maybe the chimneys, now no more than heaps of brick rubble, had once been artillery 'markers', or simply that the approach road was under observation.

My first ride to 'S' was on the morning after our move-in and I adhered strictly to the 'Drive Slowly! – Dust brings shells!!' warnings by the roadside. I located their HQ hole in the shattered ruins of the brickworks, delivered the message and had the engine running ready to leave when a batch of incoming shells announced their imminent arrival. Dust at that juncture would clearly have no effect, so I twisted the throttle wide open and roared off as fast as I could work my way through the gearbox. Behind me, bursting shells were re-arranging the heaps of rubble and I learned later that two Marines had been wounded.

Despite the frequency of bombardments, 'S' Troop's casualties were relatively light as the kilns and flues, with the added protection of a covering of brick rubble, made effective shelters. A drawback for DRs, however, was that the Troop Commander would move around his subterranean domain, so, when your sole concern was to get rid of the message and go, it was necessary to flit around from hole to hole calling down, 'Is this Troop HQ?'

Two days after our arrival in the Bulge there was a strong buzz that the Germans were pulling back and, simultaneously, we had an unexpected visit from the Brigadier, 'Jumbo' Leicester. Some said that the Brigadier had brought the rumour, but the wags averred that it was more likely that the rumour had brought the Brigadier! That, of course, was no more than a 'family' joke, as 'the Brig' was well respected. Anyhow, a strong patrol went forward to investigate and the Germans, taking it to be the start of a major attack, subjected the Commando area to a heavy pasting for the rest of the day, causing some casualties.

On the fourth day in the Bulge Frank Heggarty and Ray Stillwell arrived by truck to relieve Jack and me, taking over our bikes. Half an hour later we were back in the peace and quiet of Rear Echelon, repairing the roof of our hole which had been stove in by a truck. Then, next day, Rear Echelon moved to a new location near Pegasus Bridge, so we had to dig a new one! The move at least confirmed my acceptance as a driver as I was given the job of driving a loaded jeep to the new location.

Later in the day two incidents demonstrated that, even without enemy action, life in the rear areas had its hazards. The first incident came about whilst we were attempting to perfect an oil-and-water stove. When carefully regulated droplets of oil and water are contrived to fall onto a hot metal plate and set alight, combustion is self-perpetuating. It would have had no practical

91

application for us but it was an interesting experiment. The basic problem was to get the hearth plate hot enough to vaporize the oil, so Jack Horsfield was helping things along with a slosh of petrol when he found he had a flaming jerrican in his hands. Luckily he had the presence of mind to close the cap quickly and the flames soon died away.

Nearby, Frank Barker had the cylinder head off his bike and decided to wash out the engine's innards with petrol before putting everything back together again. He depressed the kick start to move the piston, but, unbelievably, had left the sparking plug on its lead and the bike was immediately enveloped in flames. Showers of dry earth prevented major damage, but the incident certainly prolonged Frank's maintenance work.

Next day, back at Advanced HQ in the Troarn woods, I was given a trip to a quieter part of the salient. This took me onto a deserted narrow road running along the top of a dyke, some six feet or so above the surrounding countryside, and my nose was soon wrinkling with the stench of rotting flesh. The source became apparent when I came upon a German tank keeled over on its side at the bottom of the dyke. The decomposing body of one of the crew dangled by one leg trapped in the turret hatch and he had obviously been there for quite some time as the visible flesh had rotted away until it was almost transparent. Judging from the all-pervading stink, it seemed probable that some of his pals were still inside.

The forward positions of the Troarn Bulge were as lively as ever and casualties were mounting; in six days the Commando suffered a total of forty-four, including three killed. Every man went about his duties continually deciding where he would dive for cover when the next batch came in. This meant that 'going to the heads' was a tricky business, as the latrine areas couldn't be sited below ground level. Should there be a lull in the shelling, suggesting that things would be quiet for a while, and you decided to go, only to hear more shells coming in, you had a problem. I am sure that few of us escaped the indignity of being, literally, 'caught with their trousers down'.

41 Commando's move into the Troarn Bulge had coincided with momentous happenings all along the Normandy front. By Sunday 6 August, the day before the Unit had left Sallenelles, the sweeping

American 'right hook', by no less than twenty divisions, had reached Alençon and Le Mans. That same night Von Kluge's Seventh Army had attacked in the direction of Mortain and Avranches in an attempt to cut them off from their supply base in the Cherbourg Peninsula. The British and Canadian Armies had resumed their attack to the south of Caen; with the sole exception of the Orne bridgehead, the entire Allied invasion front was in motion.

Von Kluge's counter-attack was pressed forward for five days, with his troops continually at the mercy of the omnipotent Allied air forces and suffering heavy losses. By Friday 11 August, the day on which I had returned to Advance HQ in the Bulge, they had been forced to abandon the attack and were beginning to pull back. Units of General Patton's US Third Army were then swinging northwards towards Argentan, while the British and Canadians, supported by the Polish armoured division, were attacking strongly southwards in the direction of Falaise. The jaws of the 'Falaise Gap' were beginning to close and the only questions were when and how many Germans would then be cut off, to be killed or captured.

By Tuesday 15 August the British and Canadians had reached Falaise (the gap was finally closed on the 20th) and the Americans, striking towards Paris, were rapidly approaching Chartres. It was clear that the German forces around the Orne bridgehead would soon be forced to pull back too if they were to avoid being completely outflanked. Possibly to help them make up their minds to go, the British artillery barrage rose to a crescendo during the day; it began to look as though Montgomery's hinge was at last beginning to turn.

Next morning, 16 August, conditions in the Troarn Bulge were so unusually quiet that it was generally believed that the Germans had indeed moved back. Early in afternoon, however, such thoughts were rudely dispelled when a heavy rain of shells neatly targeting the HQ area sent everyone scurrying for shelter.

Those shells, however, had been the enemy's Parthian shot. The afternoon advanced with unaccustomed peacefulness and by evening the usual sounds of bombs and shells had been replaced by birdsong. A message from Brigade advised of the imminent likelihood of a German withdrawal and shortly afterwards a deserter, who obviously preferred not to go with them, confirmed that the Germans had been alerted to pull back across the River Muance before dark that evening.

Orders were given for a strong patrol to move off early next morning, probe forward to the south-east of Troarn and re-establish contact with the enemy. 'A' and 'B' Troops were to lead and I was to be the DR to accompany them. As the noise of a motor-cycle engine would be too much of a give-away, it was understood that I would be allowed to use the CO's jeep.

Chapter 7

FORWARD FROM TROARN

During the late evening of Wednesday 16 August, and again at first light on the 17th, Commando patrols failed to make contact with the enemy and preparations to move forward were finalized. My hopes of using a jeep to accompany the patrol were dashed when I was told to report to 'A' Troop Commander, Captain Stevens, with my motorbike. I was given an explicit order not to start the engine until he gave me the instruction personally; until then the bike would be pushed. TSM Jack Hazelhurst positioned me in the long single file of men, 'A' Troop following 'B', which was already snaking its way through the trees.

Pushing a motorbike through rough woodland is no easy matter and after only the few hundred yards to the foot of a railway embankment (the line curves towards Troarn in two sinuous loops from the level crossing where we had had to leave our bikes) I was lathered in sweat. Others helped manhandle the machine to the top, bounce it across the tracks, then ease it down the other side. At the foot of the slope we passed through a narrow gap in a tall hedge on to a minor country road and turned left.

It came as a surprise to me to see just how close to Troarn our positions had been – the first buildings were less than a quarter of a mile away. In that short distance three British tanks were slumped at untidy angles in the roadside ditch; after passing those dead tanks we entered a dead town. It was seemingly intact, even to a church with a slim steeple, but many of the buildings lining the rubble-littered streets were no more than gutted shells. Apart from ourselves there was no sign of life.

My motorbike was very probably the first Allied mechanized vehicle to have entered Troarn since 6 June. In the very early hours of D-Day Major Roseveare, with a few men of 6th Airborne Division, had roared into the town in a jeep to blow the bridge over the River Dives, but he was intercepted by a German patrol and was lucky to escape with his life, on foot. My own journey was in the reverse order – I went in on foot and rode out.

After leaving the town the patrol began moving across country again and, even with some assistance from less-encumbered Marines, it was hard going. After half a mile or so, however, we joined the minor road which follows the River Muance to the small hamlet of Janville, some two miles away.

In marked contrast to the dug-outs and shattered trees of Troarn wood, the countryside was unblemished but completely empty, silent, bare. There were no houses, no people, no animals in the fields, and even the birds seemed silent. There was no sound other than the scuffling of booted feet.

The advance was slow and spasmodic. 'B' Troop was scouting ahead, alert for the first sign of the enemy; the rest followed with alternate men moving along each side of the roadway, weapons at the ready, eyes searching constantly for any sign of movement. I just pushed my bike and looked about.

Janville was reached without incident. The road should have crossed over the River Muance, which at that point has two separate courses, but both bridges had been blown. The carriageway made two V-shaped contacts with the river, but the water was only knee-deep, so men had been able to cross and were pushing on. I was given a signal to take back and allowed to start the engine after having pushed the bike back round the first bend in the road. Then I was in the saddle, bowling through the empty countryside, wondering whether any German snipers had been left behind.

I was given a reply to take back and, on regaining Janville, which I now saw comprised little more than a church, a few houses and the blown bridges, found that 'A' and 'B' Troops were still there, in a position of all-round defence. 'Y' Troop had taken over the lead and was on the other side of the river, moving towards St Pierre du Jonquet two miles further on; the Patrol Commander was with them, so I had to follow.

It wasn't too difficult a job to manoeuvre the bike across the two bridge spans resting on the river bed, through the shallow waters and do a little rough riding up the far bank to regain the road. Then once again I was like The Ancient Mariner, 'Alone, alone, all, all alone . . .', with the added knowledge that this time I was heading forward, instead of back. There was a loaded Colt 45 automatic at my belt, but that was little more than a symbolic protection, and those two miles of recently-liberated France seemed very long indeed. It was a great relief to cruise round a bend in the road and find myself looking down the muzzles of the 'Y' Troop rearguard. There was no doubt that I was back among friends when they bawled, 'For Christ's sake, shut that bloody thing off!' The bike had to be left by the roadside while I went forward on foot to find the Troop Commander.

'Y' were ranged in firing positions along both sides of the road, the bocage-type country, with hedges set upon banks of earth, providing good defensive parapets. The Marines slumped against them were delighted to divert a little of their attention towards a DR without a motorbike.

'What's up, Mitch? Lost your bike?'

'Hey, look! DRs can walk!'

'Is that my leave chit you've got there, Ray?'

'What the hell does Monty want of us this time?'

There was also some unprintable language from the less couth.

I found the Troop Commander on the high ground on the outskirts of St Pierre du Jonquet and handed him the signal. It was clearly the 'Press on!' instruction he had been expecting and, even as I turned to walk back to my bike, shouts of 'All right, "Y", on your feet, on the road, we're moving on' were passing down the line.

As I retraced my steps men were reluctantly easing themselves away from their restful positions against the banksides and adjusting their equipment. There were some 'cracks' about me going the wrong way and I may have smirked a little, but we all had our jobs to do. 'Y' Troop 'bumped' the Germans about half a mile further up the road at the River Dives, where again the bridge had been blown, but this time a rearguard had been left to cover it.

Shots were exchanged, but both sides were content to leave it at that. Brigade was awaiting further orders, so it was just a case of sitting tight. I spent the rest of the day with 'A' Troop at Janville and slept with them in a barn alongside the church.

Next morning, after stand-to, the Patrol was put at instant readiness to continue the advance, but later this was relaxed to one hour's notice. Throughout the day I had trips to HQ, still in the old position, but not until 2030 hours was the Commando given orders to move, and it was due east from Troarn, not via St Pierre du Jonquet, as had been assumed. The axis of advance given to our Brigade, and to No. 3 Parachute Brigade, was Route Nationale 815, leading to Dozulé and Pont l'Évêque. 41 Commando's immediate orders were to advance as far as St Richer, about three miles away, and assemble there. The Patrol in the Janville area was to retrace its steps to Troarn and rejoin the Unit as soon as possible next morning. Commando headquarters was set up at St Richer by 0100 hours on the 19th without having made contact with the enemy.

I passed a second night in Janville and next morning was sent off alone to report to HQ. It was Saturday 19 August, dull after a night of rain, and on reaching Troarn I found that, in 48 hours, the town had been unbelievably transformed. The N.815 was now carrying an unending stream of nose-to-tail military traffic of every conceivable type and it was fortunate that a military policeman was on hand to slot me into the flow.

To the east of Troarn the N.815 has to cross the Rivers Muance and Dives – about five hundred yards apart at that point – and both bridges had been blown. These had been replaced by floating pontoon bridges and rough tracks bulldozed down the steep river banks linked them to the N.815. The bridges, however, could carry only one lane of traffic and, as many vehicles needed attempt after attempt to negotiate the wet and slippery tracks, there was one helluva double traffic bottle-neck. All the while the neighbourhood was being subjected to intermittent shellfire and the entire column could do nothing but wait in line and hope for early release.

To be stuck motionless between a pulsating truck belching exhaust fumes in your face and the hot radiator of another monster towering behind, with cold, uninviting water on both sides and shells bursting in your field of view, is not an enviable position. It was a huge relief, therefore, to be able to ride off the end of a bridge, sit back along the luggage carrier to increase traction on the rear wheel, open the throttle and bounce and slither up the opposite bank.

Once across the rivers the congestion quickly subsided as vehicles dispersed into the countryside; then the N.815 became largely the domain of the infantry. The Paras were 'at the sharp end' a mile or so ahead and much of 41 Commando was moving forward in the traditional manner of foot-slogging. After I had reported back, I found that my own role was, largely, just to be there. On occasions I was sent up or down the marching column with messages – giving the marchers a target for more ribald remarks – but often it was just a matter of waiting by the roadside until they had passed.

Then it filtered down that the CO had been called forward to an 'Order Group' at Brigade HQ in Goustranville, about two miles ahead. It was learned that the Paras had secured the crossing of the River Doigt some three miles further on and a mile short of Dozulé, but had been unable to achieve the hill feature in front of the town. 46 RM Commando were to make an attack on this high ground that night, while 41 and 48 would initiate an out-flanking movement to the south of Dozulé at dawn. I wasn't to be involved and passed the night by the roadside, where I was able to crawl under a truck to gain protection from the overnight rain, until dawn stand-to next morning.

That Sunday dawned bright and fair. By first light elements of 48 and 41 Commandos had crossed the river via a small pedestrian bridge south-east of Goustranville. 41 advanced to Putot-en-Auge and later in the morning the Commando was moved up to fill a gap between 48 and 46 Commandos. The Germans had become very active in the area and their mortar fire was inflicting casualties. A number of 'S' were wounded, including Captain Grant, the CO who had been hard to find in the brickworks near Troarn. Patrols pushed forward to Clermont-en-Auge, taking prisoners, and by afternoon were advancing northwards from Panniers. St Léger was occupied that evening; our forward Troops remained there overnight.

While this had been going on I was shuttling up and down with the Transport Column as it moved along Route N.815 towards

Dozulé. Some distance short of the town the vehicles were halted and the officers and men of Rear Headquarters continued on foot through dank and shady woodlands, along narrow tracks, made soft and slithery by the overnight rain. For Despatch Riders it was a major achievement just to stay in the saddle and, more than once, a file of foot-sloggers had to hop rapidly off a track which wasn't wide enough for them and a motorbike.

In the late afternoon we moved into bright sunshine to find ourselves on an extensive straw-covered farmyard area, bounded by rough wooden buildings. Almost immediately a score or more of French civilians were milling around with glasses and bottles to welcome their liberators. One perspiring Marine gratefully accepted what he assumed to be a tumbler of water and had taken a gargantuan swallow before discovering that it was Calvados, the local apple brandy! His reaction verged on the cataclysmic.

HQ was set up in one of the outbuildings and despatch riders were immediately called from the liberation celebrations to deliver messages. The portable radio sets then available could be unreliable at any time, but in the woods above Dozulé they were useless and Despatch Riders had to make up the deficiency.

As the shadows lengthened, riding along slippery woodland tracks without lights and with the trees cutting off what little daylight remained became more and more difficult. In the very late dusk I was given a signal for Brigade HQ, established in a large house more than a mile away through the woods. I managed to make the delivery just as the last vestiges of daylight were fading; there was no reply, so I started back immediately, but after perhaps five minutes of slipping and sliding through a black maze of trees I had to accept defeat. A DR who just couldn't find his own way home slithered back to Brigade to spend the night on the floor of their SDO.

It was raining heavily next morning, but in full daylight I was able to negotiate the treacherous tracks and return to HQ. I learned that, at 0430 that morning, aided by the light from some burning buildings, a combined force of 41 and 47 Commandos had entered Dozulé without opposition. During a sweep through nearby orchards at first light, however, 'X' Troop and Advanced HQ had suffered casualties, including two killed. Later in the day the unit was pulled back to St Léger, leaving only a Standing Patrol in the town. For the rest of the day British troops, including the 5th Parachute Brigade, streamed through burning Dozulé in pursuit of the retreating Germans.

For most of that day much of the Commando was occupied in little more than keeping dry as rain continued to deluge down. The DRs, however, were continually out and about, but by evening conditions had deteriorated to such an extent that this couldn't be accomplished on two wheels and, with visibility down to almost zero, it became a two-man job, a driver to handle the jeep and a DR to find the way.

In the almost total darkness of those woodland tracks it was still a very dicey business and at times progress depended largely upon the driver proceeding at a snail's pace, gauging the amount of resistance he was getting from the flanking bushes to keep him on the track. The DR, meanwhile, head bent low and well inboard, strained his eyes to see as much as possible and give such directions as he could from his knowledge of track junctions and gated entrances. Surprisingly, we all got home that night.

Next morning we wondered what the previous two days' problems had been about. Even at dawn stand-to the air was sweet and dry and, as the early morning mist lifted, the sky became bright and crystal clear. We moved down into the valley, passed through shattered Dozulé and resumed a rather slow progress along the N.815. It was uneventful until reaching the high ground above the town of Pont L'Évêque, when the column moved into a confused medley of incoming missiles and nearby explosions. Pont l'Évêque – Bishop's Bridge – is a crossing point of the River Tougues, which the Germans had clearly decided was a good line on which to fight another rearguard action.

HQ was set up in a farm a short distance from the main road leading down into town where a group of French civilians appeared to have sought refuge. That night we shared with them the straw-covered stone floors of a long row of single-storey outbuildings extending from the farmhouse towards the road. The stout stone walls were probably adequate to withstand the blast and shell splinters from near-misses but the lightly-tiled roofs would have been shattered by a brick.

At some time after midnight I was called from the fuggy warmth of our communal resting place to deliver a signal to one of the

Troops. The night was filled with the rumbles of explosions and, in the valley below, the glow of many fires and clouds of red-tinged smoke hung over Pont l'Évêque. The Germans had obviously started blowing up anything that might be of use to us. The flames, reflected from low clouds, helped me find my way; I completed the delivery and returned without incident.

Morning was sunny and comparatively quiet. After stand-down a cheerful *entente cordiale* atmosphere pervaded Commando headquarters as we hunted for receptacles to hold water for a wash and shave. In this we were helped by cheerful civilians and it wasn't long before one old lady had been 'conned' into thinking that she had learned a little English.

A popular nonsense song of the day began with the 'words', 'Mairsy Dotes 'n dozy dotes 'n little lams-ee-tivy . . .' subsequently translated into 'Mares eat oats, and does eat oats, and little lambs eat ivy'. A signaller got the idea of responding to the lady's 'Bonjour' greeting with a polite 'Mairsy Dotes' and it wasn't long before she was proudly airing her 'English' by greeting others in the same way!

During the morning it became known that the Commando was to take over a sector previously held by some of the Airborne Division which, for reasons not divulged, had been withdrawn. I was sent with the leading elements to report where the positions actually were and, leaving my bike by the roadside, accompanied them on foot. We crossed a number of fields, passing scores of well-dug but empty slit trenches – many more than could have been filled by the entire Commando. The weather was now overcast and a feeling of foreboding seemed to hang over those abandoned positions, which was heightened for me during my solitary long walk back to the road. Enemy guns had opened fire again and shells were falling in the immediate neighbourhood. Back at HQ, I found that the civilians had been evacuated.

That shelling was the start of one of the most prolonged barrages we experienced there. For the remainder of the day I alternated between the comparative safety of HQ and solitary trips around the Commando area, all to the accompaniment of mortar and/or 88 fire. Despite the very good Airborne holes, the unit suffered a number of casualties in those positions, including the Medical Officer and some of his Sick Berth Attendants.

In the afternoon I was given a message for one of the Troops positioned on the high ground overlooking the River Tougues and was shown their approximate position on the map. It meant going about three-quarters of a mile or more down the main road towards Pont l'Évêque, then taking a farm track to the left, along the top edge of the river valley; the Troop would be in the third or fourth field on the left-hand side.

Three-quarters of a mile is a long way when you are completely on your own and there are no friendly troops between yourself and the enemy. I seemed to be getting uncomfortably close to Pont l'Évêque and had reached the stage of thinking 'Must have missed it – another fifty yards and I'm turning back' when I came upon a break in the hedgeline and turned on to a narrow track. A hedge ran along the left-hand side and to the right open fields fell away towards the river. At that point it was hidden by trees, but beyond a wide panorama of countryside on the enemy-held bank was clearly visible. I was counting the gateways on the left, paused at the third, but, seeing nothing, carried on and rode directly into the fourth field. It was small, largely bounded by trees, and it too appeared empty until, some 10 yards away, a head and shoulders appeared above ground level, arms waving wildly and a voice bawling, 'Drop that bloody thing QUICK! – AND GET OVER HERE!'

I didn't have to ask why. Even as I obeyed and started to run, the urgent screaming approach of shells announced that a salvo was going to land very, very close. As I fell on top of the Troop Sergeant the shells were bursting all about. 'You silly bastard!' he was spluttering angrily. 'They've got that bloody gateway taped to an inch. Any movement and we get twenty minutes of this fricking lot.' 'Sorry, sarge, but they didn't tell me.' We both used the word 'they', but I knew he meant the Germans and he knew I was talking about Commando HQ. When things had quietened down sufficiently for me to flit across to the Troop Commander's hole more heads poked above ground level and I was followed by a barrage of bad language and baleful glares. 'At least,' I reminded them, 'you lot always have holes to jump into.'

After receiving the officer's reply I was ready to go, but it was obvious that I would have to find some other way back. I righted the bike and rode into the trees at the rear of the field to find one.

It was only a small copse and soon gave way to a wide, rolling hill-side falling away from the Troop position. All was plain sailing until progress was halted by a stout wire fence, too high for me to 'topple' the bike over – a technique used in training – with the bottom strand almost at ground level. I rode back and forth, searching for a gap or a weak spot, but the posts were too stout to move and the wires were strong and unbroken, nor was there any way round, yet it was unthinkable to return the way I had come.

Trying not to panic, I reasoned that as the bike was too heavy to lift and couldn't be toppled over, it would have to go under. I laid the machine on the ground as close to the fence as possible and climbed over. Then, lying close to the fence, I began a combination of heaving up the bottom strand of wire, manoeuvring the handle-bars and other parts of the machine underneath one at a time and dragging hard. In short heaves, as handle bars, footrests, hub nuts, etc, gouged furrows in the earth, I managed to inch the bike forward. It required long pauses for deep breathing and resting muscles in between heaves, but the process was eventually successful. It probably took half an hour to complete the job, by which time I was weak and wringing with perspiration.

When my thumping heart had settled down I started off again and was soon riding down a hillside falling steeply into a grass-covered valley a few hundred feet deep. At the bottom, near the hedge boundary, a battery of field guns was set up, the gunners apparently getting ready for a shoot. Barely had I been heartened by the sight of British troops than a salvo of shells shrieked over-head to burst, in puffs of black smoke, about midway between me and the guns. Instinctively, I opened the throttle, zoomed down through the drifting smoke, flew past gaping artillerymen picking themselves up off the ground and slithered through a muddy gateway on to a farm track.

The track led me to a farmyard from which I regained the N.815 and returned to HQ. In the Signals Despatch Office a radio set had been tuned to receive the BBC Home Service News and I was just in time to hear cultured tones announce, 'This morning, our troops entered the town of Pont l'Évêque'!

The Germans knew that Allied troops would soon be moving into the town and were continuing their demolitions. They were still at it when, in the darkness of late evening, I was handed a signal for another of our Troops. Their HQ was in a house on the outskirts of the town, standing isolated at the top of a steep *pavé* street leading down towards the river. My trip was probably in connection with a crossing of the river at Pierrefitte-en-Auge, a few miles to the south of Pont l'Évêque, which had been planned for that night.

I was sitting in the kitchen, awaiting a signal to take back, when a batch of particularly large high explosives blasted off. They were so close that the building shook to its foundations, as we did to ours. We surmised that it had been a salvo from one of the German large-calibre multi-barrelled Nebelwerfer mortars, some of which fired rocket-propelled missiles up to 32 cm calibre – as big as 12" shells. As has been mentioned previously , the translation of 'Nebelwerfer' is 'Smoke thrower', something of a misnomer, but at least those ones hadn't had our names on them.

Back at HQ, my tour as Duty DR was finished for the day, another one would sleep in the SDO, so I was forced to spend the night in the open, in the transport lines. It was an extremely noisy night. The German rearguard must have had lots of ammunition left and, rather than carrying it away, were blasting it off in our direction.

There were no holes available so I crawled under a truck as protection against falling bomb and shell splinters, despite realizing that it could be a foolhardy thing to do. Suppose the truck was hit and the petrol tank blew up? I didn't go too far under. Then what if shell splinters slashed the tyres, dropping the thing on top of me? I kept away from the sump and differential housing. A combination of such thoughts, plus the whines and explosions of shells, kept me awake much of the night, but it all helped to pass the hours of darkness.

Chapter 8

ACROSS THE RIVERS TOUGUES AND SEINE

By dawn, however, all the threatening noises had gone and an un-accustomed blanket of silence lay over the countryside. Pont l'Évêque was still burning, but, as hour followed hour without any enemy activity, it was clear that the Germans had pulled out. It was learned that the crossing of the Tougues at Pierrefitte planned for the previous night had been called off at the very last moment when the Commando was actually moving up to the jumping-off point. News also filtered down that elements of Sixth Airborne were already across the river, pushing forward to regain contact.

Throughout the day the Commando remained in position, waiting and wondering. That night I was Duty DR again, so at the nub of things when, at half past four in the morning, the Commando received orders to make an immediate move forward. The Fighting Troops were roused, to climb into TCVs and be taken forward some eight miles beyond Pont l'Évêque. They debussed in the vicinity of Beuzeville and began an early morning pursuit on foot. The 8th Parachute Battalion, advancing on the same axis, was ahead of 41 and I was ordered forward to report to their HQ to act as liaison link for Brigadier Leicester.

The Paras had set up their Headquarters in a recently-vacated German bunker built in the corner of a wood where it had commanded the approaches to an adjacent crossroads. The location, shown on a map, posed no problem, but to reach it circumspectly from the rear entailed a final approach ride of about two miles over rough farm roads meandering between high hedges

1. Ply/x 111113 Marine H.T.W.B. 'Geordie' Swindale, killed on D-Day. Taken in Catania, Sicily, after the Salerno operation, September 1943. This book is dedicated to his memory.

Royal Marine Commandos embark on LCI(S) – Landing Craft Infantry (Small) – at the *Rising Sun* jetty, Warsash on the River Hamble, 5 June 1944. *(Royal Marines Museum)*

3. LCI(S) carrying Royal Marine Commandos, nearing *Sword* Beach, Normandy, D-Day, 6 June 1944. *(Royal Marines Museum)*

4. Royal Marines coming ashore from LCI(S). The man at the foot of second ramp is being helped carry a parascooter.

5. Sword beach on D-Day; men take brief shelter behind an AVRE.

6. Prisoners taken by Royal Marines at St Aubin being marched away.

7. The outskirts of Lion-sur-Mer. On D-Day the shop bearing the name 'Martin' was the Post Office. The Author's small group of stragglers took the road leading straight ahead. *(Photo taken by the Author in 1976)*

8. Ranville, where 6th Airborne Division had their Headquarters, commemorates the fact that it was the first village in France to be liberated. *(Photo by Author)*

RANVILLE
LE PREMIER VILLAGE DE FRANCE
LIBERÉ A ÉTÉ PRIS AUX ALLEMANDS
A 2H30 LE 6 JUIN 1944
PAR
LE 13TH (LANCASHIRE) BATTALION
THE PARACHUTE REGIMENT

WIN OR DIE

THIS MEMORIAL IS RAISED BY ALL RANKS IN MEMORY
OF THEIR COMRADES WHO FELL IN THE CAMPAIGN

9.Pegasus Bridge in June 1944. (British vehicles are still driving on the left!). In the background are two gliders of the 6th Airlanding Brigade.

10. and 11. Pegasus Bridge in 1976. Open for road traffic (left) and canal traffic (right). *(Photos by Author)*

12. The station house at Cany-Barville, standing derelict in 1976. In August 1944 Signallers and DRs of 41 RM Commando were billeted on the ground floor, while the stationmaster and his family lived in the upper storey. *(Photo by Author)*

13. A Welbike is taken from its container, having been dropped by parachute. *(Airborne Forces Museum)*

14. Squatting on their loaded Buffaloes, men of the Commando wait as their LCT approaches Walcheren. *(IWM)*

15. An LCT of 41 RM Commando nearing Westkapelle.

16. An LCT touches down after passing through the breach in the sea dyke.

17. The Buffalo blown up by a German mine at Serooskerke on 8 November 1944, with the loss of 20 lives, including 14 men of No.48 Royal Marines Commando. *(Jacob van Winkelen)*

and tortuous muddy tracks snaking through intermittent stretches of woodland.

As at Troarn, I was instructed to leave the machine at the edge of the wood lest the noise of the engine should alert the enemy. Long before reaching there, however, the futility of such an instruction was obvious. Almost continuous explosions were splattering the area and the rattling of automatic small arms fire, uncomfortably close by, made any other noise irrelevant. Nevertheless, I dropped the machine and doubled the few score yards to a massive blockhouse, nodded to a paratrooper sheltering in the doorway and headed down a flight of concrete steps.

At the bottom I entered a completely different world, but my eyes needed time to adjust to the gloom. It was a confined, dim, shadowy place, illuminated only by a few hurricane lamps, around which indistinct figures were poring over maps or talking into microphones. The crashing noises above ground had been replaced by no more than the low mumbling of voices of officers discussing the situation and signallers reciting call signs and dictating messages.

I reported to the Signals Officer and was told to wait while a message for Brigade was finalized, so there was time for a smoke and to absorb the absolute safety engendered by a yard or two of reinforced concrete. In due course I was handed the message, but on starting back up the stairs the Para at the top called down, 'Hang on a bit, DR, its rather noisy up here.' After a while he came back with 'OK, it's quiet now,' and I was on my way.

On emerging into daylight it was clear that his 'quiet' was only relative as there were still many unfriendly noises in the real world. With them came the realization that my brief stay in complete safety had engendered a degree of reluctance to get back to the 'normality' of bombs and shells. The feeling returned each time I had to leave the Paras' bunker, but apparently, like stage fright, it evaporated once back into things. There was no major problem in being 'outside' when that was the only way of life you knew, but having it interspersed with periods of complete safety brought home a realization of how dicey the whole business was.

After that first trip to 8 Paras I spent the day shuttling back and forth between their bunker and Brigade along those rough, muddy tracks. In marked contrast with the Paras' bunker, Brigadier

Leicester's 'Headquarters' was no more than a small clearing in a wood. There, sitting on logs near a wood fire where a dixie of tea was constantly kept hot, he, with some of his officers, map cases on knees, conducted the Brigade's business.

After delivering one message from the bunker, the Brig asked if it would be possible to take his Intelligence Officer back with me for a discussion with the Paras. I replied that it could be done, but the ride was rough and often touch and go whether I could keep the bike on an even keel, so there was an even chance of him coming off. The Brigadier clearly thought the risk was worth taking, so the officer straddled the luggage rack and off we went.

Nearing 'bunker wood', I was engrossed in watching the track and keeping the pair of us on the bike, and it was only at the last moment that a glance forward revealed a figure in German field grey emerging from the trees. Then I saw a rifle and bayonet at his back, in the hands of a grinning parachutist.

After conducting the Officer to the bunker and waiting until he had completed his discussion, I delivered him unscathed back into the presence of the Brigadier. The two officers exchanged welcoming pleasantries, then the IO dipped a mug into the dixie of tea, but, before allowing him to make his report, 'Jumbo' dipped another mug into the dixie and handed it to me, saying, 'I think the DR deserves one too'.

After that tea break I returned with a signal to 8 Paras which could have been the order to put in an attack. In any event the Germans pulled back and when 8 Para HQ vacated the bunker and moved forward about two miles I accompanied them. When they were settled in their new positions I was given a signal for Jumbo to inform him where they were.

It was evening when I reported once more to Para HQ and artillery and mortar fire had subsided to a 'desultory' stage. The entire countryside was quietening down so that the noise of my engine had become an embarrassment. I was thanked kindly for my efforts during the day and politely told to return to my own Unit.

The rest of the Commando hadn't been idle either. In the morning our scouting patrols had bumped the Germans between Beuzeville and St Maclou, then maintained contact during the day. When I returned to HQ it was dusk, dull and overcast, and some of our Troops were moving forward. 'A' was to be accompanied by tanks, therefore the noise of a motorbike engine wouldn't be any problem, and I was sent along with them.

Tanks and Marines moved together along a narrow country road with hedges set high on dikes along both sides. The column turned through a gateway on the right-hand side of the road up a steep track which turned almost immediately sharp left into a field of stubble. One tank slithered sideways, crushing TSM Hazelhurst against the stone gatepost; he was crippled for the rest of his life. A short while later the tanks laagered up for the night and I was sent back to Commando HQ.

It was then about nine o'clock and I was dismayed to learn that 41 and 48 Commandos had been alerted to set off at two o'clock in the morning on a cross-country march on St Maclou, some six miles away. However, Colonel Palmer must have been aware of my very full day as he motioned me across to him and said, 'You needn't come, Mitchell. Stay here for the night and catch up in the morning.' I snuggled down into the straw of a barn and knew no more until the cocks were crowing next morning.

The operation had been a complete success. After the approach march in almost complete darkness the two Commandos had descended upon St Maclou in the early hours, only to find that the Germans had decamped. 48 had been given the job of leading the way and their Commanding Officer, Lieutenant Colonel 'Mouldy' Moulton, came up with an effective way of keeping the long file of men on the right track. Individual Officers had been given stretches of the route to commit to memory and they moved forward in turn to act as 'point'. Even amidst the many major news items of the time, that night march of 48 and 41 warranted a few column inches in the National Press.

Immediately after breakfast I set off to catch up, riding alone along deserted country roads, the verges littered with the aftermath of infantry activity. Unlike the outskirts of Caen, there were no shattered wrecks of tanks or trucks. The debris of war this time was no more than scattered odds and ends of military equipment – water bottles, steel helmets, ammunition carriers, etc, with, here and there, bodies of the dead. I passed perhaps a dozen or so; two, I noted, were Canadians, lying side by side on the grass verge, but the rest were German. One still remains in memory as a short, podgy youngster, lying face down in a shallow ditch, steel-rimmed spectacles and coal-scuttle helmet still in place.

My introduction to St Maclou was having to find my way around a very large crater where there had recently been a major cross-roads. Then I became engulfed in the jubilation of people liberated after four years of enemy occupation – cheers and smiles, hugs and handshakes, tears of joy and kisses, with some glasses of wine, cider or calvados. The Commando would be staying in St Maclou for a few days; it was Saturday, so there were hopes of a weekend off the war. Quite a lot had happened in the week since leaving Troarn.

The Despatch Riders and some Signallers had been allocated a recently-vacated terrace house as their billet. All furnishings, fittings, crockery and cutlery, even to a well-stocked drinks cabinet on the living-room wall, were still in place. Presumably the absence of the previous occupants had been linked with the precipitate departure of the Germans. We quickly adapted to living in a house again, for the first time since leaving Hastings three months earlier.

It was said that, in consequence of all the to-ings and fro-ings of the previous day, Colonel Palmer had put my name forward for a commendation. Whatever the reason, in due course I did receive a certificate which reads:

'It has been brought to my notice that you have performed out-standing good service, and shown great devotion to duty, during the campaign in North West Europe. I award you this certificate as a token of my appreciation, and I have given instructions that this shall be noted in your Record of Service'. It bears the signature, 'B.L. Montgomery, Field Marshal, Commander-in-Chief, 21st Army Group', so that was one occasion when Monty's instructions weren't carried out. My Record of Service bears no mention of the certificate!

For men in the Fighting Troops it *was* a weekend off because, in the words of the Unit's War Diary, theirs was to 'rest, wash and recuperate'. That didn't apply to the DRs as there were still messages to deliver. To make matters worse, it started to rain next morning and it continued almost non-stop for two days; while the troops sheltered indoors, we travelled the wet roads of France. Nevertheless, it was enough to have a house in which to sleep and a drinks cabinet on the wall.

As usual, the easing of tension and our static situation opened the flood gates of rumour; the buzz-mongers came into their own again. 'Home next week!' some said. 'SS Brigades are to be re-organized as ordinary Infantry Brigades.' 'Not so,' said others, 'We will become Mobile Reconnaissance Brigades.' The 'hottest' buzz of all was that the Airborne Division and No 1 SS Brigade were to be sent back to Blighty.

Wednesday came, with no positive news nor developments until, out of the blue after lunch, transport was laid on for 'shore leave' in Honfleur, the coastal resort some eight miles distant. The town had been liberated by the Canadians on the same day as the Marines reached St Maclou and was still in festive mood. Streets and buildings were decorated with flags and bunting, while every Allied vehicle received spontaneous waves and cheers. Café owners and restaurateurs, however, had returned to 'business as usual' and the prices being charged verged on highway robbery.

On our return to St Maclou that evening we found that the withdrawal of Sixth Airborne Division and No. 1 SS Brigade was a *fait accompli*; they were on their way home. No. 4 SS was to 'soldier on', apparently to demonstrate the unofficial motto of the Royal Marines – 'First in, last out'.

The DRs at least received 'sweeteners' by inheriting some of the Airborne Division's motorcycles. In place of the long-in-the-tooth Ariels we each became the proud possessor of a state-of-the-art 350cc Matchless, with teledraulic (telescopic hydraulic) front forks. As if to stress that it was 'all change', the operational element of the unit was moving forward next day, leaving me behind as the DR with Rear Echelon.

On the Thursday morning I was quite happy to wave 'Cheerio' to the other DRs as they rode away, shepherding the Unit convoy towards 'the front'. My stay in St Maclou was short-lived, however, as next morning I was handed a despatch for Advanced Headquarters, which I would find in Yvetot, a small town on the far side of the River Seine, beyond Barentin. In 1944 the first bridge over the Seine was at Rouen, but I was to make for a point opposite Duclair to be ferried across.

I set off with a mixture of glee at being able to try out the Matchless on a trip of almost fifty miles and some trepidation as to what conditions might be like so far away. For the first twenty miles via Pont Audemer the road was awash with a continuous flow

111

of military vehicles all heading for the Rouen bridges. At Bourg-Achard, however, I had to turn off onto the minor road leading into the horseshoe loop of the river towards Berville-sur-Seine, my ferry point. Then, for ten long miles, I was completely alone on a deserted forest road, passing more and more wrecked German vehicles as I drew nearer to the river and with the stench of rotting flesh growing ever stronger in my nostrils.

During the previous two weeks German troops in headlong flight had been trapped in such loops of the Seine and, at the mercy of Allied aircraft, untold numbers had perished. In the adjacent larger loop of the Forêt de Brotonne, where even more German troops had been trying to escape, the carnage had been particularly horrendous. As I drew near the river I passed lines of those German vehicles which had managed to survive the air attacks. The lines continued down to the water's edge and some vehicles had even been driven deep into the water, as though the drivers hoped that their trucks would float and carry them to safety.

The 'ferry' turned out to be no more than one of the pontoons used for building floating bridges, fitted with an outboard motor and being operated by two REs. Despite having seen no sign of life during my ride, there were files of British infantrymen lined up waiting to board, but they were halted until my bike had been manhandled over the gunwale. An Army DR with bike was already on board, so there wasn't much room left for infantrymen. The crossing, of about five hundred yards, was rather hairy as the pontoon was buffetted by the adverse current of the river. We were hard put to keep our bikes on an even keel, but eventually grounded safely within a few hundred yards of Duclair. 'Vive les REs!'

Only then did it sink in that the Commando had not gone forward into shot and shell, but into vin blanc and kisses. I had to join a long string of military vehicles moving slowly through the streets lined with cheering people waving flags and bottles of wine. If any vehicle stopped, even momentarily, the occupants were deluged with hugs, kisses and glasses of wine; the air was filled with 'Vive les Tommies'.

Motorcyclists were particularly vulnerable as children lining the kerb poked Union Flags and Tricolours into their faces. The obvious defence was to stop and accept a drink, but more positive evasive action was needed if my message was to be delivered. Even beyond the town there was little easing off in the rapturous welcome being accorded the stream of vehicles by groups of people gathered by the roadside. The six-mile journey to Barentin was a continuous triumphal procession, but then I had to turn out of line. The main flood of traffic was heading northeast towards Pavilly and Tôtes, following the German retreat, but my route to Yvetot was 'back' to the north-west. The road was only sparsely trafficked, but I still encountered group after group of French folks wanting to say 'Thank you' to any passing Allied serviceman. The sight of a waving wine bottle seemed to bring my machine to a rapid halt automatically, until I steeled myself to resist temptation.

Yvetot was in a state of euphoric turmoil, the streets were thronged with a noisy, boisterous *mélange* of Marines and civilians. I located the Signals Despatch Office with some difficulty and delivered my message. It evinced no great stir, so I regretted not having delayed longer. I was simply told to find the other DRs and stick around. By the simple process of grabbing every passing jolly Royal and bawling, 'Where are the DRs?' I eventually located them. The Commando had been the first Allied troops to enter Barentin and Yvetot, so had been welcomed as liberators. The square outside the Barentin Mairie has been renamed Place de la Libération and the building itself bears a plaque attesting to the fact that 41 RM Commando were the first to arrive.

In Yvetot hundreds of Royal Marines were almost inextricably mixed up with the local population. The top brass were undoubtedly aware of this and may have been a little concerned about the unit getting too attached to the place. During the evening orders were passed around by word of mouth that 41 would be moving out next morning and all ranks had better be there.

Chapter 9

CANY-BARVILLE, LE HAVRE AND DUNKIRK

On Saturday, 2 September, together with 46 and Brigade HQ, the Commando marched to Fauville-en-Caux, some ten miles away. Commando Headquarters had been allocated the Château de Bourville on the outskirts of town and arrived to find a main gate guard already in position, courtesy of the French Forces of the Interior (FFI), all armed with German light automatic weapons.

The FFI were much in evidence, as their major preoccupation was to organize public 'shearings' of French females who had consorted with Germans. 'Stages' had been set up in the market square of every town and village and, one after another, struggling women and young girls would be held down in a chair in full public view while a barber went about the job. As each handful of hair was snipped off he would twirl it around above his head to rounds of applause and cheers from the crowd, before casting it to one side and taking hold of another. After that he resorted to hand shears and finally removed the last vestiges with a razor leaving the victim's pate as bald as a billiard ball. Only then was she released to fight her hysterical way through the spitting, buffeting, jeers and catcalls of the crowd.

Even before one victim had managed to escape the concentrated hate of her townsfolk, those nearer the platform were starting up with new rounds of cheers as more handfuls of hair were being waved aloft. I witnessed only a small part of one of those ceremonies; they were too much like the citizenesses of the French Revolution knitting beside 'Madame Guillotine' as the heads dropped. For months afterwards a headsquare was the hallmark of a shorn collaboratress.

Although the Brigade was on 4 hours' notice to move, nothing had happened by Monday afternoon, so Jack Horsfield and I, being off-duty, sallied forth in search of eggs to supplement the compo rations. With Jack riding pillion, some tins of food for bartering purposes and a supply of 'invasion money', we set off. However, as Rouen was only about thirty-five miles away, we decided to make a detour there first.

As we drew near the city centre the bike was sucked into a main street awash with nose-to-tail traffic before there could be any thought of evasive action. Two Bailey bridges, built across the Seine to replace those demolished by the Germans, were carrying endless streams of vehicles into the city. Clouds of dust raised by the multitudinous wheels and tracks soon clogged our noses and throats, and Rouen's bombed buildings looked no different from any others. I took the first opportunity to turn into a side street and escape. Back in the quietness of Seine Maritime, we soon located a farmer's wife who was happy to exchange eggs for some of our tins of food and we returned to the thanks of our oppos for a successful egging expedition.

The following day began quietly, but around mid-morning the Commando received 'Immediate' orders to move out. The journey was again of the order of ten miles and Headquarters, with 'S' Troop, were located in Cany-Barville, five miles from the Channel coast and twelve miles due east of Fécamp, home of the Benedictine monastery and its liqueur. The rest of the Commando was spread out in nearby villages, with Brigade Headquarters in Ourville, some four miles away, all in an attractive rural area completely untouched by the war.

The Despatch Riders and some Signallers, about a dozen of us in all, were billeted in the empty ground floor of the house of the station-master who, with wife and two children, was still in occupation of the upper part. It stood on a triangular grass plot bounded by a low, wooden pale fence, one side of which abutted an irregularly shaped station yard, while it backed on to a narrow unmade road separating it from some disused railway tracks. An interesting feature of the station yard was a small café in the far corner.

Although the Unit was 'resting', the flow of messages continued and the DRs were kept busy, pleasantly riding around in the warm sunshine. I was soon doing much more riding than any of the others, especially on my off-duty days because my smattering of French had cast me in the role of unofficial egg procurer. I became known around the nearby farms and quickly established a 'round' of likely suppliers, where negotiations invariably started with a glass of wine or a nip of calvados.

Sardines and corned beef were most sought after by the French, but there was also an insatiable demand for petrol. With the area around the station house littered with motorbikes, jeeps and trucks, it was obvious that there was petrol somewhere around; no sooner had we moved in, than enquiries were being received for, '*D'essence?*' I was invariably called to the fore and soon adopted the Gallic attitude of hunching the shoulders, head on one side, displaying empty hands saying, '*Je regret, M'sieur . . . !*' The DRs received a jerricanful of petrol when necessary to top up their tanks, but there was none to spare for the black market business.

Two days after our arrival, however, I was turning away an enquirer when someone called out, 'Hey, Mitch, if it's petrol he's after, there's a jerricanful here you can flog'. I agreed a price for the twenty litres and told the Frenchman to bring his vehicle along the track behind the house. It was a gigantic 'camion', which pruned most of the trees en route, and it was crammed with dozens of passengers.

The driver jumped down, whipped off the vehicle's petrol filler cap, then took a quick sniff at the jerrican I handed him before pouring the contents into his tank. I had received the money and the big truck was trundling away when I saw that my comrades were 'rolling in the aisles'. They had conned me into selling four gallons of water with a few inches of petrol on top! That was my first and last petrol sale. For days thereafter I kept out of sight, with one eye always on the lookout for a big French truck.

Friday was a red letter day – our first pay parade on French soil! Each man received 100 francs – equivalent to ten shillings or six pints of beer in the UK – and we didn't have far to go to spend it. The café in the station yard was little more than two rows of five or six marble-topped tables along the sides of a strip of carpet leading to the bar. Both walls were lined with mirrors bearing adverts for such French beverages as Byrrh and Dubonnet, but we wanted to try Benedictine. Madame was apologetic, she would have to charge 20 francs a glass as she had to buy on the black market, but we accepted. After four, one more would make us penniless, so we changed to cider at one franc a tumblerful and still had a few francs left when wandering back to our billet.

At 0800 hrs next morning I began a twenty-four-hour tour as Duty DR. It was Saturday and business was slack and, around noon, I told the signallers where they could find me and wandered across to the café. Before I had time to order anything, a Frenchman asked me to join him in a particular apéritif. My French didn't extend to 'I have never tasted it', so M. André Lecop, I still have his visiting card, taught me the words '*Je ne l'ai jamais bu*'. He also invited me to his home for a meal the following Wednesday evening, with the suggestion that I might perhaps take a tin or two of British rations.

Next morning, minutes before relief, I was handed a signal for Brigade and, as there was no answer, decided to take an 'exploratory' route back. I didn't have my map and became doubtful of the way, so stopped in a village to ask. The man I approached had been on his way to a café for an 'eye opener' coffee and he invited me to join him, which I was pleased to accept. He insisted that it should be 'un café/cognac', then suggested that I joined him for breakfast – he lived with his sister. Afterwards he changed into his 'Sunday best' and we went to meet his girlfriend coming out of church. Thereafter I was happy to be drawn into a succession of visits to family and friends, but, after a late lunch, insisted that I really must report back to HQ. My new-found friend was reluctant to let me out of his sight – he had arranged more involvements for me – so rode pillion back to Cany. He waited while I washed, shaved and changed into best battledress, then we returned to the fray. The finale was a formal dinner, with more wine glasses on the table than I had seen in my life, at the home of one of his girl-friend's bosses. She worked in the Town Hall.

Whilst I had been enjoying those junketings, some thirty-five miles away at Le Havre, British and Canadian troops were finalizing the surrender of the Germans still holding out there. When Allied forces had swept forward from the beachhead substantial garrisons had remained in all the major Channel ports to deny their use by the Allies and Le Havre was the first to be liquidated. At

Cany we learned of the imminent fall of the port on Monday 11 September, when the unit was alerted to move into the city immediately after German capitulation. 48 Commando was to take care of prisoners, but 41's job would be to 'Act in Support of the Civil Power' or 'keeping the peace'. It seemed incredible that there were fears of disturbances by civilians, but it was even said that there could be French *francs-tireurs* firing upon us.

The garrison of Le Havre capitulated on Tuesday 12 September and early the following morning the long convoy carrying 41 Commando moved off. It was a slow and, especially for the DRs escorting it, a very dusty journey. When the string of vehicles started to negotiate the ruins of the city progress became desultory and spasmodic. The nearer the convoy came to the centre the damage encountered was progressively worse; in places it was impossible even to distinguish where streets had been. The very few civilians encountered gave us nothing but blank stares or glares of hatred.

The trucks finally came to a halt in the docks area, the very centre of the desolation, and just stayed there. By the time the brass hats were satisfied that there wasn't going to be any civilian uprising it was late afternoon; the convoy turned around and returned to Cany. Our arrival came as a surprise, but everyone seemed pleased to see us, especially Madame at the café.

At the time we simply assumed that hostile French reaction had been feared because their city had been destroyed to force the Germans out and thought no more about it. Not until many years later did I learn that, only a few days before our arrival, no less than three thousand French civilians had been killed in a single air raid, the culmination of a week of unnecessary bombing. Allied ground commanders had made it clear that they did not want air attacks, being confident of effecting the surrender of the city without any. In addition, offers by the German commander, Colonel Wildermuth, to allow civilians to leave and ensure that none of his troops would be in the city centre, where most of the civilians were gathered, were refused. For some reason the RAF not only went ahead with unwanted attacks, but concentrated upon the city centre, rather than the German defensive positions on the outskirts.

Nevertheless, that chance return to Cany enabled me to take up the invitation to supper given by M. Lecop the previous Saturday.

We had a pleasant meal in his home in the village of Theuville-aux-Maillots, four miles from Cany along the Fécamp road. He pressed me to call on him again and thrust a bottle of calvados into my hands as a parting gift.

Three days later came the final farewell to Cany-Barville, with the DRs conducting the road convoy to an unknown destination. The first town en route was Yvetot and 41 Commando rumbled through its narrow streets with no reaction whatsoever from the people who had been so ecstatic only two weeks earlier. Liberation was already a thing of the past.

As the journey continued it became clear to those of us with maps that the convoy was making a wide detour around Dieppe, still occupied by the Germans. An overnight stop, sleeping in barns, sheds and outhouses, was made in a small town with the even smaller French name of Eu, three miles inland from Tréport. By 0700 hours next morning, we were on our way again; it was a very chilly morning for the DRs, but M. Lecop's calvados helped. It was young, raw stuff, very different from the pleasant café/cognacs of the previous Sunday morning, but we endured the taste for the warming effect.

The convoy meandered on, crossing the Somme at St Valéry, then via St Omer and Cassel to come to a final halt, in the dank dark dusk of a September evening, outside another of those massive German reinforced concrete bunkers. 41 HQ had arrived in Loon Plage, a small town about two and a half miles from the coast, straddling the road to Dunkirk, another port still held by the Germans, which lay some six miles further east. Our Brigade, now under command of the Canadian First Army, was to take over the job of 'containing' the garrison. The Commando was relieving the Calgary Highlanders and the first order given in our new location was 'No green berets'. The Germans could find out for themselves who was their new opposition.

The Commando had inherited the blockhouse, dimly lit with hurricane lamps as the power was cut off, for their Headquarters building and the DRs were allocated one of the many small compartments as sleeping quarters. Hardly had we settled down on the concrete floor, however, than it was reported that the German garrison in Calais, eighteen miles to our rear, had broken out and we were in danger of being surrounded. The unit was put on 50%

119

stand-to throughout the night, increased to 100% for the hour before dawn, and everyone spent most of the night in extremely cold firing positions in the open. Then it transpired that it had been a false alarm; the Germans were still in Calais. There may have been no connection, but that Sunday had seen the start of Operation MARKET GARDEN, which secured the river crossings at Eindhoven and Nijmegen, but failed to capture Arnhem, 'a bridge too far'.

It was understood that the Dunkirk garrison numbered about ten thousand men, while No. 4 Brigade couldn't muster two thousand, and these were very thin on the ground. 41, with less than 450 men, had almost six miles of front to cover, a line running almost due south from the Channel coast east of Mardick to the left flank of 48 Commando at Brouckerke. It being impossible to form a continuous perimeter, the Rifle Troops held small, widely spaced positions based upon farmhouses and other buildings, with the gaps covered by mines and frequent patrolling.

As well as getting back into an active role, the Commando had moved into a completely different environment. Instead of the rolling, wooded countryside around Cany-Barville, our new location was an empty, flat terrain, criss-crossed by innumerable canals, dykes and watercourses. The featureless landscape was relieved only by almost leafless roadside trees and a few widely scattered farm buildings. The weather too had changed almost beyond belief. The warm bright sunshine of Seine Maritime had been replaced by leaden skies, dank mists and cold drizzle.

From a DRs point of view the situation was very similar to that which had prevailed at the radar stations. With the Commando strung out along the perimeter of a large German position, long detours were necessary to get to the various Troop headquarters. All trips to Troops positioned to the south of the road to Dunkirk had to start by heading inland for three miles to Bourbourgville, then working your way around to the east, before riding in towards the coast.

There were no such complications in getting to 'B' Troop, as their Headquarters was close to the road to Dunkirk. Shortly after our arrival the Troop had probed forward for almost two and a half miles without meeting any opposition, therefore Captain Sturgis had positioned his Troop in that area and established his

Headquarters in adjacent Ferme Hameral. As the road was almost perfectly straight and under German observation, a 'limit of visibility' had been created by stretching a wire hawser across the road and draping it with camouflage netting.

On the coastal flank were 'X' with Headquarters in the handful of houses known as Mardick (Fort Mardick, two miles further east, was in German hands) and 'S' was a little further on in Le Clipon. Unfortunately a short length of the road to Mardick was completely open and under German observation, which meant speedy runs to get out of harm's way before the inevitable began to arrive.

In Mardick, in addition to 'X' HQ, there were some of the local FFI. They were militarily dressed in knee breeches and jackboots, had Lüger pistols at their belts and carried Schmeissers over their shoulders – and they were female! I didn't learn if they had any military duties, but did wonder whether their get-up might be more of a deterrent to advances from Allied troops rather than German.

After one running of the gauntlet return from 'X', the SDO received an emergency call from them – a knocked-out German truck and a defunct British Bren Gun Carrier were blocking a strategically important road and a breakdown truck was required immediately to clear the way. I led a massive recovery vehicle to the spot, which, luckily, wasn't under direct observation, but it was clear that the Germans were aware that something was happening and were doing their best to make things uncomfortable. For a disconcerting half-hour I could only stand by as truck and carrier were slowly manoeuvred on to the narrow road for towing away, while the Germans sent over salvoes of 'Hope these catch you in the open' shells.

A few days after our arrival a battery of Bofors Light ack-ack guns came under unit command. The gunners had never previously fired their weapons at the enemy and were delighted to join us. Although their normal role was against low-flying aircraft, the 40 mm calibre guns, firing 2 lb shells at a rate of 120 a minute, were quickly brought into action against German ground targets. A farm occupied by the enemy was soon burned to the ground and we began to get deserters protesting about the 'new weapon', which was much feared by the Germans.

The Fighting Troops were sending probing patrols to seek out and harry German positions, and the Germans were doing very

121

much the same thing. On the Wednesday 'Y' moved up, bumped a German patrol, suffering one casualty. That same day 'B' pushed a patrol almost two miles up the road towards Dunkirk and they managed to collect a German prisoner. Ironically, on their return journey he trod on one of his own people's mines; he was killed and his two NCO escorts were badly wounded.

More often than not these patrol clashes were nocturnal affairs and on most nights there would be noisy confrontations in the darkness. At times our men were involved in hand-to-hand clashes close to their sleeping quarters, when infiltrating Germans were detected and pounced upon. One such incident took place during the night of Wednesday/Thursday.

I was Duty DR and shortly before dawn was roused from sleep on the SDO floor. 'B' troop was requesting transport and an escort for three German prisoners taken in a night encounter. The Duty Officer arranged for a jeep and driver, and ordered me to be the escort. I left the drowsy warmth of the HQ bunker for a freezing cold ride to Ferme Hameral in an open jeep. On arrival we learned there were only two prisoners to take back as the other one had 'got himself shot'.

There was just sufficient light in the early morning sky to make out the young, rather bristly, expressionless faces of my two charges as I waved them into the back of the jeep with my Colt 45. When they were settled, I squeezed in too, facing them with gun at the ready. They looked so small and inoffensive that the whole affair seemed rather ludicrous, but I waited until we were all back inside the HQ bunker before handing each of them a cigarette and returning to my disturbed sleep.

At 0800 I was off-duty, so could undertake an egging expedition. Around Loon Plage my smattering of French was no longer so effective as most of the farmers spoke only Flemish, but I had managed to pick up enough words to stay in business. When I knocked on a farmhouse door, whether or not there were eggs available, I was invariably made welcome. Even without eggs, there would be a drink or two, now beer rather than wine, and I would reciprocate with cigarettes.

At one farm I found the lady owner still incensed by the fact that when the Germans had pulled back into Dunkirk they had taken three of her horses. She told me that the commander of the Dunkirk garrison had lost an arm on the Russian Front and she knew how she would deal with him: 'I'd cut off the other one,' she said, 'and let the . . . starve to death.'

Another advantage of the DR job was to be able to stop at cafés to get warm and practise the language. There weren't any in the immediate vicinity, but on Saturday evening I was given a trip to Brigade HQ and on the return journey decided to stop at a café in Wormhoudt. I got into conversation with two Frenchmen, one of whom said that he had spent four years as a prisoner in Germany. I couldn't work out just how he had managed to get home, but was pleased to drink to his achievement.

On Monday buzzes about a move started again. The hot one was that we were heading for Holland to support the First Airborne Division at Arnhem. We never did learn if there had been any truth in that one because that was the very day the airborne troops were pulled back across the Rhine. Nevertheless movement orders did come through and we were bound, not for Holland, but Ostend in Belgium. The Commando's positions around Dunkirk were to be handed over at midnight next day, Tuesday, 26 September, after which we would 'proceed' to Ostend during the night. By a remarkable coincidence, the relieving unit was to be none other than the Black Watch, from whom 41 Commando had taken over responsibility for the radar stations at Douvres/La Délivrande shortly after D-Day. Now, four months later, at Loon Plage they were to take over a similar pocket of enemy resistance from us and we repaid the compliment with interest. The radar stations had yielded little more than two hundred Germans, but at Dunkirk we gave them a quarter share of ten thousand!

Chapter 10

INTO BELGIUM, TRAINING FOR WALCHEREN

The handover took place at midnight 26 September as planned, but it wasn't until an hour later, after many tricky manoeuvres in fitful moonlight, that the long convoy of more than fifty vehicles was finally assembled. Twelve 3-ton trucks had been borrowed from nearby units to enable the Commando, with all weapons and stores, to be moved all at once. A Despatch Rider rode down the line giving the 'Start up!' signal and the long string of vehicles rumbled off into the night. The DRs rode behind the 'Pathfinder' jeep until a doubtful part of the route required one of them to remain behind to ensure that all vehicles kept to the planned route. Then came the hair-raising job of regaining position at the head of the convoy.

The truck drivers, travelling without lights along unfamiliar roads made slippery by drizzle, tended to hog the crown of the carriageway; therefore, for DRs needing to get past, with only a few feet between a swaying 3-tonner and a muddy ditch, it was a leap in the dark every time. A few trucks slithered off the carriageway, then one DR would stand-by while another went for assistance, but, surprisingly, no Despatch Riders came to grief that night. With only the drivers, DRs and a handful of officers awake, the convoy rumbled on throughout the hours of darkness, travelling via St Omer, Cassel and Poperinghe. It was still trundling forward when the wet night gave way to warm September sunshine.

Around mid-morning the convoy came to a halt in sight of

Ostend. Then, as hour succeeded hour, rumours passed up and down the line that Commandos weren't wanted there. It was late afternoon before the unit eventually moved into town – Other Ranks to an empty convent building, with parts of the outer walls missing and devoid of any glass in the windows, Officers to the Hotel Manchester. Next morning the Commandos moved on, 41 and 48 to the coastal town of De Haan, some six miles further east, while 47 travelled three miles further along the coast to Wenduyne, and Brigade Headquarters carried on ten miles inland to Bruges.

De Haan (Le Coq) had been used by the German Gestapo as a Headquarters and Recreational Area, and a number of hotels had remained fully operational. These, however, had long since been taken over by the Headquarters staffs of the Canadian Army and the RAF Tactical Air Force, so empty buildings, which had provided seasonal pre-war holiday accommodation, were opened up for the Commandos. One such building, the Pension du Nord, became 41's HQ offices, plus living quarters for the Signals Section and Intelligence personnel, the DRs' being allocated a room on the top floor. It contained a single item of furniture – an iron bedstead with wire base – which Frank Heggarty and I, who got there first, promptly appropriated. It seemed fitting that the Auberge des Rois – Inn of the Kings – became the Officers' Mess!

All ranks were warned that, before pulling out, the Germans had carried out extensive and indiscriminate booby-trapping and every-thing in and about the buildings should be carefully examined before touching. Despite this, only sloppy German workmanship saved one of the Sick Bay staff from injury when he opened an oven door and out came a length of fuse with pull-igniter attached, which hadn't been securely fastened to the explosive charge. Two men of 'X' Troop weren't so lucky and were injured by a booby-trap fitted to the roller shutter of an empty house they were investigating.

Once settled in, the CO's first Daily Orders stressed that the Commando was in De Haan for 'rigorous training and general toughening-up'; it was understood by all that a specific operation was already in mind. Details of German defence works were needed for training purposes, so the Intelligence Sections of both 41 and 48 Commandos collaborated in surveying those in the neighbourhood and preparing plans. Two Royal Engineers clearing a beach to be used in training were badly wounded when a mine they were working on exploded.

Morning parades were re-instigated; boots and uniforms had to be clean, webbing equipment scrubbed and there was a ceremonial sentry at the entrance to Commando Headquarters, to the great delight of children when he sprang to attention to salute officers. The DRs received a jolt when told that they too were expected to get fit and a few route marches and other strenuous pursuits were interspersed with delivering messages.

Twice a day there was a round of delivery runs beginning with the various Headquarters offices in De Haan, then continuing along the coast to Wenduyne, inland to Nieuwmunster, where other elements of the Brigade were stationed, and on to Brigade HQ in Bruges. The round trip back to base involved some 25 miles. Brigade had taken over a medieval convent near the town centre, standing close to a main road but completely screened from view by a frontage of tall buildings of a very much more recent vintage. Access was gained via an unremarkable archway in the street façade, but, only a few score yards further on you had travelled back in time some six hundred years to a secluded courtyard bounded by shady cloisters, with a statuary centre-piece.

Shortly after our arrival those of us who frequently travelled from De Haan to Wenduyne began to notice that unfamiliar tracked vehicles were being accumulated on the lower slopes of the dunes bounding the seaward side of the road. In shape they were similar to Churchill tanks, but had open 'holds' in place of gun turrets and were very lightly armoured. They were parked nose to tail in tight rows and completely covered with camouflage netting. In time we learned that they were amphibious landing craft, officially designated 'Landing Vehicles, Tracked' (LVTs) but generally known as Buffaloes. They stood eight feet high, were twenty-five feet long, and could carry twenty-four fully equipped men or three tons of supplies on land at twenty-five miles an hour and in water, floating with a freeboard of barely two feet, at about five knots.

The vehicles being assembled near Wenduyne belonged to the 11th Battalion Royal Tank Regiment and were arriving as and when released from active operations with the Canadian 3rd

126

Division, little more than twenty miles away. Buffaloes had proved invaluable in a slogging battle to clear the Germans from their last foothold south of the river, the flooded countryside at the mouth of the Scheldt estuary, around the port of Breskens, the so-called 'Breskens Pocket'. Their next job was already lined up – to carry commandos ashore, somewhere.

A smaller amphibious tracked vehicle, the 'Weasel', was also to be used in the coming operation. Although sometimes looked upon as an amphibious jeep, there was no development nor manufacturing link between the two vehicles, the only similarity being their size and carrying capability. The load limit of a Weasel was about half a ton, including crew, and, like the Buffalo, it could travel at 25 mph on land and 5 knots in water. Weasels were to be handled by our own drivers and those selected for the job began training immediately. Paradoxically, one of them was 'Pegler' Palmer, driver of Gunga Din, the unit's water truck, so he who had spent much of his time transporting water was now learning to drive a vehicle where water would be transporting him!

For the Fighting Troops a much more strenuous programme had been drawn up by Major Wood, the Second-in-Command. This covered every aspect of fitness and military training and laid down precisely what each Troop would do every morning and afternoon during the coming weeks. They were even required to indulge in sessions of battle drill or Troop attacks before attending noon church parade on Sundays.

A large proportion of the programme, naturally, involved weapon handling. First, 'zeroing', i.e. having the sights checked and adjusted, then the whole range of small arms weapons (automatic pistol, rifle, Bren gun, Tommy gun, Sten gun, Vickers medium machine-gun) had to be fired to set proficiency standards. For some there were sessions operating flamethrowers, hurling hand-grenades and firing 2" and 3" mortars, while others handled explosives – fixing beehives onto concrete fortifications, thrusting pole charges through gun slits and detonating Bangalore torpedoes to explode mines and blow gaps in barbed wire defences.

An important weapon in the Commando's armoury was its only anti-tank weapon, the PIAT mortar – an acronym for Projector, Infantry, Anti-Tank. This was a very effective close-range weapon capable of penetrating 4 inches of armour plate at 120 yards, although, despite its name, it wasn't strictly a mortar at all, being fired in the prone position by means of a trigger. Tragically, practice with this weapon at De Haan resulted in four of our men being killed – three when a bomb exploded prematurely and the fourth when another ricocheted off the German strongpoint being used as a target.

In addition to the training programme within the Commando there were exercises involving the rest of the Brigade and other units earmarked to take part in the operation. Tank support would be provided by Shermans and Flails of the 1st Lothian and Border Yeomanry, and there would also be armoured vehicles of 87 Assault Squadron RE, while the Canadian First Army Corps would be providing medical teams. As it was to be, largely, a mechanized landing, everyone had to become accustomed to working with both Buffaloes and Weasels – loading them, boarding them and getting in and out of them in a hurry!

As usual, no sooner had the Commando become settled than the 'buzzmongers' became active. As usual too, each of them knew just where the landing was going to take place and could forecast that it would be either 'a piece of cake' or 'a bloody suicide job'. One of the names frequently bandied about was Walcheren, the Dutch island at the mouth of the River Scheldt, but it was given no more credence than a number of others being put forward.

Walcheren had 'hit the headlines' in the English-speaking Press on 3 October, a week after our move from Dunkirk, as the 'Tea saucer island'. On that day, at the instigation of General Guy Symonds, Commander of the Canadian First Army, No. 84 Bomber Group RAF had blasted the first gap in the sea dyke at Westkapelle. As the greater part of Walcheren lies below sea level, once the protective dyke was breached the North Sea poured in and much of the interior of the island 'filled up like a saucer of tea'. The great military importance of the island of Walcheren lay in the fact that German gun batteries, particularly those at Westkapelle and Domburg, prevented vessels from entering the River Scheldt, thus preventing the use of the port of Antwerp, which had been in Allied hands since September.

As day succeeded day, with the fighting echelon of the Commando deeply involved in the training programme, the off-duty DRs were able to exploit their mobility to explore adjacent towns and villages. With three months' back pay to draw on, they were also able to investigate what lay behind such signs as 'Café' and 'Bieren'. On one such occasion, in a café near Jabbeke, our group was surprised to be greeted by the girl behind the bar, not in French nor Flemish, but in English! She was an American, about nineteen years old, who had been staying with relatives in the area at the outbreak of war and had been unable to return home.

Such local runs were generally made in the company of two or three others, but I also indulged in more protracted solo trips – generally on the pretext of 'trying her out', after some minor repair or adjustment! The first of these was a probe of about 35 miles to Ghent, which was subsequently extended by another 20 miles to St Niklaas. The most protracted was a 150-mile round trip to Brussels, where peace had already broken out, but the most memorable was a tour of some of the places familiar to my father during the First World War.

This one took in 'Wipers' (Ypres), with its sadly impressive Menin Gate bearing the names of tens of thousands of men with no known graves, then on to 'Popperingee' (Poperinghe) and Armentières, passing many awesomely extensive military cemeteries en route. In stationers' shops, too, I found evidence of that earlier war. Picture postcards of Hellfire Corner, Plugstreet Wood, Hill 60 and The Menin Road were still on sale. As I rode back to De Haan in the dusk of an autumn evening I could almost imagine the shades of my father's generation of soldiers travelling at my shoulder.

At De Haan I renewed contact with Ben, our Moroccan volunteer. In the moves of the Commando immediately before, during and after the breakout from Normandy, our paths hadn't crossed, but, with the Unit settled down again, Ben's cheerful face was once more in evidence. We had only a few brief encounters and never got back to more language-swapping sessions, but there was always a spontaneous exchange of greetings on meeting. By this time Ben was unquestionably 'on the strength', attached to the Intelligence Section, presumably because some of them spoke a little French. Sadly, some weeks later, it was probably after my first leave, I returned to the unit to learn that Ben had been fooling around with a primed hand-grenade when the pin came out and he had been evacuated to hospital, badly wounded. I never saw him again.

During the last days of October the likelihood of the island of Walcheren being our objective seemed to have evaporated. Breskens had been captured by the Canadian 3rd Division on the 22nd and units of the 52nd (Lowland) Division had then crossed the East Scheldt to land on South Beveland. It is ironic that the 52nd, specifically trained for a possible invasion of Norway and bearing the word 'Mountaineer' on their shoulder flashes, should first go into action on the flattest terrain in Europe! By the 26th they had linked up with the Canadian 2nd Division, attacking along the peninsula, and these combined British and Canadian forces were nearing the causeway linking Walcheren with the mainland. It looked as though the island was already 'in the bag' and that No. 4 Special Service Brigade would be going elsewhere.

By then it was known that only four DRs would be going with the assault force – Tuckwell, Thompson, Barker and Mitchell. Also, that there would be no motorbikes; the Despatch Riders would be primarily employed as 'ammunition wallahs', getting ammunition up to the forward Troops. Colt automatics would be left behind and the four of us were to be issued with rifles and bayonets. Like all those taking part in the landing, we painted our names on big packs, filled with a change of clothing, greatcoat, etc, which would go ashore sometime after the initial landing.

Towards the end of October the 'FOO' and 'FOB' people joined us. These were the teams of the Forward Observation Officer (Royal Artillery) and the Forward Officer, Bombardment (Royal Navy) who would call up and direct artillery fire when and where required. Their arrival was invariably an indication that an operation was 'on' and that its start would not be long delayed.

On Friday 27 October Colonel Palmer breezed through the Orderly Room in the Pension du Nord with a bundle of maps under his arm. As he passed a group of us – DRs and Signallers – he teasingly remarked, 'I bet you'd like to have a look at these!' The 'top brass' already knew what our objective was to be, but the rest would have to wait until De Haan had been turned into a top security camp before being let into the secret. Royal Engineers were erecting a high wire-mesh fence to enclose the entire northern part of the town between the tramway and the sea. When complete, and with everyone to be involved brought inside, the gates would be closed and armed patrols would ensure that no one entered or left until the planned operation was under way.

On the morning of Sunday 29 October it was announced that De Haan would be sealed off that evening. Killer and I were off-duty and, after lunch, we decided to pay a farewell visit to a café in Breedene, about a mile from Ostend, which, due largely to the landlord's two pretty daughters, had become the favourite retreat of Despatch Riders. We left the café in good time to get back for the evening meal, but I collected a puncture. It was decided that Killer should carry on to ensure that some food was kept for us, while I set about the repair. Before the job was half-way through, however, he was back – our bikes were to be loaded after all and all HQ had been hunting high and low for us! I sweated to complete the repair and rushed back, but found that the loading had had to go ahead and another machine had been sent. Fortunately, in the overall 'flap' of preparations, there were no repercussions; the motorcycles were never landed, perhaps they never even left Ostend.

On Monday 30 October, with the 'concentration camp' of De Haan sealed, it was safe for us to be 'put in the picture'. We were marched across the road to the Auberge des Rois, where an Operations Rooms had been set up, and briefed for the coming landing. Only then was it learned that the objective was, after all, to be the capture of Walcheren.

In retrospect, it is difficult to comprehend why the operation which No. 4 Special Service Brigade and units of the 52nd Lowland Division were called upon to undertake on 1 November 1944 had ever been allowed to become necessary. Had the pressure on the Germany Army, fleeing in chaos through the coastal regions of Holland and Belgium in the early days of September, been kept up for only a few more days it wouldn't have been required.

On 4 September, after a swift advance from Brussels, tanks of the British Second Army had entered Antwerp. The Belgian Resistance Army, alerted in advance by a seemingly innocent message broadcast by the BBC – *Pour François: La lune est clair* – (For François: the moon is clear), had risen against the German garrison and, heroically, had managed to preserve the vast docks area of the city intact.

Next day, Tuesday 5 September, the Dutch of South Beveland, seeing their roads crammed with retreating Germans and knowing that advancing Allied armies were almost on their doorstep, believed that their day of liberation was at hand. They went crazy with joy and chased their oppressors from towns and villages.

But the rapid Allied advance came to an abrupt and unexpected halt. Had it progressed only a dozen miles beyond Antwerp the many thousands of Germans streaming across the Scheldt from Breskens to Flushing, and those who had already managed to get across, would have been trapped on the peninsula of South Beveland. The subsequent bloody battles of the next two months, on both sides of the estuary, would have been avoided.

In the event, the retreating Germans, realizing that the pursuit had stopped dead, returned to exact their revenge. The euphoria of that *Dolle Dinsdag* (Mad Tuesday), when the Dutch had belaboured retreating Germans, evaporated and they had to suffer German retribution, bemoaning the halted Allied advance.

Even now it wasn't entirely clear whether the failure to continue the advance beyond Antwerp wasn't due more to chance than having arisen from any need or design. A variety of suggestions have been put forward, such as: time was needed to build up supplies; the British Second Army had become too involved in celebrating the capture of the city; the Canadian First Army, responsible for the extreme left flank of the Allied advance, was more interested in organizing a memorial service for the five hundred of their countrymen who had lost their lives on the ill-fated Dieppe raid of 1942. What cannot be disputed, however, is that General Eisenhower, who had just assumed personal command of all the Allied land forces in place of General Montgomery, was more than 400 miles from the front, near Granville on the Cherbourg Peninsula, nursing a wrenched knee.

Whatever the truth of the matter, the net result was that, for two months, the only major port with the capability of supporting an Allied thrust into Germany had rested in Allied hands, completely intact, but unusable. The German guns on Walcheren guarding the Scheldt estuary made it impossible for ships to approach.

On 30 October 1944, in the 'Ops Room' in the Auberge des Rois, individual Troops of 41 Commando took it in turn to study maps and aerial photographs of Walcheren, were given 'the overall picture' and learned of their own parts in the coming operation.

Four gaps had been blown in the sea dyke protecting the island from the North Sea. In addition to the first one at Westkapelle on the western tip of the island, there was another immediately to the west of Flushing, a third at Rammekens between Flushing and the causeway, and a fourth just west of Veere on the north-east coast. In consequence, most of the centre of the island was under water, which had inundated some minor German positions and also seriously hampered the manoeuvrability of the island's defenders by confining them to such parts as still remained above water, but heavy coastal batteries, sited on the massive sea dyke, were unaffected.

The seaborne assault was to be carried out by No. 4 Special Service Brigade (later re-styled 'Commando Brigade') under Brigadier 'Jumbo' Leicester. It comprised four Commandos, each of less than 450 men – No. 4 (Army) and Nos. 41, 47 and 48 (Royal Marines). The Belgian and Norwegian Troops of No. 10 Inter-Allied Commando (about 60 men in each) were to be attached to 41.

The attack was to be three-pronged. No. 4 Commando would make an early morning crossing of the Scheldt in LCAs (Landing Craft Assault) to land at Flushing, (this operation was code-named INFATUATE I) with the Royal Marines going ashore on both sides of the four hundred-yard wide gap in the dyke at Westkapelle (INFATUATE II).

No. 4 Commando would be spearheading a follow-up force of elements of 52 Division, whose task would be to strike towards the causeway and link up with the forces already attacking it from South Beveland. At Westkapelle 41 would land to the north of the gap, capture Westkapelle and the neighbouring heavy coast defence battery, then push on to Domburg and beyond. The task of 47 and 48, going ashore to the south of the gap, would be to deal with the German batteries between there and the Flushing gap, where they would link up with No. 4 Commando.

The attack of 41 Commando was to be 'double-barreled'. 'B' and 'P' Troops would land from LCI(S)s (Landing Craft Infantry, Small) on the face of the dyke immediately to the west of the gap, then move towards the gun battery W15. 'S' Troop would also land there and set up their mortars on the dyke top to give support where required. Five minutes later HQ, 'A', 'X' and 'Y' Troops would go ashore in Buffaloes and Weasels from Tank Landing Craft which would sail through the gap and beach themselves at the edge of the bomb-shattered town.

For INFATUATE II the Royal Navy would be laying down a massive softening-up barrage, to be initiated by the 15" guns of the battleship *Warspite* and the monitors *Erebus* and *Roberts*. As the range shortened, smaller naval vessels would join in, then close inshore support would be provided by a special squadron of small craft, 'firing down the gun slits'. All in all, the fleet carrying the assault force to Westkapelle would total over 180 vessels.

All of this was reassuring, but eyebrows were raised when it was revealed that the assault was to take place in full daylight. H-hour had been set at 0945 to ensure that the pilots of rocket-firing Typhoon aircraft would have a clear view of their targets. It was also disconcerting to learn of the 150-feet-high lantern tower at Westkapelle, which would ensure that the German defenders would have full knowledge of the size of the attacking force long before any vessel came within range.

While the Commando seaborne assaults on Walcheren were proceeding, the Canadian and 52 Division forces in South Beveland would be attacking the island via the causeway. This narrow strip of land, wide enough only to accommodate a two-lane carriageway, a railway line and a cycle track, some fifteen feet above sea level and twelve hundred yards long, provided the only link between island and mainland. Even as the Commando was being briefed a series of costly head-on attacks along the causeway had been under way, but without success.

INFATUATE had been set for Wednesday 1 November, two days hence, and we would leave De Haan next day, Tuesday 31 October, to join our Buffaloes, already loaded and waiting on LCTs in Ostend harbour. In the evening, when everyone had been briefed, the Officers of the Commando invited the Senior NCOs of the unit to the Auberge des Rois for 'Good Luck' drinks. I was Duty DR in the SDO just across the road, without the possibility of any such conviviality, so was feeling a little 'Bolshie' about it. Then a message came through for the Signals Officer. It was quite innocuous and totally irrelevant at that time, but I saw my chance. Donning riding gear and crash helmet, I walked across to the Officers' Mess. Then, as I eased my way into a maelstrom of boisterous, loud-talking, drinking humanity, I began calling out,

'Message for the Signals Officer! Message for the Signals Officer!' Before he had been located the anticipated had happened; one of the throng had started shouts of, 'How about a drink for the Dog Rodger?'

After lunch next day 'the Walcheren party' was fallen in outside HQ while those who had not been chosen to go looked on with a mixture of relief and chagrin which we could very well appreciate. It was something of a surprise to learn that there was to be no transport, so we marched off, to lots of unprintable advice and an exchange of vulgar 'V' signs, which we knew was the Rear Party's way of saying, 'Keep your heads down, lads, and come back safe'. Two hours later we were marching through the bustling, café-lined streets of Ostend, thronged with off-duty military personnel. The wags had their inevitable last quips, 'Hey, Sarge! How about a quick one?' 'Can I grab a couple of bottles for the boat?'

At the docks we were directed to our allocated LCTs, then assigned to the specific Buffaloes which would carry us ashore next morning. I was among those given the rearmost vehicle on the port side, an unenviable position, as it could very well be the last one to move ashore. In the well of the LCT we had to squeeze our way along narrow alleyways between the LVTs to reach our vehicles. Their gunwales were almost three feet above our heads and, at such close quarters, they looked huge monsters. Using the tracks, we clambered up the vertical side to find that the hold was already full, almost to the top, with boxes of ammunition, jerricans of petrol and other stores. We would be steaming towards the enemy guns perched on top of powder kegs.

After dumping weapons and equipment on the vehicles we were given 'the freedom of the ship', although there was very little of that – no more than a small upper deck, with a few capstans and winches, the open tank deck where the Buffaloes and Weasels were parked and the ablutions. In the early dusk of an end of October afternoon there was little time, and not much light, to study the nearby vessels which would accompany us, but they were reassuring. There were LCTs loaded with Sherman tanks and flail tanks to detonate mines on the beach, AVREs (Armoured Vehicles Royal Engineers) to attack concrete fortifications and armoured bulldozers to clear the way if Buffaloes couldn't negotiate a beach exit.

After an evening meal of the inevitable 'Compo' one blanket per man was issued, which was as much as our Royal Navy hosts could provide towards easing the overnight accommodation. Harry Tuckwell and I chose the upper deck and decided to squeeze into the confined space between a winch drum and its housing, which we felt would at least shield us from the cold breeze created by the craft's forward motion during the night. We were asleep before very long, but stirred into semi-consciousness in the early hours of the morning when the reverberating throb of engines signalled that we were on our way. The island of Walcheren lay only thirty-five miles distant and 'tomorrow is another day'.

Chapter 11

THE WALCHEREN LANDING

For Harry and me, squeezed together for warmth in the winch drum housing, the night passed quietly and not too uncomfortably. It was still dark when we were roused to stand in line for our turn to make use of the ablutions, then wait for a breakfast of tinned sausage and Compo biscuits, washed down with tea. Once those preliminaries were out of the way, it was 'All right, on your Buffaloes and get rigged!' – despite the fact that it would be more than two hours before we went ashore.

At first light that Wednesday morning, 1 November 1944, it was heartening to receive confirmation that our LCT had not been travelling alone in the darkness. Perched on top of the load of military supplies in our Buffalo we had an unrestricted view ahead and, as visibility gradually increased, more and more vessels came into view. With full daylight a vast armada of vessels could be seen, spaced out some hundreds of yards apart, covering many square miles of ocean, the more distant ones little more than dark smudges on the horizon; we appeared to be somewhere in the middle.

The impressive fleet moving towards the assault on Westkapelle, designated Naval Force 'T', under the command of Captain A.F. Pugsley RN, totalled 182 vessels. However, unlike the earlier landings of Sicily, Salerno and D-Day, when many tens of thousands of men had been put ashore, the total to be involved in Operation INFATUATE II would be only about two thousand. This made the overall ship-to-man ratio of 1:12 far greater than on any of those

WALCHEREN
November 1944

Battery W 19
Battery W 18
Vrouwenpolder
Battery W 17
GAP
Domburg
Veere
Battery W 15
Westkapelle
GAP
W 13
Zoutelande
Middelburg
Arnemuiden
Nieuwland
Flooded areas
W 4
Rammekens
GAP
Miles
0 1 2 3
Flushing
GAP
West Scheldt
Breskens

previous occasions, a consequence of the fact that the assault of
Westkapelle was to be largely mechanized.

More than a hundred Buffaloes and some eighty Weasels would
carry most of the men ashore, together with their food, stores and
reserves of ammunition, and these were being transported in LCTs
(Landing Craft, Tank) of only 600 tons displacement. Other
LCTs carried tanks of the 1st Lothian and Border Yeomanry, of
the 79th Armoured Division and the Armoured Vehicles Royal
Engineers (AVREs), which, for this operation, were equipped with
bridging equipment and fascines to cross streams and ditches, and
also armoured bulldozers to create exits from the beach if need be.

Close inshore support would be provided by twenty-seven similarly sized vessels of the SSEF (Support Squadron, Eastern Flank),
a naval unit which had been created specifically to protect the
eastern flank of the vast amount of sea traffic needed to transport,
reinforce and supply the Allied armies involved in the invasion of
France. The craft were crewed by six hundred officers and men
of the Royal Navy, with five hundred Royal Marines to handle the
guns. The squadron, under the command of Commander K.A.

138

18/19. German battery (W 15) on the dyke at Westkapelle after naval bombardment *(H. Sakkers and J. Tuynman)*.

20. Lieutenant D.F. Murray (later Sir Donald Murray KCVO CMG DL) a Section Commander of 'A' Troop, outside a German bunker on Walcheren. *(Charles Leonard)*

21. Royal Marines returning from a patrol on the Maas Front. *(IWM)*

22. The author, second from right, outside his Dutch billet in Goes, Zeeland, in May 1945 with Marine Barker and the children of the Smallegange family.

23. Wesel, Germany, 19 May 1945. *(Photo by Author)*

24. Königs Allee, Düsseldorf, 19 May 1945: the only feature amid a wasteland of rubble.

25. Essen, 19 May 1945: the ruins of a Krupp factory. *(Photo by Author)*

26. The author in Cologne, 20 May 1945. The cathedral is in the background.

27. Cologne: the wrecked Hohenzollern Bridge. *(Photo by Author)*

28. Cologne: the skeleton of the railway station. *(Photo by Author)*

29. Cologne, the Cathedral Square: a German tank is just part of the litter.
    (Photo by Author)

30. Parachuting course at Ringway,
Manchester, August 1945. The
Author with Marine Leggett.

31. Taking part in a Brigade motorcycle
rally at Erkenschwick, September 1945.

2. Major William Cunningham DSO RM, acting-CO of the unit, presenting a contingent
of 41 Commando to Prince Bernhard of the Netherlands at a Royal Navy week in
Rotterdam, August 1945. *(Charles Leonard)*

33/34. Dortmund, September 1945. *(Photos by Author)*

Sellar RN, hadn't long been released from duties in the Channel and men had to be recalled from leave to sail for Walcheren.

The bulk of the fire power of the squadron was housed in various adaptations of LCT hulls – LCG(L)s (Landing Craft, Gun (Large)) fitted with 4.7 inch guns, LCFs (Landing Craft, Flak) with 2-pounder pompoms and 20mm Oerlikon anti-aircraft guns, and the deadly LCT(R)s (Landing Craft Tank (Rocket)), of which there were five at Walcheren. The last-named launched 1080 (Mark 1), or 936 (Mark 2), 29lb rockets, with 7lb bursters, in a rapid succession of salvoes of twenty-four. The result was a carpet of missiles, one to every 100 square yards of ground, over an area of some 700 by 150 yards. There were also two smaller types of vessel, LCSs (Landing Craft, Support) with quick-firing 6-pounders, Oerlikons and machine guns and, in action for the first time, LCG(M)s (Medium) armed with quick-firing 17-pounders.

The invasion fleet was steaming unhurriedly towards the rising sun, which soon cleared away the early morning mists, giving almost unlimited visibility at sea level, although the sky overhead continued to be obscured by almost total cloud cover. We were still some fifteen miles away, with about one and a half hours before touchdown, when we gained our first sighting of the Westkapelle tower. It was no more than the top of the lantern, seeming to poke out of the sea on the horizon dead ahead, the rest of its 150-foot-tall bulk still hidden from our view by the curvature of the earth.

The craft moved inexorably forward in comparative silence, the only sounds being the low throb of the engines, the slap of the sea against blunt bows and our own small talk as we squatted on the military stores piled high in the Buffaloes. Minute by minute the lantern tower grew taller as it emerged above the sea and was soon standing like an admonitory finger, attracting us towards itself like a powerful magnet.

We had been briefed on the overall pattern of the assault. While the SSEF engaged the shore batteries, LCI(S)s (Landing Craft Infantry, (Small)) would put 'B', 'P' and 'S' Troops of 41 Commando ashore on the face of Westkapelle dyke, immediately to the north of the breach. 'B' and 'P' would clear the northern part of the town, then move towards battery W15, on the dyke top a few hundred yards away, leaving 'S' to set up their 3" mortars and machine guns to cover the landing of the rest of the

Commando. Meanwhile, the LCTs carrying the armoured vehicles and amphibians would be heading for the breach in the dyke and, five minutes after first wave, 'A', 'X' and HQ would go ashore to secure the southern part of Westkapelle, including the lantern tower. 'Y' and the attached Belgian and Norwegian Troops of 10 I-A Commando would land, in reserve, 25 minutes later.

The craft carrying 47 and 48 Commandos, together with Brigade Headquarters and Canadian medical units, were on the starboard flank of the task force, heading towards the southerly edge of the Westkapelle gap, their 'aiming point' being the ruins of a radar dish on the dyke top. The initial assault there would be by 48, followed by Brigade HQ and the medics, while 47 would land in support one hour later. Somewhere in the North Sea, far to port of the task force, the 'heavies', the battleship *Warspite* and the monitors *Erebus* and *Roberts*, would be heading towards their bombardment positions.

As the lantern tower continued to grow out of the sea ahead of us we could imagine German defenders having a leisurely breakfast before making final preparations for our reception. For us there was ample time to consider an unexpected snippet of 'information', that RAF airfields in Britain were fog-bound, making it impossible for aircraft to take off; therefore we couldn't expect any heavy bomber 'softening-up' prior to the landing.

At the time this announcement was accepted as 'Just the luck of the draw', but it transpired later that Air Marshals Tedder and Harris had flatly refused the Canadian Army's request for such assistance. Tedder is reported to have referred to the Walcheren defences as 'a part-worn battery' and added that the Canadians were 'drugged with bombs'. 'Bomber' Harris, for his part, is reported to have boasted that, after all the bombs dropped there, 'he could have taken the island with his batman'. It was a great pity that those two weren't with us. Nevertheless the fog in England had been real and it is possible that bombers couldn't have taken off in any case. More significant at the time was that the assistance of rocket-firing Tiffies, for whose benefit the attack had been scheduled for full daylight, also appeared to be in doubt.

With the mesmerizing Westkapelle tower pulling us forward, the overall quietude prevailed until about 0820 hrs when action was initiated by the *Warspite* and the two monitors opening fire. Far away to the north we saw the muzzle flashes of their guns and fluffy white mushrooms began to spurt above the horizon to the left of the Westkapelle tower. There was no land visible, but the position of the shell bursts in relation to the tower indicated targets on the north-west coast of the island, which was defended by the string of German strongpoints and gun batteries, from W15 at Westkapelle to W19 at the northern tip of the island, all of which it was 41's job to liquidate. Ironically, in the W15 and W19 batteries there were a total of nine 3.7 inch guns, which had been captured from the British in 1940. This may have been the source of Tedder's reference to a 'part-worn battery'. Not until about half a minute after the muzzle flashes did the booms of the fifteen-inch guns reach us, followed quickly by the rumbling crumps of exploding one-ton shells.

For the next hour the fleet sailed irrevocably on, with the lantern tower growing taller by the minute. We could only sit and watch the spectacle, as more and more guns came into action, until the billowing puffs of exploding shells had built up into an ominous white curtain wall along the horizon. This began to grow darker in colour from the smoke of burning buildings, and then from ships, as the van of the task force sailed within range. The crashing explosions ashore and afloat grew in number and intensity. Waterspouts from bursting shells could be seen dotting the sea ahead.

At first all this was happening some distance from us, but, all too soon, our section of the convoy came within range. Shells began falling among the nearby ships and the sea ahead became a jumble of burning landing craft, shell splashes, smoke and noises. Walcheren, perhaps a mile away, was visible only as a low smudge on the surface of the sea, when the whole shoreline appeared to erupt into a continuous wall of waterspouts. My heart probably wasn't the only one to skip a few beats at the thought of having to pass through that sort of barrage until someone remarked 'Rockets!' It was a huge relief to realize that what we had seen had been the effect of our own rocket craft. It later transpired that a German shell had caused the premature release of an entire launch of rockets, which had fallen into the sea. There was another rocket mishap later, when a control fault caused salvoes to fall short, among our own craft, but enough rockets were on target to have a dramatic effect upon the enemy and many dazed and bemused Germans were taken prisoner as a result.

During our approach the SSEF had been moving ahead to engage the German shore batteries at close range, consciously attracting enemy fire upon themselves, and the squadron was badly mauled in the process. Of the original twenty-seven craft nine were sunk and only five escaped being completely disabled. The two craft fitted with 17-pounders, the first of their type to go into action during the war, had beached themselves close to German fortifications and both vessels, as well as most of their crews, were lost.

It must have been towards the end of the SSEF's sacrifice that our section of the assault force sailed within range of the smaller enemy guns. Shells began to shriek down, splashing into the sea around nearby vessels, sending up spouts of spray and solid water. Craft ahead could be seen to have been hit, were on fire, some belching smoke and drifting helplessly. Despite the shelling, there was no suggestion of taking evasive action. The landing craft held course, steaming steadily and exasperatingly slowly towards the shore.

Unknown to us, a stroke of good fortune had eased the final stages of our approach. Battery W13 to the south of the gap, comprising four 150mm guns and the one responsible for much of the havoc to the SSEF, had run out of ammunition, which couldn't be replenished because of the flooding. Fortunately, too, the Typhoons had after all been able to take off from fog-bound England. They came swooping low over the coast, the high-pitched scream of their engines and the deadly swishes of their rockets adding to the general turmoil of noise.

Throughout it all every ear had been attuned to detect that short, sharp, high-pitched swissshh which we knew meant that a shell was going to plummet down uncomfortably close. Each time that happened our bodies reacted automatically, but, sitting as we were, out in the open, perched on a load of military supplies, all that was possible by way of self-preservation was to hunch our shoulders and keep our heads down.

The approach of the Infantry Landing Craft carrying the dyke Assault Party had been more to the north than had been expected, putting them in clearer view of W15, and in consequence they had attracted more enemy fire than anticipated. Twice the craft were forced to turn away, first when some rockets fell among them and

then when two were hit and casualties were suffered. In consequence the initial landing didn't take place until 1012 hours,
27 minutes behind schedule.

The LCTs carrying the rest of the Commando also approached
the gap in the dyke from the north, with smoke from burning shore
installations drifting seawards towards them. The craft then
made a sharp turn to port, to pass through the smoke and into the
400-yard-wide stretch of North Sea pouring through the breach.
To the left came a brief glimpse of a wrecked windmill perched on
the crest of the stone-faced dyke, while, to the right, the bombed
radar station was clearly visible on the far side of the gap. All
forward vision was cut off by the high landing ramp, where a
matelot was positioned to ensure that it dropped rapidly on touchdown.

By this time most of the 'outside' noises were being drowned out
by the impatient revving-up of Buffalo and Weasel engines. Drivers
had been given the start-up signal and were eager to move off the
instant the order was given. Like the rest of us, they were itching
to get the hell out of there to the relative safety of dry land.

Then came another abrupt swing to port as the helmsman
squared-up for landing and, almost immediately, the bows
crunched ashore; the bow doors flopped open and the ramp
splashed down into the shallows of a sandy beach which only a few
weeks earlier had been rear gardens. Landing vehicles began to
trundle ashore and we gained our first close-up view of Holland a
few hundred yards away – the rear elevation of bomb-wrecked
houses lining the main street of Westkapelle.

As the deckmaster regulated the rapid exit of Weasels and
Buffaloes engine noises lessened and we again heard the swishes
and bursts of shells. Our vehicle, being at the rear of the LCT, was
last to clatter down the ramp, but we were finally ashore on
Walcheren. Surprisingly, the drive up-beach was exceedingly brief;
the LVT stopped more than a hundred yards short of the houses;
we dropped the eight feet to the ground and raced across the sand
to take shelter against the nearest ones.

Surprisingly too, there wasn't a great deal of activity going on. The
LCT which we had just left was already pulling off and one other
was still disgorging LVTs. Three or four Buffaloes had been hit and
were abandoned in odd positions here and there. There was a dead

143

Weasel in the shallows at the water's edge and a knocked-out flail tank lay half-way between the sea and the town. The rest of the Buffaloes must have moved somewhere inland. We could see that a few craft had been sunk in shallow water and others were beached at awkward angles against the shore on the far side of the breach. No shells were coming very close to us, however, thanks to the fact, as we learned later, that the barrels of nearby German guns could not be depressed sufficiently to enable them to be brought to bear.

As we crouched against walls of houses, awaiting the next order, a Buffalo, moving rapidly up the beach towards us, suddenly stopped dead; all aboard her precipitately baled out and headed for cover. It wasn't apparent just what had caused the demise of that particular vehicle, but there was no time to ponder the question. Hardly had we caught our breath, still thanking our lucky stars for having seen us ashore unscathed, than we were summoned forward on to the road at the front of the houses.

We quickly formed up in single file, facing the familiar lantern tower, now visible for its full height at the end of the street perhaps half a mile away. Just as the Troop received the order to move off a British military policeman, webbing and gauntlets gleaming white, appeared on the far pavement, heading in the opposite direction. To the nimble brain of Frank Barker it was a heaven-sent opportunity. As we started marching, he sang out, in his perky Cockney accent, 'All coppers are BAH-stards!' and, raked with laughter, our column moved off, leaving a frustrated MP glaring impotently after us.

That main street of Westkapelle was little more than a succession of bomb and shell craters passing through a devastation of ruined houses. At one point, where probably a 4,000-pounder had landed, the carriageway, footways and flanking houses had been completely obliterated. In their place was an enormous crater, seven or eight feet deep and about thirty in diameter with a pool of water at the bottom, and edged with a jumble of brick rubble and splintered wood. Beyond the empty shells of buildings lining the left-hand side of the road there was nothing but an undulating wasteland of bricks and roof timbers, with only a handful of houses remaining recognizable as such. Close behind the houses to our right lapped the waters of an extension of the North Sea which now covered most of the low-lying island.

We moved forward slowly and spasmodically with intermittent minor explosions and bursts of small arms fire coming from ahead, as the Fighting Troops searched the ruins of the town, while the sounds of spasmodic heavier explosions reached us from the rear. On reaching the lantern tower we found that it stood at a staggered junction of four roads, although two of them led only into an inland sea, and our small party was on its own. At close quarters the massive brick-built structure looked higher than ever and much less slender than it had appeared from the sea. The entrance door, at the top of a short flight of external steps, stood half-open and I was one of a party of six detailed off to 'Search it!'

Thoughts of Schmeisser machine-pistols, booby traps and hand-grenades flashed through my mind as we started up the stairs, automatically doing it all 'according to the book', with covering parties and search parties leap-frogging from floor to floor, kicking doors open, weapons at the ready. The building was devoid of Germans, but the indescribable litter of clothing, equipment and general rubbish in every room told of a panic exodus. On reaching the top, puffing and panting after our rapid ascent, we found a single Spandau machine gun pointing seawards through the metal balustrading around the lantern. The view from the top was largely of sea, but there was only time to catch a glimpse; no sooner had we signalled the 'All clear!' than the bawling voice of authority came back up to us, 'All right then, don't loaf around up there! Come down out of it'. We trooped back down the stairs, glancing ruefully into the littered rooms where there would undoubtedly have been many interesting souvenirs.

Back at ground level again there was no immediate rush to go anywhere, so we wondered why we had been brought down so quickly. Later we learned that, after a few Piat bombs and an exchange of small arms fire, the garrison of the tower had surrendered to 'A' Troop some time before we had arrived. We were allowed to 'Carry on smoking' and gazed over an apparently limitless inland sea, dotted with the flooded farms and homes of the people who had lived there. In most cases no more than chimneys and ridge tiles were visible, but here and there the top storey of a 'Dutch bungalow' protruded above the water. Single lines of the skeletons of trees showed field boundaries and two rows close together marked the routes of submerged roads. Then came the order 'Out pipes!' and we began to retrace our steps through Westkapelle until reaching the vicinity of the huge bomb crater, where we were fallen out again to 'Wait here'. It was probably around noon by that time.

Another unexplained wait before we marched back through the ruins of the seaward side of the town, parts of which merged into the sea without any demarcation other than the line of seaweed and flotsam left by the receding tide. We crossed the 'foreshore' and climbed to the top of the dyke protecting the north-western coast of the island. A knocked-out armoured bulldozer stood half-way up the stone-clad face close to the slumped ruins of the windmill we had seen from the LCT.

It was in that area that Sergeant Musgrove, in command of his section of 'B' Troop after the officer, Lieutenant McKenzie, had been killed during the run-in, captured a German pillbox with a handful of men, for which he was awarded the Military Medal. 'Muscleman Musgrove' we used to call him when he was a lance-corporal PT instructor at Thurlestone in 1941 and I was Orderly Room Clerk. Then we were skirting the shattered masses of concrete which had once been German fortifications, and the more pathetic tangles of wrecked Dutch homes. Everywhere there was an air of deserted emptiness which, as the aftermath of a successful landing, was something completely new to us. On previous occasions the beach areas had been swarming with activity – ships being unloaded, supplies pouring ashore, Royal Engineers constructing steel roadways across the sand – but this time there was nothing. The task force had been put ashore and all craft still seaworthy had been withdrawn. There would be no streams of supplies, no back-up and no reinforcements; the Brigade was on its own.

After only a short march we were fallen out once again and 'put in the picture'. 'B' and 'P' Troops, after clearing the northern part of the town, had come under heavy fire from the W15 battery – a complex of artillery positions and strongpoints around the main coast defence guns. 'Y' Troop had been moved up from reserve to put in a flanking attack from the flooded side of the dyke, under covering fire from the others, and by 1230 the battery had been taken with a 'bag' of 120 prisoners. By the time we arrived on the dunes all German resistance in Westkapelle was at an end and

146

the Commando had been halted by the Brigade Commander to await his order to continue the advance.

The area in which we waited had obviously been an assembly point for Buffaloes. About a dozen of them, knocked out by mortars or shellfire, lay abandoned amongst the dunes and stunted trees. One was completely intact, but a neat hole had been drilled in the narrow bulkhead between driving compartment and hold by a shell which had failed to explode. There was no sign of any casualties, so they had obviously been evacuated to the south side of the gap where the Canadian medical teams and Brigade HQ were located.

The heavy guns of battery W17 at Domburg, less than four miles away, which had continued to fire upon the Westkapelle area, were silenced for a while by a Tiffie rocket strike early in the afternoon, but they came back into action shortly afterwards. That battery was the Commando's next main objective, but it wasn't until 1500 hours that Brigadier Leicester gave the order to move forward. The bulk of the Commando then began to move up the road which topped the broad dyke forming the rim of the flooded island, leaving 'A' and 'S' Troops, together with the two attached Troops of 10 I-A, in defensive positions around Westkapelle.

The Commando was soon passing some shattered casemates of W15. Massive concrete roofs had been sliced off their supporting walls by the devastating concussions of large-calibre shells. Guns, torn from their mountings, were slumped as long fingers of scrap steel in the ruins of their turrets. Gun crews must have been blasted into eternity or lay buried beneath the mangled wreckage, but we passed a remarkable exception. A German gunner sat in the devastation of his concrete emplacement, seemingly untouched by all that had happened around him, but obviously very much dead. Still cradled in his arms was the shell (it was about the size of those I had once handled for the 'twin four-incher' on HMS *Cleveland*, so it was probably a 3.7) he had been about to load into the breech at the very moment he had ceased to exist. 'Better you than me,' was my only thought.

For an infantry unit advancing against unknown enemy defences four miles can be a long way. The total width of the dyke base between the North Sea, hidden from us by sand dunes to our left and the water filling 'the tea saucer island' stretching away to our right and some ten feet below the road, was only a few hundred yards, but that provided ample room for a variety of defensive positions, mines and booby traps, so progress was slow.

HQ Troop was generally positioned behind the leading Troop, which was alternated from time to time, and when the width of dry land widened into more open country 'X' Troop moved out into the dunes on the right flank. Darkness was falling when word came back that Domburg had been reached; the garrisons of both W17 and of a smaller battery immediately inland were surrendering and the advance was being slowed up by having to deal with the large numbers of potentially hostile enemy giving themselves up.

'B' Troop was left to deal with them, while 'P' and 'Y' moved into Domburg, reaching the centre at about 1830 hours. It was then completely dark, apart from the light given by buildings still burning as a result of the naval bombardment. A few German stragglers were dealt with en route, but many others had withdrawn into the wooded sand dune country beyond the town. Major Wood, the 2 i/c, decided that it would be inadvisable to pursue them in the darkness, so 'P' and 'Y' were formed into a defence line between the sea and the edge of the flooded interior, with 'B' to their rear in reserve.

The group of HQ I was with marched back to spend the night in Westkapelle where a two-storey shop premises at the seaward end of the main street had been taken over as a combined Quartermaster's store and HQ billet. Only the ground floor was reasonably intact, although, with neither doors nor any glass in the large windows, it was a cold, draughty place in which to spend a winter's night. Fortunately, we four DRs were able to appropriate the narrow space between a shop counter and an internal wall at the end of which was a fireplace, albeit completely sealed off with a thin steel sheet. We set to to remove it, but, despite strenuous efforts, could do no more than prise free one top corner. Nevertheless, that proved sufficient to enable us to kindle a fire in the hearth and, with an abundance of shattered timber close to hand, the steel was soon glowing warmly.

As we settled down for the night another difference between Walcheren and previous landings became apparent. With no fleet of supply ships lying off-shore, there was no air activity. Enemy action in our area was confined to sessions of shelling, which were noisy, but the explosions remained sufficiently far away to assure us that the guns weren't being trained in our direction. Apart from a cold two-hour stint on watch outside, we passed a reasonably comfortable night, squashed together for warmth behind the shop counter.

It was a raw awakening next morning. The fire was out and the shop was filled with cold, damp air. The QMs managed to produce a mug of tea each and we finished off the remnants of the 24-hour ration pack each man had carried ashore the previous day. Then came a protracted delay, awaiting the anticipated order to move back up the dyke road to re-join the Troops in Domburg. German artillery continued to be very active and we had a clear view across the gap where most of the incoming shells were landing. There we saw that two Buffaloes had been hit and they began to burn; men baled out in a great hurry. Joined by a flurry of other figures, they raced for cover as ammunition in the vehicles began to explode and for half an hour or more we were treated to a spectacular fireworks display. Only later did we learn how deadly that 'entertainment' had been. The exploding mortar bombs and small-arms ammunition had been raking a crowded open beach area and a dozen or more British and Canadians, as well as ten German POWs who had been doing the unloading, had been killed.

We marched back along the dyke road and, just before entering Domburg, gained a glimpse of one of the guns of W17 to the left of the road. A large barrel, no doubt a '220mm-er', poked above a tall hedge, its ragged muzzle end indicating that it had been 'spiked' by its own gunners. Historically, muzzle-loading guns had been rendered useless to the enemy by driving a spike into the vent hole. Then, with the advent of breech-loaders, it became the practice to insert a shell nose first into the muzzle and, with a very long lanyard, fire another round from the breech. Something much less drastic must have been resorted to at W17!

By the time we arrived in Domburg the Fighting Troops were somewhere ahead, pursuing the enemy into a maze of gun emplacements and strongpoints in the wooded dune country to the north-east of the town. They had, however, left behind some two or three hundred prisoners and the DRs were among those assigned to guarding them. The Germans were being held in a large school, where the children's playground, secure behind high metal railings, provided an ideal exercise yard. We assiduously patrolled the perimeter of the building, but felt that our presence was largely symbolic, as none of the inmates appeared to show any interest in wanting to escape, being only too happy to buy, or barter for, cigarettes, knowing that for them the war was over.

We learned that 'X' Troop's advance the previous evening had been held up by determined Germans in a wired-in position on a high dune. As the Marines went forward the Troop Commander, Major Brind-Sheridan, and one Marine had been wounded, but their absence hadn't been immediately noticed when the Troop pulled back. Attempts to reach them during the night had been frustrated when the Germans lit fires near where they lay. Early next morning the garrison broke out to the north, coming under fire from 'B' who inflicted casualties. When the position was occupied the pair were found inside the enemy wire; the Marine was still alive but Major Brind-Sheridan had died of his wounds.

Information had also come through that 47 and 48 Commandos, on the other side of the gap, were having problems in their push towards Zoutelande. 47 Commando alone had lost more than twenty men killed in a series of abortive attacks on battery W4 and 41 was to go to their assistance. The two Troops of 10 I-A were to remain to continue engaging the Germans in the dunes, but the rest were to be pulled back, to march to Westkapelle and cross the gap by Buffalo. That night, while the German prisoners passed an undisturbed night in their intact prison building, we alternated between periods of guard duty in the open and trying to sleep in the empty shell of a house with no windows and no fire.

Next day, 3 November, was my 24th birthday and my fifth in uniform. I was growing old in the Service! On such a day, even in wartime, a Marine on one of HM ships would have had 'sippers' of rum from his messmates and there would have been the likelihood of 'big eats' at the messtable. For Marine Commandos serving ashore there was no rum ration and, for those on Walcheren, few rations of any description. A severe storm was making it impossible for landing craft to cross the ten miles of open water from Breskens to replenish food supplies and we were getting hungry.

During the morning the DRs were abruptly relieved of their POW guard duties, told to assemble equipment, clean weapons and stand by to join the last batch of 41, as riflemen, when it passed through Domburg en route to reinforce 47 and 48. An apparent increase in enemy activity north of Domburg had made the CO of 10 I-A reluctant to remain there with only his own two Troops and, in consequence, two Troops of 41 were to stay with them. Maybe we were 'make-weights'!

The afternoon was well advanced when we tagged on to the end of a column of marching men and it was dusk by the time we were fallen out at the edge of a torrent of black water scudding through the Westkapelle gap. It was high tide and the North Sea was pouring into the interior of the island like a mill race. There was a shortage of LVTs, so it was quite dark by the time our turn, as 'tail-end Charlies', came to be ferried across.

No sooner had we all climbed up the tall side and dropped into the hold than the Buffalo trundled back down the beach and into the swirling water. It was our first trip afloat in an LVT and we were surprised to see just how little freeboard there was between the gunwale and the sloshing sea. As we buffeted the current the windscreen of the driver's compartment was continually awash and every other second it disappeared completely beneath the water. With its 200hp engine racing at full throttle, our noisy splashing craft was tossed about alarmingly, but in only a minute or so we were nearing the indistinct blackness of the far side. Then, completely unexpectedly, the driver switched on powerful headlights and, at a stroke, the indistinct blackness ahead was transformed into ranges of brightly-lit fairytale sand mountains. From that moment the trip became a fantastic Jules Verne journey.

Our roaring amphibian grounded in the shallows, slewed sharply to the left and, engines still at full throttle, began to follow the water's edge along the dyke foot. One track remained splashing through shallow water while the other churned through soft sand a few feet up the slope. As we bucked and plunged forward the headlights would suddenly pick out a grass-tufted hummock, bright and clear against the dark sky. Then that would disappear as we climbed to the top of the rise, with headlights becoming searchlights sweeping the heavens until, flopping over the crest, the Buffalo would crash down into a shallow inlet to send a shower of illuminated spray over the Marines packed in its belly.

High tide had lengthened our watery trip to Zoutelande, as so much more of the island was submerged, but the intriguing journey came to an end much too soon. The LVT crawled clear of the inland sea and came to a halt on a metalled roadway. The dream-like interlude was over and we jumped down. If ever a vehicle was in the right place at the right time it was surely the 'Landing Vehicle, Tracked' on the island of Walcheren in November, 1944.

We marched off and soon found ourselves moving from the raw darkness of a November evening into the cosy brightness of a spacious German bunker, made even more attractive by an issue of hot food. Briefing for the attack next morning began immediately after the meal, but, within minutes, it was terminated by the announcement that the Germans had already surrendered! Our presence in Zoutelande wasn't required after all, so my birthday ended on an unexpected high note, as well as a hot meal, a night of warm safe sleep and the knowledge that there would be no early reveille for a dawn attack next day.

The surrender of W4 and the subsequent link-up by 47 and 48 with No. 4 Commando, who were on the other side of the Flushing gap, had put all of south-western Walcheren in Allied hands. A substantial enemy force, however, still held the centre of the island, including Middelburg, which had remained above water. The north-western part of the island too remained in German hands, so next morning 41 headed back across the gap to resume its operations there.

On reaching Domburg it was learned that the CO of 10 I-A had planned an attack by his joint force for that afternoon, to be supported by two Sherman tanks and two AVREs. These were the only serviceable armoured vehicles to have made it ashore out of the original twenty (2 Shermans, 6 flails, 8 AVREs and 4 armoured bulldozers). Our CO and 2i/c immediately went forward to witness the attack, leaving the rest to be allocated billets for the night.

Commando HQ had taken over the Bad Hotel, a large country-mansion-type building set in its own grounds, which had recently been vacated by German HQ personnel. The DRs' bedroom was fully furnished, even down to an unbelievable collection of toiletries on the dressing table. The cellars had clearly been well stocked with liquor of many varieties and in vast quantities, much of it by the carboy rather than the bottle, but stocks had been greatly depleted. Nevertheless, the fortunes of war had given us a very cushy billet for a change, the only drawback being the scarcity of food, of which we had received very little that day.

Hardly had we moved in than I was handed a message for Brigade Headquarters; there being no transport available, I had to walk the four miles back to the Westkapelle gap. While waiting for an LVT to take me across, I spotted a cake of 'dehydrated porridge', still in its cellophane wrapping, lying on the sand. Manna from Heaven! I quickly scooped it up and, stifling pangs of conscience at keeping it all to myself, started to eat. A Buffalo was preparing to come across for me, so I did it quickly!

Brigade Headquarters had been set up in the reinforced concrete control centre built into the sea dyke which had formed the base of the radar dish, so delivery was quickly effected. As there was no answer, before starting back I had a look at Brigade HQ's two open air 'annexes', neither of which would have been there had not stormy seas isolated Westkapelle from mainland Europe. The first was the prisoner of war cage, no more than a depression in the sand, bounded by a few strands of barbed wire and covered by Bren guns. There hundreds of German troops, packed shoulder to shoulder squatting on the ground, had to spend their November days and nights with no more creature comforts than they had been able to provide for themselves. Only a few hundred yards away a much more saddening 'annexe' was the mortuary. There, arranged in neat military rows, lay some scores of Allied and German dead. Each man was shrouded in an army blanket, many still on the stretcher used to carry them there, all awaiting transport across the Scheldt.

It was evening by the time I arrived back in Domburg, to be greeted by the other side of war. The entire town was buzzing with noise and jollification and at the Bad Hotel it was 'Saturday night in the Enemy HQ' with a vengeance. There was very little food but plenty of liquor; such wines, spirits and liqueurs as the Germans had left behind were flowing freely. I luxuriated in the first wash and shave for four days before joining in.

German artillery continued to be active, demonstrating that Domburg was still within range of their guns, but we were too occupied with other things to worry much about such things. Before going to bed that night the DRs decided to 'clear the decks' and, opening the windows of their bedroom, spent an enjoyable few minutes hurling bottle after bottle of perfume, face cream and body lotion into the darkness.

Next morning, despite it being Sunday and 'the morning after the night before', we had to return to serious business. As DRs without motorbikes, we were put to our assigned task of 'ammunition wallahs', getting ammunition up to the forward Troops. Under the command of a sergeant, we loaded a Buffalo with a lethal assortment of mortar bombs, PIAT bombs, 303 cartridges, hand grenades and Bangalore torpedoes, then climbed on top of the load for the ride.

We had learned that the attack of the previous afternoon had been halted when 'B' Troop was enfiladed by heavy machine-gun fire from woods on their left flank. Further advance would have been impossible without incurring heavy casualties, so they had been ordered to pull back a few hundred yards to consolidate and await the return of the Troops sent to Zoutelande. While we were loading up the reserve ammunition these Troops had moved out of Domburg to participate in an attack on W18, the next major battery along the coast.

Our Buffalo headed out of town towards the coast, then turned off the road and began ploughing its way over undulating sand dunes. We caught glimpses of the North Sea over the dunes to our left, while, to the right, there was little more than extensive straggling woodland. After a bumpy journey of about a mile or so the LVT climbed to the top of a particularly long, steep, sandy incline and came to a halt near one of the many bunkers the Germans had constructed in the area.

We began to off-load our explosive cargo and carry it into the protection of the interior. This seemed to be the signal for German artillery to open fire and shells were soon falling in the vicinity. We were allowed to take shelter in the narrow entrance passageway, but no further, so remained near the doorway, with the LVT standing in the open, directly in front of us. That particular Sunday happened to be Guy Fawkes Day in the UK, but we were under no illusions about what sort of fireworks display would ensue if a shell were to fall on or near that load of ammunition.

The worst of the barrage was over when accustomed ears warned of the approach of another missile, which was undoubtedly coming to earth unpleasantly close. We were still looking out towards the LVT at the moment when there should have been a shattering explosion, but saw only a vicious spurt of sand kick up on the brow

154

of the dune, only feet beyond the vehicle. Seconds later an explosion blasted off near the bottom of the hill. The bloody thing had bounced! Had it pitched only a little to the right there could very well have been a few more stretchers to line up outside Brigade HQ.

Things quietened down after that, the off-loading was completed and the Buffalo returned empty to Domburg. We were set marching forward with the rest of HQ Troop to maintain contact with the Fighting Troops advancing towards the battery. Breasting another dune, we suddenly gained a wide panoramic view ahead. The narrow sandy track along which we were trudging in single file led downhill until being lost in an extensive band of trees perhaps a mile ahead. Far beyond the dunes to our left were blue patches of the North Sea, while more dunes and trees stretched away to the right. Almost concurrently, the overall stillness was broken by the increasing roar of aircraft engines rapidly approaching from the rear. With rockets slung under their wings, they were instantly recognizable as Typhoons and they were clearly coming in for a strike.

As each plane in turn swooped low, directly above our heads, its engine noise rose to a high-pitched scream, quickly joined by flesh-tingling swwiiisssshes as two deadly rockets left the aircraft's wings. Our eyes followed their converging trails until the white puffs of exploding warheads rose above the trees, followed a few seconds later by the crump of explosions. My reaction at the time was similar to that expressed by the Duke of Wellington on receiving a draft of recruits during the Peninsular War: 'I don't know what effect these (men) will have upon the enemy, but, by God, they terrify me'.

The effect of that Tiffie strike on battery W18 was to pave the way for a completely successful assault by 'A' and 'Y' Troops, but, sadly, there had been casualties. Two of the four killed were Captain Peter Haydon DSO, who had been my Section Officer in 'Q' Troop, and his MOA Byron Moses, who had gone forward to help him. Three more died of wounds two days later, including a signaller friend, Harry Page. By dusk all local opposition was at an end and HQ had moved into one of the evacuated bunkers of W18. Apart from a spell of guard duty, the DRs passed a warm, peaceful night, with some assistance from a part-bottle of cherry whisky found in there.

The influx of prisoners resulting from the capture of W18 had over-stretched the accommodation available in the Domburg school, so next morning, 6 November, the DRs and two Signallers were sent back to town by Buffalo to act as escorts in transferring some of them to the Brigade POW cage. We reported to the Sergeant-in-Charge, then waited outside the school while he completed arrangements. Soon our charges began shuffling out and, for interest's sake, we started to count – ten, twenty, thirty, forty – but gave up when it go to two hundred, and they were still coming.

Our charges were of all shapes and sizes, but, almost to a man, they carried what we called a 'surrender suitcase' containing their belongings. We had to search the prisoners for hidden weapons, but found no more than a few forbidden penknives; all wrist watches had disappeared. As the long, straggling column of threes moved off it was obvious that six men with rifles and bayonets, plus a Sergeant with a Colt 45 automatic, would be hard-pushed to control them should they decide to get awkward. In the event the only awkward person was the Sergeant. He started to make the POWs double march, but we made it clear that *we* weren't prisoners.

At the Westkapelle gap the prisoners were fallen out while the slow process of ferrying them across got under way. The Germans were well prepared and, from suitcases and haversacks, produced bread and sausage for lunch, more food than we had seen in days. I was standing alone, some twenty yards or so from a group of them, wondering whether it would be British to pinch some of their grub, when a party of seven or eight started moving towards me. I waited, bayonet loosely pointing in their general direction, wondering 'What the heck?', until I saw that one of them had a loaf of bread in one hand and was making cutting motions with the other, saying, '*Messer? Messer?*' They needed a knife to cut the bread and we had taken all theirs!

There had been no guidance as to what to do in such a situation, but as the Germans were obviously more amused than aggressive I fumbled for my jack-knife and handed it over. The bread-holder inclined his head as he said '*Danke*', opened the knife and proceeded to hack off rough slices for his comrades. I watched closely lest he should try to cut anything else, but as soon as he had finished he snapped the knife shut, handed it back to me with a grin, a slight flourish and a *'Danke sehr'*. Throughout this pantomime my hungry stomach had been suggesting that I should 'liberate' at least one slice of bread, but I persuaded it that it would have been *infra dig* to show the defeated enemy that we were hungry.

Only two LVTs were available to shuttle the horde of prisoners across the gap, so it was late afternoon before the last ones were off our hands. By the time we had marched back to Domburg it was pitch dark and there was no LVT to take us up to HQ. So, instead of a comfortable bunk bed in a cosy German bunker as on the previous might, we had to make do with the bare floorboards of a cold, small room in the school/prisoner-of-war building. Once again parsimonious rations sent us to sleep with rumbling stomachs and this time there wasn't any cherry whisky to help things along.

It was a relief next morning to climb on board a Buffalo and be taken back into the bosom of the family. On the previous day, although we hadn't known it at the time, the 52nd (Lowland) Division, as the culmination of their joint attacks with the Canadian 2nd Division, had accepted the surrender of General Daser, the overall German Commander on the island, with his remaining force of 2000 men. This meant that only in 41's sector beyond Domburg were the Germans continuing to offer resistance.

During our absence the previous day REs had been striving to open up a supply route to the forward troops, to enable them to continue their advance towards the next enemy positions, 'The Black Hut' and W19. So many mines had been encountered, however, that an alternative route had had to be found and this had occupied the entire morning. In view of these supply difficulties and the few hours of daylight remaining, Brigadier Leicester had decided to postpone the attack until next day and use the afternoon to build up stores. As a preliminary move, the Belgians of 10 I-A had cleared the adjacent woods and taken up forward positions near the line of the proposed attack. It was rumoured that the Germans had evacuated W19 and pulled back into the wooded country beyond.

After an early morning recce on 7 November the Commando put in its attack at 1000 hours with armoured support and 25 pdrs and by noon the first stage, taking the Black Hut, had been achieved. Unfortunately, when moving forward towards W19, the leading

AVRE was destroyed by a placed charge, completely blocking the track. The attack was continued without fire support, but after 400 yards, when 'A' had taken over the lead from 'B', they encountered a minefield and, when seeking a way around it, came under heavy and accurate mortar fire. They suffered a dozen casualties, so the CO decided to call off the attack until armoured support became available. It took the Adjutant, Captain De Lash, three hours to evacuate the casualties under fire.

Before daylight next morning, Wednesday 8 November, while we were still in the comfort of the HQ bunker, the attack was resumed. By 0715 an enemy position between the inland scrub and W19 on the seaward dunes had been taken and movement within the battery indicated that, contrary to previous reports, the battery was still occupied. Just before eight o'clock, in full daylight, an assault was launched, which took the Germans completely by surprise and they quickly surrendered. The advance and mopping up continued with No. 4 Commando, coming from the other side of the island, linking up and moving forward on 41's right flank.

At about 1000 hrs the 2i/c of No. 4 came across to 41 with the Brigadier's orders to cease fire, as the surrender of the entire German garrison on Walcheren had been arranged. This information clearly hadn't reached the Germans in the next strongpoint, codenamed FUJIYAMA, as our leading Troop came under heavy fire when approaching it. They were halted while a German officer was brought from Vrouwenpolder to explain the situation to the Germans and by noon it was all over. The area around FUJIYAMA had been cleared and all prisoners, said to number over a thousand, were on their way to the No. 4 Commando POW cage. Our men began moving back to W18.

With the news that INFATUATE was over, we DRs and Signallers began poking around German bunkers and other buildings in search of food. We found some rock-hard Knackerbrot, which wasn't at all exciting, then came upon a food store which had received a direct hit. Most of its contents had been splattered around the ruins, but, after digging deep, we eventually located a few undamaged tins of the German equivalent of spam (the American name for their Lend-Lease wartime food delicacy of spiced ham!). Thick slices were soon sizzling in a German frying pan and the meat made even Knackerbrot seem palatable.

We returned to Domburg next morning, into the same room in the Bad Hotel and were allowed time for a wash and shave before resuming the job of guarding prisoners. Off duty that evening, there was still some liquor left in the cellar but before long the more palatable ones had run out, leaving only arrack – the liquid distilled from dates or coco-palm – and Dutch gin. Both of these 'fire-waters' appeal only to their devotees or to really dedicated drinkers, so most of us were quite happy to call it a day at that stage. One of our number, however, had apparently kept at it, as he came prancing around the cellar dangling a cat by its tail. We were obliged to ensure that he acted more humanely, after which he quickly passed out. Next day Harry had to be kept away from the eyes of authority until regaining normality.

On the afternoon of that next day the burial ceremony of those who had been killed during the final stages of the Walcheren operation took place. I was one of the detail sent, with an LVT as communal hearse, to pick up the bodies from the mortuary of the local hospital and transport them to Domburg churchyard. There were over twenty, sewn up in army blankets, and identified only by a plain white card pinned to their chests bearing 'Name, Rank and Unit'. An imperishable identity disc, around the neck, where it had dangled throughout their Service careers, would be buried with them.

Apart from an RAMC man all were from 41 and 48 Royal Marine Commandos and the Royal Engineers, in roughly equal numbers. We piled the blanket-shrouded corpses one on top of another in the hold of the LVT for the short journey to the grave-yard. One parcel was particularly pathetic, no more than two feet long yet containing all the earthly remains of a man whose vehicle had been blown up by a mine. The name, rank and regiment are indelibly imprinted upon my memory, yet, unlike the others recorded as having been buried at Domburg that day, no such person was later re-interred in the Bergen op Zoom War Cemetery. More than that, neither his Corps nor the Commonwealth War Graves Commission has any record of such a man. It remains, for me, one of the war's little mysteries.

At the churchyard a burial party took over to carry the bodies to their communal grave, a rectangular excavation barely two feet deep, alongside a boundary hedge overhung by the branches of leafless trees. The bottom was awash with water, but, with most of the island flooded, the water table was everywhere very close to the surface, so that was unavoidable. Nevertheless, it didn't seem fitting that our dead comrades should be put to rest in such a wet place. The bitterest thought in most minds, however, was that if the Germans had surrendered only a few days earlier these men would have still been alive.

Volleys of rifle fire crackled out over the grave and a bugler sounded the Last Post. It took my mind back, five years almost to the day, when my eldest brother, Rex, had been buried with military honours in Heaton and Byker cemetery, Newcastle upon Tyne, on Armistice Day 1939. A Sergeant-Pilot in Coastal Command of the RAF, he had been killed when the Lockheed Hudson of which he was second pilot had crashed on returning to its base at Thornaby-on-Tees after a patrol over the North Sea.

The day after the Domburg mass burial was Armistice Day 1944. 41 RM Commando marched out of Domburg to the cheers, waves, thanks and good wishes of the Dutch inhabitants, free at last after four and a half years of German occupation. We were bound for Flushing, twelve miles away, from there to cross the River Scheldt to Breskens and return to De Haan.

The Unit marched along the dyke road for the last time, passing the defunct batteries of W17 and W15, and at Westkapelle Buffaloes again acted as ferries to take us across the gap. The march continued via Zoutelande. At the Flushing gap there were more Buffaloes to effect the crossing and they trundled through the flooded outskirts of the town to set us down on dry land again. Daylight was fading by the time the last mile or so had been covered and we were halted alongside an LCT tied up at the dockside.

As the Commando trooped on board all eyes opened wide with disbelief and the air turned blue with lurid Royal Marine epithets. Stacked seven or eight layers high, and about twenty rows wide down much of the centre of the tank deck, were hundreds and hundreds of boxes of Compo rations. Seeing all that food heading away from Walcheren, when we had just spent a week on short rations, was enough to cause a riot! Ropes were cast off, bells clanged, engine noises rose to a crescendo, racing propellers thrashed the water, but nothing happened. The flow of bad language quickly changed to ironic cheers and gales of laughter as

160

it was realized that the heavily laden LCT had missed the tide and was firmly aground. Everyone about-turned and trooped ashore again. Then it was realized that there wasn't a lot to laugh about. There was some food, tins of cold Compo were handed out, but for overnight accommodation it was simply a matter of being marched to nearby streets of bombed and derelict houses and told to make ourselves comfortable.

All the houses were lacking doors, windows, parts of the walls and roofs, even the entire upper storey, but a group of us finally came upon a reasonably intact rear room. It was just large enough to accommodate about ten, stretched out on the floor, and was approached through the shattered front room by picking a way along such floorboards as still remained in place. Where there was no flooring, the cold, black waters of the Scheldt could be seen lapping less than two feet below.

In the corner behind the door of our bedroom there was a very small fireplace and it was soon roaring with a fire of bomb-shattered timber. We ate our cold rations in the resulting warmth and, with nothing else to do, were soon cocooned in sleep and wood smoke, but it wasn't to be an undisturbed night. In the early hours urgent yells of 'Fire! Fire!' had us rushing out into the very chill night air to find that the wall outside our room was a sheet of flames. With water close to hand under the floor, the rapid use of mugs and messtins quickly doused the flames and we returned to sleep. Perhaps the fire was no more than an accumulation of wallpaper, dried out by the heat of our fire and ignited by a tongue of flame licking through a crack in the brickwork, but it could have become serious.

Sunday morning was bright and sunny when the Commando marched back to the harbour. The LCT, with its countless boxes of Compo, was still there and floating this time. There were no hitches; it left Flushing to a round of spontaneous cheers and forty minutes later nosed up on to a beach near Breskens. The ramp flopped down and we trooped ashore to find a beach bustling with activity. LCTs were being unloaded by German prisoners in field grey, while numerous trucks shuffled back and forth. There was even a Church Army mobile canteen parked near the water's edge serving tea and buns, so it felt very much like the last day of a 'stunt' back in the UK.

TCVs to move the Commando the forty-odd miles back to De Haan hadn't arrived, so there was time to queue up for tea and buns. Then it was realized that we were still in Holland, would have to pay in Dutch guilders and we had sailed from Antwerp with only Belgian francs in our pockets. Fortunately, some of our number had persuaded Germans taken prisoner on Walcheren to surrender their guilders as well as themselves, so we were all able to pay.

Reasonably refreshed, we watched, with little interest, as German prisoners continued to unload the hoard of food with which we had travelled from Flushing. One after another they filed on board, humped a box onto a shoulder, carried it some two hundred yards from the sea and dumped it on another growing stack. Then a 15-cwt truck belonging to the Commando's Signals Section arrived, simply to make contact, and Operation COMPO was rapidly initiated, the objective being to acquire some of those boxes.

The truck was positioned close to the route taken by the POWs from LCT to stack, while two of our number wandered down to the water's edge and nonchalantly positioned themselves one on either side of the foot of the ramp. This was to be quite sure that, on whichever German shoulder a box might be carried, the reference letter could be read. We had decided to go only for 'A' boxes, containing steak and kidney pudding for main course, with mixed fruit pudding for 'afters'.

When a prisoner stepped off the ramp with an 'A' on his shoulder an almost imperceptible nod alerted those by truck. That particular POW was then followed by six pairs of eyes as he drew nearer and, after a quick check that no one in authority was looking in our direction, all that was needed was for one of us to step in front of him and point, commandingly, to the back of the truck. The German had no option but to drop his box inside, where it was immediately covered with camouflage netting, as he headed back to the LCT.

Not wanting to be too greedy, we called a halt at six, or it may have been seven or eight, boxes. It was only a 15-cwt, so there wasn't room to hide too many. However, with a full day's rations for fourteen men in each box, we reckoned that the Signallers and DRs had adequately, and justifiably, recouped themselves for those hungry days on the other side of the Scheldt!

The TCVs arrived during the afternoon and by 1630 hours we four DRs were back in the top floor room of the Pension du Nord, exchanging news with those who had been left behind. They listened attentively to a bare-bones account of what had transpired since leaving them – a lifetime of thirteen days previously – before jumping in with the latest buzz that De Haan was destined to be used as a military convalescent area and 41 was to be pushed out, probably up to the front.

Chapter 12

RETURN TO HOLLAND, AND V-WEAPONS

During our absence from De Haan the power supply had been restored to the Pension du Nord, so, with electric lighting and a radio set, one of 'the spoils of war' brought back from Holland, the DRs room was becoming less spartan. However, the weather had turned decidedly chilly and, with the imminent onset of winter, and that of 1944/45 was destined to be one of the coldest for many years, some form of heating had become top priority. Next day the off-duty DRs set out on a rummaging expedition.

After poking around the ruins of bombed buildings in the neighbourhood a small pot-bellied stove with some lengths of metal piping were unearthed and hauled gleefully up the four flights of stairs to our room. As there was neither fireplace nor chimney, an outlet for the flue pipe was provided by the simple expedient of knocking a hole in a window pane. Fuel, in the form of coal briquettes, was 'won' from a nearby Army cookhouse, but, despite repeated attempts to kindle a fire, it proved impossible to get the stove to draw properly, the only result being a roomful of smoke.

The following morning the stove was jettisoned out of the window and a second expedition returned with a replacement, but that too refused to function properly. Four days and a succession of stoves later, by which time the garden below our window was well covered with shattered cast iron, success was achieved. Then, with a working stove, electric light and the radio, although not quite in the lap of luxury, we felt that we were at least perched on its knee.

During our first few days back in Belgium the Unit was given a succession of, 'Jolly good show, chaps' talks, first by our Commanding Officer, Lieutenant Colonel E.C.E. 'Pegler' Palmer, then by Brigadier B.W. 'Jumbo' Leicester, and finally by Major-General Sturges, GOC of the Special Service Group. The General, on our return from the Mediterranean in January, had apologized for being late and he had another apology this time – for not being able to send us on leave. Instead he talked about 'polishing-off a few more islands' and 'going into the line in Holland', so we knew just where we stood.

In consequence of the casualties suffered on Walcheren, there were insufficient Officers and Other Ranks to form five effective Fighting Troops, so the number was reduced to four by amalgamating 'A' and 'X' as 'Q'. The original 'Q Troop' had ceased to exist at Salerno in September 1943 for the very same reason that this second one had had to be created, casualties. The newly-formed 'Q', together with Headquarters Troop, became the core of FORCE PALMER, which was immediately put on two hours' notice to react to any German incursion which might take place.

To mark the end of a successful operation, the Fighting Troops were granted a week to 'Rest and Re-equip', but for the 'Ammunition Wallahs-cum-DRs' return to De Haan simply meant a resumption of the rota of duty trips. Nevertheless, for all there was a new facet to life – currency exchange. Those who had arrived back with pockets bulging with Dutch guilders had to decide whether to cash in at once or keep them for a likely return to Holland. Then there was the problem of getting money back to the UK in sterling. At one time it had been possible to buy British postal orders at the Orderly Room using local currency, but the authorities had cottoned on to the possibility of 'fiddles', after which such transactions had to be entered in your Pay Book as debits against pay. The affluent set about devising ways of getting around this!

The few guilders I had managed to acquire – the circumstances are lost to memory – caused me no such heart-searching and they were largely consumed as fish suppers! In Ostend at that time even the most prestigious hotels were attempting to attract the 'Tommy Trade' by displaying prominent FISH AND CHIPS signs in their windows. With a white linen table cloth and waiter service, it was on a rather higher level than a normal British 'Chippy' and the cost of almost a week's pay would have been prohibitive had it not been for our temporary affluence.

On 23 November, ten days after our return, the Commando was put under two days' notice to move back to Walcheren. On that day, too, the Belgian Troop of 10 I-A Commando was again placed under command and seven officer replacements joined the Unit. One of them was Lieutenant R.S. Bate of the South African Union Defence Force, killed in a raid across the Maas less than three months later; another, Lieutenant J.B.R. Grindrod of the Manchester Regiment took up Holy Orders after the war and ended up as Archbishop and Primate of Australia, while a third, Lieutenant John Cameron Stewart, was to lose part of a leg by a German *Schuh* mine, also in a raid across the Maas, and he too emigrated to Australia.

The return to the 'Tea Saucer Island' was to be by land, via Antwerp, into Holland at Putte, then along the South Beveland peninsula to the Walcheren causeway. Although the total distance was only of the order of 150 miles, an overnight stop en route was planned, in view of the slow overall speed when shepherding a long convoy of vehicles. On Friday 24th, therefore, Lieutenant 'Bud' Abbott, the Intelligence Officer, with Corporal Latimer of 10 I-A Commando as interpreter, left De Haan by jeep to arrange accommodation for the following night; I was the DR chosen to accompany them.

Our little party reached Antwerp in less than two hours and were surprised to find that the vehicular tunnel under the river was still intact, although the entrance had been damaged by one near miss. The city centre was thronged with Allied military traffic and personnel; it was time for 'stand-easy' tea and buns and we had soon located a very up-market NAAFI/EFI canteen. These establishments were strictly 'off limits' for commissioned officers, but, muffled up in my riding coat Bud's pips were hidden, so he passed as one of a quartet of Other Ranks.

When we arrived, more than two weeks after the surrender of Walcheren, the Royal Navy still needed a few more days in which to complete the work of clearing mines from the approaches to the port. Nevertheless, even without there being supply ships unloading, Antwerp was already being targeted by German V-weapons, so it wasn't a place in which to linger unnecessarily.

The first two V2s had fallen on the city on 13 October, killing forty-two civilians, and on 16 November ten V-weapons had killed 263. Three weeks after our NAAFI stop, on 16 December, the Germans launched their Ardennes offensive, the so-called Battle of the Bulge, aimed at the city, and the main weight of V-bomb attacks was switched from London to Antwerp. In the afternoon of that same day a V2 rocket fell on the Rex Cinema in the Avenue de Keyser, killing 567 people, including 296 Allied Service personnel. When Antwerp became the major inflow point for Allied supplies, it remained a prime target for V1s and V2s. By March 1945 no less than 1200 V-weapons had fallen on the 65 square miles of Greater Antwerp, of which 150 V1s and 152 V2s actually hit the port area.

The first of those *Vergeltungswaffen*, Reprisal Weapons, had been used against London on 13 June, and the even larger and more expensive way of delivering a similar load of death, the V2, became operational in September 1944.

The V1 was simply a flying bomb, an unmanned aeroplane; some were launched from aircraft but the usual method was from concrete or steel ramps on the ground. After being aimed in the chosen direction by its launch ramp, the V1 was kept on course by a gyroscopic autopilot linked with a compass pre-set to the required bearing, the range being determined by a log actuated by a propeller in the bomb's nose. However, any manufacturing defect (such as slave-worker sabotage), deviation of the flying controls or unexpected wind change could put the bomb off course. In consequence, most of southern Holland and northern Belgium was at the mercy of 'strays' intended for more distant destinations, in addition to those actually targeted on the area.

V1s were variously sized between 20 and 30 feet in length, had a wing span of around 16 feet and a fuselage diameter of the order of 2.5 feet. The ram-jet engine, fitted on top of the fuselage, emitted an unmistakable 'tonk-tonk-tonk-tonk-tonk' noise as it ejected a pulsating comet's tail of fire from its single jet tube. Commonly known a 'buzz bombs' or 'doodle bugs', the V1s carried a warhead of one ton of high explosive, had a range of about 200 miles and flew at an altitude of some 2500 feet at a speed in excess of 400 mph. On one surprising occasion, through a momentary break in a blanket of cloud cover over 's Hertogenbosch, I saw a doodle bug easily overtake an unsuspecting Spitfire in full flight.

The fiery tails of flying bombs made them easy to spot in a clear sky by day or by night, but when it was cloudy or if confined indoors there was only the engine noise to reveal their presence. When the tonk-tonk-tonk-tonk of a V1's engine heralded its approach, time stood still for everyone within earshot, holding their breath and wondering where it was heading. If the engine noise began to die away, it had passed over and everyone breathed freely again, but if the tonk-tonk-tonk-tonk kept growing louder you were near its flight path. Your brain crossed its mental fingers, hoping that the devilish thing would keep on going. Should the engine noise stop abruptly, one ton of high explosive was plummeting earthwards and nothing could prevent it from impacting somewhere nearby. It was time to dive for whatever cover might be available, until the juddering blast of an explosion signalled another lucky escape.

In marked contrast, the V2 was a rocket bomb which impacted at a velocity of more than twice the speed of sound, so there was absolutely no warning of its approach. The first intimation of the arrival of a V2 was the explosion, which might be no more than a heavy 'Thump!' in the distance, but could be the building in which you happened to be being shaken to its foundations, or worse.

The V2 stood 46 feet high, had a mid-height diameter of some 5.5 feet, a take-off weight (made up largely of fuel) approaching 15 tons and had a range of 250 miles. The rocket's initial vertical take-off lifted it to about 12 miles above the earth's surface, when a radio signal turned it into its calculated trajectory. The rocket continued its arc of ascent to a height of about 70 miles, then tilted earthwards to impact within a mile or so of its pin-point target, so, on balance, it was probably the more accurate weapon. There was no preferred way of having one ton of death delivered and it was no consolation to know that, if one of them 'had your name on it', you would never be aware of the fact.

The place chosen for 'overnighting' the Unit was the small village of Hoogerheide, some twenty miles over the Belgian/Dutch border, where allocation of sleeping quarters was to be arranged with the local Burgomaster. For the night we three other ranks were given the rubble-strewn front room of a small, shell-blasted terrace house. The previous occupiers were safe, living with their next-door neighbours whose house was relatively undamaged. We were later invited in to share the warmth of the stove and pass a pleasant evening conversing in a mixture of English, Dutch, French and mime. One thing that seemed international was the instinctive hunching of shoulders and exchange of rueful glances at every nearby explosion.

When the main body of the Commando arrived next day we were able to direct them to the various empty buildings in which they would spend the night. Early on Sunday morning I re-joined the DRs and we began shepherding the convoy towards Middelburg, some forty miles away. It was a slow, cold business, most of our time being spent on the roadside directing the trucks along the right road. All went smoothly until, around noon, the convoy came to an unexpected halt outside Nieuwland, a small village some two miles short of our destination.

Hardly had the noise of our engines died away, however, than a dozen or more Dutch youngsters, brandishing wads of guilder notes, besieged the trucks, wanting to buy almost anything. With kit packed for the move, there was little immediately available for sale other than the cans of Compo carried for lunch and some bars of chocolate, but, at the prices being offered, many elected to go hungry for a while. Chocolate was *the* big sell. Two ounce (57 gramme) bars were snapped up at the going rate of 3 guilders, no less than thirty times their retail price in the UK. Over the next months civilians would be seen wearing a number of items of 'War Office issue' which had been put to new uses – blankets reappeared as overcoats, towels turned into blouses and innumerable sets of ladies' underwear were created from parachute silk.

The unexplained wait by the roadside became prolonged. Those who hadn't sold their lunch ate it, and still we waited. Then, from time to time, wavering trails of white smoke could be seen snaking high into the sky a few score miles to the north of us over occupied Holland and we realized that we were witnessing the initial ascent of V2 rockets. On a subsequent occasion, when V2s were being launched in the gathering dusk, bright flashes of light seen near the peak of their ascent were puzzling until it was realized that the rockets had been passing from the shadow of the earth to be momentarily illuminated by the sun, which had already set so far as our earthbound eyes were concerned.

On that Sunday afternoon outside Nieuwland the message

eventually trickled down to us that the unit we had come to relieve, the 4/5th Battalion Royal Scots Fusiliers, would not be moving out until next day and we would have to double up with them in their barns, garages and attics. Two Troops carried on to Middelburg and the Belgians moved into Arnemuiden, while HQ and the remaining three Troops stayed in the Nieuwland area. The Signals Despatch Office and Signal Section billets were located in a two-storey building at the corner of the main road to Middelburg, where the DRs were allocated a draughty attic as sleeping quarters, but at least it had a workable stove.

We were aware that the Commando's new job would be in general guard duties for the island and the provision of a mobile striking force. As all the islands in the Scheldt estuary, apart from Walcheren, were still in German hands, and North Beveland lay less than a mile distant, this was rather more than a perfunctory assignment. Brigade Headquarters had been set up in Goes, the main town of South Beveland, some twelve miles away.

When the RSFs had departed, a primitive form of electric lighting was installed by utilizing one of the Signal Section's petrol-driven battery-charging sets. However, it soon became possible to use the original lighting system when a nearby Searchlight Unit sent one of their men with a Lister diesel/electric generator to hook up to the mains electricity circuit.

During the following few days 'S' Troops moved to Middelburg and 'P' and 'Y' to Veere on the north-east coast of the island, vacating a nearby school, which became the HQ billet. The DRs were allocated one of the classrooms, which was quickly reorganized by extending the flue pipe of the stove and moving it into the centre of the room. We had inherited straw palliasses, then managed to ferret out some bedsteads and, with a table draped with a spare blanket, had a very passable barrack-room. Jackie Horsfield had come across a paint store and set to work emblazoning our names in red and gold on the wall above each of our beds.

In very marked contrast to these improved living quarters, our working life was becoming daily more unpleasant as the weather deteriorated. Unprotected faces were buffeted by snow or sleet and, with many of the roads under water, we were obliged to use unmade tracks and, within minutes of leaving the SDO, our lower legs would be soaked to the skin. In an effort to combat this I hunted around, found a sheet of aluminium, cut and bent it to shape, and fixed it between petrol tank and footrests as a mud splash. Preliminary trials indicated that it was a practical proposition, but before it could be given a 'field trial' we were moved to Middelburg, although the Signals Office remained in Nieuwland.

The new billet had a central location on the 'Canal through Walcheren', close to the Bailey bridge which replaced the one which had linked the town with the road to Flushing and Goes, demolished by the Germans. As at De Haan, the room had neither heating nor fireplace, so the rigmarole of finding a stove and poking a hole in the window for the flue pipe started again. We soon achieved warmth, but during my first short stay there the room was never completely free from smoke.

Next day I had the noon trip to 'P' Troop at Veere, barely five miles from the Signals Despatch Office, but at that time a completely isolated community. The flooding of the island had drowned the road to the town, which could only be reached by using an unpaved track. Arrival in Veere, after a solitary struggle against the elements through a bleak and empty landscape, seemed like reaching the end of the world. Troop Headquarters was in a stark, stone-faced building on a deserted quayside which seemed always to be lashed by stinging rain or sleet; Captain Sloley, the Troop Commander, was dubbed by his fellow officers 'The Hermit of Veere'.

On that December Friday in 1944 I didn't complete the journey. Nearing the end of the track, threading my way between water-filled potholes, I saw a jeep and trailer coming towards me at speed. It was travelling much too fast for the state of the road and the trailer was bouncing about like a mad thing, so I pulled off the track to let it pass. I obviously hadn't gone far enough, because the trailer dealt me and my bike a swingeing blow; I landed in the mud, moaning involuntarily from the pain in my left shoulder, while the trailer ended upside down with its wheels describing ineffectual circles in the air. It was a jeep of the Dutch Grenzwacht, frontier guards, who bundled me inside, righting the trailer, heaved my motorbike aboard, new mudsplash crumpled out of all recognition, and took me to Middelburg.

The Medical Officer didn't think that there was very much

wrong with me, but when I reported back next day, after a sleepless night with a shoulder that was still as painful as ever, he decided to send me to hospital for an X-ray. Transport was laid on to take me to No. 82 CRS (Casualty Receiving Station), set up in a school in Goes (without empty school buildings it is doubtful whether wars could be fought at all!) but it was too late to be examined that day. The shoulder was inspected next morning and arrangements were made to transfer me to No. 9 BGH (British General Hospital), in the centre of Antwerp, for X-ray.

Arrival there on Sunday evening was again too late to be seen by a doctor, but in good time for the nightly session of V-weapon attacks, which could be guaranteed to divert a mind from lesser personal problems. All too often the menacing tonk-tonk-tonk-tonk of a flying bomb could be heard, while spasmodic violent explosions and dull thumps told of either V1s or V2s impacting in the City area. On more than one occasion the entire hospital shuddered to its foundations. That was Sunday, 17 December 1944, the day following the launch of Von Rundstedt's 'last fling' Ardennes offensive, and only the previous day the Rex cinema had been hit, with the heavy loss of life mentioned earlier.

Next morning a lady doctor examined the shoulder; she seemed satisfied that there was no dislocation, although no X-ray was taken to verify this. I remained confined to bed, with nothing more than regular checks of pulse rate and temperature by two young Belgian nurses, until Wednesday afternoon. Then, after an abrupt transfer, I found myself in bed in the British General Hospital in Duffel (the town which gave its name to the Royal Navy's bridge coat) some ten miles away.

At that time I was totally unaware of the strategic implications of the German offensive, so didn't appreciate that I had been moved ten miles down the line of their planned attack. In any case, with a score or more V1s per day coming within earshot, Duffel was not an ideal place in which to be confined to a hospital bed. Like the clock inside the crocodile in *Peter Pan*, V1s gave warning of their approach, but nothing could be done about it, except to put your head under the pillow if the engine cut out.

On 21 December, six days after the event, an X-ray finally confirmed that all my pain had been arising from no more than 'a contusion'. By that time too, on a wider scale, it had become clear that the Germans had caught the Americans completely off-guard and advances of up to 50 miles had been made. General Montgomery had been given command of all British and American troops in the sector to stabilize the situation. The American 101st Airborne Division, cut off at Bastogne, was completely surrounded for a week and had to be supplied from the air. This occasion attracted public attention by US General McAuliffe's single-worded reply when called upon to surrender – 'Nuts!' For many years after the war the Military Museum at Bastogne went under the name of The 'Nuts' Museum.

With confirmation of the contusion, I became an 'up-patient' (which meant a hospital dogsbody, taking meals to bed patients, etc) but had to report to the gym twice a day to exercise the shoulder, which was still unpleasantly painful. By that time I felt sure that there was no chance of rejoining the Commando before Christmas, but consoled myself with the feeling that Christmas dinner in hospital could very well be better than anything to be found in a box of Compo rations.

On Christmas Eve, as the hospital was settling down for the night, from the corridor outside the ward came the sound of voices singing a Christmas Carol. It grew louder as the singers drew near; then, as they filed into the ward, we saw that they were carolers with a very sad difference. It was a mixed choir of all ages, but with one thing in common – they were all amputees. Some were on crutches, some had parts of two limbs missing; all were civilian war casualties. They stayed in the ward to sing another carol, then distributed hand-made Christmas cards, courtesy of the Belgian Red Cross; I still have mine.

The Christmas Dinner fully measured-up to expectations. A meal of chicken and pork was undoubtedly much better fare than most troops in NW Europe would have been getting that day and few civilians in meat-rationed Britain could have enjoyed a comparable meal. It is a long-standing tradition in the British Armed Forces that, on Christmas Day, commissioned officers serve the meal to the other ranks and this was faithfully observed on that occasion. What was far 'over and above' tradition was the barrage of popping corks as bottles of champagne were opened for the Loyal Toast! No doubt that luxury came under the heading of 'spoils of war' and, despite being drunk from enamel mugs rather than fine glassware, the toast of 'The King' was none the less sincere!

After the celebration of Christmas, hospital life seemed even more restrictive. The shoulder was by now almost pain-free; my only wish was to escape, but, despite being officially discharged on the Friday, it was early Monday Morning, New Year's Day 1945, before transport arrived from Brigade HQ to return Commando personnel to their Units.

It was a bright, frosty morning, with a slight overcast and, something which hadn't been seen since beachhead days, German aircraft scooting about the sky. The German Ardennes offensive had coincided with a period of cloud and low visibility, which had greatly assisted the Luftwaffe in avoiding the attention of Allied fighters. On top of this, early morning mists over the more southerly German airfields had cleared long before Allied planes in England were able to take off, giving the enemy pilots a head start before Allied fighters could be brought into action.

The air activity on 1 January 1945, however, wasn't in support of the ground troops, as the German thrust had been halted on Christmas Day. It had been a 'last fling' of air attacks on forward Allied airfields in France, Holland and Belgium, in which, the Germans claimed, 400 out of a total of 579 Allied aircraft destroyed that day were caught on the ground. At Brussels' Zaventem aerodrome alone losses on the ground amounted to 180 aircraft, including Monty's own Dakota. The Allies' counter-claim was that, of 500 German planes which had taken part in the attacks, 364 were destroyed.

Back in Middelburg, I found that the smoking stove problem had been solved, but the major 'welcome home' news was of the intro-duction of a Home Leave Ballot. Everyone with six months' service in the War Zone had become entitled to seven days' leave, albeit in dribs and drabs. The names of all those so entitled had been 'put in the hat' and the first to be drawn had already left; my name had been drawn for the beginning of February, four weeks ahead.

For those with surplus Dutch currency, acquired during the Walcheren operation or from selling NAAFI rations, etc, the link with the UK created by this leave system proved to be an added blessing. Their money was only of real value if it could be converted into sterling and it soon became common knowledge that the currency exchange offices at the Channel Transit Camps weren't concerned with the amount nor the source of the money they changed. With men going back to the UK on a regular basis, an efficient 'courier service' was now available.

The New Year of 1945 brought a snowy freeze-up which rapidly transformed flooded Walcheren, and the rest of Holland, into a white winter wonderland, but made living conditions for front-line troops so much the worse. Despatch Riding became a cold and hazardous occupation, so jeeps were made available for longer trips; four wheels and four-wheel drive kept us moving, but the vehicles did little so far as warmth was concerned. The wartime models were open to the elements, apart from the windscreen and a flimsy canvas rear cover and, notwithstanding an issue of sleeve-less sheepskin jackets donated by individual benefactors in South Africa, conditions were quite bleak. In addition, with a manually-operated windscreen wiper, one hand had to relinquish the steering wheel every time the screen became obscured by rain or snow, which could be a tricky business on ice-bound roads.

Nevertheless, the four-wheel drive and slick manoeuvrability of the Willys World War Two Jeep were qualities much appreciated by friend and foe alike. In Normandy we came across some, abandoned at the time of Dunkirk, which had been 'upgraded' for use by German officers, with the sides fully boxed-in, fitted with doors and the canvas of the seats re-covered with luxurious padded upholstery.

During the second week of January rumours about 'moving up' began to circulate and, on the 18th, the Despatch Riders shepherded a long string of vehicles away from Walcheren. After negotiating the completely deserted thirty miles of road along the South Beveland peninsula, the convoy turned left and, a few miles later, halted in Bergen op Zoom. 41 was to take over a sector of the Maas River front from 47 Royal Marines Commando.

Chapter 13

THE MAAS RIVER FRONT

In Bergen op Zoom, as in Deal some twelve months previously, the bulk of the Commando was housed in a barracks. It was an extensive, single-storeyed timber structure, built in the form of a large open square, and housed a multiplicity of barrack rooms, ablutions, cook-houses, messrooms, recreation rooms, offices and stores. A particularly welcome feature, in view of the wintry weather, was that it was well-provided with efficient solid fuel stoves and the complex was comfortably warm throughout.

Although some of the Troop Offices were now under the same roof as the Signals Despatch Office and a number of the DRs' 'trips' were reduced to no more than indoor walks, the greater part of our time was still spent on ice-bound roads. Offices in the vicinity of Bergen had to be visited by motorcycle, but, with Brigade HQ still in Goes and a number of other formations located between Bergen and Tilburg some forty miles away, round trips of 50–80 miles by jeep were not uncommon. These longer journeys were, inevitably, cold and lonely affairs, relieved only by tea and buns at any NAAFI/EFI canteens found en route.

The Commando's Operational Instructions in Bergen op Zoom were to be ready to move in support of No. 4 Special Service Brigade in Beveland, or of No. 1 Polish Armoured Regiment in the Tholen/Sint Philipsland area, and also to plan and execute raids across to the north bank of the Maas. Each Troop, therefore, had to familiarize itself with an allotted section of the river, between the island of Schouwen in the Scheldt Estuary and Geertruidenberg, a stretch of no less than thirty miles.

In addition to giving the Commando a more active role in the war, the move to Bergen had put it squarely on the V1 routes to Antwerp and more distant targets. On the day of our arrival six of them fell into the Scheldt near the town and that set the pattern. By day and by night the sound of doodlebug engines became commonplace and on too many occasions an engine would cut out close enough to freeze all movement until the thing had exploded. By day they could be seen passing over or heading earthwards and by night their routes were marked by their fiery tails. On solo drives along the deserted road to Goes it wasn't uncommon to see a doodlebug heading in the same general direction and, more than once, the engine stopped and the bomb crashed to earth in a blast of smoke and debris in a field, or as a spout of sand and seawater in the shallows of the East Scheldt.

Four days after the Commando's arrival in Bergen Captain Stevens of 'A' Troop led a raiding party across the river with the object of bringing back a prisoner from a known German position. The party, comprising two officers, sixteen men and a Dutch guide, started off from Drimmeln harbour in two assault boats at 0245 hrs. Impeded by the adverse current, however, and by having to laboriously break a passage through ice in order to reach the north bank, it took them an hour and a half to cover a distance of no more than 1200 yards. Then, once ashore, it was found impossible to move quietly across the icy marshlands of frozen reeds and willows.

Nevertheless, the patrol pressed on, cutting trip wires encountered en route, and they also cut a way through the double apron fence found to be protecting the German position. The first four men had passed through the gap when flares illuminated the area, two machine guns opened fire and grenades began bursting amongst them. Captain Stevens who, along with the Dutch guide and one of the Marines, had been wounded by this fire, ordered a withdrawal to a position nearer the river.

The patrol pulled back under mortar and machine-gun fire, but when they had re-grouped it was found that the wounded Marine was no longer with them. It was then 0550 hrs and, with two men remaining behind to wait for the wounded man, the others returned to the 'firm base' by the boats at the river's edge. At 0630, the wounded man not having shown up, the patrol started back across the Maas and, helped by the current this time, were back in Drimmeln harbour by 0705 hrs. On learning of the impossibility of moving quietly over frozen ground, the Corps Commander immediately issued instructions that there should be no further raids until after the thaw.

On Sunday 28 January Lieutenant Colonel P.C.W. Hellings RM took over as Commanding Officer and Lieutenant Colonel Palmer returned to the UK. The very next morning the unit was placed under the command of 10 Canadian Infantry Brigade and given 'immediate' orders to join them somewhere beyond Geertruidenberg, about 35 miles further up the Maas. The entire barracks was immediately enveloped in a frenzy of packing kit and stores. As Corporal Angel, the NCO-in-Charge of Despatch Riders, was on UK leave, I was detailed off to take two other DRs and accompany the Unit road convoy when it left that afternoon. All jeeps would be needed to transport personnel and stores, so we would have to use our motorcycles.

After lunch, with all my kit packed and stowed in a Signals truck, I went off on a final duty trip around the Bergen area. Returning in late afternoon, I was concentrating on keeping control of the Matchless 350, slipping and slithering on the icy road; consequently it wasn't until turning to enter the main gate that I noticed smoke and flames arising from the barracks. Propping my bike against the outer railings, I ran forward to see what was happening. A corner of the wooden building was already well alight; men were hurling kit, boxes of ammunition and stores out of windows on to the snow and others were humping them away; more men were rigging up hoses to fight the flames.

As I drew near, there came an urgent shout from Jan Maley, 'Hey, Mitch! – over here quick – *the petrol!!*' Flames were licking perilously close to our stock of 40-gallon drums of fuel, standing on end close to the building, and I spent a frantic few minutes helping to topple them on their side and roll them out of harm's way. That accomplished, I joined a chain of men passing stores, hand-to-hand, away from the building, until called upon to get hold of a hosepipe.

By that time the fire was gaining strength and had reached some remnants of ammunition still inside the building. The crackling of the flames was now punctuated by staccato bursts of exploding small arms cartridges and the intermittent thumps of hand-grenades. As we played hoses on the flames, an icy wind blew back the lesser droplets of water which, despite the heat of the fire, froze into a film of ice on the revers of our sheepskin jackets. Before long it was decided that nothing we could do was going to save the barracks. The fire had eaten its way over the main gateway and was rapidly and relentlessly consuming the timber structure in two directions; the order was given to 'Let it burn!'. In the failing daylight we began to collect a miscellany of articles strewn far and wide over the snow.

Fortunately the loading had been going on since morning and all the Unit's weapons as well as the bulk of its ammunition and supplies were already packed on the vehicles lined up on the road outside. In the gathering darkness of a bitingly cold winter's evening, wet and dirty Marines boarded their vehicles. Rather later than expected, the convoy moved off towards the front, leaving the barracks, which had been our home for only ten days, no more than a glowing square of red-hot ashes.

The three DRs conducted the string of vehicles from the barracks, through the town and on to the Breda road at the start of their journey into the night. By that time, however, we were all riding behind 'Tail-end Charlie', the last truck in the convoy. Normally we would have been working our way up to the head of the column again, but, as things were, that was manifestly impossible. In the darkness, without any lights, and all drivers 'hogging' the crown of a narrow road, slithering on the hard-packed snow, any attempt to overtake would have been foolhardy in the extreme. Even continuing to tag along behind the trucks, on a barely visible icy road, was to risk broken legs or worse. I decided that it was impossible to carry on and, after telling the men on the last truck what I was doing, led the DRs back to Bergen.

I knew that the Rear Party had been accommodated in one of the town's hotels, so made my way there to report to the Officer-in-Charge. He was, with the handful of others, in a bright, warm, basement kitchen, the complete antithesis of the freezing darkness outside. My explanation of the reason for our return was accepted without question and we were allocated an area of the kitchen floor on which to pass the night. Civilian cooks were busy preparing a meal, obviously for the Rear Party, but we weren't included.

Next morning a jeep was made available to enable us to re-join the Main Body and (as OC DRs!) I elected to drive. By daylight there was a vastly different world outside. It was still freezing cold, but, instead of the blackness of the previous night, there was bright sunlight with a light morning mist, and the white, slippery road to Breda was now carrying a continuous flood of military traffic. The mist soon produced a coating of ice on the windscreen and it had to be swung up out of the way to enable me to see where we were going. As to our intended destination, all the information available was that the Commando would be 'near the Maas, beyond Oosterhout and east of Geertruidenberg', and on reaching that area we would have to make enquiries.

At Breda, after a 'stand easy' interlude at a NAAFI canteen, we had to turn off the road to Tilburg where, presumably, all the other vehicles were heading, and head for Oosterhout and the River Maas. From that point we were completely alone, travelling along a deserted road through a bleak white wilderness, relieved only by fences, hedgerows and leafless tress. Before long the unmistakable 'whoomps' of artillery fire confirmed that we were indeed heading in the right direction.

A few miles beyond Breda we entered Oosterhout and for a short while made contact with the human race again. The drive along the main street of the small town, white under a blanket of snow, was rather like passing a series of Christmas card scenes. Cafés were brightly lit with their doors open and muffled-up figures moved about the streets or warmed themselves at bonfires crackling cheerfully on open spaces. The fact that virtually all the figures were British or Canadian military personnel, whose guns and vehicles littered the streets, didn't destroy the illusion.

We didn't stop and were soon back in the barren whiteness beyond. I drove slowly and cautiously for mile after mile, eyes searching for some sign of life, or where some might be found, with the sound of the guns growing louder. Eventually we spotted a small sign at the roadside, bearing the name of a Canadian Artillery Unit and an arrow pointing up a narrow track. In a few hundred yards it led us to a farmyard crammed with trucks and jeeps, while the abutting buildings bustled with Headquarters Staff. On reporting to the Orderly Room the Duty Officer had no hesitation in saying, '41 Commando HQ? They're in Waspik. I'll give you a guide'. He immediately summoned a stumpy, roly-poly sort of Canadian private to show us the way. The Canuck led us back to the farmyard, grinned a cheerful 'Just follow me, Bub!' as he hopped into a jeep and shot out of the farmyard as though it was a Le Mans start.

There had been no opportunity to explain that I was something of a novice driver, but to be left behind would have been a sad reflection upon the British, so I too had to put my foot down. The freezing cold soon became a thing of the past. I sweated profusely as we slid along narrow ribbons of ice between menacingly deep roadside ditches, slithered round ninety degree bends and jolted over rough, crunchy snow. Eventually we arrived in a small town, where my escort skidded to a brief halt. He indicated the adjacent building with his thumb, gave a typical North American 'See you!' salute, executed a rapid three-point turn and disappeared in the direction from whence we had come before there was time to say 'Thank you'.

Commando HQ in Waspik had been established in the Gemeentehuis, the local council offices. The standard architectural pattern for such buildings was for the main entrance to be about five feet above pavement level, approached from both sides by flights of balustraded stone steps. Probably this was to provide a podium from which the Burgomaster could make public announcements. At Waspik directly below the main entrance was the doorway to a cellar which, I found, was 'home' for the HQ Signallers.

The cellar had obviously been a storeroom for the Town Engineer, as signboards bearing the name WASPIK, red warning lamps, picks, shovels, coils of rope, etc, had been heaped to one side to clear part of the cobblestone floor. This had been covered with straw to provide a communal sleeping area for about fifteen men, and the 'kitchen', a roaring pressure stove sited near the doorway, made it a haven of warmth. I reported to the Signals Officer, who was quite happy with my explanation of our late arrival and about receiving one jeep instead of three motorcycles.

On the previous evening lack of visibility and road conditions had kept the speed of the convoy down to little more than walking pace and it had been almost 2300 hrs before they reached Waspik. After that it took a further two and a half hours for men of the Fighting Troops to take over the forward positions. It was probably as well that they had been unaware of the Despatch Riders sleeping in the hotel kitchen in Bergen!

The reason for the Commando's precipitate departure from Bergen op Zoom had now been made known. 41 was needed by 10 Canadian Brigade to secure their flank for an attack upon a stubborn German position on an island between two arms of the River Maas. The roughly diamond-shaped island, some five miles long and one and a half wide, lies between the main river, the Bergsche Maas, and the more southerly, and narrower, Oude Maasje (little old Maas), one and a half miles north of Waspik. The island was known to Allied troops as 'Capelsche Veer' but 'veer' is the Dutch word for 'ferry' and that name relates to the ferry which, in peacetime, crossed the Bergsche Maas just beyond the point where the Oude Maasje joins the main river, on the line of the road leading north from Capelle, two miles east of Waspik.

For some time the Canadians had been trying to eliminate the German garrison of the island in order to regularize the Allied front along the line of the main river. Only two weeks earlier 47 RM Commando had almost managed the job, but, badly outnumbered and suffering heavy casualties, just couldn't make it. They had, however, confined the Germans to the eastern end of the island and 10 Canadian Brigade were engaged in completing the job.

Preliminary infantry attacks had started on 26 January while Engineers went ahead with building a bridge across the Oude Maasje. During the night of the 29th, when 41 was moving in, the Canadians built up a tank force on the island and, next evening, the day the DRs reached Waspik, they attacked the German positions once more. Two battalions of Canadians, the Argyll and Sutherland Highlanders and the Lincoln and Welland Regiment, supported by tanks of the South Alberta Regiment, were involved. It took most of the night, but by dawn on the 31st the island had been cleared, leaving 145 Germans lying dead and sixty-nine taken prisoner, the rest having escaped across the main river. After the capture of the island, 41 Commando was given the job of holding on to it.

That action had coincided with the thaw, but this proved a mixed blessing for the troops in forward positions, adding the problems of mud to those of ice and snow. Those of us back in the Gemeentehuis cellar were thankful that we could pass our nights, apart from spells of guard duty and the inevitable dawn stand-to, in our cellar with nothing to disturb us apart from the sounds of distant gunfire. On that occasion I had only two such nights as, on 1 February, it was my turn for Home Leave!

Late in the afternoon a truck deposited the leave party, washed, shaved and wearing best battle dress, at the Antwerp railway station. It was some hours too early for the 2030 hrs 'Blighty Express' for Calais, so there was ample time for a meal in the station canteen, then to wander into town for a few beers. By the time we were settled down with our glass of rather fizzy Belgian brew the city's nightly session of V-weapon attacks had begun and our minds became a turmoil of unpleasant thoughts. What could be worse than 'catching a packet' with a leave chit in your pocket, just waiting for the train to take you home?

We sat with eyes continually drawn towards the clock behind the bar as random explosions shook the city. Each time a V1 engine cut out I was probably not alone in offering up the silent prayer of 'Please come down somewhere else, I'm going on leave'. With still an hour or more before train time a crashing explosion shook the whole building, all the windows rattled and the swing doors squeaked open. A phlegmatic Scot at a nearby table, who was obviously one of those unfortunate souls for whom Antwerp was 'home', looked towards us and explained, succinctly, 'Vee-ee Too-oo'. We decided to get back to the station, in the vain hope that the train might leave early.

We pulled out on time, but, on bare wooden seats, in an unheated compartment and with one window completely missing, it wasn't a pleasant journey. It was also inordinately slow; the journey of 120 miles took ten and a half hours. At 0700 next morning, cold, stiff and hungry, we stumbled across numerous rail tracks into the vast Calais Transit Camp to tag on to the end of a succession of seemingly endless queues for breakfast, document checking and changing guilders into sterling.

Hopes of a ship that day lingered on until late afternoon. Then we were given shore leave until 2200 hrs and told that our ship would sail at 0600 next morning, Saturday 3 February. A hurried black market currency deal was necessary to provide French francs to ensure an enjoyable run ashore. It was bleak and shivery next morning, but the trooper left on time and eight hours later docked at Harwich. By 1500 hrs a 'Leave Special' was steaming towards Newcastle 'and all points north'. We gazed rapturously out of the windows, drinking in every detail of the bare winter landscape – not much more than innumerable hedges, gaunt trees and ordinary houses, towns and villages, but it was 'Blighty'! Only when fading daylight made it fruitless to strain the eyes further did we settle down to sleep or to play cards, using English money for a change.

It was just half an hour short of midnight by the time the familiar arch of the Tyne Bridge, then a moon-glint on the river far below, confirmed that this was indeed 'home'. A few minutes later the fuggy carriages were disgorging streams of sleepy, shivering uniformed Geordies onto platform eight of Newcastle Central Station. We waved cheerio to our Scottish pals, who had still more hours of travel ahead of them, then rushed outside to see if the tramcars were still running.

That leave followed the normal pattern of wartime visits home – luxuriating in hot baths, stoking up on home cooking, undressing and changing into pyjamas then curling up between white sheets in a real bed. Predictably, almost without exception, immediately after a first greeting, people would ask, '. . . and when do you go back?' I'm sure that I wasn't the only one who felt like thumping some of them.

Home leave in wartime was subject to the vagaries of travel and, in particular, the state of the sea in the English Channel. Our leave entitlement was 'seven days at home' and, on arrival in the UK, everyone received a chit bearing a 'Leave Party Number' and the date, time and port to which he was required to report for the return crossing. As the day of return drew near, all service personnel on leave from the continent would pay particular attention to weather forecasts and news bulletins on the radio. Storms in the Channel would raise the hopes of tens of thousands of men and women, all waiting to hear, 'The following Leave Parties will report to their embarkation ports twenty-four (or maybe even more) hours later than shown on their leave chits . . .'

On that occasion I was fortunate in getting a forty-eight hour extension, so it wasn't until the early hours of Shrove Tuesday, 13 February, that I was back in the dark, cold, almost-deserted Newcastle Central station to catch the 0230 train to Harwich, where we arrived around noon. The next sailing wasn't until 0100 next morning and I passed the crossing with no more accommodation than a steel deck, made a little more bearable by occasional sips from a half bottle of whisky which my father had somehow managed to obtain as a 'going back present'. The crossing took ten hours, then came another wait in Calais for the 2230 train which deposited us at Antwerp railway station at 0930 the following morning.

Congregated outside the office of the RTO (Railway Transport Officer) were six or seven men of 41 Commando all needing to get back to Waspik, and we obtained permission to try hitch-hiking, rather than waiting around indefinitely for a truck from the Unit. We found an Army driver heading for Bergen op Zoom who took us to our Brigade Rear Echelon there and they arranged onward transport to Waspik. By 1800 hrs I was back in the cellar from which I had departed fourteen days earlier to go on seven days' leave. With the best part of half a bottle of Scotch to pass around for 'sippers', I was made very welcome.

During my absence the Waspik sector of the Maas River front had been generally quiet, with little more than the spasmodic exchange of shelling, mortaring and machine-gunning across the river. The Fighting Troops had continued to take turns in occupying the forward positions on the island of Capelsche Veer and there had been a few patrols across the main river, the Bergsche Maas, to check on enemy positions. A few days after I went on leave three men were crossing the Oude Maasje to the island when their boat capsized. Two were immediately swept away and drowned and, although the third was pulled from the water, he failed to revive after two hours' artificial respiration. In a very much lighter vein, one cross-river patrol, charged with finding out whether a particular German position was occupied, had reported in the affirmative, adding a rider to the effect that 'it was also established that at least one man of the Unit holding the north bank of the Maas is called Wilhelm.'

On the night of my return from leave 'B' Troop mounted Operation 'HUSSAR', a crossing to the north bank of the river, with a view to capturing a prisoner for interrogation. They landed without incident, but, when moving towards their objective, came under heavy enemy fire which inflicted a number of casualties and forced the Patrol Commander to order a withdrawal. One officer and one Other Rank, both badly wounded, had to be left behind. Two nights later Operation 'HUSSAR II', another 'prisoner snatch', was mounted by 'X' Troop, under Captain Cunningham.

The patrol crossed the river in two LCAs, touching down on the north bank just before midnight. After a five-minute softening-up barrage by medium artillery and mortars, followed by close-in fire from five Brens raking the top of the dyke, they stormed up. On reaching the top, the first party came upon seven or eight of the enemy running towards their stand-to trenches. They opened fire with TSMGs at 5 yards range and, as the Patrol Report records laconically, 'all went down'. The second party saw four Germans running towards their positions and opened fire with a Bren at 30 yards range; 'two went down'. Then a German was found crouching in a trench and, having 'bagged' their prisoner, the Patrol withdrew. It was all over in fifteen minutes, with eight or ten Germans having been killed or wounded and one taken prisoner, with no casualties to our men.

The prisoner was a Franz Neuhauser, an Austrian by birth, who had celebrated his eighteenth birthday only three weeks previously. Under interrogation he volunteered much more information than just his own 'name, rank and number', giving the names of his Section, Troop, Company, Battalion and Regimental Commanders. He also revealed that Lieutenant Bate, the Officer reported missing on the previous HUSSAR raid, had been found badly wounded and evacuated to hospital, but the man, Corporal Joe McKenna, had been dead when found, and was buried with Military Honours at Hank. It was learned later that the officer, Lieutenant Bate, a young volunteer from the South African Union Defence Force, died of his wounds; both he and Joe McKenna are now buried in Werkendam Protestant Cemetery.

That successful attack was a fitting finale to the Commando's tenure of the Waspik Sector of the Maas Front. Later that same day Commando Advance Parties reconnoitred fresh positions to be taken over some fifteen miles further up river. On 19 February the Unit pulled out of Waspik and moved to 's Hertogenbosch, there to take over a sector of river from the Canadian Lake Superior Regiment. Since going on UK leave, almost three weeks previously, the snow had practically disappeared and the Despatch Riders were back in the saddle again.

At that late stage of the war Allied Armies were moving forward on most fronts. The 'Ardennes Bulge' had been nipped out by the end of January and, during the first days of February US troops had cleared the last occupied areas of Belgium. In Holland things had begun moving again on 8 February, when the Canadian First Army launched an attack SE of Nijmegen, crossing the German frontier through the Reichswald and striking towards Kleve and Goch. This, the nearest offensive activity to 41 Commando's position, was some thirty miles to the east of us; on the Maas the front remained static.

At 's Hertogenbosch the Commando was given responsibility for about eight miles of the river between Bokhoven and Het Gewande so, with less than four hundred men to deploy, a continuous defensive line was out of the question. The tactics adopted, therefore, were to have three Troops 'up', manning secure front line positions and observation posts on the river bank, and covering the gaps with minefields, booby traps and patrols. The 'up' Troops were based in the almost deserted villages of Bokhoven, Crevecoeur and Empel, while the other two Troops were held 'back' in nearby Voordijk and Orten, ready to provide assistance, if required. 'S' Troop, was centrally located at Engelen where their mortars and machine guns could provide support in both directions, while further firing positions were prepared and ammunitioned, so that their weapons could be rapidly redeployed there, ready for immediate use.

Commando Headquarters was set up in 's Hertogenbosch ('Bois le Duc' or 'Duke's Wood'), a town of some 60,000 inhabitants lying less than three miles from the river. The various offices were located in vacant houses on the northern fringes of the town, while most HQ personnel were billeted with Dutch families. Unlike 'civvy billets' in the UK, however, this was on an accommodation only basis, all food being issued from Section cookhouses. Initially we took our food back to the billet to eat, but the ordeal of having every bite followed by the envious eyes of young Dutch children, who seemed to exist on sugared bread and vegetables, proved too much. Thereafter we ate our meals standing around the hydro burners in the 'cookhouse', an empty private garage where the tins of compo were heated, until a messroom was organized. Any food that was surplus, or could be scrounged, was gratefully received in the billets.

Every day would see some kind of harassing activity somewhere along our river frontage. Most fixed German positions had been pinpointed and some of these would be engaged by the Commando's mortars or machine guns, or, on occasions, HQ would ask for supporting artillery to carry out shoots on specific targets. Then, from time to time, a squadron of tanks would roll within range to do a shoot of their own. The Germans had similar patterns of harassment, so Despatch Riders delivering messages around the Troop positions or to nearby units could suddenly find themselves involved in a 'hate session'.

The Commando's immediate artillery support was provided by a Polish Field Battery, to whom we delivered frequent messages. These, no doubt, gave map references, times, rates of fire, etc, for the employment of their guns, so presumably someone in their HQ was able to read them! Personally, I never came across anyone who spoke more than one or two words of English, although even that was much more than my command of Polish.

In addition to these long-range exchanges, both sides engaged in patrol activity into the other's territory to check whether known positions were still occupied, to determine if routes for future planned incursions had been mined, or just to see if the enemy was on his toes. The Commando had been in its new location for about a week when orders were received to plan two more 'Prisoner Snatching' Patrols to be code-named MOUSETRAP and FLYCATCHER.

Reconnaissance Patrols for both operations were successfully carried out during the night of 2 March and MOUSETRAP was put in motion two nights later. During the crossing one of the assault boats was found to have sprung a leak and it sank some ten yards from the enemy shore, but there was no loss of men or equipment and the Patrol carried on. Moving up the dyke face towards the German position, however, mines were encountered which had not been there at the time of the reconnaissance and the Patrol Commander was wounded. Surprise having been lost, he ordered a withdrawal and the one serviceable assault boat managed to make two crossings to bring all men back. Next evening a Patrol went across to bring back one of the mines, which confirmed that they were, indeed, 'Schuh' anti-personnel.

FLYCATCHER went ahead on 10 March. 'A' Troop crossed the Maas in two LCAs and, after some softening-up artillery fire on an area known to be held by German troops, moved along the dyke. They used the standard 'Trench clearing drill' of throwing a hand grenade into a bunker position, then following it up with bursts of TSMG fire. After seven or eight positions had drawn blank, they were rewarded with a cry of pain and dragged out a wounded German – mission accomplished. On their return one Marine was reported missing, but he later swam across; there were no British casualties.

The NOIC (Naval Officer-in-Charge) of landing craft on that stretch of the River Maas, Lieutenant R.O.S. Salmon RNVR, was something of an extrovert. In his opinion, taking his craft across the river constituted a formal occasion, so he opted to wear a top hat and white gloves. He also considered that it was correct to leave a 'visiting card', so he had prepared a notice board which was erected on the north bank, proclaiming, in German, that the 'Rosstiny Taxi Service' was offering trips to England for enemy personnel at – Wehrmacht (Army) 2 Marks and Volksstürm (Home Guard) 1 Mark. It ended with the words 'Look out for the top hat' and was 'signed' with a drawing of one.

The German prisoner was *Oberwachtmeister* Georg Fickenster, who had suffered wounds in the arm and the thigh. He was interrogated in hospital soon after capture and, not unnaturally, as the interrogation report put it, 'he found concentration extremely difficult'! Only after being assured several times that there were no other Germans present did he agree to talk, and then he said that he was 31 years old, came from Frankfurt am Main and that his Unit was 3 Coy of 1 SS Polizei, but he stressed that he was no Storm-trooper. He had been given only two months' infantry training and, like all the others of his unit, considered himself to be a policeman, not a soldier. He gave information about his Company's arms and equipment, communications system, ration deliveries, etc, and alleged that the Commanding Officer spent most of his time in a cellar under Company HQ.

It wasn't only the Germans who took shelter in cellars, of course; the civilians in 's Hertogenbosch made good use of all that were available. Lying, as it did, so close to the front line, the town suffered frequent shelling by German artillery, which caused numerous casualties. The Signals Despatch Office had been set up in the front room of an empty house on the main road leading out of town and in the direction of a nearby cemetery. Frequently, whilst awaiting the next despatch, a funeral cortège would pass the window, and most of them were much more macabre affairs than in the UK. The horse-drawn hearse was virtually a glass-walled tank, with the ornately carved wooden framing painted in sombre black, but with each corner post surmounted with a grinning white skull!

As well as the civilians, the Commando was also suffering casualties, but more often from mortar bombs machine-gun fire and snipers, rather than artillery, although we also had one man killed when he trod on one of our own mines. An open-sided outhouse at the rear of the HQ building was used as a mortuary. It was a sobering experience, going out on a trip, to pass another blanket-shrouded figure awaiting burial, and particularly poignant when you had known the dead man, as was the case when one of our Signallers had been killed on the Maas the previous evening.

Despatch Riders were part of the Signals Section of the Commando and one of our jobs was to undertake spells of duty at the 'Advance Signals Post'. This had been set up in a house, one of a long terrace at the extreme northern edge of the town, which had an unimpeded outlook over the flat countryside stretching towards the river and far beyond. That was the direction in which we would look expectantly for the first morning flight of V1 flying bombs, launched from ramps far to the north in German-occupied Holland.

The show would start just before the sun began to put any brightness into the sky, when a number of small orange-red lights appeared above the horizon. Then, as they gradually increased in size, it could be distinguished that the lights were propelling black blobs through the dawn sky. Soon the tonk-tonk-tonk-tonk-tonk noise of engines would reach us and it became possible to discern the double-barrelled shape of the missile – an aircraft fuselage forming the bomb body and the ram jet engine perched on top.

190

It was commonplace to see a dozen or more 'buzz bombs' in flight at the same time, ranging far and wide across the morning sky, but we could watch them in safety, knowing that they were heading further afield, for Antwerp or London. Only rarely did we see a 'maverick' bomb drop out of the sky and never very close.

Another 'once in a lifetime' spectacle, during our stay in 's Hertogenboscsh, was to see the roads of southern Holland carrying many more boats than the rivers and canals! The British and Canadian armies were building up for an assault across the Rhine and appeared to be transporting anything and everything that would float through Holland into Germany. Canvas boats, pontoon floats, motor boats and infantry landing craft of all descriptions were travelling piggy-back on every kind of military vehicle capable of bearing the load. Huge tank transporters, massive enough to carry the biggest and heaviest of tanks, were dwarfed by large steamers strapped to their backs. To manoeuvre such loads through the tortuous narrow streets of Dutch towns, especially around sharp corners, took much time, patience and effort, leaving more than one scraped building to mark their passage.

A week after the FLYCATCHER raid it looked as though 41 Commando was all set to be relieved by 48 Royal Marines Commando and moved back to South Beveland. Advance Parties left to reconnoitre billets in Goes, the capital of the province; then, abruptly, the move was cancelled. That same day we suffered three casualties during a German mortar attack on Crevecoeur, which sparked off a prolonged 'hate sessions' by both sides. Typhoon aircraft attacked the Germans in Ammersooien, a town a mile or so from the river, and in turn the enemy moved a battery of guns into Hedel and proceeded to shell Crevecoeur. Cross-river activity remained at a high level during the next day when one Troop of 48 Commando joined 41 to take over 'A' Troop's positions, seeming to confirm that they would soon be inheriting our 's Hertogenbosch sector.

The increased belligerent activity could possibly have had some bearing upon the decision, which had already been made, to send one of our Troops across the Maas to destroy a known enemy post. The operation had been code-named HELEN; a preliminary reconnaissance of the area to be attacked was carried out and other

191

preparations put in hand. Immediately before the assault went in there would be the usual artillery softening-up and, in addition, two more Fighting Troops and the Support Troop would provide a strong 'firm base' on our side of the river, ready to assist in the attack, or to facilitate a withdrawal if either course of action might prove necessary.

A further Patrol reconnoitred the chosen route to the enemy position, to verify that it was mine-free and, at 0345 on 22 March, 'Y' Troop landed on the north bank from two LCAs. The position scheduled for the attack was found to have been evacuated, so the Troop Commander immediately ordered an assault on another one, a short distance further along the dyke, achieving complete success, with all the occupants being killed. The Patrol then searched nearby houses and, finding that the enemy had decamped, were returning along the dyke when fired upon by a machine gun which inflicted a casualty. The position was immediately attacked and the gun silenced; then the patrol went on to assault another gun position where, once again, the occupants were killed. At that point the Troop was heavily engaged by a number of machine guns, suffering more casualties, and the Patrol Commander ordered a withdrawal.

On that occasion, too, Lieutenant Salmon had been in charge of the landing craft, wearing his top hat and white gloves, and once again he left a notice board on the north bank of the river. This time he advertised an 'amazing special offer, for one week only' of a free passage to England for all Germans! It continued with the admonition that 'This offer cannot be repeated – the bombardment is coming'. Again it ended with 'look out for the top hat'. On 19 June 1945 Lieutenant Salmon was awarded the DSC for 'services to the 509th LCA Flotilla'.

Later in the morning German medical orderlies and stretcher bearers could be seen collecting casualties and our men were ordered not to open fire. In the afternoon, under cover of a white flag, the Germans sent a party across to the front of the dyke where the action had taken place and were seen to carry away a British casualty who was still alive. The Germans searched the area but found no more. 41 had suffered two killed, four wounded and two missing; nine Germans were confirmed killed.

Two days after HELEN, on 24 March, the Germans sent over an

early morning patrol of five or six men which was soon spotted and fired on; the enemy quickly withdrew under smoke. As usual, the Germans retaliated with a mortar attack on the Commando positions, killing one man and badly wounding three more, two of whom died soon afterwards.

That turned out to be the day on which the boats we had seen being moved through Holland by road returned to their own element – General Montgomery had launched the 2nd Army's assault across the Rhine. Airborne Troops and No. 1 Special Service Brigade spearheaded four landings in the vicinity of Wesel, the town being captured by No. 1 Special Service Brigade.

On that day, too, the Advance Party of 48 Commando arrived in 's Hertogenbosch and ours left for Goes. The main body of 48 arrived next day and the two units double-banked in Troop locations until midnight, when 41 relinquished responsibility for that sector of the river. On 26 March the DRs shepherded the Unit convoy out of 's Hertogenbosch, away from the war zone, and back to Zeeland.

Chapter 14

THE END OF THE WAR AND
OCCUPATION DUTIES IN GERMANY

In South Beveland the unit was to take over the civilian billets previously occupied by 48 Royal Marines Commando and, as suitable accommodation was at a premium in the area, the number one priority of the Advance Party had been to ensure that none of those billets was lost to another unit! Headquarters and two Fighting Troops were stationed in Goes (pronounced 'hoose'), the capital, and the other Troops were housed in the nearby small towns of 's Heer Hendrikskinderen, 's Heer Arendskerke, Heinkenzand and Wemeldinge. Wemeldinge stands at the northern end of the South Beveland Canal, the only shipping link between the east and west arms of the river Scheldt, so it was vital that the lock gates there should be guarded night and day.

Initially, Frank Barker and I were allocated to the home of Mevrouw van Opstal, a neat, modern house in Violenstraat on the outskirts of town. It was comfortable and we felt very fortunate with our situation, but it lasted only a few days, because the husband came home! Mijnheer van Opstal, a merchant seaman, had been at sea at the outbreak of war and ever since then had been serving with the British Merchant Navy. It was understandable that he didn't want a couple of foreign servicemen sleeping in his second-best bedroom, so we had to move.

Our next billet, in the home of Mijnheer Smallegange, a baker with house and shop premises at Oud Vismarkt 4 (No. 4 Old Fishmarket), proved to be even better. It was very conveniently located in town, barely fifty yards from the market square, and we were given a commodious room at the front of the building, over the shop. We soon discovered that we had become part of a large Dutch household, as, in addition to five children aged six to twenty, a local girl lived in to help in the house and shop, and there was also a young girl evacuee. The elder children spoke good English and, apart from taking our meals at Headquarters, we became part of the family, even to obeying Heer Smallegange's command, 'Boven!' (Upstairs!) each evening when he felt that it was time to go to bed. He had to get up early to start his baking.

The Commando hadn't been moved back to Zeeland for a rest cure but to train as a mobile striking force for employment in the 'war of movement' which was expected to develop on the plains of northern Germany once the Allies had established themselves across the Rhine. In addition, with the Germans still occupying the islands in the estuary of the East Scheldt, strategic installations in the area were at risk and the Commando was required to provide a defence force for South Beveland.

The new mobile role envisaged for the Commando would require rapid and efficient radio communication between Headquarters and the Troops whilst on the move, so all command jeeps were fitted with brackets to take the more powerful '68' sets. Then Officers and Signals Personnel began perfecting signals procedures to maintain overall control of the Commando and to operate in conjunction with other units, including tank and artillery support.

For the men in the Fighting Troops, being part of a mobile force wouldn't make a great deal of difference to the basic infantry tactics to be employed once they had de-bussed in close proximity to the enemy. However, within a few days of arrival, they started on another serious 'refresher course', as laid down in a detailed day-by-day programme drawn up by Major Young. Once again, too, great emphasis was laid on the zeroing and firing of all infantry weapons to set proficiency standards. In addition, another weapon had been added to the armament of the Commando and two men per Troop were sent for training in the use of flame-throwers.

The Troops also brushed up on their infantry tactics, practising the various 'drills' for assaulting enemy positions, clearing bunkers, etc, but not at the expense of the parade ground aspect of Royal Marine life and 'saluting was to be punctiliously carried out'. There

195

were also the usual 'Keep Fit' occupations such as P.E. and route marches, some of which, on occasions, included the Despatch Riders.

Commando Headquarters had taken over the vacant Oude Mensenhuis (Old Men's Home) and the main entrance was flanked with a pair of highly polished shell cases. It was also graced by a ceremonial sentry with rifle and fixed bayonet; during the hours of daylight the Union Flag flew above the doorway. The local children never tired of watching the sentry spring to attention, bring his rifle up to the slope and give a smart butt salute to every officer who entered the building.

Directly across the narrow street fronting the Mensenhuis stood a row of small workshops where our motor cycles were garaged, while the Signals Despatch Office was located in a room at the rear of the main building, looking out on to a secluded courtyard garden. The SDO was distinguishable by the score or so of telephone wires issuing from the top of the window, linking the hand-cranked exchange inside to the outlying Troops and other units on the Commando's network. DRs would also visit these local HQs daily, but in addition there was an appreciable number of much longer journeys to Army and Royal Marines Headquarters in Middelburg, Bergen op Zoom, Tilburg, Breda and Antwerp.

The run to Antwerp involved a hundred-mile round trip and, if the weather was particularly bad, the DRs might be allowed to use a jeep; if the bar of the Officers' Mess needed replenishment, a jeep was mandatory. On one such DR-cum-drinks journey, I managed to squeeze in a meeting with my brother-in-law Horace, who was stationed in Antwerp docks with an RAF Embarkation Unit. There wasn't much time to spare, so it was probably as well that he was teetotal and our meeting amounted to no more than a 'hello and goodbye' over a cup of tea in the rather basic dockyard NAAFI.

In the market square of Goes there was a much more attractive tea-and-biscuits canteen where, on some evenings, Mies, the eldest daughter of the Smallegange family, would help out as a volunteer waitress. There was little control over the number of packets of biscuits we could buy so on those nights I would head back to Oud Vismarkt 4 with my battledress blouse bulging more like an ATS girl than a Royal Marine. Arrival at the billet would be to the great delight of the younger Smalleganges.

196

In Goes the unit had become eligible to participate in a Second Army scheme of 48-hour leaves in Brussels and, only a week after arriving there, Frank and I were lucky. A three-tonner truck took the leave party of some twenty men the eighty miles to the Belgian capital, to be accommodated with full board, as non-paying guests, at the fully-staffed Hotel Metropole in Place Rogier.

We were given a list of Do's and Don't's for the leave period and a major one of the latter was 'Not to eat in any civilian establishment other than your leave hotel' because this would upset the city's food distribution arrangements. There were no restrictions on drinking in civilian cafés and bars, however, but this proved to be an overrated and expensive pastime. The simple matter of buying a beer was bedevilled by the compressed air delivery system which produced very much more 'head' than beer. Behind every bar counter there would be rows of partially-filled glasses waiting for the froth to settle before being topped up again, then after another squirt from the pump a wooden spatula would be used to scrape off the surplus head before the glass went back for a further period of settling down.

Spirits could be obtained much more quickly, but a combination of basically high prices, the inevitable 'hostess' system and a ten percent service charge made them exorbitant to us. That first evening Frank suggested cognacs as a finale, so we entered a café and he ordered two. A 'floozie' hostess sidled up to him saying, 'One for me too, soldier?' Frank reluctantly agreed and three very small glasses were lined up on the bar counter, hers no doubt containing only coloured water. When asked the price, the barman said 'Two hundred francs', about a week's pay to us, which Frank promptly queried. The barman pointed to each drink in turn saying, 'Sixty, sixty, sixty, plus service – two hundred francs'. Frank repeated the barman's words in amazement, put his money back in his pocket and said, 'C'mon, Mitch, let's get out of here!' We did.

Back in Goes the training programme went on apace, but, as the Allied armies continued to advance into Germany from east and west, it was becoming clear the Commando wouldn't see any action in Germany. On 5 April, the very day on which we went to Brussels, 45 Royal Marines Commando of No. 1 Special Service Brigade had taken Osnabruck and troops of the 6th Airborne Division had entered Minden. Further south, American troops were daily moving further east, while the Russians pushed inexorably west-wards.

By 21 April the Russians had reached the suburbs of Berlin and it was clear that the end was near. On 4 May, on Lüneberg Heath, General Montgomery accepted the surrender of all German forces in North Germany, Holland and Denmark.

In Goes we had been able to follow the progress of the Allied Armies on a map displayed in the window of a small newsagent's shop close to Commando HQ, which the proprietor had updated daily by moving lines of coloured pins. On the day the war in Europe came to an end, this service was terminated with the single word 'KAPUT!' – 'Finished!' – written in large letters over the map of Germany.

The surrender of the German Armies in North-West Europe came into effect at 0800 hrs on 5 May 1945; Holland was completely free again, after five years of occupation. That evening the market square of Goes, illuminated by a blazing 'Victory Bonfire', became thronged with a jubilant, dancing, singing mass of civilians and servicemen. Long fingers of searchlight beams circled the sky to demonstrate the end of the long wartime blackout and the celebrations continued into the early hours of the morning.

Three days later the war with Germany came to an 'official' end, when the British Government declared 8 May a national holiday – 'Victory in Europe Day'. To mark the occasion the Commando organized a Victory Dance in a church hall near the market square, with a local band to provide the music and bar supplies trucked in from Antwerp, the liquor capital of the area.

The dance was in full swing and all was going as planned when the bartenders surprisingly announced that stocks of beer had run out. There was, however, still a goodly supply of spirits and liqueurs, and these the amateur barmen, having only one size of glass to hand, continued to dispense in liberal quantities. At some point during the evening we realized that Bill Smith was no longer with us and simply assumed that he had wandered off on his own. On making our way billet-wards very much later we discovered that this had indeed been the case, but he hadn't wandered very far. We almost tripped over him, stretched out flat on the pavement outside the hall, dead to the world. He was hauled to his feet and manoeuvred into headquarters to sleep it off. He should have been

Duty DR next day, but was in no fit state to ride, so we covered for him.

That there was no longer a war in Europe had no marked effect upon the Despatch Riders' work load. Bill and I, however, were soon to receive an unexpected bonus when, less than two weeks after VE-Day, we were abruptly detailed off to join a 'leave party' going to Germany next day on a purely sightseeing trip!

Those who were able borrowed cameras from their Dutch hosts and, on the morning of Whit Saturday 19 May, two 3-tonner trucks, packed with twenty or more boisterous Marines, together with a pile of blankets and some boxes of Compo rations, rolled out of Goes. The weather was warm and sunny, and the canvas sides of the trucks were rolled up to give an all-round view. The journey started off along the Despatch Riders' 'canteen trail' of Breda, Tilburg and Nijmegen, then, a few miles further on, we entered Germany and jolted in turn through the ruins of Kleve, Kalkar and Xanten, heading for the Rhine. We crossed via a floating pontoon bridge, leading directly to Wesel, but, before entering the town, experienced our first encounter with 'D.P.s'. Displaced Persons, people who had been separated from their homes by the war, whether confined in concentration camps, used as forced labourers in Germany or simply having been in the wrong country when war broke out, were to prove a major problem for Allied governments for many years thereafter.

In 1945, to ensure that none of those travelling from Eastern Europe were carrying any unwanted bugs on their persons, the River Rhine had been constituted as a *cordon sanitaire* and, before being allowed to cross over, all civilians were made to suffer the indignity of de-lousing. Long lines of men and women waited their turn to have a rubber hose attached to a hand pump inserted between underclothing and skin to be given generous squirts of anti-louse powder, downwards and upwards, back and front.

As we passed through Wesel the borrowed cameras clicked, even though there was little to see other than mounds of rubble, obliterated streets and shrivelled, leafless trees; there was no sign of life of any kind. Beyond the city the countryside, although unmarked by the ravages of war, was equally deserted; the entire land seemed empty and dead.

We were heading for Essen and for a while our route lay along one of Hitler's much-vaunted autobahns. It was devoid of any other traffic, so the drivers were able to indulge in an unaccustomed spree of speeding. To arrive in 'Kruppsville' was to enter another grave-yard of a city, but one with a difference. The vast expanse of masonry rubble and the empty shells of buildings were interspersed with acres of twisted steelwork which had once been armaments factories.

The trucks made a 'photo stop' outside the ruins of one of these Krupp works, as two German girls were approaching it from the opposite direction, walking down an otherwise completely deserted street. In any other country of the world, notwithstanding any language problem, they would have been greeted with a barrage of wolf-whistles and facetious remarks, but not in Germany at that time. Immediately after the German surrender a strict Non-Fraternization ('Non-frat') Order had been imposed, making it a serious offence for Allied Service personnel to have any form of social contact with enemy nationals, of either sex, except as re-quired in connection with their duties. The girls walked past, we looked at them and they looked back at us, but, apart from the clicking of cameras, all in complete silence. By dusk we were happy to have moved away from a succession of such scenes of devastation into unscarred countryside and spent the night in a vacant school put at our disposal by the local American Military Authorities.

Next day, Whit Sunday, was another gloriously sunny day as we moved on to Düsseldorf, there to find yet another empty, desolate wasteland of rubble and the sickly stench of rotting flesh. Where the original street pattern had been obliterated, Army engineers had bulldozed access roads through the ruins. During one brief halt in our bouncing progress through the city I looked around for some-thing distinctive to photograph. The best I could find was a column of masonry some fifteen feet high, which had obviously been the corner of a substantial building at a road junction, the street name-plates were still in place. The names meant nothing to me, but, many years after the war, visiting a re-built Düsseldorf, I recognized one of those names, Königs Allee, the most prestigious shopping street of the city.

From Düsseldorf the trucks travelled back towards the Rhine, heading for Neuss and Cologne. We re-crossed the river by way of another pontoon bridge, but American-built this time, named the

Ernie Pyle Bridge after one of their most popular writers. Here we met up with more DPs when our 3-tonners had to join a long string of trucks heading for the bridge, taking hundreds of them to the West; no doubt they had all been properly de-loused.

Cologne was also a dead and virtually deserted city, although, like Essen, many substantial buildings were still standing as empty, roofless shells. The trucks trundled through the ruined streets to the Cathedral. The massive edifice, although scarred and slashed by bomb and shell splinters in a number of places, towered high above us, still amazingly intact. The cathedral square was a litter of broken masonry, felled lamp posts and a solitary German tank. On the far side stood the ruins of the Hauptbahnhof, the main railway station, no more than an arched steelwork skeleton rising from a carpet of shattered bricks and glass fragments.

Bill and I walked around the Dom, inspecting the external damage, then, finding the main door standing open, went inside. There were a few civilians moving around, some in clerical garb, but others seemed to be, like ourselves, merely sightseeing. Outside again, we walked to the rear of the building and found ourselves directly in line with the Hohenzollern Bridge. Like every other Rhine bridge, it had been blown and the roadway led down into the river instead of across it. We took photographs of each other with the huge twin spires of the Cathedral as a backdrop, marvelling at its survival in the midst of the destruction all around.

From Cologne it is about one hundred and fifty miles to Goes, so the trucks started back early in the afternoon. En route to Aachen, we passed close to another heap of rubble that had once been Düren, probably the ultimate example of 'saturation bombing'; the original street pattern appeared to have been completely obliterated.

Moving from Germany into Belgium at Aachen was to pass from an empty, dead country into one bustling with life. Although the frontier towns had been bombed and shelled, and were badly damaged, they were nevertheless crowded with people. It was Whit Sunday, everyone was dressed in their 'Sunday best' and religious processions were encountered in every town. In Hasselt it took half an hour for a procession to pass and the streets to clear sufficiently to enable our trucks to proceed. A brief halt was made in Antwerp for tea and buns, then it was over the border into Holland at

Putte and the drive through South Beveland back to Goes.

The very next day our Brigade received a Move Order with the unambiguous codename of Operation DEUTSCHLAND. We were to take up occupation duties in Germany. By the following Saturday morning all was ready and the DRs began their task of shepherding the long road convoy away from Zeeland. The 'specifics' were – Speed 15 MIH (Miles in Hour): Road Spacing 40 VPM (Vehicles per mile) and, as a rider: *The attention of all troops is drawn to the Non-Fraternization Order, and the severity of the punishment following a breach of the Order cannot be over-emphasized.*

Once again the route lay through Nijmegen and into Germany via Kleve and Kalkar, but on this occasion the Rhine was crossed at Rees. Once across, the snake of trucks was guided north east to Bocholt, where it split up, distributing the various elements of the Commando to a number of different locations around Borken, a small town which lies only six miles from the Dutch border near the town of Winterswijk.

The basic duties of the Commando in that area of North Rhine-Westphalia were to guard vital services, in particular the trains operating on the main railway line between Borken and Rheine some fifty miles away, and the local distillery! In immediate post-war Germany these weren't the perfunctory tasks that might be imagined, because the country was in a turmoil. Gangs of Russian DPs, many of whom had armed themselves, were roaming far and wide, engaged in murder, rape and pillage, hell-bent on exacting revenge upon the enemy which had incarcerated and maltreated them.

To go some way towards providing protection for the civilian population, the operational Troops of the Commando and 'B' Echelon were stationed in eight small towns scattered over more than a hundred square miles of Germany – Borken, Gemen, Heiden, Holthausen, Lembeck, Oding, Rhade and Weseke. By a strange twist of fate, Borken had been the home town of one of the German-born 10-IA Commando men who had been attached to 41 since just before D-Day, and it was soon common knowledge that the welcome home from his ex-girl friend had been anything but friendly.

In addition to providing a deterrent to roving bands of DPs, the widespread distribution of the Commando was also designed to 'Show the Flag'. During the hours of daylight the Union Flag was flown outside every Troop Headquarters and beneath it a large notice-board instructed all German males over the age of fourteen to doff their caps as they passed. Anyone caught trying to sneak past without complying could be dragged back and made to stand bareheaded, facing the flag, for as long as the Officer-of-the-Day deemed appropriate. Teenage cyclists, naturally, pedalled furiously past, shouting incomprehensible remarks and any driver or DR in the vicinity would be ordered off in pursuit of them. Such an order couldn't be disobeyed, but most of us 'came the old soldier' by simply keeping out of sight for a while then reporting back, 'Sorry, sir, but they got away.'

For those men detailed off for train guards sixty were needed every day to start a tour of duty lasting two and a half days; living and messing conditions en route, mainly on the train, were primitive. We weren't involved in these guards, but had our own problems, one of which was the potential danger from Werewolves. These were said to be Hitler Youth fanatics who had banded together to prey upon Allied occupation troops. A solitary Despatch Rider on a deserted road was particularly vulnerable as a baulk of timber flung on the road would catapult him out of the saddle, while a length of invisible piano wire, stretched taut between two trees, could probably take off a head as neatly as Madame Guillotine.

This latter possibility was taken seriously by the High Command and for a while DRs were permitted to use jeeps. This didn't last for very long, however – possibly Despatch Riders could be replaced more easily than jeeps – and we went back to our bikes. For some time thereafter we tended to ride more slowly than usual, bent low over the petrol tank.

A further problem was that the roads were in an appalling state of disrepair, necessitating a continual look-out for potholes. Nevertheless it was easy to forget about piano wire and potholes if you had passed safely down a particular stretch of road only an hour or so previously, as was brought home to me when returning from a trip to Wesel, some twenty-five miles from Borken.

The road was, as usual, completely empty and the throttle was quite wide open as I swept around a bend to be suddenly confronted by a deep pothole. I managed to steer the front wheel clear, but the rear wheel struck with a jarring blow. The impact was so great that the pillion stays crumpled, squashing the mudguard hard down on the tyre and, with a dead rear wheel, and a strong smell of scorched rubber, the bike slithered to a halt. In the gathering gloom of dusk, on a completely deserted woodland road, I could almost hear the howls of Werewolves scenting a kill! Extreme loneliness, and a dash of panic, must have supplied the brute strength needed to enable me to reduce the bending of the mudguard stays sufficiently to free the wheel and allow me to ride back to Borken.

The quirk of national pride, requiring the doffing of caps to the British flag, didn't last for long, but the 'Non-frat' Order remained in force for a full three months. For some time before it was rescinded, however, it had been, as Horatio remarked to Hamlet, 'more honoured in the breach than in the observance'. While it lasted, however, it had been pleasant to be able to cross into Holland and talk freely with the locals – within the limits of one's vocabulary.

One drawback, however, was that the invariable topic of conversation of every Dutchman was bicycle tyres. With so much of their individual transport based upon push-bikes, replacing tyres worn out during the years of war was top priority for them. Presumably, being a motorcyclist, they thought that I might supply their needs, but I was asked so many times that, whenever I saw a purposeful Dutchman approaching me, I would get in first with *Het spijt me, geen fietsbanden!*' – 'I'm sorry, no bicycle tyres'; they invariably shrugged and turned away.

The Germans too had bicycles, but most of theirs were seen, hooked by the handlebars, dangling over the backs of the massive leviathans of the road then being used to move people about the country. Those huge vehicles with slatted timber sides, rising to perhaps eight feet above the road, were often towing one, or even two, similarly-sized monster trailers, all jam-packed with humanity. On the narrow roads of the area they were things to be given a very wide berth, but it was an Allied, not German, truck which almost put me back in hospital one day as I crossed from Germany into Holland at Gronau.

I had zipped over the border – there were no customs or any other formalities for DRs – and was approaching a long line of military vehicles parked facing in my direction on my side of the road. I was almost abreast of the first in line when it started to move off, turning directly into my path. Instinctively, I yanked the handle-bars away from it and effectively executed the self-preservation manoeuvre of 'riding to ground'. The bike and I covered the next few dozen yards of carriageway in a horizontal position, with me still in the saddle and holding on to the handlebars, as showers of sparks streamed from all parts of the machine in contact with the concrete. Surprisingly, neither bike nor I suffered any real damage and, when getting to my feet, it was to see the truck responsible had completed its U-turn without pause and was speeding off into Germany.

Our billet in Borken was a large empty house fronting onto the main street, where we slept on bare boards and ate compo rations out of mess tins. Despite the minimal labour content of cooking compo, those who had the job were given the benefit of some elderly German prisoners-of-war as a fatigue party. One luxury we were all able to enjoy, however, was being able to take baths in the local hospital, where a uniformed attendant was on hand to run the water and clean the bath afterwards!

In mid-June, some two weeks after our move, a scheme for releasing people from the Armed Forces back into civilian life came into operation. Initially it was restricted to skilled craftsmen needed in UK industry to continue the war with Japan and to produce exports to get the country earning foreign exchange again, and building workers to make a start on the reconstruction of bomb-damaged cities; after that it was to be on a 'first in – first out' basis. There was also talk about 'training for civilian life', so we began to think that there might really be an 'after the war' for us. Throughout our Service life we had been singing, 'When this blinking war is over, oh, how happy I will be . . .', but, as year followed year, many had come to wonder if their luck would hold out until then.

The war against Japan was, of course, still very much in progress and, concurrently with releasing men from the Forces, there were 'Far East Drafts' to transfer Servicemen from Europe to the Pacific. Lists of names were posted on notice-boards and it was generally reassuring to see that these appeared to be based upon length of service in the Corps. Those who had survived four or five years of war began to feel reasonably confident of being passed over for drafting, but one couldn't breathe easily until??! On 26 June the first Far East draft from the Commando, of three Troop Commanders, the Padre, six Subalterns, seven SNCOs and eighty-four Other Ranks left, and no one knew when the next one would be.

For Despatch Riders life had settled down to a routine signals delivery service, interesting enough in its way as we were operating in enemy territory, but, basically, still just shuffling paper. The possibility of leaving all that behind for a few weeks appeared attractive, so, on 3 July, I volunteered for a parachuting course in the UK, which had the bonus of a leave at home afterwards. Two days later, however, all such extraneous thoughts were pushed from the mind when an Advance Party left Borken to reconnoitre a new location – Recklinghausen, in the Ruhr.

This move was code-named Operation BELSEN, obviously chosen because the Commando's next task, together with No. 4 Army Commando, would be to guard almost four thousand German prisoners being held in No. 4 Internment Camp. It wasn't learned whether any of the inmates had in fact had any connection with Belsen, but undoubtedly many of them had been guards at equally infamous extermination camps. One of the inmates was Alfried Krupp the 'armaments king', who remained in captivity until 1951.

In Recklinghausen most of the Commando was billeted in blocks of flats near the camp, but HQ troop was given an estate of detached houses, surrounded by a high chain-link fence topped with barbed wire. This was probably not so much as a deterrent to Germans, although talk of Werewolves were still prevalent, but as protection against marauding DPs. It would appear that the Occupation Forces had created some 'Displaced Persons' on their own account, as the previous occupants of the houses were still in the vicinity and, on occasion, were allowed to enter the compound to harvest their garden produce. Some, however, seemed to find more to interest them in the swill bins outside the cookhouse. The houses were unfurnished, but had been provided with beds and the mains electricity was functioning, so it was an up-market move. The houses had cellars, accessed by a very steep ramp from the back garden, and ours proved ideal as a workshop and garage for the bikes.

In marked contrast with practically deserted rural Borken, industrialized Recklinghausen was bustling with civilian activity. Despite having been extensively bombed, the town was still relatively intact and the coal mine was in full production. There was work for the civilian population, and shops and cafés were open for business, although not available to us because of the Non-frat Order. There was, however, one civilian establishment available to us which didn't involve fraternization, the pithead baths. Bathing parades, when we were marched there in parties, became part of our weekly routine.

The 'changing room' was no more than a large expanse of tiled floor, above which dangled hundreds of metal baskets attached to ropes passing over pulley blocks fixed high on the ceiling. After being allocated a basket, each man would lower his to the floor, strip to the buff and, with clothing and towel inside, it would be hauled up out of harm's way, before heading for the showers. More often than not a few dozen yards away there would be another group of naked men, looking very little different from ourselves, who had been our enemies only a few weeks earlier.

As a motorcyclist, one of the things I had been looking forward to doing in Germany was to ride my Matchless 350cc machine 'flat-out' on an autobahn. We had been given no more than an 'outline' map of the area, with little detail, but it did indicate that the Rhineland-Magdeburg motorway crossed the road to Bochum, very close to Recklinghausen and, at the first opportunity, I set off to find it. I rode slowly for mile after mile without any sign of a bridge over the road and had covered the entire nine miles to Bochum before accepting the fact that there just wasn't one. On the return journey I continued to look out for the elusive bridge and was almost back at HQ before noticing massive masonry walls at either side of the road, clearly the abutments of a bridge which no longer existed. I later found the access to the autobahn, a slip road nearer town, but, after a brief inspection, immediately abandoned any idea of speeding along it. Without exception the bridges over all minor roads had been blown and very few of the gaps had been fenced off. Only some time later did it dawn on me that the grassy mound topped with a line of trees which skirted our HQ Troop compound, only a few hundred yards away, was the autobahn!

Ten days after moving to Recklinghausen my name had reached the top of the leave roster again and, early on Sunday 15 July, a truckload of boisterous bootnecks set off, 'bound for Old Blighty's shore', and seven days' at home. The first leg of the journey was an 80-mile run to the 'railhead' at the Dutch border town of Gennep, where we endured a dispiriting six-hour wait before boarding the 'Leave Special'. Its standard of comfort – wooden slatted seating, a few broken windows and no heating – was typical, as was its speed. The journey to Calais, barely one hundred and eighty miles away as the crow flies, took a full twelve hours.

At 0400 on the Monday morning we once again stumbled over the multiplicity of rail tracks to the adjacent transit camp. As early bird arrivals, we felt confident that our trainload of troops would be on the next ferry to leave, and so it was, but that wasn't until 0900 the following morning. On that occasion it was the short sea crossing to Folkestone, and by late Tuesday evening I was back in Newcastle to hear my first, 'Hallo Ray! Home again? When do you go back?'

Conditions in the English Channel gave me a 'windfall' extension of 72 hours, so I was in Newcastle until mid-afternoon on Monday 30 July; it was Wednesday evening when I arrived back to Recklinghausen, seventeen days after leaving.

After reporting in at the Orderly Room, my 'Welcome Home' was a bit of a shocker, 'Just in time, Mitch! You're off to Manchester in the morning, for that parachute course,' and someone added comfortingly, 'I hear they're crying out for paras in the Far East!' It was no consolation to me to know that I was probably the only man in the entire Commando Brigade who possessed a slim volume entitled *Colloquial Japanese*, bought for interest's sake some years earlier! Another piece of news was that the Non-frat Order had been rescinded during my absence, but that was of no consequence at the time, as I didn't even have time to say 'Hello' to my motorbike.

The start back next morning gave every indication of the journey to England being very much smoother than my previous one. There were only eight of us bound for Ringway Airport, Manchester, and a 15-cwt truck with driver had been laid on to take us straight to our port of departure, Ostend, some two hundred miles away. At a NAAFI stop en route, purely by chance, we met up with a Belgian youth who was also on his way to England, but his trip wasn't in any way connected with the war, or Service life – he was off to enrol at one of our universities! It gave us some food for thought, as we couldn't even guess when we might get back to civilian life.

In the event, the truck managed to cover barely half of the journey that day. We ended up almost a hundred miles short and passed the night in a monastery-cum-transit camp at Bourg Léopold. Next morning our driver had to return to Reckling-hausen, so we were left to hitch lifts on passing vehicles, and it was evening before we reached the Ostend transit camp. There were no more ferries that day so we had to acquire some Belgian francs for a night ashore. We found Ostend to be a much more lively place than it had been some ten months previously after our return from Walcheren when we had to pay so much for fish and chip suppers.

Next day was a hot Saturday in August, but there was no ship for us. Instead we were able to visit those beaches previously fenced off with German barbed wire, carrying skull and crossbones *Achtung minen!* warning signs. Wearing thick battledress, we mingled with crowds of barefoot Belgians in bathing costumes and mused about men of military age drinking beer beneath striped umbrellas, sunning themselves on the beach or bathing in the sea, while we still soldiered on.

Sunday was another gloriously sunny day and, as our troop ship sailed out of Ostend harbour, it was given a stirring farewell from crowds of holidaymakers lining the piers. It was the long sea crossing to Tilbury this time and our 2100 hours arrival was too late for trains, so we were bedded down in the docks area. Next morning we left on an early morning train, but it was late evening before our party eventually arrived at No. 1 Parachute Training School at Ringway Airport.

Only then, when trying to find someone to whom we could report, did it impinge upon us that it was August Bank Holiday Monday and virtually everyone was away on leave. Eventually we were marched to a satellite camp some distance from the airport, allocated to a Nissen hut, told where to find the mess-hall, then advised that it wouldn't be open until after 0545 reveille next morning!

Immediately after breakfast we met the RAF Corporal who was

209

to be our instructor, presumably awaiting his third stripe, as all the others were Sergeants. Our squad of about two dozen was a mixed bag of all ranks, including commissioned officers, but there was no distinction in the training and when Corporal McLean gave the order 'Jump!', whether Major or Marine, you jumped or risked being RTU'd. The rule book didn't seem to be entirely specific on the subject, but it was generally accepted that, if a man refused his first jump, he was simply classed as 'unsuitable for parachuting' and left the course. After the first jump, however, refusal was a serious matter, warranting the ultimate disgrace of being 'Returned to Unit'. The vast majority would rather have broken their necks than refuse and be sent back to their unit with 'RTU' on their chit.

Parachute Training courses normally began with a week of 'toughening up', including lots of P.T. and other strenuous pursuits, but, being from a Commando unit, we were excused this. No one raised the point that for the previous eighteen months I had been a Despatch Rider, not a foot-slogger in a Fighting Troop. The course would consist of eight jumps in all, starting with two from a tethered balloon, followed by five from an aircraft and ending with a 'night balloon'. Before any parachuting began, however, there had to be lots of lesser jumping, to perfect the correct 'roll over' method of hitting the ground without injury. The first jumps were therefore from a height of no more than nine inches above ground; then we progressed to more realistic landings in a parachute harness hauled by pulley block a few feet above the floor of the aircraft hangar which served as gymnasium and training shed. Once the victim had fastened his harness he was hoisted up, his mates giving him a few hefty swings, and the instructor, choosing the right moment, pulled a quick released cord, then there was no option but to make a landing.

Next came 'the fan', designed to give a realistic simulation of an actual parachute landing, which was a bit more scary. No larger than the cooling fan of a car but with its blades fitted square-on to the axis of rotation, it was attached to the end of a steel cylinder around which was wound a steel cable with a parachute harness at the end. The fan was bolted on to the steel framework of the hangar at eaves level, some thirty feet above the floor, and in operation it was simply a matter of fitting the harness and jumping off. As the cable unwound, the cylinder spun the fan which generated sufficient air resistance to slow a man's descent to the landing speed of a real jump. The coming down was great; it was the climbing up that was a bit scary.

All 'real' jumps would be by a 'static line' hooked onto a rail inside the balloon basket or aircraft fuselage, which automatically pulled the parachute out of its pack. We had sessions of practising hooking up to the static line, the correct way to 'stand to the door', moving quickly along the aircraft and, most importantly, making a good exit. Aircraft jumps were made in 'sticks' of from two to ten men, and the longer the stick the greater the need for rapid movement along the aircraft and quick exits to ensure that, in action, the men landed in a cohesive group or, in our case, didn't end up in the trees at the edge of the DZ (Dropping Zone).

The order 'stand to the door' applied only to the first man in a stick, the rest simply lined up closely behind and followed him through the doorway as quickly as possible. When the command was given, No. 1 would move to the doorway, stand with his left hand on the edge of the opening, left foot on the edge of nothing and right hand grasping his right trouser leg about half-way down the thigh. When the red light alongside the door changed to green the Despatcher would slap him on the shoulder and bawl 'GO!!' in his ear; he went. Once outside the aircraft, the drill was to get your feet together as quickly as possible and bring the left hand over to clasp the right wrist. If you weren't slick enough, the slipstream would catch any outflung limb and spin you round like a top, 'corkscrewing' the rigging lines, which could result in an uncontrolled landing. The parachutes of the time didn't have the 'steerability' possessed by modern ones; all that could be done was to pull down on the front or rear pair of lift webs, spilling some air out of the canopy and so urging your descent in the chosen direction. If the rigging was twisted up, you were likely to come down 'all of a heap'!

One of the aircraft jumps was with a kit bag containing 50lbs of sand to simulate ammunition or other supplies, strapped to the right leg, so it was necessary to practise moving with this encumbrance. The bag had to be heaved forward with the right arm in harmony with a kick forward with the right leg, and a line of men practising the 'left foot forward, right kick and heave', routine was always good for a laugh by those involved. Invariably someone

211

would start singing the dwarfs' song from *Snow White* and all would soon be chanting, 'Heigh-ho, heigh-ho, it's off to work we go!' as they thumped along. Jumping with it attached to the leg was practised from an aircraft fuselage about two feet above the ground.

Time and again, for a week, we repeated the various 'drills', for moving along an aircraft, standing to the door, exiting and landing. Interspersed with practical training sessions were instructional lectures, attending film shows to give us some insight into parachute manufacture and operation, including shots of German parachutists (who seemed to have a completely uncontrollable 'chute), what to do if you landed in water and watching WAAFS packing them at long tables in an aircraft hangar.

Our first two real parachute jumps were from 'balloons'. These were standard wartime barrage balloons, in essence a form of the helium-filled airship which in earlier days had been known as 'Blimps'. This name had arisen during the 1920s, when the British government was experimenting with two types of airship – those with an aluminium framework encasing the gas bags, classed as Type 'A' (Rigid) – hence the reference letters of the only two built – the R100 and the ill-fated R101 – while those without any metal framework were Type 'B' (Limp), so 'Blimps' they were!

During the war balloons, or more correctly their steel anchor cables, were a useful deterrent against low-level air attack. Single balloons would be tethered to merchant ships, while the forest of cables created by scores of them, strategically sited, could protect a large area. For parachute training a metal cage capable of holding eight men, with a 'door' – simply an opening in the side – was attached below the gas bag. A steel cable tethered the balloon to a winch on the back of a standard 'anchor vehicle', which could let the balloon float up, haul it down and transport it where required.

We had been warned that the programme of live jumps was at the mercy of the weather, as there had to be little wind so that we wouldn't be blown away, and good visibility to enable instructors to see men coming down and so be able to give any necessary instructions by loud-hailer. On the Monday, therefore, after a truck had taken us to the DZ for the first balloon jump, it wasn't a great surprise to be told that the wind was too strong, so we were taken back to Ringway. We were returned to the DZ in the afternoon and conditions were suitable, although, with a backlog of jumps to work off, there was a long wait before a balloon became available.

Eventually our turn came for the first jump and we filed into the cage; the RAF crew of the anchor vehicle released the winch; the cable started to unwind, allowing the balloon to rise, slowly but irrevocably. During the silent ascent Corporal McLean did his best to keep minds occupied with innocuous chit-chat and reiterating points made in the training. At the same time there were the inevitable 'wise-guy' comments, such as 'Third floor – ladies underwear, bed pans and potties' or 'Stop the balloon, Corp! I've changed my mind, I wanna be in submarines'. The balloon just kept going up and up until halted at about seven hundred feet, tethered to mother earth by no more than a long length of very slim cable.

Balloon jumps, we later appreciated, are quite different from those made from aircraft. The static line was attached by a short length of thin nylon string to a small pilot 'chute, designed to open the canopy, affixed to the top of the main parachute, and everything was pulled out of the parachute pack until the nylon snapped under the man's weight. After exiting the basket, therefore, a man had to fall the combined length of the static line, pilot chute, main canopy, parachute rigging and parachute harness, a vertical drop of about 150 feet, before a reassuring tug under the armpits signalled that all was well. From an aircraft, on the other hand, the slipstream opens the canopy almost immediately and, in a good 'tight' stick, there is time to nod 'Hiya' to your nearest neighbour as you float in the air, before being wafted away from each other. There were no reserve chutes, so it had to be right first time, but, once reassured on that point, you could enjoy floating down to earth – until the time came to prepare for landing! The cup of tea after that first jump, bought at a mobile Salvation Army Canteen at the edge of the DZ, was one of the best ever! Late that same afternoon we were also able to accomplish the second jump and could progress to our first aircraft jump.

This was scheduled for the next day, but first we were given a dummy run over the DZ to show us how it looked from the air, before having to get down there on our own. For most of us that was our first ever flight so we weren't surprised to learn that there was also a 'take-off drill'. The aircraft used for parachute training were 'Good old Daks', Dakota DC3s, the ubiquitous aerial work-horse of WW2. The interior was just as it had left the factory, with all the construction ribs exposed, the only fitments being the slatted timber seating running along both sides of the fuselage and a steel rail for the static lines along the 'ceiling'. With a full load of parachutists these aircraft had a problem in getting their tails off the ground in order to take off. So, when it was time to go, the command 'Prepare for take-off' would be given. Then we all shuffled forward along the seating, squeezing together as tightly as possible towards the nose of the plane to take the weight off the tail. The plane could then proceed to take-off and, once airborne, the 'passengers' could spread themselves out, in comfort, along the seating.

When it came to that first aircraft jump I was somewhere in the middle of the stick and, following closely behind the man in front, was out of the door and floating on air with my parachute opening in the slipstream before really knowing what had happened. The descent was uneventful and, luckily, a front-facing approach to the ground made it just right for a copy-book roll-over landing. After the usual cup of tea, our truckload of budding parachutists returned to camp glowing with a sense of achievement, to be greeted with news that capped even that momentous day – Japan had accepted unconditional surrender and the war was over!

The government had designated the following day, Wednesday 15 August, as Victory over Japan (VJ) Day and declared it a public holiday, but this had no immediate effect upon our set routine. We kitted up as usual and drew parachutes, but it was declared too misty for jumping, so we spent the entire morning just waiting to be taken to the aircraft. Lunchtime came and went with no improvement, then, abruptly, we were given three days' leave! There followed a flurry of collecting leave chits, ration cards and rail warrants, being transported to the railway station and we were off.

It was mid-evening when I arrived in Newcastle Central Station and took a tramcar to High Heaton. From all sides came the crackling of fireworks and the swoosh of rockets criss-crossing a sky made bright with the glow of many bonfires; the air was filled with the smell of wood smoke. As I neared the family home I could see the silhouettes of my parents, elbows resting on their garden gate, absorbed in the spectacle. I was able to get right up to them before saying, 'Hello, Mum; Hello, Dad!' and see the amazement on their faces at my sudden appearance. Until that moment they believed that I was hundreds of miles away 'Somewhere in Germany', as I had left home to return there only two weeks previously. I explained that I had been sent back to England on a course at Manchester and they were quite content to accept that without pressing for details.

Like all periods of leave, that one passed all too quickly; on the Sunday I returned to Ringway for 0545 reveille next morning to carry on with the parachuting course. The first jump that day was a stick of four when it was my turn to be No. 1 and I had to stand to the door. Looking down from the open doorway of the aircraft, with a bird's eye view of the English countryside some 500 feet below, was a very different experience from simply tagging along in a string of men moving down the aircraft and suddenly finding yourself outside. It looked an awful long way down to mother earth and I wondered what I was doing up there. Then the dispatcher slapped me on the shoulder, bawled '**GO!!**' in my left ear and I went.

That afternoon it was much more comfortable to be near the middle of a stick of ten and simply go with the rest, but my exit must have been sloppy. I was spun around by the slipstream until the rigging lines became corkscrewed almost up to the canopy. As I began the drill of kicking in the opposite direction, starting to unscrew, a loud-hailer voice came up to me saying, 'That's right, No. 6 – kick them out'. The job wasn't more than half-finished, however, when the voice came again, 'Stop kicking, No. 6 – you're almost down – take up landing position'. The twisted lines brought me to earth backwards and, unable to perform a roll-over landing, all the air was knocked out of my lungs and I probably collected another bruise or two.

The most potentially dangerous landings, however, arose from the kitbag jumps. The bag, strapped to the leg with a quick-release toggle, was fitted with a twenty-foot line, but some men hadn't attached these to their belts, so, immediately after landing, heads would swivel skyward, ears cocked for yells of 'Kitbag!' which meant that another fifty pounds of sand was hurtling down to the DZ with potentially lethal results.

By this time, with a few jumps to our credit, we could consider all those who hadn't progressed as far as we had to be 'rookies'. Some even went to the extent of collecting pieces of the nylon string used to attach the pilot 'chute to the static line – which would be scattered over the DZ – and fixing a strip for each jump to their smocks, like long-service medals! However, we did feel justified in singing the 'para' songs and, surprisingly, one still in vogue was 'Jumping through the Hole', despite the fact that all jumps were then being made from a doorway in the side of an aircraft, not through a hole in the floor. The most popular one was undoubtedly 'I ain't gonna jump any more', the words which ended every 'verse'. These verses were no more than the repetition, three times, of such gems as 'I'm looking for the WAAF who put a blanket in my chute', 'I'm looking for the Sergeant who forgot to hook me up' and 'They scraped him off the tarmac like a lump of raspberry jam', so, naturally, 'I ain't gonna jump any more'. But, of course, we did.

The eighth and final jump was the 'Night Balloon', which proved to be a rather eerie business. Standing on the edge of the DZ, awaiting your turn to use it, the balloon, floating at 700 feet, was visible only as a dark smudge against a slightly lighter sky. Every few seconds the single bawled out word **'GO!!'** came down from the dark smudge, but there was nothing to be seen until, with a sharp crack, which hadn't been noticed in the daylight jumps, another parachute opened and could be seen oscillating earthwards.

The ascent in the balloon and exiting from the basket were much less traumatic than the daylight jumps because you couldn't see anything! However, coming down and not being able to distinguish the ground was disconcerting as you didn't know when to prepare for landing. More than once it was a case of thinking 'Here it comes!', pulling down on the lift webs ready for a roll-over landing, but nothing happened. Then, suddenly, when you weren't expecting it, you hit the ground with a sprawling thump. We returned to camp in high glee, with a group of Belgians who had also just completed their course, and joined in with them singing *Je te plumerais*.

Next morning, without any ceremony, we were handed our parachutist's wings and, after a speedy session with needle and thread, hied to the nearby airport hotel to 'wet' them. A camera was produced for photographs with the newly-adorned right shoulders of battle dress blouses prominently displayed, then it was off on another seven days' leave which, of course, had been one of the incentives for volunteering for parachute training in the first place.

The return journey to Recklinghausen was fraught with transport delays and took almost as long as the leave. In consequence, we didn't get back to base until Saturday 8 September; I had been 'otherwise engaged' for precisely eight weeks since first setting off for 'seven days' leave at home'. During that time my haircuts hadn't been strictly 'Royal Marine', so it seemed advisable to put matters to rights by visiting a nearby civilian barber shop. The shop was empty apart from two men standing talking near the chair, the barber and an exceedingly tall German. I was motioned to sit down and, nearing the chair, saw that the latter had the unmistakable scar of a sabre cut on his cheek. In turn he had obviously spotted the bright new parachutist wings on my sleeve and uttered a single word to the barber, '*Fallschirmist*!!' I knew enough German to know that he had said 'Parachutist' and I wasn't too happy about the tone in which he said it, which seemed to imply, 'I know what I'd like to do with *that* lot!', so my sojourn in the barber's chair was slightly uncomfortable.

During my absence a scheme of 'Civilian Work Experience' had been instigated whereby men could start getting used to their peacetime jobs again, e.g. ex-butchers would spend one day a week in the local abattoir and miners went to work in the local pit. There were also 'organized entertainments' designed to keep the troops interested and, a week after returning, I was selected for the Commando's team in a 4 SS Brigade Motorcycle Rally. It had been organized by 47 RM Commando near their home base of Erkenschwick, and each Commando (41, 47 and 48 Royal Marines and No. 4 Army) plus Brigade Headquarters, fielded a team of six riders. The particularly muddy course began with a steep hill climb, followed by a tortuous cross-country circuit through a wood, which brought us back to descend the same hill. 41 finished second to 47, but we consoled ourselves with the thought that 'If only we'd had as much time to get used to the course as they had'!

A few days later a middle-of-the-night spot check of an outlying district of the town had the entire Commando out on the streets at 0100 hrs, fully rigged and armed. In small groups, each with a German speaker of 10-IA Commando, we roused all the occupants

217

and searched every house. The net result of four hours' lost sleep was one antiquated shotgun, a barrel of illegally acquired pickled pork and the discovery that a few people had been spending the night in beds that weren't their own.

Towards the end of the month the Corporal-in-charge of DRs was returned to the UK for release and I was promoted in his place. This didn't relieve me of the job of taking my turn as Duty DR, but it did enable me to take the off-duty DRs on what I classed, officially, as 'Training Runs', but a more correct description would have been 'Fun Runs'. With two or three of the others following, I would set off along the autobahn, looking for an inviting exit point where I could take off, up or down a grassy embankment, and head for the open country. Surprisingly there were few fences to impede our progress and the runs could go on for miles and miles, across fields and through woods, until I found my way on to another road and we could map-read our way back or to any likely place for tea and buns.

There were, however, some nasty moments. More than once I roared up a steep embankment only to find that it carried a railway line and the sleepers were almost at the edge of the slope. Then it might prove possible to make a sharp turn, bounce over a few sleepers and head back down again, but not for everyone. Those who didn't make it either did a rapid 'back-pedal' to keep their machines upright while they went down the slope backwards or fell off and bike and rider rolled to the bottom.

One incident did make me more circumspect for subsequent occasions. We had had a good run from the autobahn, through woods and open country, then came upon a narrow beaten earth track leading up a low grassy hill. With three others following, I speeded over the top and had no option but to carry on down a track on the other side which led only to a floating walkway of timber battens, about three feet wide, chained end to end, across a wide expanse of water. If I had tried to stop most of us would probably have ended up in the water anyhow, so the only thing to do was to trust that the battens would have buoyancy enough to support the weight of a man and a motorbike.

They had, but only just. The first length tipped slightly as I moved on to it, then sank until it was awash, leaving a four-inch step at the far end where it was linked to the next in line. Scarcely breathing, I rode on, with each section in turn settling down in the water as it took the weight. At the far side there was another steep narrow track up an embankment and I zoomed thankfully to the top before daring to look back to see how the others were faring. By great good fortune, or good training!, they all got across safely and were soon up alongside me, giving my ears a pounding. Consulting our maps to determine the route back, we found that we had just crossed the Dortmund-Ems canal.

On other off-duty trips we roamed far and wide, and on one occasion I was persuaded by less mobile comrades, to ride to Mönchen Gladbach some fifty miles away. There was an immense prisoner-of-war camp there and I was commissioned to barter cigarettes for wrist watches with the inmates. It was too depressing an experience to repeat.

On another of our exploratory journeys around Recklinghausen we would come upon deserted ash-surfaced horse-trotting tracks. Then we would race around them, picturing ourselves as speedway riders, and there could be one German lady, who was nine or ten years old at the time, who retains a vivid memory of one of those occasions. As our quartette of motorcyclists came roaring round a blind bend we saw her walking across the track only a short distance ahead. Fortunately for all of our sakes, she didn't attempt to run, but simply froze in her tracks. We flashed past, two on either side of her, and next time round she was gone.

At the beginning of November the Commando was uprooted from industrial Recklinghausen and transplanted a hundred miles deeper into Germany, in the afforested countryside between Paderborn and Kassel. Headquarters and most of the Troops were stationed in the small town of Warburg, with two 'outlying Troops' in Lichtenau and Hardehausen, small villages on the edge of the extensive Hardehausen Forest. Brigade Headquarters was in Paderborn, some twenty-five miles away through the forest, and every ride there filled the mind of a solitary motorcyclist with thoughts of Werewolves and piano wires.

Warburg, because of its rail links, was a major transfer point for DPs being moved around the country and the Commando's job was the overall control of the town. This involved patrols by day and night, enforcing the curfew, carrying out traffic checks and house searches, providing round-the-clock guards for food dumps, including the Warburg sugar factory and, primarily, controlling the railway station and the DPs passing through. Headquarters Troop was billeted immediately adjacent to the station in a large two-storey building which had probably been a school before being taken over as a barracks. A few days after our arrival in Warburg the Commando was given another job, codenamed Operation BUTCHER – the killing of deer in the nearby forests to provide food for the Ruhr.

The boundary between the British and American zones of occupation crossed the road to Kassel a dozen or so miles to the south of Warburg, so a few of us decided that it would be a good idea to make contact with our Allies. We sought out a Yankee unit, found their cookhouse and made the point that it was extremely cold outside. Mugs of coffee were eventually produced, but so grudgingly that it was abundantly clear that they just didn't want to know us. We got the message and thereafter stayed near the comfort of the barrack-room stove instead of riding around a freezing countryside on any 'Hands across the Ocean' expeditions.

I was Duty DR on Sunday 11 November and so had the morning trip to Brigade Headquarters in Paderborn. It was the usual cold, lonely ride through the forest and, on Sunday morning, there was no sign of movement in the town either. I was nearing the city centre, riding along a deserted street, when a German policeman, resplendent in ornate Prussian helmet, stepped off the footpath and waved me down. 'Who the bloody hell does *he* think he is?' I thought, 'stopping a British Despatch Rider', but I pulled up beside him. He didn't speak, simply pointed to a nearby church clock, which was beginning to strike eleven o'clock – the eleventh hour of the eleventh day of the eleventh month – reminding me that it was Armistice Day. For two minutes we stood together in silence, at that time the customary commemoration of the end of the First World War, until a siren signalled 'back to normal'. The policeman saluted; I gave one in return and we carried on with our respective duties without having spoken a word.

As had been happening for many weeks, long-familiar faces were disappearing as more and more release groups of H.Os, Hostilities Only men, left for the UK and 'Civvy Street'. The C.Ss, Continuous Service Marines, would have to soldier on until the end of their individual twelve-year engagements, but there was no doubt that the Commando was running down. The year was also running down and, as the end of November drew near, it looked as if the Unit would have another Christmas away from home. Then, out of the blue, came the order to pack all kit for return to the UK, leaving all vehicles behind. Within 48 hours the unit marched to the station and entrained for the start of the journey home.

Chapter 15

FROM SERVICEMAN TO CIVILIAN

On 29 November we arrived at Borde Hill Camp, Haywards Heath, Sussex, and the DRs were allocated some ropey old motorbikes to go through the motions of carrying on a normal routine, but the Commando was dying on its feet. On 2 December we were paraded to hear Colonel Sanders give his farewell speech on leaving the unit to take over No. 46 Royal Marines Commando. Then, on 7 December, the entire Commando, less a small rear party, left camp on 21 days' disembarkation leave. For the first time since 1941 I had the pleasure of spending Christmas at home.

Two days after our return, on 30 December, Major General Wildman-Lushington, GOC Commando Group, and all officers and men of No. 4 Commando Brigade, from Brigadier 'Mouldy' Moulton (who had taken over from 'Jumbo' Leicester) to the lowliest Marine, attended a church service to mark the completion of the Brigade's wartime service. Next day, New Year's Eve, we were surprised to find that the regulation issue of turkey had been kept for us, so we had our second Christmas Dinner that year, although it wasn't served by the officers.

A few days later the Commando moved from Borde Hill to the Royal Marines' Training Camp at Wrexham, where the disintegration of the unit continued. My turn to say farewell to 41 Royal Marines Commando came on 11 January 1946 when I bade adieu to those friends still around who had a few more weeks or months yet to serve. It was time for those in my 'Release Group No. 32' (we weren't demobilized, just 'released to civilian life', which meant we could be recalled) to begin the discharge formalities and I was returned to my 'Home Division' of Chatham for the process.

The Royal Marines Barracks itself hadn't changed at all since I had worked in the Records Office there for a few weeks in October 1940. However, the complete absence of air raid warnings, which had then occurred a dozen or more times a day, made Chatham itself a very different place. Another major change was being able to sleep in a barrack room and not have to 'Proceed to the Tunnel', which had been mandatory in 1940, there to sleep on the concrete floor, if all the wooden forms set against the walls had been taken.

Then followed a week of standing in line with other Chatham Marines who had been brought back from whatever part of the globe they happened to have been serving in when their 'number came up'. Each separate step of our transition from servicemen to civilians required a different queue. The first was for the Quartermaster's Store, to return service clothing and equipment (apart from one set of clothing and a uniform to wear on the journey home); the Records Office, to make sure that you really were the person entitled to be released; medical and dental inspections, the issue of civilian clothes, release document, civilian identity card, ration book, leave chit, rail warrant, back-pay and authorization documents to draw war gratuity and post-war credit entitlements in your home town. They seemed endless.

In one of those queues occurred a coincidence which few people would accept in a work of fiction, but which obviously do happen in real life. It was a bright, not too cold, January day and a string of men were waiting in line for the next stage in their move into civilian life. All had the appropriate document in their hands, ready to be checked and stamped after completing whatever process it happened to be. Purely by chance I happened to notice the regimental number of the sheet of paper being held by the man immediately in front of me and my eyes popped when I saw 'Ch/X 100976'. Almost five and a half years previously, on 8 August 1940, I had been standing behind that very same man, in a very similar queue, when we were both waiting to be processed **into** the Royal Marines. I had been given the next number – Ch/X 100977.

It was Ron Walker. We had done our six weeks' initial training together in No. 48 squad at the Royal Marines Reserve Depot, Exton, Devon (which has since been completely redeveloped as the

223

Commando Training Centre Royal Marines, Lympstone), but we had never met again during our service lives. After our squad passing-out, I was posted to Chatham Barracks as a Records Clerk, while he had gone off with the bulk of the others for field-firing in Wales. By the time I had managed to get back to Exton, some three weeks later, in a vain attempt to catch up with them, they had moved on. Many of my squadmates, including Ron, had been posted to MNBDO1 (Mobile Naval Base Defence Organization, but often ragged as 'Men Not to Be Drafted Overseas'!) and were in Crete when German parachutists swamped the Allied defenders. A number of the squad were taken prisoner, but Ron had evaded capture and was later with Tito's guerrillas in Yugoslavia. Others of my squad would have been in the same release group, but I saw no other familiar face.

Moving about the barracks, going through the long release processes, we naturally came upon many youngsters who were in their early days of being processed in the opposite direction. I passed the King's Squad, doing their impeccable close order drill, and remember thinking to myself, 'What's the point of all that now? The war's over!' Later I realized that I had already been thinking like a civilian, as Rudyard Kipling shrewdly wrote: 'Oh, it's Tommy this, an' Tommy that, an' "Tommy go away" But it's "Thank you, Mr Atkins", when the band begins to play.'

The most difficult episode of the release procedure for me was selecting a 'civvy suit'. Every man heading back to civilian life was provided with a complete rigout of civilian clothes – shoes, socks, underwear, shirt, tie, hat – and a suit. I wandered along racks and racks of jackets, waistcoats and trousers of innumerable colours and patterns, and all with the same invisible price-tag of 'free', but hadn't the vaguest notion of what might be appropriate. In desperation, I picked a double-breasted navy-blue herringbone, as it was described to me later, which proved to be very suitable and gave good service during the next few years.

The complete rigout was packed in what was probably listed in military terms as 'Box, cardboard, brown, civilian clothes for the carrying of'. Those boxes were unmistakable and were the target of civilian touts and wide boys, looking for a quick profit. 'Ere, myte! I'll give yer ten quid fer yer civvies!' – and quite a lot of men succumbed and went home without a suit.

By 18 January all military procedures had been completed. I was transported to Chatham railway station, where I too received an offer to sell my civvies, but, realizing that there had to be some kind of life after the war, wasn't tempted.

Only when I had boarded the train for London, with the cardboard box of clothing stashed on the luggage rack above my head and was settling down for the long journey home, did the finality of the situation impinge upon me. The ticket in my pocket was for one way only; never again would I have to 'Report back at 2359 hrs'; my five-and-a-half year stint of service in the Royal Marines was over.

INDEX

226

229

231

234

940. 5486 MIT
commando units
special services
world war 2.

FROM CHINA
WITH LOVE

FROM CHINA
WITH LOVE

Margaret Pemberton

Severn
House

This title first published in Great Britain 2000 by
SEVERN HOUSE PUBLISHERS LTD of
9–15 High Street, Sutton, Surrey SM1 1DF.
Originally published by Robert Hale Limited as
Party in Peking under the pseudonym *Carris Carlisle*.
This title first published in the USA 2000 by
SEVERN HOUSE PUBLISHERS INC., of
595 Madison Avenue, New York, NY 10022.

British Library Cataloguing in Publication Data

Pemberton, Margaret
    From China with love
    1. China - History - Boxer Rebellion, 1899-1901 - Fiction
    2. Love stories
    I. Title
    823.9'14 [F]

    ISBN 0-7278-5576-X

Printed and bound in Great Britain by
MPG Books Ltd, Bodmin, Cornwall.

For Edgar Ramsden,
in loving memory

One

Olivia Harland leaned back against the soft leather upholstery of the open carriage as it swayed ponderously up the dusty track. The dry, oppressive heat of Peking was behind them now. They would soon be high in the Western Hills and would remain there, at the exquisite villa that her uncle had converted from an ancient temple, until the cool season returned and Peking became once more habitable.

'I wonder if our dear Queen enjoyed her eighty-first birthday celebrations?' her aunt, Letitia Harland, asked musingly as the great North China Plain receded behind them and they entered the welcoming shade of a belt of trees.

William Harland assured his wife that Queen Victoria would have indeed enjoyed her birthday celebrations and Lady Glencarty, who was seated beside Olivia, replied vehemently that she only wished that *she* had been able to enjoy the revelry in the blessed beauty of her native Scotland and had not had to endure them in the stifling heat of Sir Claude MacDonald's salon. Sir Claude was Her Majesty's Minister at the Manchu Court and the previous evening, 24 May 1900, had hosted a party in order that the British community in Peking could suitably toast their sovereign.

The guests had numbered over sixty. Dinner had been served in a small theatre at the British Legation and afterwards there had been dancing on the tennis courts beneath the soft glow of paper lanterns hanging in the trees.

Olivia's aunt and Lady Glencarty continued to discuss the soirée, but Olivia remained silent, her thoughts full of Phillippe. How handsome he had looked as he sat across from her at Sir Claude's dining table, the light from the chandeliers gleaming on his sun-gold hair. Involuntarily she touched the square cut emerald that sparkled on the third finger of her left hand. Their engagement had pleased her aunt and uncle. Phillippe Casanaeve was one of the most eligible bachelors in the diplomatic corps. His arrival six months ago as a junior diplomat at the French Legation had caused many a female heart to flutter.

Tall, slim, sleekly moustached and elegantly dressed, he had attracted all eyes at the parties and picnics that were the backbone of diplomatic social life. He had singled her out almost from the very first, and her aunt and uncle had encouraged his attentions. Childless themselves, they had gallantly assumed responsibility for her when her parents had died, but it was a responsibility that had been unsought and Olivia knew that her marriage would come as a relief to them.

'Sir Claude seemed most perturbed yesterday evening when mention was made of the mountebanks in the northern provinces,' Lady Glencarty said as a vermilion and gold-plumaged bird darted from the trees, startling Olivia from her thoughts.

'Not mountebanks, Clarissa. Rebels,' William Harland corrected, his gloved hand resting lightly on the silver top of his malacca cane. 'The French Minister, Monsieur Pichon, is so alarmed by them that he has suggested the foreign powers in Peking send for a naval attachment from Tientsin to serve as protection, should it be needed.'

Lady Glencarty's heavy eyebrows shot upwards. 'I hope this suggestion was vetoed!' she said with asperity. 'To go to such lengths because of bands of superstitious peasants would be intolerable! We should become a laughing stock!'

'His suggestion *was* vetoed, but I am not too sure the decision was a wise one,' William Harland said gravely.

'The rebels are no longer confining their burning and looting of missions to the northern provinces of Chihli and Shansi. There have been reports of missionaries murdered a mere forty miles from Peking.'

His wife laid a hand restrainingly on his arm, her face pale. 'Please do not speak of it, my dear. It makes me feel quite ill.'

William Harland smiled reassuringly. 'Do not worry, Letitia. The danger does not extend to ourselves. No Chinese, Boxer or otherwise, would dare to lay violent hands on a member of one of the foreign legations.'

'Why are the rebels referred to as Boxers?' Olivia asked curiously, grateful for the light breeze which stirred the leaves on the trees and blew a tendril of soft dark hair against her cheek.

William Harland's obscure features softened. He was extremely fond of his intelligent and pretty niece. 'The sobriquet was given to them by missionaries. The rebels refer to themselves by a much more splendid name: The Fists of Righteous Harmony.'

Lady Glencarty snorted in derision.

'They object strongly to the western practice of building churches with spires,' William Harland continued, undeterred. 'Their own architecture refrains from anything they think will interfere with the *feng-shui*, the spirits of wind and water.'

'Poppycock!' Lady Glencarty said vigorously, 'And against such native superstition the French minister was prepared to make fools of us all by sending to Tientsin for a naval detachment!'

'It is, unfortunately, dangerous superstition,' William Harland said, a faint frown furrowing his brow. 'The Boxers and their followers believe that it is the presence of Europeans in China that is the cause of the present drought. They say that our presence has offended the spirits of wind and water and until they are appeased, that no rain will fall.'

Lady Glencarty's thin lips tightened disdainfully. 'Is it true that they believe they are invincible?' Letitia Harland asked nervously, adjusting her veil with a net-gloved hand. 'Lady MacDonald says that the spirits of heroes render them immune to death and that they cannot be killed.'

A slight smile tugged at the corners of her husband's mouth. 'I am not sure if even the Boxers are so credulous, my dear. It would make them a formidable fighting force if they were.'

'*Nothing* can turn ill-trained, illiterate peasants into a formidable fighting force,' Lady Glencarty said tartly.

William Harland politely refrained from replying and thereby antagonizing his guest further. But Olivia could tell that he was not convinced.

'We really must talk of them no longer,' Letitia Harland said with a shudder. 'When I think of the poor missionaries in Chihli and Shansi and what they have suffered, I feel quite faint. I cannot understand why the Empress does not intervene. She has power of life and death over her subjects, does she not?'

'She does indeed, Letitia,' said Lady Glencarty, carefully removing a speck of dust from the sweeping folds of her skirt. 'Though I refuse to believe that she exercises it in a manner that rumour would have us believe.'

A chill ran down Olivia's spine. Gossip said that there were days when the Inner Courtyard of the Imperial City ran red with blood. That not only did Empress Dowager Tzu-hsi command the execution of those who displeased her, but that she actually witnessed the executions in person. Olivia could well believe it. She had met the Empress Dowager only once, but it was an occasion that she would not soon forget.

In an unprecedented gesture, Empress Dowager Tzu-hsi had invited the diplomatic ladies to tea at the Winter Palace, and had presented each and every one of them with a generous gift of a ring. Olivia had accepted her present reluctantly. There was something unpleasant in the

Empress's hooded eyes. An expression which did not accord with her overtures of friendship.

She sat on a divan, flanked by eunuchs, her short, stout figure robed in stiff, yellow silk. Her hair was dark and sleek, parted down the centre and pulled tightly back over her ears, secured on the top of her head with a long, jade pin. Lady Glencarty had gushingly whispered to Olivia that she reminded her of their own, dear Queen, but Olivia had been unable to find any resemblance. There was something evil about the doll-like figure, her grotesquely long fingernails protected by jewelled nail shields. However much her actions might seem to belie it, Olivia was sure that the Empress despised the gaily chattering European women thronging her court. She had been relieved when the audience was over and they had been carried by sedan chair out of the Forbidden City and through the straight, dust-blown streets that led to the Legation district.

In Peking, as in other oriental cities, custom had always decreed that various trades were located separately and in their own areas. Silversmiths were to be found in one street, jewellers in another, and saddlers in a third. When diplomats arrived in Peking they, too, had been concentrated into their own area. Their legations were large houses set in vast, high-walled grounds. There were eleven of them together with an hotel, the Russo-Chinese Bank, the offices of Jardine Matheson, the inevitable club and a handful of European residences, occupying an area nearly three quarters of a mile square.

When Olivia had first arrived in Peking, she had been fascinated by how one part of the city had been walled inside another. In Peking's heart was the Winter Palace. The walls of the Forbidden City surrounded it and in turn was surrounded by the pink walls of the Imperial City. Beyond the gates of the Imperial City lay the Tartar City, the legations and cathedral, and the various missions. The walls of the Tartar City were massive and crenellated, more than forty feet high and forty feet thick. Beyond their gates lay the Chinese City, colourful and crowded and noisy.

Small shops huddled three-deep, gay flags announcing their wares. Craftsmen followed their professions in streets, mending delicate porcelain with nimble dexterity. Rope-dancers twirled and spun. Fortune-tellers vied with beggars for attention of the crowd. Pedlars whistled, carrying heavy paniers of sweets and cakes and household necessities. There were acrobats, jugglers, storytellers. Mule-drawn carts, and donkeys and camels. It was a teeming, raucous circus, and alongside it was the other China. The China of fluttering doves and almond blossom; of tinkling bells and the clear notes of trumpets as they blew in fanfare to welcome important personages at the Tien An Men Gate. All of it held Olivia in thrall. The gentle, passive faces of the Chinese charmed her, and she hated to think of the violence which flared in the North.

Despite the stories she had heard, she had scarcely been able to believe in the existence of the Boxers until the day that she met the Empress Dowager. The veiled hostility had been palpable, and looking into the raisin-black slits of her eyes, Olivia had been seized with a sudden sense of foreboding. With such a woman as Empress, any barbarity would be credible. Phillippe had teased her, and told her that her fears were groundless, but the uneasiness had persisted and even now, high amidst the peace and tranquillity of the Western Hills, it reached out and touched her, spoiling the beauty of the day.

'Lewis Sinclair is back in Peking,' William Harland said as the trees thinned, and they neared the marble lion-dogs flanking the gateway of the villa. 'He will have first-hand news of the situation in Shansi and no doubt Sir Claude will be grateful for it.'

'Is Mr Sinclair the reckless young man who married a Chinese girl?' his wife asked enquiringly.

William Harland nodded.

'I shall be most surprised if Sir Claude pays any attention to information coming from *that* source,' Lady Glencarty said. 'Do you know that he had the *effrontery* to assume that social invitations would be extended to his wife, and was unspeakably insolent when none were forthcoming?'

'It was a regrettable marriage,' William Harland agreed as the coach shuddered to a halt. 'It resulted in his leaving Peking, and that was a great loss. Despite his unfortunate go-to-the-devil manner, I am told he is a remarkably fine doctor, and speaks Chinese like a native.'

'He probably *lives* like a native now,' Lady Glencarty said with a shiver of distaste.

As Olivia stepped from the carriage, she glanced down at her engagement ring, glad that her marriage to Phillippe would not be discussed in such a way. She felt a surge of compassion for the unknown Chinese girl not welcome at social functions with her husband.

'Tea, Lin Pei,' Letitia said in relief as a pig-tailed Chinese hurried forward to greet them. 'Oh dear, my poor head. I shall never accustom myself to the summer heat.'

Parasols were closed, net gloves discarded. Olivia had no desire to sit sipping tea with Lady Glencarty. Her limbs were stiff from sitting for so long in the cramped confines of the carriage, and she yearned for exercise.

'Would you excuse me, Aunt Letitia? I would like to take a walk before dinner.'

'Yes, of course, my dear. But don't overtire yourself,' Letitia Harland added, wanting to do nothing more than rest and free herself from her too-tight Parisian corseting.

Olivia retired to her room to freshen her face with eau de Cologne. The afternoon sunlight filtered through lattice screens. Behind the delicately carved K'ang bed were embroidered hangings of full-blown peonies, crested pheasants, pomegranates and peaches. The former temple never failed to exercise its magic on her. She gazed around her with pleasure, then hurried downstairs, past the marble lion-dogs guarding the doorway, and out into the garden where ornamental ponds were crammed with lilies.

The scent of flowering trees filled the air. Exotic shrubs

bordered the gravel pathways. In the clear light the villa glowed like a jewel. Its roofs were rose-red, the ornate eaves upturned as if defying gravity. Scarlet and emerald and azure enamelling decorated the walls and balconies in an explosion of colour, perfectly offset by the stark purity of the groves of white pines rising behind it. She looked up into their cool depths longingly. Tomorrow she would ride high amongst them. It was too late in the day to ask that a horse be made ready for her now. She suppressed a sigh of regret. Riding was her greatest pleasure, and one she could not indulge in as often as she would have liked. A smile curved her lips. She would be able to ride and to walk to her heart's content when she was married to Phillippe.

She was beyond the large garden now, walking through a fragrant wilderness of knee-high grass. A little-used track led up into the groves of pines, beckoning her temptingly. Her aunt and Lady Glencarty would be resting. Her absence would not be noticed if she indulged herself.

She walked at a swift pace, enjoying her freedom and the pine-scented air. Not until she was well out of sight of the villa did she rest, leaning breathlessly against the silver bark of a tree. A hoopoe swooped low into the valley, the sun flashing on its gaudily coloured wings. She sighed contentedly, hoping that Philippe's government would not transfer him too soon from Peking. She did not want to leave China. She wanted to discover more about it. She smiled to herself, wondering if she was succumbing to what Lady Glencarty referred derisively as 'the strange fascination which a Chinese environment so often exercises over a European mind'. If she was, she was uncaring. She was nineteen, engaged to an incredibly handsome man, and living in one of the least visited and most exotic countries in the world.

There was no sound; no movement; even the clouds seemed motionless in the high blue bowl of the sky. She closed her eyes, enjoying the warmth of the sun on her face, and her daydream of what life would be like when she was Mrs Phillippe Casanaeve. Then came the scream. Her eyes flew open. For a second she thought she had been dreaming, and then it came again, terrified and high-pitched, followed immediately by shouts and cries and the distant whinnying of horses.

With a gasp of dismay she ran from the shelter of the trees, desperately seeking a vantage point that would enable her to see down into the valley.

The track had curved round and away from the villa, and all that she could see were the ranks of pines and a wisp of cloud. Fear made her cry out loud. It wasn't a trail of cirrus trapped in the fold of the hills: it was smoke.

'Oh no!' she whispered, her hand clutching her throat as the shouts and cries intensified. 'The villa! The villa is on fire!'

She began to run downhill, her momentum hurtling her into the trunks of the trees, her palms becoming scratched and bloodied as she clutched at the rough bark. The shouts grew louder, more demented, and the smell of burning wood hung heavy in the air. The way seemed endless. It was impossible to imagine that it was the same track she had climbed so enjoyably only a short time before. Beneath the hem of her gown, her small booted feet gouged out clouds of dust as she slipped and slid heedlessly over the dry, parched earth. With a sob of relief, she saw that the track veered round the shoulder of the hill. Another twenty yards and she would have a clear view of the cause of smoke now billowing upwards in acrid density.

She hurtled forward and then the track turned and she slithered to a halt, seizing a tree-trunk for support, gazing in stupefied disbelief at the scene before her.

The fairy-tale roofs were barely discernible in the smoke. The colonnade fronting the villa was burning furiously, the filigree carved wood cracking and splintering, the flames shooting skywards, the breeze carrying the sparks so that they fell on her hair and skirt. But it was not the ravaging fire that rooted her to the spot in horror. The immaculately laidout gardens, with their lily ponds and dwarf trees and flowering shrubs were overrun by yelling, exultant Chinese. Scarlet sashes swathed their heads and waists. Monstrous swords flashed in the late afternoon sunlight.

'No!' she cried in protest. 'Oh, dear God, *no!*'

She ran towards the villa as if there were devils at her heels. How she would chase off the nightmare figures once she arrived, she had no idea. She had no thoughts other than that her aunt and uncle were trapped inside the burning inferno, and that she had to reach them; had to do something before it was too late. The breath hammered in her chest, the blood pounded in her ears. The trees thinned, the ground levelled and the long, bristled stalks of the grass clung to her skirt, hampering her speed.

Through the shimmering heat, she saw Lady Glencarty's purple clad figure try to run from the smoke and flames, an arm shielding her face. As she did so, the grotesque Grand Guignol figures whooped with triumph and surged forward, weapons high. Lady's Glencarty's screams rent the air and then the smoke obscured her, and there was nothing but heat and noise and the hideous flare as the villa's eaves ignited.

Olivia was aware of her own screams, of the smoke stinging her eyes and catching at the back of her throat and then she heard the unmistakable sound of hoofbeats bearing down behind her. She was going to die. Unprepared and ignominiously and at the hands of crazed fanatics. Rage flooded through her. If she was going to die, she would die fighting, resisting with every ounce of strength she possessed.

She was dimly aware of a furious voice commanding her to halt and still she ran, the frenzied shouts of the rampaging Boxers reverberating through the air.

The ground throbbed before the onslaught of galloping hooves.

'*For the love of God!*' a voice shouted exasperatedly.

She could sense the horse bearing down on her; feel the

heat of the flames on her face. Sparks fell around her, sizzling and cracking.

'Aunt Letitia!' she cried vainly, and then the horse veered past her and the rider sprang from its back, hurling her bodily to the ground.

She tried to struggle free, but iron-strong hands pinioned her fast.

'*What the hell do you think you're doing?*' a furious voice demanded. '*Are you trying to kill yourself?*'

She gasped in bewilderment. It wasn't a red-garbed Boxer holding her prisoner, but a European. His face was savage, the cheekbones high, the mouth hard.

'My aunt and uncle!' she panted. 'They're in the villa!'

'Sweet Christ!' He released her abruptly, thick black hair tumbling low over his brow as he wheeled to view the burning villa and the frenzied figures ringing it in whooping exultation. '*Stay here and don't move.*'

The words were flung at her as he leapt to his feet, running towards his horse and the rifle jammed in his saddlebag. The Boxers were a mere fifty yards away, distorted figures eddying and surging in the heat haze. Their whole attention was fixed on the burning villa and when the first rifle shot rang out there were cries of alarm and bewilderment. The unwieldy swords being swung vengefully around their heads faltered and dropped. A white-robed figure, red scarves flying from waist and wrists, plummeted to the ground. There was another shot, and another. Olivia pushed herself to her knees. The Boxers were in disarray, unsure from what direction the unexpected attack was coming.

By her side the horse whinnied and reared as, shielded by the long grass, its rider fired a volley of rifle shots which sounded as if an army was bearing down in avenging fury. Olivia saw another demonic figure fall, and then another and then, as she stumbled to her feet, sobbing in relief, the whole host turned on its heels, fleeing in full retreat.

Her rescuer began to sprint towards the blazing inferno

and she picked up her skirts, racing with a pounding heart in his wake.

He turned his head, yelling at her again to stay where she was. At any other time, the fierce command would have instantly halted her, but above the roaring of the flames there came a woman's cry, and she ignored him, running even faster, every nerve in her body raw with fear.

At the main entrance the heat beat them back; the marble lions grinning grotesquely at their helplessness.

'This way!' she shouted desperately, pressing a handkerchief against her nose and mouth, running with all her remaining strength towards the rear of the villa.

A beam fell with a shudder, tongues of fire shooting off it. A volley of sparks rained down on her and the silk of her skirt sizzled and burst into flame. She beat at it with her hands, still running, running, running. Smoke billowed round her. No matter how hard she tried, she could not keep pace with him. She saw him take a flight of steps two at a time and disappear into the roaring conflagration. She pressed her arm against her face, shielding it from the heat, determined to follow and then, with a sob of relief, she saw the servants run screaming on to the lawns, the stumbling figure of Lady Glencarty in their wake. Seconds later her uncle followed, the Englishman at his heels, her aunt senseless in his arms.

As they fled towards Olivia, there was a massive rumble and the delicate, upturned eaves succumbed to the inferno, toppling in on themselves.

At a safe distance, the formidable Englishman laid Letitia Harland on to the grass and began to loosen her tight bodice with indecent expertise.

Olivia knelt down at her aunt's side, her hair curling wispily in damp tendrils around her frightened face. 'Is she alive?' she asked urgently.

He nodded, rolling Letitia Harland unceremoniously over on to her side, his fingers resting on the pulse beat at her wrist. As he did so, Letitia Harland shuddered, her eyelids flickering open. Olivia grasped her aunt's hand, weak with relief.

If her aunt's rescuer also felt relief, he showed no sign of it. The black bars of his eyebrows were pulled together in a frown as her uncle stepped shakily towards them, saying incredulously, 'Sinclair! By all that's wonderful, Lewis Sinclair!' He grasped him fervently by the hand. 'Sinclair, my good chap! How can I thank you enough?'

With eyes suspiciously bright, he dropped to his knees beside the prostrate figure of his wife. 'It's all over, my love,' he said, circling her shoulders with his arm. 'You are safe now. There is no more danger.'

As her aunt moaned and clung piteously to him, Olivia saw a flicker of impatience cross Lewis Sinclair's face and then he was saying in a tightly controlled voice, 'I doubt if that is quite the case, Sir William.'

William Harland looked up at him in bewilderment, his usual self-assurance pathetically absent. 'I'm afraid that I don't understand ...'

'Are there no more men in your party?'

Sir William shook his head and Olivia saw comprehension dawn in his eyes. She felt suddenly faint. They were fifteen miles from Peking. Their servants had scattered. The countryside was alive with Boxers, and only Mr Sinclair was armed. She swayed dizzily and Lewis Sinclair sprang forward, catching hold of her in strong arms as she fell into a vortex of darkness and black rushing winds.

As she returned to consciousness she was aware that she was lying on the grass, her head resting on the linen of a jacket that carried a faint but pleasing smell of cologne. Male cologne. She could hear her Uncle William saying, 'Poor child' and a rich, deep voice retort dryly, 'A little more than that, Sir William. Your niece was intent on beating off the Boxers single-handed when I came to her aid.'

Her cheeks warmed and she stirred hastily in order to

bring the conversation to a halt before she should be embarrassed further. Her uncle immediately rushed to her side, but Lewis Sinclair remained where he was, his dark brows pulled together, white lines of impatience edging his mouth.

His jacket had been discarded and beneath the white silk of his shirt, Olivia was uncomfortably aware of exceedingly broad shoulders and lean, hard muscles. There was a sense of power under restraint about him, a brooding restlessness that was palpable.

She remembered the conversation that had taken place in the carriage and marvelled that it had been only a few hours ago. Since then the whole world seemed to have tilted on its axis. Her uncle had said that Lewis Sinclair had married a Chinese girl and had left Peking when it became obvious that his marriage would never be countenanced by the European community there.

She looked across at him in the gathering dusk as her uncle solicitously asked after her well-being. She could well imagine that he would be uncaring of what society thought of him. There was a fearlessness about him, a daring and an insolence towards life that she had never encountered before, and which she found strangely attractive.

She saw the muscles along his jaw line flex and then his gaze inadvertently met hers. Shock ran through her. His eyes were almost as dark as his hair and the expression in them was one of inner pain, searing in its intensity.

Distinctly shaken, and telling herself she must have been mistaken, she looked away hastily, saying to her uncle, 'Is Aunt Letitia quite recovered?'

William Harland's face was white and drawn. 'Yes, thanks to Doctor Sinclair.'

Olivia looked up at him startled, and then remembered. Lewis Sinclair was a doctor. It certainly explained the no-nonsense way in which he had loosened her aunt's corseting.

'And Lady Glencarty?'

'Only too well,' her uncle replied dryly, and Olivia became aware of Lady Gencarty's voice a little distance away, raised in outraged indignation. 'I've never *heard* of such an insulting suggestion! The man must be mad! To *walk* to Peking! I would rather die first.'

'The choice is yours,' Lewis Sinclair said indifferently, rising to his feet and walking across to his horse. 'If you stay here, you will almost certainly be dead by morning.'

'Poppycock,' Lady Glencarty retorted, but there was a trace of uncertainty in her voice. She turned to William Harland. 'Sir William, please inform ... this ... *gentleman* ... that troops will already be on their way here from Peking to avenge this outrage.'

'There are no troops,' William Harland said wearily.

'Then the minister should have seen to it that troops were sent for,' Lady Glencarty said, conveniently forgetting that only hours before she had derided the thought of any such action.

Sir William struggled for patience. 'We are in an exceedingly difficult situation,' he siad tensely, 'The Boxers will have realized by now that they were not being attacked by a large force and one rifle will not deter them for long if they return.'

Lady Glencarty glared at him. 'I will *not* walk to Peking as if I were a peasant.'

'Nor will I, William,' Letitia Harland said, her voice trembling. 'We would become the talk of the community. Lady MacDonald would think it most odd.'

With an expletive of impatience that made Sir William blanch, Lewis Sinclair pivotted on his heel and strode away from them.

William Harland regarded his retreating back nervously and grasped his wife's arm. 'Calm yourself, Letitia. Lady MacDonald will say that you have been very gallant.'

'But I do not want to be gallant, William,' Letitia Harland said, tears streaking her face. 'I want to wait here as Clarissa suggests, until help arrives.'

'No help is going to be forthcoming, my dear,' William Harland said quietly. 'There are no troops and ...'

'But the Empress has soldiers! When she hears what has taken place, she will send her soldiers ...'

William Harland doubted very much whether Empress Tzu-hsi would send soldiers, even if she knew of their predicament. And she would not get to know of their predicament, as Sinclair had informed him that all the telegraph wires had been cut by the rebels. Gently he told his wife of the impossibility of making contact with Peking.

With an underlying note of fear in her voice, Lady Glencarty said, 'Rubbish! I refuse to believe it! I ...'

William Harland mopped his forehead with his handkerchief. Behind them the flames from the burning villa continued to leap skywards. The servants had fled. The horses had bolted. He was responsible for the lives of three people, two of whom he loved dearly. Common sense told him that he could only save those lives with the help of Lewis Sinclair, and Sinclair had told him that he had been travelling *away* from Peking when he had come to their aid. A cold shiver ran down his spine. If Sinclair continued on his journey, leaving them to their fate, that fate would almost certainly be death. Letitia grew beathless walking the short distance from the carriage to the coolness of her rooms. She would never be able to complete the hot, dusty, return trip to Peking on foot. She needed Sinclair's horse, and she needed the protection afforded by his rifle.

He fixed Lady Glencarty with a steely stare. 'As my guest, Clarissa, you will oblige me by doing what I request.'

Lady Glencarty gasped, opened her mouth to speak, and then, for the first and only time in her life, thought better of it.

William Harland turned on his heel. 'Where did Doctor Sinclair go?' he asked Olivia.

'He strode off in the direction of the gatehouse,' Olivia said, her eyes troubled. 'Uncle William, if the telegraph wires have been cut, the countryside between here and

Peking could very well be teeming with Boxers.'

'That is a risk we have to take,' her uncle said, making sure his wife could not overhear him. 'To remain here would be folly. The Boxers cannot have retreated far and will be back to see what, if anything, remains to be looted.'

Olivia looked over her shoulder apprehensively, half expecting to see red-sashed figures once more bearing down on them.

Her uncle continued, 'It is also our duty to ensure that Peking is informed of what has taken place. When I last spoke to Sir Claude, he believed the Boxers were contained in Chihli and Shansi. Their presence so far south can only mean that they are intent on launching an attack on the city.'

Olivia paled. There were over four hundred Europeans resident in the city. Many of them were missionaries, their lives revolving around the cathedrals and churches, the hospitals and orphanages. The others were diplomats: men like Sir Claude MacDonald and Mr Edwin Conger, the American Minister, both of whom had their wives and children with them. Men like Phillippe. She felt her heart contract. Even now the Boxers could very well be marching on Peking, and they were unwarned and unprepared.

'What is it that Mr Sinclair wishes us to do, Uncle?'

William Harland thanked God for her quick grasp of the situation and her lack of hysteria. 'He thinks that we should set off for Peking on foot. If we walk through the night, we can be there by dawn.'

'But Aunt Letitia cannot walk so far over rough ground!' Olivia protested.

'Your aunt will ride on Doctor Sinclair's horse.'

'And Lady Glencarty?'

Sir William passed a hand wearily across his eyes. 'Perhaps another horse can be obtained,' he said, turning in relief as Lewis Sinclair strode towards them, throwing a pile of clothing on to the ground.

'I salvaged these from the gatehouse,' he said curtly.

'There's no sign of the gatekeeper or his wife. I imagine they fled with the rest of the servants.'

Sir William regarded the Chinese clothing in perplexity. 'I'm sorry, Sinclair. I don't quite understand ...'

'The ladies will find the trek easier in native dress. Their long skirts make it impossible for them to walk far, much less to ride.'

Letitia Harland gazed at the bundle of cast-off clothing in horror. 'I couldn't, William. I couldn't ...' she said with a shudder.

Lady Glencarty's rocking-horse nosrils flared. 'No!' she snapped, her head high, splendidly regal despite her dishevelled coiffure and the smoke smuts on her cheeks. '*Never!*'

Olivia saw Lewis Sinclair's jaw tighten in impatience. 'Lady Glencarty, it is fifteen miles to Peking. Your present skirt is not only long and straight, it has a ridiculous train that I have nearly fallen over twice. You will be able to walk far quicker in native dress.'

'No,' Lady Glencarty repeated, and then with ice-cold clarity added, 'Those clothes, Doctor Sinclair, are *Chinese!*'

The insult to his wife was blatant. Olivia saw the skin stretch like parchment across his cheekbones. His knuckles clenched white and then he swung on his heels, striding quickly away, towards his horse.

Olivia took one look at her uncle's stricken face and picked up her skirt, running after him. 'Please, Doctor Sinclair! Lady Glencarty did not mean ...'

He spun around and she flinched at the expressiion in his eyes. 'I am well aware of what Lady Glencarty meant,' he said, his voice a whiplash in the growing darkness.

'But it would not have done,' Olivia protested. 'All the garments are too small for my aunt and Lady Glencarty. They could not wear them even if they tried. They would not fit.'

Lewis Sinclair frowned, and then looked across to the plump figure of Letitia Harland and the Junoesque proportions of Lady Glencarty. There was no disputing the truth of what she said. He swore savagely to himself and then said with barely controlled patience, 'You are quite right, Miss Harland. They would not fit at all.'

'If I tear a rent in my aunt's skirt to the knee, it will enable her to ride.'

He nodded, releasing his hold of the horse, and William Harland let out a sigh of relief.

'Come, my dear,' he said to his wife. 'There is no further time to spare. Let Olivia do as she suggests and let me help you mount Doctor Sinclair's horse.'

'Olivia, no!' her aunt cried as Olivia seized the hem of her ankle-length skirt, 'It is Indian silk!'

Olivia ignored her, ripping the skirt to the knee.

Lady Glencarty glared, 'My gown,' she said freezingly, 'will remain as it is.'

Lewis Sinclair disregarded her. If she broke her ankle trying to descend the hillside, she would have no one to blame but herself.

He turned instead to Olivia. 'You will find Chinese dress easier to walk in.'

She nodded, and as there was nowhere else to change, walked quickly towards the gatehouse.

The flames from the burning villa cast a lurid red glow over the surrounding hills and trees. Somewhere, in their depths, were the Boxers. Perhaps even at this very moment they were watching them. She shivered, and in the deserted gatehouse quickly abandoned her apple-green dress with its long skirt, and stepped into the strange and oddly comfortble coarse blue cotton garments. The smock was long, falling narrowly over loose trousers that enabled her to move with ease.

When she returned, Lady Glencarty said scathingly, 'You look a disgrace, Olivia.'

'No you don't,' Lewis Sinclair said, 'Chinese dress suits you.'

She looked up at him and as their eyes met, a curious

sensation ran down her spine. 'It would be even better if your hair was unpinned,' he continued, eyeing her speculatively. 'Then if we *are* attacked you won't look at all European.'

He stepped towards her, reaching out, taking the pins deftly from her hair. She felt her cheeks flame, and then he was saying in a voice that sounded oddly gentle, 'Now you really do look Chinese.'

She moved away from him sharply, curiously disconcerted, reminded abruptly of the existence of his wife. Where was she now? Had he been journeying to meet her? She tilted her chin upwards. It was no concern of hers if he had. She would not think of Lewis Sinclair or his Chinese wife. Instead, she would think of Phillippe. Tall and blond and devastatingly charming. His face seemed a little indistinct, but that was because she was tired. She braced her shoulders. There was a fifteen-mile walk ahead of her, most of it over rough terrain. She could not afford to feel tired. Again she tried to think of Phillippe, but as she followed Lewis Sinclair's broad-shouldered figure away from the villa and into the darkness, she was aware that she was once more remembering the flash of pain she had surprised in his eyes, when he had thought himself unobserved. It had been so raw, so deep, it had almost taken her breath away. She wondered what had occasioned it. What kind of life he lived in the countryside far from Peking.

'Are you all right, my dear?' her uncle asked her as they made their way carefully down the roughly made track that they had ascended with such ease in the carriage only hours ago.

'Yes,' Olivia replied, but her voice was vague, her thoughts elsewhere.

Two

Olivia had never before realized how quiet the night could be. In the surrounding silence their footsteps on the roughly made track sounded deafening. She looked around apprehensively as the horse sent a flurry of pebbles tumbling into the undergrowth. Surely they would be heard? The Boxers could not have reteated far.

Lady Glencarty was breathing heavily, keeping pace with them in a manner that earned her Olivia's grudging admiration as first one arduous mile was covered, and then two.

The moon scudded out from a bank of cloud. The trees receded and the great, parched plain spread out before them. Ahead of them Lewis Sinclair halted and Lady Glencarty collapsed on to a boulder in relief.

Sir William hurried forward and stood beside Lewis Sinclair, regarding the vast expanse of open country with anxious eyes. 'No sign of Boxers?' he asked queryingly, struggling to regulate his breathing and appear unaffected by the tiring descent.

Lewis Sinclair shook his head.

'That's good,' Sir William said, resisting the temptation to emulate Lady Glencarty. He had not realized that he was so unfit. His heart hammered painfully and the muscles in his legs ached.

Lewis Sinclair turned and regarded the perspiring Lady Glencarty with a slight frown. He was well aware that Sir William had found the way down the hillside arduous, and certainly Lady Glencarty must have done so. She was a heavily-built woman in her early sixties, unused to exertion.

He glanced across at Olivia. She, alone, was showing no signs of tiredness. Her hair was thick and dark, hanging down freely, almost to her waist, her slenderness heightened by the native dress she wore. His heart contracted violently. For a moment it was as if Pearl Moon was once more at his side. Pearl Moon, whom he had buried with his bare hands after the Boxers had razed to the ground the village in which they were living. Pearl Moon, with her sweetness and gentleness and happy laughter. Pearl Moon, whom he had loved and irrevocably lost. His hands bunched into fists and a muscle jerked savagely at the corner of his clenched jaw.

Pearl Moon had been a Christian, and Chinese converts to Christianity were hated by the Boxers almost as much as Europeans. He had been at a distant village when the attack had taken place, setting the broken leg of a young peasant boy. He had not been with her when she had died, and he wondered, in a sea of pain that he was barely able to conquer, if he would ever be able to forgive himself.

'I think the ladies need a rest,' Sir William was saying.

Lewis passed a hand over his eyes. After Pearl Moon's death he had ridden hard to Peking, leaving his five-year-old son in the care of the Vicar-Apostolic of Peking, Monseigneur Favier. Then, for five long months, he had done his best to summon aid for the hapless Chinese converts unprotected against the Boxers' wrath.

He had been unsuccessful. Sir Claude MacDonald had expressed his condolences on being told of the death of Pearl Moon, but had been unable to provide him with even a small body of men. If the Chinese converts needed the protection of Peking, they would have to find their own way inside the city walls.

He had approached the other legations: the American, the Belgian, the Italian. The response had been the same. They were not responsible for the numberless Chinese who had abandoned their own faith and gods for Christianity. His eyes darkened as he remembered the insolent young diplomat at the French legation who had dismissed Pearl Moon's death as being only that of 'another native'. His fist had shot out and he had floored the suavely dressed Frenchman with a savage blow to the jaw, storming from the legation before anyone could have the satisfaction of evicting him.

Disgusted by the apathy which he had met, appalled at the inability of the ministers to grasp just how many innocent Chinese were about to lose their lives, he had ridden to outlying missions himself, escorting as many converts as he could to the relative safety of the city. The Boxers were now only days, perhaps hours away and he could ill afford to waste time shepherding the Harlands and lady Glencarty to Peking when so many others required his help.

'I think the ladies need a rest,' Sir William repeated, not liking the grim expression of Lewis Sinclair's face.

This time Lewis heard him. 'Of course,' he said tersely, walking over to his horse and removing a bottle of water from his saddlebag.

Sir William helped his wife to dismount, and the water was passed round. Letitia Harland accepted the bottle and held it gingerly, unaccustomed to drinking without the benefit of a glass.

'For goodness' sake, hurry up, Letitia,' Lady Glencarty said bad-temperedly, 'You're spilling more than you're drinking!'

'Yes, of course. I am sorry, Clarissa,' Letitia said apologetically, tipping the leather bottle once more to her lips, and this time spilling only a little water on to her bodice.

'Are there any other European villas nearby?' Lewis asked Sir William abruptly.

'The Hoggett-Smythes hve a summer home half a mile away on the rim of the trees, but they aren't in residence, thank God. One of the children has chicken pox and was too ill to travel.'

'But there will be servants there, preparing the villa for their arrival?' Lewis persisted.

'Well, yes, I suppose so,' Sir William said, not understanding the reason for his interest.

Lewis picked up his rifle. The chances were that the Hoggett-Smythes' servants were Christians. Half a mile there and back would take him very little time. It would enable Lady Glencarty to rest before they set out across the plain and, if the Hoggett-Smythes' villa had not already been attacked, it would enable him to warn the inmates and offer them the chance of returning to Peking.

'I say, Sinclair ... What the devil ...?' Sir William began as he prepared to leave.

'I'll be ten minutes, perhaps less.'

'But you can't leave us here, unprotected!' Sir William protested in alarm. 'I've told you, the Hoggett-Smythes are still in Peking. The villa is deserted.'

'Except for the servants,' Lewis said dryly. He took the water bottle from Lady Glencarty's startled grasp. 'I'll take this with me. I may be able to refill it.'

Olivia, remembering the dead and wounded that might have so easily have been left in the wake of the Boxer attack on their own villa, stepped towards him. 'I'll come with you,' she said quietly. 'You may need help.'

A flash of surprise crossed his eyes, and then he merely nodded.

'Olivia, you must *not* go into the woods with Mr Sinclair! It is quite improper,' Letitia Harland remonstrated tearfully.

'I must go, Aunt Letitia. There may be people hurt. I shall be perfectly safe with Doctor Sinclair to escort me.'

'No, Olivia! I forbid it!' her aunt said, but Olivia's mind was made up and she simply squeezed Letitia Harland's hand and turned, following Lewis Sinclair into the depths of the trees.

Letitia Harland pressed her hand against her mouth, smothering a cry of anguish, wishing desperately that they had never left Peking; that they had never left England. Never even *heard* of China.

'I shall complain about Doctor Sinclair's attitude to Sir Claude,' Lady Glencarty said, when he was safely out of earshot. 'His manner is unpardonably overbearing.'

'I hope that you will also inform Sir Claude that he saved our lives,' Sir William said dryly. 'And now, if you please Clarissa, I think it would be best if you were to remain silent. We don't want to attract any unwelcome attention.'

Olivia's heart beat light and fast as she wallked quickly along at Lewis Sinclair's side. The track was dry and sandy, the trees pressing in closely all around them. There was a rustle in the undergrowth as a small wild animal darted for cover and she drew in her breath sharply. He looked down at her, the expression in his eyes unreadable in the darkness.

'Are you afraid?'

'A little,' she answered as he slapped a low-lying branch out of the way. She wasn't sure, but she thought that a slight smile had softened the harsh contours of his mouth. After a while she said hesitantly, 'Doctor Sinclair, why do the Boxers hate us so?'

'China has always discouraged foreigners, Miss Harland, and the treaties that she has been forced to make with other countries over recent years has opened the gates to a flood of them.' He paused and then said with a curious edge to his voice, 'Unwittingly, it has been the missionaries who have most offended the peasant population from which the Boxers have sprung.'

She remembered that his parents had been missionaries and said tentatively, 'Because of the church spires that offend the *feng-shui*?'

He nodded and though she could not see, she knew that his face was once again sombre. 'We have paid far too little heed to the deeply ingrained superstitions of the peasantry. The telegraph poles that we have strung across the country also pierce the sky and offend the spirits. Unfortunately, when the wind blows the wires make a low moaning noise and the country people believe that it is the sound of the spirits in pain. They also rust and the rainwater dripping from them is tinged a dark red.'

A small frown creased Olivia's brow. 'I can understand why the noise would distress them, but I do not understand about the rainwater.'

'They believe that the rusted rainwater is blood,' Lewis Sinclair said with stark simplicity.

Olivia gasped. 'But that is terrible!' Has no one taken the trouble to explain to them? To set their minds at rest?'

'No, Miss Harland,' Lewis said, aware that Pearl Moon would have liked Olivia Harland exceedingly. 'No one has.'

The path curved and dipped and Olivia said, 'Are there other things, too? Do the railway lines offend them?'

'Being flat, they do not offend the *feng-shui* in the same way as the telegraph lines do, but hardly a mile of track can be laid without the grave of someone's ancestors being disturbed and ancestor worship is the most deep-rooted of all Chinese superstition.'

They continued on in a silence that was curiously companionable and then Olivia said, 'I understand now why the Boxers savaged the telegraph lines between here and Peking, but I still don't understand why the missionaries are hated so. They do so much good. In Peking, unwanted girl babies are simply left outside the city walls to die and the missionaries take them in and shelter them, and school them.'

A spasm of pain crossed Lewis Sinclair's handsome face. Pearl Moon had been just such an unwanted child. Left to die of exposure and saved by his parents. For the first few years of his life, he had believed that she was his sister and been puzzled that she looked so different from himself. Then he had understood and they had become friends, the bond between them as deep as any filial bond could possibly have been. When he had been sent away to school in England it had been Pearl Moon that he had missed. Pearl Moon that he had been homesick for.

'So how,' Olivia was saying, 'can the Chinese possibly object to them? They save hundreds and hundreds of babies every year.'

Lewis closed his eyes to the painful images of the past and said, 'The Chinese have exposed unwanted girl babies at birth since time immemorial. They cannot, and do not, believe that the missionaries save the babies for no other reason than the sheer goodness of their hearts.'

Olivia's frown of perplexity deepened. 'Then what on earth do they believe?' she asked, brushing a tangle of undergrowth out of her way.

Lewis glanced across at her. She was an intelligent girl and she deserved the truth. 'That they have an ulterior motive,' he said, his voice grim. 'It is a widely held belief that Europeans can turn lead into silver. Because so many of the babies rescued are in advanced states of malnutrition, large numbers of them die. The Chinese do not believe that their deaths are due to natural causes. They believe that they are killed by the missionaries for the purpose of alchemy.'

Olivia halted abruptly, her eyes wide. 'They can't! It's too horrible!'

'I'm sorry,' he said gently. 'But you asked me for the truth and there it is. There are other things, too, equally horrible. The Christian rites of baptism for the dead and Extreme Unction are similarly misunderstood.'

Somehow she forced herself once more to walk, fighting down a wave of nausea. At last she said unsteadily, 'Do people know this? Does Uncle William? Does Sir Claude?'

'I'm not sure about your uncle. Sir Claude does, certainly. And he regards it as another example of peasant ignorance not to be taken seriously.'

'But it must be taken seriously,' Olivia said aghast.

'People are dying because of it! Missionaries in Chihli and Shansi, and now missionaries nearer to Peking.'

'And their converts,' Lewis said, and at the savagery in his voice, she looked across at him, startled. His mouth had compressed into a hard, bitter line and the skin across his cheekbones was taut, white as parchment.

He had withdrawn from her. Lost in the hellish world that she had glimpsed so briefly when she had caught him unawares and the suffering in his eyes had been exposed to her gaze.

She fell silent, wondering what it was that had happened to cause him such pain. Perhaps his parents had been murdered by the Boxers. Perhaps the Chinese that they had converted to Christianity had suffered death and worse.

Her heart tightened. Only that very morning she had been intoxicated by the beauty of China. By the hoopoe swooping low across the valley; by the cloudless sky and the serried ranks of endless pine. Now the beauty was destroyed. Transfigured into ugliness and monstrosity.

The white stone of the Hoggett-Smythes' villa gleamed palely between the trees. She felt a prickle of fear run down her spine. It was very quiet. Very still. But that did not mean that the Boxers had not been there before them. That bodies were not strewn upon the grass.

They broke free of the trees and Lewis surveyed the silent house through narrowed eyes. The windows were naked, devoid of blinds; the flowerbeds, barely discernible in the moonlight, were gouged and trampled by scores of rampaging feet.

'Stay here,' he said quietly.

'But why ...'

'The Boxers have been here and it's just possible that they are still here. Now do as I say.'

She shivered, despite the airless heat as he strode away from her, watching as he mounted the long flight of steps that led to the entrance with panther-like agility. A night owl gave a raucous cry and she gritted her teeth. It would do no good at all to panic. There was nowhere to run; nowhere to hide.

Lewis strode swiftly through the deserted, ransacked rooms. He had known instinctively, before he had entered, that the Hoggett- Smythes were not in residence. It had been the sight of dead and mutilated bodies that he wished to spare Olivia by insisting that she remain outside. There were no bodies on the ground-floor rooms. No smell of blood. He mounted the stairs, striding along the delicately tilted corridors, flinging open door after door. In the nursery, a rocking-horse lay overturned on its side, great glass eyes staring.

'Thank God for the chicken pox,' he said to himself, retreating to the disordered kitchen, refilling his water bottle, rifling through the cupboards for packets of biscuits.

To Olivia it seemed an eternity before his tall, broad-shouldered figure took shape once more in the darkness.

'Can you carry these?' He thrust several packets of biscuits into her arms. 'The villa has been ransacked but there's no sign of anyone killed or injured.'

'But the servants must have been there when the Boxers attacked,' Olivia said as he began to lead the way round the back of the villa and towards the stables. 'Where can they have gone?'

'If they were Christians, back to their villages. If not, they may have joined forces with the Boxers.'

Olivia's eyes widened in disbelief. 'They wouldn't do that! The Hoggett-Smythes' servants have been with them for years and are devoted to them!'

His face was grim as he began to fling open the door of first one empty stall and then another. 'When the Boxers reach Peking, I think you may be surprised at just how quickly their ranks are swelled by Chinese "devoted" to Europeans,' he said dryly.

She stared at him. He had been born in China; brought

up in China. He had married a Chinese girl and had chosen to devote his life working among the Chinese. Yet he spoke of them as if he hated them.

'Do you not like the Chinese?' she asked incredulously.

He opened the door of the last stall and stared down at her, raising a dark eyebrow. 'Do you?' he asked, a note of surprise in his voice.

'Yes,' she said, uncomfortably aware of his nearness in the darkness.

'Even after the Boxers did their best to massacre your family?' His gaze was disturbingly intense.

'All Chinese are not Boxers, and I do not believe that all Chinese are sympathetic to them.'

His eyes were appraising. 'Perhaps you are right,' he said, and for the first time she saw something approaching a smile touch his lips. 'But when news of what has taken place reaches Peking, I doubt if many of your friends and family will be in agreement with you.'

He swung open the door of the last stall and a short, sturdy Mongol pony regarded them indifferently.

'You're not quite what I had hoped for,' Lewis said to it as he led the pony from the stall and searched for a bit and bridle.

'Will he be strong enough to carry Lady Glencarty?' Olivia asked doubtfully, stroking the pony's soft muzzle.

Lewis grinned, his white teeth flashing in the darkness. 'Ponies like this are accustomed to heavy loads, Miss Harland.'

'But not quite such *illustrious* loads,' Olivia murmured mischievously.

The amusement in his eyes deepened. 'No,' he agreed, 'and I doubt if the lady in question is going to be very impressed with her mount.'

They began to walk back along the soft, dry track and as the trees began to thin, revealing the expanse of the plain, she said, suddenly shy, 'I haven't thanked you yet for saving my life.'

He felt a ripple run through him, a tensing of his muscles and then he shrugged dismissively and she knew that the lean, dark face was once more harsh and abrasive. Perhaps he had not wanted to be reminded of that hideous moment when he had ridden to her aid. She wondered how many other men would have done so. Phillippe, of course. But she could not imagine many other gentlemen riding full pelt and single-handed into a ferocious Boxer attack.

Lewis continued to march along the track in silence. He had saved Olivia Harland, her aunt and her uncle and the obnoxious Lady Glencarty, but he had not been able to save his own wife. The burden of that failure weighed so heavily on him that he could scarcely breathe.

He was overcome with hatred for the country he had always loved so passionately. His knuckles whitened. He would make a new life for himself elsewhere. But where? England, with its neat fields and polite society gave him claustrophobia. He had never wanted to be anywhere else but China. It was China that needed him; China that was in his blood, and China that had betrayed him.

'What,' said Lady Glencarty, as they emerged from the trees, 'is that?' Her glare was directed at the pony.

'It was the only mount that we could find,' Lewis said tersely.

'It's a Mongol pony and very strong,' Olivia said, patting it affectionately.

'And am I to ride it?' Lady Glencarty asked, regarding it resentfully.

'Oh please do, Clarissa,' Letitia Harland said, eyeing the pony apprehensively. 'Although it is small, it looks quite fierce and I do not think that I would like to ride it at all.'

Lady Glencarty glowered at her friend and Lewis said dispassionately, 'You will have to make some alteration to your skirt in order to mount.'

Lady Glencarty clenched her teeth and then, accepting defeat, bent down and with a strength born of fury ripped the seam of her skirt wide, mounting the pony with as much dignity as she could muster.

Surprisingly, Olivia did not feel tired as she resumed the journey, walking at Lewis Sinclair's side. Her aunt and Lady Glencarty swayed ponderously behind them on their respective mounts and her uncle brought up the rear, walking with a briskness he was far from feeling.

'How far is it to the main highway south?' she asked Lewis as the great plain stretched out before them, vast and parched and silent. There had been no rain all spring. No corn had been sown. No fields tilled. In some parts of the country the drought had lasted two years.

'A mile, perhaps less,' Lewis replied. 'If you listen, you will be able to hear the rumble of carts.'

She stood still for a moment, listening intently. Very faintly she could hear the unmistakable clatter of Peking carts trundling over the dry earth.

'Could it be Boxers?' she asked with a sudden surge of fear.

He shook his head. 'I don't think so. Boxers would be travelling on horseback and at a much quicker pace.'

'Then who is it? Chinese seldom travel at night. Why should so many people be on the road?'

In the moonlight, his handsome face hardened and contracted. 'Refugees,' he said tersely. 'Converts fleeing south.'

The noise grew slowly louder and gradually a long line of figures could be seen trudging southwards. Only a lucky few were in carts, the pale, frightened faces of their occupants peering out over the high wooden sides. Donkeys and mules staggered by under mountainous loads. Women carried babies on their backs. Children walked wearily.

'Where have all these people come from?' Letitia Harland asked bewilderedly as the narrow track they had been following merged into the great confluence south.

No one answered her. Lewis was talking earnestly to an aged Chinaman with a stout birch staff, and Olivia was watching him, her face anxious. When at last the old man raised his hand in farewell, she hurried to Lewis's side, her heart sinking when she saw the sombre expression on his face.

'Are they fleeing from the Boxers?' she asked urgently as they were jostled by the crush.

He nodded. 'They are from Shanfu. The town has several missions and a large hospital and most of the community is Christian.'

Somewhere in the mêlée behind them a baby began to cry.

'And have they all left?' she asked incredulously.

'All those that can walk,' Lewis said, and at the tone of his voice horror touched her spine. There would have been patients in the hospital. Women and children. She swayed slightly and he looked across at her, his eyes darkening in concern.

She had had a long and hideous day, and had walked uncomplainingly over rough terrain for the last four miles. He knew that she must be tired, but she showed no signs of it.

She was not very tall: five foot two or three, and with her dark hair hanging loose and her Parisian coutured day dress exchanged for garments of coarse linen she looked more Chinese than European. He could smell the cleanness of her hair, see the delicate outline of her cheekbones and jaw, and was aware of a deep protective feeling that he had never expected to feel again. A feeling that he had thought had died with Pearl Moon. The realization filled him with deep disquiet. He glanced away from her quickly, and as he did so, Lady Glencarty's strident voice rang out.

'Doctor Sinclair, kindly inform the peasant in front of us that we are in need of his cart.'

The peasant in question, wearily pushing a cart carrying a woman and child, looked around apprehensively, and then increased his pace.

'For goodness' sake, stop him,' Lady Glencarty shrieked at Lewis. 'I refuse to ride this wretched animal any longer. Demand that he gives us his cart!'

'And let his wife and child walk?' Lewis asked witheringly.

'Peasants are accustomed to walking,' Lady Glencarty snapped, goading her pony in the peasant's direction and leaning forward to seize his shoulder.

The peasant howled in outrage and twisted away, nearly unseating her.

'Stop, this minute!' Lady Glencarty shouted, her eyes flashing, her bosom heaving.

The intimidated peasant did as he was told. Lady Glencarty victoriously clambered down from her mount and marched across to the cart. As she did so, Lewis strode past Olivia and seized Lady Glencarty, whipping her round to face him, his fury making even Sir William flinch.

'You'll not commandeer this cart, or any other cart!' he hissed between clenched teeth. 'Now get back on the pony, or walk!'

Lady Glencarty tried to wrench her wrist away, and failed. 'How *dare* you speak to me in such a manner!' she demanded, but her voice had lost its authority and was nervously high-pitched. 'I demand an apology at once. Sir William! Insist that he apologize to me.'

Sir William said stiffly, 'Doctor Sinclair is quite right. The cart could not accommodate us all. Our party would be dangerously divided and the woman and child do not look as if they have the strength to walk.'

'But there are other carts! Lots of carts!' Lady Glencarty persisted as the peasant, sensing a reprieve, set off again at a desperate trot.

'And they are not ours,' Sir William said with austere finality. 'I have not sunk so low as to evict women and children from their only means of transport. Remount your pony, Clarissa, and let us continue.'

Lady Glencarty glared venomously at him and snapped her hand from Lewis's grasp, marching back towards her pony. When she had remounted, she dug her heels savagely into the pony's flanks and the pony, annoyed at the maltreatment and his unaccustomed load, snorted in protest and sprang forward, knocking Olivia to the ground.

She fell heavily, hitting the bare earth with such force that for a second she couldn't breathe. Dimly she heard Lewis Sinclair utter a savage expletive and then he was kneeling beside her, his hands on her shoulders, saying with startling depth of feeling, 'Are you hurt?'

She shook her head and he raised her forward, holding her against his chest. There was the same faint aroma of cologne that she had been aware of when her head had rested on his jacket; an indefinable smell of maleness that sent a pulse beating wildly in her throat. Not even Phillippe had held her so close and so intimately. Her cheeks flushed and she tried to pull away from him, but he held her easily.

'Stay still,' he said, his voice catching and deepening. 'You're bleeding.'

Holding her so close that her hair brushed his cheek, he pressed a handkerchief against her temple. she began to tremble and then he said, 'It's not deep. Only a graze.'

Her hair had fallen around her shoulders in wild disarray, black and silky. He felt it brush his hands and wrist and once again, he felt as if he were holding Pearl Moon. Pearl Moon, with her sweetness and gentleness and eager, pleasing body.

In an agony of grief and longing, he sank his fingers into her shoulders, pressing his mouth against her hair.

She tried to cry out in protest but no sound came. She was seized by a feeling so deep, so primeval, that it robbed her of coherent thought. She wanted to press herself closer and closer to him, wind her arms around his neck, feel his lips on her cheek, her mouth, her breasts.

'Is she badly hurt?' she heard her uncle ask, and it was as if his voice came from another life, another world.

'Olivia! Oh my dear child!' Her aunt was dismounting clumsily.

The arms around her froze into rigidity. Olivia. Not Pearl Moon. Olivia: a girl he barely knew. He released her with such suddenness that she gasped out loud. There was no longer any heat in his eyes, no tenderness in his voice.

'We must hurry if we are to reach the city by morning,' he said tersely, turning away from her as her uncle helped her unsteadily to her feet.

Dazedly she pressed his handkerchief against her temple, staring after him, her heart slamming against her breastbone, the blood pounding in her ears.

Three

'Olivia, my dear, are you all right?' her aunt was asking solicitously, brushing the dust from the Chinese garment with a net-gloved hand.

'Yes thank you, Aunt Letitia,' Olivia replied, her voice unsteady, a pulse beating wildly in her throat.

'Perhaps you should ride Doctor Sinclair's horse for a little while,' Letitia Harland suggested gallantly.

'No thank you, Aunt Letitia, that won't be necessary.'

Her emotions were in such turmoil that she couldn't separate one from another. How long had he held her close against his chest? She shook her head, trying to think clearly. It had seemed like an eternity, but it could have been no more than a few seconds. A minute at the most. And in that moment her whole body had flamed with such a shameless desire that it had shaken her to the roots of her being. His lips had sought her hair, and his fingers had burned her flesh, and she had not pulled away. Had not even cried out in protest.

She stood alone as her uncle helped her aunt to remount, her cheeks burning with shame. How *could* she have behaved so? She had displayed a wantonness that she had never even suspected lay within her nature. Had her aunt and uncle been aware of her disgraceful response to Lewis Sinclairs embrace? An ice-cold flood replaced the heat of her mortification. If they had, she would not be able to bear it.

Her uncle looked across at her, his eyes full of concern.

'Are you able to walk, Olivia?'

'Yes.' Relief flooded through her. There was no censure in his eyes. No disappointment. 'I am not hurt, Uncle William. I only grazed myself.'

'And got quite a fright,' William Harland said grimly. 'I only hope Clarissa has come to no harm, but if she has, she has only herself to blame. Our situation is difficult enough without such displays of petulant temper.'

'Where is Clarissa, William,?' his wife asked, once more nervously astride Lewis Sinclair's powerful stallion.

'A little ahead of us. It's too dark for me to see clearly, but the pony didn't gallop far and now Sinclair is holding the reins.'

'Doctor Sinclair will be very angry with her,' Letitia said, with a little shiver.

'And quite rightly,' William Harland said without sympathy. 'Olivia could have been badly hurt. Even killed.'

They began to walk forward once more, hemmed in on either side by trudging peasants, their bundles of belongings on their backs. Olivia tilted her head a fraction higher as they neared the bulky shape of Lady Glencarty and the fractious Mongol pony. Every line of Lewis Sinclair's lithe body was taut with anger, and Lady Glencarty was looking distinctly cowed.

'I did not intend ... It was an accident ...' she was saying pathetically, as he vented his wrath on her, the whipcord muscles bulging under the linen of his shirt.

Olivia halted a little distance away as her uncle went up and spoke quietly to him. She never wanted to see him again. He had changed her in a way she had not thought possible. How nearly she had circled his neck with her arms! The very thought made her want to drown in a sea of humiliation.

Had he known? Had he guessed? He had turned and was looking directly at her.

She kept her gaze firmly fixed on the ground, shame and longing fighting for supremacy. At last, after what seemed an eternity, she was aware that his eyes were no longer upon her and she slowly lifted her head. He was talking to her uncle. Though she tried to look away, she could not do so until she had noticed how straight and tall he stood; how snugly his breeches fitted about his narrow hips; how his shirt, gashed open at the throat, revealed a chest wide and deep. How the black hair tumbling low over his brows had taken on a blue sheen.

He moved away, not looking at her, striding on ahead of them. She felt suddenly weak, as if only now was she experiencing the effect of being hurled so violently to the ground.

'Doctor Sinclair says that the Boxers are sheltering in Shanfu ten miles to the north. If we want to make Peking by daybreak, we must increase our speed,' her uncle said to her apologetically.

She nodded, her eyes darkening with concern. Her uncle was no longer a fit man. There were beads of perspiration on his brow, and she wondered apprehensively for how much longer he would be able to keep pace with the frighteningly agile Lewis Sinclair.

Lady Glencarty offered gruff apologies and managed to keep the unhappy pony under a measure of control. Behind her, William Harland marched stoically at the side of his mounted wife, Olivia walked a little apart from them, struggling to get her emotions in order.

The shame that she had initially felt had intensified and deepened. She was not in love with Lewis Sinclair. She was in love with Phillippe. The engagement ring on her finger seemed to sear her flesh in reproach. She had been taken by surprise. Shocked by her fall. And he had taken ungentlemanly advantage of the fact.

Her shame began to be coupled with anger. He had pressed her indecently close to him. Had taken unforgivable liberties, and all within sight of her aunt and uncle! Her anger blazed white hot. What might he have done if they had not been there? He was a libertine and a lecher. She stumbled as another realization hit her with breathtaking impact.

He was a *married* libertine and lecher! She began to shake. He had left his wife, probably in the deadliest of danger, and in his absence from her had had the effrontery to hold another woman in indecent closeness against him and press his lips feveredly to her hair! And to think that she, Olivia Harland, had viewed him as a romantic hero who had forsaken all for love. Why, Dr Lewis Sinclair did not even know the meaning of the word!

With her head held high she marched in his wake. He had saved her life and she had thanked him for it. She owed him nothing more. Her friendliness towards him had obviously been grossly misunderstood. From now on she would be cool and impersonal, and do her best to ignore him.

She stumbled again, this time on a stone she had not seen. Tears of tiredness and frustration stung her eyes. It was not easy to be cool and impersonal when she still felt the heat of shame and rage. And not when a small voice at the back of her mind kept prompting her to relive the few minutes after she had fallen.

Had his behaviour been so outrageous? He had lifted her from the ground, steadied her until she had regained her breath – surely it was not his actions, but her own response to them that was at fault. Her jaw tightened. No. She would not believe it. He had seized her by the shoulders and pressed her to him with a passionate intensity that had been real and not imagined. His lips *had* sought her hair! Even now she could feel where his fingers had sunk into her flesh. No wonder such a man had been ostracized by polite society.

She no longer felt the slightest sympathy for him. His presence would have to be tolerated until they reached Peking, but once there she would make sure that she never set eyes on him again.

Phillippe would be waiting for her in Peking. Phillippe

with his blond hair and blue eyes; blue like a summer sky. Not a deep, night-black that flared and flashed and intimidated even her uncle. She wondered if he was wrong in assuming that Peking knew nothing of the Boxers' nearness. Perhaps Phillippe was already aware that European villas in the Western Hills had come under attack. Perhaps even now he was in a fever of anxiety about her safety.

She narrowly sidestepped a deep rut in the road. In another few hours she would be able to reassure him as to her safety. She would be able to have a reviving bath, change once more into her own clothes; eat a hot meal; slip between cool sheets and sleep until her body and her mind were rested.

'Why has Doctor Sinclair stopped, William?' her aunt was saying. 'Why has he picked up that child? Oh, do hurry ahead and ask him what he is doing. I'm so frightened that the Boxers are behind us and will catch up with us.'

With an anxious frown, Sir William hurried forward. Olivia hesitated and then continued walking to where Lewis Sinclair stood, a child in his arms, his head bent low as he listened to a small, dark figure. It was none of her affair who he stopped to talk to. Perhaps he was negotiating for another pony or maybe even an unused cart. Steeling herself for the moment when their eyes should once again meet, she heard her uncle say fretfully, 'It is madness, Sinclair, we will be slowed down alarmingly.'

The child in Lewis's arms began to whimper. Forgetting the scathing glance she had been about to subject him to, Olivia said in horror, 'His feet are bleeding!'

'No doubt ours would be too, if we were barefoot,' Lewis said dryly.

There was another snuffle, somewhere to her right, and Olivia turned swiftly, seeing clearly for the first time the small figure that Lewis had been talking to. It was an elderly nun, no taller than herself, her face lined and weary beneath her dust-covered coif. Clinging to her habit was a small boy, barely old enough to walk.

'The children can go no further,' the nun said tiredly. 'Ch'un is five and he has carried Cheng-yu but he can do so no longer. I have tried to carry him myself, but we have covered only a hundred yards in the last hour.'

She swayed, and Olivia caught her arm, steadying her, her eyes flying to Lewis's. 'She's on the point of collapse! She can't possibly walk any further.'

Lewis didn't disagree. He lowered the child gently to the ground and looked reflectively at Letitia Harland and Lady Glencarty.

'Can I give them a drink of water?' Olivia asked, and at his brief nod, hurriedly retrieved the water bottle from his saddle pack and handed it to the aged nun. She took it with shaking, arthritic hands.

'Kwangtei has been burned,' she said, her eyes bright with tears. 'I was out in the fields with Ch'un and Cheng-yu. There was nothing we could do.'

'Where is Kwangtei?' Olivia asked Lewis, passing the water bottle to the eldest child.

'About twenty miles north. God knows how they managed to make it this far.'

'Are there other refugees from Kwangtei on the road?' Olivia asked, turning her attention once more to the fragile figure at her side.

The old nun shook her head. 'No,' she said simply. 'Everyone was killed. Nuns. Children. Even the old Chinese who cleaned the chapel for us.'

Olivia fought down the overwhelming urge to be sick. Lewis had told her that no mission was safe, but it had seemed a thing too monstrous to be true. Now she was faced with the reality. There would be other missions besides Kwangtei. Missions as yet unattacked and unprepared. Once they reached Peking, escorts could be sent from the city to bring the occupants to safety. But there was very little time. Even now, as they stood in a motley group in the middle of the unmade highway, precious minutes were ticking by.

'We must give them some biscuits,' William Harland was saying impatiently. 'We have plenty to share. And now Sinclair, for the love of God, let us be on our way.'

Olivia bent down and picked up the child squatting at the nun's feet. She had never held a child before and was not quite sure how to go about it. Awkwardly she cradled it in her arms. It lay passively, large, eloquent eyes holding hers.

'Olivia! What are you doing?' her aunt shrieked in anguish.

'Carrying him,' Olivia said succinctly. 'He's little more than a baby, Aunt Letitia. He can't possibly walk all the way to Peking.'

'William! Tell her to put that child down! Tell her to ...'

'Sister Angelique cannot walk any further either,' Lewis interrupted tersely, eyeing his horse.

'Oh no, I couldn't,' Letitia Harland said, clutching at her heart. 'Tell Doctor Sinclair I couldn't walk, William. It would kill me!'

'It won't kill me,' Lady Glencarty said briskly, and to everyone's stunned amazement, she dismounted, squaring her jaw and eyeing them defiantly.

'Thank you,' Lewis said, striving to keep the surprise from his voice. 'If I can find another mount for you, I will.'

Lady Glencarty shrugged her massive shoulders as if it were of very little interest to her whether he did or not, and tried not to look too discomfited as Sister Angelique took her hands in hers and thanked her with tears in her eyes.

'Ch'un can ride behind you,' Lewis said as he led Sister Angelique away from Lady Glencarty and towards the pony. With ease he swung her astride the pony's broad back, and lifted Ch'un up behind, then he turned to Olivia. 'I think I may find the task of carrying Cheng-yu a little easier than you will,' he said, a curious expression in his eyes as he removed the near-naked child from her arms.

She nodded stiffly, averting her eyes from his, walking speedily away from him until she was abreast of Lady Glencarty.

Lewis swung Cheng-yu up on to his back, a frown marring his brow. He had wanted to tell her that her willingness to carry Cheng-yu the remaining eleven or twelve miles to Peking had touched him deeply, but the hostility in the set of her shoulders deterred him. He had hoped that she had been too dazed from her fall to have been aware of the spasm of desire and grief that had swept over him when he had held her in his arms. He knew now that she had not been. She had been acutely aware of it, and she had misunderstood it.

Sir William walked past him, his face white and drawn and Lewis saw that there were tears on Letitia Harland's plump cheeks. He remained where he was, staring at Olivia's retreating figure, his face sombre. He could speak to her; explain. Tell her about Pearl Moon. The moment came and went, and he knew that he would not do so. He could speak to no one about Pearl Moon. The hurt was still too naked, too raw. He began to walk forward quickly, to take the lead once more, aware that if he did ever talk to anyone about the woman he had loved, it would be to Olivia Harland with her refreshing directness, her impulsiveness, and her heart-catching kindness.

She froze as he approached her and passed her and his face tightened. He had inadvertently alienated and offended her and he wished to God that he had not done so. 'Damn,' he muttered under his breath as he led his motley party past an overloaded Peking cart, 'Damn, damn, *damn*!'

There were other nuns amongst the long straggle trudging across the airless plain. All had the same story to tell. Attacks on their missions, attacks on nearby missions, warnings by the local peasantry of proposed attacks. Peking, with its stout walls and its representatives of their respective governments, was the only place that offered refuge.

'The city will be overflowing with refugees,' William Harland said as he made a gallant effort to keep abreast of Lewis. 'They'll all have to be fed and watered. God, what a mess it all is.'

Lewis shifted Cheng-yu to a slightly more comfortable position on his back. 'It will be even worse if the Empress Dowager comes out in open support of the Boxers.'

William Harland paled. 'Do you think there is a serious possibility that she might?'

Lewis shrugged. 'There is no telling what Empress Tzu-hsi might or might not do. She certainly hasn't come down too hard on the Boxers so far.'

'But if they run riot in her own city, surely she will suppress them?' William Harland asked, determining to remove Letitia and Olivia to Tientsin and the coast at the earliest opportunity.

'Peking also houses all the heads of all the foreign legations,' Lewis said tersely. 'She might quite like it if the Boxers made an end of them once and for all.'

William Harland inserted a finger between his collar and his neck, trying to ease the restrictive tightness. 'But why should she want to do such a monstrous thing?' he demanded.

Lewis looked across at him and suppressed a sigh. Sir William Harland was a not-unintelligent man and was an official at the British Legation. Yet his knowledge of China and Chinese grievances was minimal.

He said with strained patience, 'Over the last fifty years, China has been divided piecemeal among other nations, including Britain. Is it inconceivable that she should resent the fact, Sir William?'

'There have been certain treaties,' Sir William said reluctantly, 'but all conducted most fairly, I can assure you.'

A cart lumbered past them. A child began to cry and turning his head, Lewis saw Olivia bend low and offer it a biscuit from her rations. His eyes lingered on her for a few moments. In the moonlight, in native dress and with her dark hair streaming freely down her back, she looked far more Chinese than European. Only when she raised her head and her eyes briefly met his, was the illusion destroyed. There was nothing Chinese about the delicate oval face with its high cheekbones and full, generous mouth. The look she gave him before turning to Lady Glencarty, was cool and freezingly indifferent. Bleakly he turned his attention once more to Sir Wiliam.

'In eighteen fifty-eight, Russia seized vast territories in the north. In eighteen sixty-two, Portugal occupied Macao, France occupied Annan and Britain annexed Lower Burma. Since then, Russia has occupied a vast tract of Chinese Turkistan, Japan has taken the Liuchiu Islands, and France has gained control of the Mekong basin. The list is endless and it will surely seem to China's rulers that the countries respected in Peking are not going to be satisfied until the whole of China has been carved up between them.

'And do you think that is the reason for the uprising?'

Lewis shook his head. 'No. The Boxers are peasants. I doubt that they are politically motivated. Their concern is with gods and spirits and their hatred is directed against Christians, but Christians are also foreigners, and such a vast, unpaid army could be put to very good use by the Empress.'

The past few hours had etched deep lines around Sir William's eyes and mouth. He felt – and looked – like an old man. 'Then you think that there is a very real danger that the Boxers might attack Peking, and that the Empress will not deter them?'

'I think there is a very real danger that not only will she do nothing to deter them, but that she might order the Imperial Army to join forces with them,' Lewis said briefly.

'If she does that,' William Harland said, his voice trembling slightly, 'then we are all dead men.'

Lewis did not contradict him. Sir William Harland was

at last aware of the extreme gravity of the situation and he only hoped that together they would be able to convince Sir Claude MacDonald that the time for polite notes between the legations and the Winter Palace was at an end. Troops had to be called for, and called for without the slightest delay.

'Are you a friend of Doctor Sinclair's,?' Sister Angelique asked Olivia as she walked tiredly along at the pony's side.

Olivia looked up into the kindly face and shook her head. 'No. I had not met him until yesterday.'

'And you were travelling south, as we were?'

'No.' Olivia patted the pony's flank, her eyes dark. 'We only left Peking yesterday morning. My aunt and uncle leave the city every year in late May to avoid the sweltering heat. They have a villa in the Western Hills. It used to be a Chinese temple, and was very pretty.'

Sister Angelique nodded, and waited as Olivia paused. Had it only been yesterday morning that they had travelled out from Peking in comfortable carriages, chattering light-heartedly about the party that Sir Claude had given in honour of Queen Victoria's birthday? After a little while, she continued, 'When we arrived, I went for a walk while my aunt and Lady Glencarty rested. It was then that the Boxers attacked.'

'I see,' Sister Angelique said quietly. 'And Doctor Sinclair?'

Tears stung Olivia's eyes. 'The Boxers had set fire to the villa and my aunt and uncle and Lady Glencarty were trapped inside. I was running down the hillside, screaming, when Doctor Sinclair overtook me on his horse. When I told him about my aunt and uncle, he ran forward with his rifle.' She faltered. 'I think he killed one of them. Perhaps two. I can't remember. I can only remember running towards the villa, and the heat, and the smell of the smoke ...'

Sister Angelique leaned towards her and pressed a frail hand lightly on her shoulder. 'It must have been very distressing for you, little one.'

Olivia remembered the flames beating her back; the awful

seconds when she had been convinced that her aunt and uncle were dead.

'Doctor Sinclair was very brave,' she said unsteadily. 'He rushed into the villa through all the flames and smoke, and carried my aunt to safety.'

A small smile touched Sister Angelique's lips. 'Yes, Doctor Sinclair is a very brave man. A brave man and a good man.'

Olivia looked up at her with surprise. 'Do you know him, Sister Angelique?'

Sister Angelique's smile deepened. 'Everyone in Chihli and Shansi knows of Doctor Sinclair. He is a remarkable doctor. I doubt if any of his patients would *dare* die. He is also one of the few men who can speak the northern dialects with ease. He loves China and the Chinese, and the Chinese love him.'

'Yes,' Olivia said thoughtfully, regarding his lean, lithe silhouette as he marched on a little way ahead of them. 'He seems to understand them far more than any other European that I have talked to.'

'He has patience and tolerance,' Sister Angelica said. 'He accepts people for what they are and that is a very rare quality.'

Olivia regarded her doubtfully. It seemed to her that Lewis Sinclair had a remarkably small amount of patience.

'He is also a man of honour,' Sister Angelique continued, 'and the Chinese respect honour.'

Olivia was just about to indignantly say that Lewis Sinclair was most certainly *not* a man of honour, when the expression on Sister Angelique's face stopped her. It was cruel and pointless to destroy the elderly nun's illusions. Whatever his more worldly faults, he had behaved with great courage in saving the lives of her aunt and uncle and Lady Glencarty, and he had behaved with great kindness in not bypassing Sister Angelique and her two small charges.

She found her eyes resting on him with increasing frequency. Cheng-yu's small arms were firmly around his neck, his chubby legs tucked beneath his arms. It was a long walk, and she knew from her own brief experience that Cheng-yu was surprisingly heavy.

Beside her, Lady Glencarty stumbled and paused, panting heavily. Olivia took her arm, her face anxious. 'Are you all right, Lady Glencarty? Would you like me to ask Doctor Sinclair to rest for a few moments?'

'I am *not* all right,' Lady Glencarty replied tartly. 'I fail to see how I can be, in the circumstances.'

Her breathing was harsh and rasping, and Olivia's concern deepened. Even as she was speaking she was clutching a hand to her side, and Olivia saw that her face was tight and drawn with pain. Breaking her resolve not to speak again to Lewis Sinclair, she hurried forward, saying urgently, 'Lady Glencarty looks most ill. I don't think she can continue much further.'

He halted in his tracks, staring down at her grim-faced.

'She has tried very hard,' Olivia said defensively, aware of a disconcerting sensation as his eyes held hers.

Lewis turned, walking back to where Lady Glencarty stood, panting for breath, the endless line of peasants filing past her on either side.

'You have done your best,' Olivia heard him say to her with surprising gentleness, and then, to her aunt, 'Lady Harland, I think there is room behind you for Ch'un.'

Letitia Harland nodded and Lewis lifted Ch'un from behind Sister Angelique, and placed him astride his own horse where he clung incongruously to Letitia Harland's plump figure.

'Now what?' William Harland asked.

'Sister Angelique weighs little more than a child,' Lewis said brusquely, 'and Mongol ponies are extraordinarily strong. I think it quite possible that Lady Glencarty and Sister Angelique can ride together.'

Lady Glencarty was too exhausted to protest, but she did regain some of her former tartness just before Lewis helped her to mount.

'I hope,' she said imperiously to the gentle-faced Sister Angelique, 'that you are of the Anglican persuasion and not a Roman?'

Lewis's mouth twitched suspiciously, and Olivia felt her own mouth tug into a smile as Sister Angelique assured Lady Glencarty that she was indeed an Anglican and Lady Glencarty, with a nod of approval, allowed herself to be seated once again on the uncomplaining pony.

'Splendid,' William Harland said as they set off again. 'How many miles do you think we have covered, Lewis?'

'About six. Can you see that dark shape looming up ahead of us? That is Tongku, but I doubt very much that the gates will be open, and even if they are, I think we should give it a wide berth.'

'To do so will put extra miles on our journey,' Sir William said with a slight frown.

'Better that than finding ourselves trapped with no means of escape if the Boxers attack,' Lewis said dryly.

Sir William glanced at him sharply. 'You think it likely then? At night?'

'Anything is likely,' Lewis said uncompromisingly. 'Our best bet lies in reaching Peking in the shortest possible time. If Tongku has opened its gates to the refugees, it will be so packed it will be virtually impossible to move in it, and there's a great risk that we might become irrevocably separated.'

Sir William could well imagine what the overcrowded, fetid, sweltering streets of the village would be like and he nodded in agreement. There wouldn't be only refugees crowding the narrow, dust-blown street seeking shelter; there would be pickpockets and thieves taking advantage of the crush.

They could smell Tongku well before they could see it. Lewis halted, catching the reins of both the pony and his horse. 'This is where we make a detour, I think,' he said.

Straining her eyes in the darkness, Olivia could make out a mass of seething humanity encamped outside Tongku's walls.

'Shouldn't we rest also?' Letitia Harland asked waveringly.

Lewis shook his head. 'They are not resting, Lady Harland. They're simply too exhausted to continue. You'll have to remember that a lot of the missionaries and the converts have travelled from as far away as Shansi. All those who have the strength will be continuing on to Peking, not waiting for Tongku to open its gates at dawn.'

Sir William regarded the not very substantial walls surrounding the village. 'They won't be much protection if the Boxers should attack.'

'But why should they attack Tongku?' his wife asked bewilderedly. 'There isn't a mission or a hosptial there.'

'True enough,' Lewis said, leading the way into a wilderness of scrub that surrounded the village. 'But it is on the direct route to Peking, and the Boxers will hardly avoid it. They may even find recruits among the local peasantry. Whether they do or not, they most certainly will not leave alive any Europeans taking shelter there.'

Letitia Harland gave a little moan and her husband patted her hand reassuringly. Olivia, gazing round at the all-enveloping darkness, said with a catch in her voice, 'I think there is a fire a little way to the west.'

The clamour of carts and the wailing of the many tired and hungry children outside Tongku's walls made it nearly impossible to hear anything out of the ordinary, but as they looked to the west, they all saw the unmistakable rose-red hue of flames staining the night sky.

'How far away do you think it is?' Sir William asked Lewis, his face strained.

'Three miles, perhaps four.'

'Then they are right behind us!' Letitia Harland sobbed in alarm.

Unwillingly, Olivia allowed her eyes to slide across to Lewis Sinclair. His lean, dark face revealed very little. His eyes had narrowed and she found something strangely reassuring about the firmness of his jaw, the strong, finely chiselled lines of his mouth.

'There's a railway line to the west,' he said. 'I imagine that is what we can see burning. With a little luck it will keep them occupied for the next few hours.'

'We must go faster,' William Harland said, beads of perspiration streaming down his face.

Lewis nodded and said to Olivia, 'Will you be able to manage?'

'Yes,' she replied coldly.

He seemed about to say something more, and then thought better of it, merely nodding.

They continued at an exhaustive pace and Olivia was uncomfortably aware of his eyes resting on her with disquieting frequency. She felt a surge of anger. No doubt he wanted her to say that she could *not* manage. That she required his arm about her waist. Even, perhaps, like Cheng-yu, that she required to be carried! Sparks flared in her eyes. She would drop with fatigue before she would give him the slightest excuse for manhandling her again!

'Be careful,' he said suddenly, his rich dark voice rasping across her nerve-ends. 'There is a deep hole in the road ahead of you.'

'I can see it perfectly,' she lied, narrowly missing falling full length into it. His hand shot out to save her, and she snatched it away from her. 'That was not necessary,' she said furiously as Lady Glencarty and Sister Angelique trotted close by them.

'Perhaps not, but it saved you twisting your ankle and being left behind,' he said, a dangerous edge to his voice.

She glared at him, rubbing her wrist where his hand had circled it.

'I have no intention of doing anything so foolish,' she said with as much dignity as she could muster, painfully aware that, because of him, her hair was falling in wild disarray about her shoulders and that she had not even the respectability of a skirt.

'Good,' he said tersely, his mouth a hard line, the skin taut across his cheekbones.

She flashed him a glance of withering contempt and spun on her heel, her back rigid, her head held high. His whole manner bordered on insolence. She could not even begin to imagine why Sister Angelique should consider him a man of honour. As for him being a man of tolerance and patience! She wanted to laugh, but her throat was painfully tight. Lewis Sinclair possessed neither virtue. He was brusque to the point of rudeness; arrogantly overbearing, and the most objectionable man she had ever had the misfortune to meet. He was also the most disturbing. It was impossible to ignore his presence; to pretend that he did not exist. He was behind her now, talking to her uncle. She closed her eyes, blinking back weary tears, longing for Phillippe.

From the direction of the distant railway station there came the unmistakable sound of rifle fire. Noise broke out among the peasants surrounding them. Children were urged on faster, carts rattled past with little regard for those in their path. A young Chinese girl gasped in exhaustion, swaying against Olivia, a baby in her arms. She muttered a half-audible apology and instinctively Olivia reached out, taking the baby from her grasp.

'Let me,' she said, hoisting the baby up against her shoulder.

'Thank you.' The words were in English, the gratitude in the lustrous dark eyes, intense.

'Where have you come from?' Olivia asked, slowing her pace fractionally to match that of her companion.

'Lupao. The Boxers attacked the village yesterday afternoon. They were seeking out all the missionaries and Christians. The priest at Lupao refused to leave, but he told me to make for Peking. He said that in Peking we would be safe.'

The baby was heavy, but Olivia had no intention of handing him back. Lupao was eighteen miles away. Her own tiredness could be nothing compared to that of the girl at her side.

'My name is Olivia,' she said, aware that Lady Glencarty and her aunt and uncle were already several yards ahead of them.

'And mine is Lan Kuei,' the girl said with a smile that illuminated her tired face.

'Olivia! Hurry!' her uncle called out as a surge of peasants hurried into the space that had distanced them.

Lewis Sinclair turned his head, saw the child in her arms, the girl at her side, and slowed his pace. Olivia was aware of a grudging feeling of gratitude. She had no desire to be left behind but she knew that now she had befriended Lan Kuei, she could not leave her.

Lan Kuei eyed Lewis's tall, broad figure and Cheng-yu sleeping snugly on his back. 'Your husband is very kind,' she said shyly.

Olivia gasped, the blood surging into her face. 'Doctor Sinclair is *not* my husband,' she said with such heat that Lan Kuei was overcome with confusion. 'He is … He is not even a friend!'

Her words carried clearly. She saw Lewis Sinclair's shoulders stiffen and was uncaring. It was unbearable that anyone should imagine that they were married. He was the last man on earth she would even consider as a husband.

'My fiancé is in Peking,' she said, her voice throbbing with suppressed emotion. 'We were to be married in September, but now that circumstances have changed, I hope we shall be able to be married much sooner.'

'I hope that you will be very happy,' Lan Kuei said timidly, aware that she had inadvertently angered her new-found friend.

'Thank you,' Olivia said stiffly, wishing that her pulse would return to normal and that she did not feel so disturbingly disconcerted. For the first time she wondered if she really would be able to marry Phillippe sooner than they had planned. Her aunt would be disapproving if she suggested it, but surely Phillippe would be pleased? She tried to imagine his reaction, but just as his face began to take shape in her mind, Lewis Sinclair shattered the image by saying, 'The sky is lightening in the east. It will be dawn in another hour.'

'The Boxers always attack at dawn,' Sister Angelique said quietly. 'If Peking is their goal, they will be riding south as soon as the sun rises.'

Olivia felt her throat tighten. If the Boxers attacked, she might never see Phillippe again. Involuntarily she glanced across at Lewis. Sister Angelique and her aunt and Lan Kuei were looking at him with childlike trust, and even Lady Glencarty and her uncle were regarding him with quiet confidence.

She felt suddenly deeply ashamed of herself. If he had wanted he could have been many miles away; instead he was risking his life by shepherding them across the plains to Peking, and she had declared that he was not even a friend. She hugged the baby tighter, knowing that he had overheard her, and that she had no alternative but to apologize.

She bit her lip. It was really most unfair. *He* should have been apologizing to her. But then, perhaps a renegade like Lewis Sinclair thought nothing of taking liberties with any female who happened his way. The sky was pearling to grey. She looked covertly across at him. The commanding profile and strong, assertive jawline did not look like those of a womanizer. She experienced a moment's doubt and then, remembering his wife, banished it. He was not a man to be trusted. But neither, in view of his courage, was he a man to be maligned. Taking a deep breath, she stepped purposefully towards him.

Four

He looked down at her, his eyes inscrutable in the darkness, his eyebrows slightly raised in silent query.

'I wanted to apologize to you,' Olivia said, forcing her voice to be steady. 'Lan Kuei took me by surprise a moment ago and I answered her too hastily. When I said that you were not even a friend, I did not mean ... I was trying to explain that we had not known each other long ... That ...' She floundered helplessly, disconcerted by his nearness.

'*I understand*,' he said, putting an end to her embarrassment with a kindness she was grateful for.

Looking up at him, she forgot that he was a libertine and a womanizer, and was aware only that he exuded a sensation of safety. For a second, she thought that he was going to speak to her further and of something personal, but he merely checked himself, saying, 'The sun will be up within the hour.'

'Yes.' She no longer wanted to distance herself from him. Her anger and fury at his earlier actions were already ebbing. She had misunderstood them. She wanted to tell him so, but the words would not come. The very thought of her reaction to his embrace made her cheeks burn scarlet. He must never know. He would think her lewd and shameless. It had not been an embrace of tenderness or passion as she had thought. He had simply held her against him in concern until she had recovered her breath and he had ascertained that she was not seriously hurt. In just such a way would he have held her aunt or Lady Glencarty. That his lips had pressed against her hair had been an accident and nothing more.

He gave her a down-slanting smile and regret rushed through her. In a moment of stark and painful clarity she knew that she would have liked his embrace to have been occasioned by passion for her. She turned away from him quickly, confused by shame and bewilderment.

She was betrothed to Phillippe and she had fallen in love with Lewis Sinclair. Lewis Sinclair, a man who was married and whose existence, forty-eight hours ago, she had been unaware of. She began to walk once again by Lan Kuei's side.

How had it happened? How could she, Olivia Harland, intelligent and level-headed, have allowed herself to fall so completely under the spell of a man she scarcely knew?

She pressed a hand to her throbbing brow and her aunt, seeing the action, asked anxiously, 'Are you all right, Olivia?'

Olivia summoned up a reassuring smile. 'Yes, Aunt Letitia. Please don't worry about me. We shall be in Peking before very long.'

Peking. Her head ached. In Peking she would be reunited with Phillippe. Could she still marry him? Her feelings towards him had not changed. She still thought him the most handsome, charming man she had ever met. But he did not arouse in her the fevered longings that Lewis Sinclair's presence aroused.

The sun rose, bathing the plain in golden light. In the far distance the massive crenellated walls of Peking shimmered in the early morning heat. Lady Glencarty straightened her shoulders and brushed untidy wisps of steel-grey hair into a measure of neatness. Letitia Harland stifled a sob of relief and vowed that she would never, ever again leave the safety of the legation district. Sir William closed his mind to the pain in his calf and thigh muscles and kept walking stoically on. There was still at least a two-hour trek ahead of them; a two-hour trek in which the Boxers could attack at any moment. Olivia held Lan Kuei's baby tighter against her chest, her mind in too much of a turmoil to be overcome with relief at the sight of Peking.

In Peking, Lewis Sinclair would take his leave of them. She would never see him again. Perhaps then, free of his disturbing presence, she would be able to resume her relationship with Phillippe with equanimity. A cold chill seemed to settle on her, despite her fatigue. Not seeing him would not prevent her from thinking about him. Wondering where he was and what he was doing. She could not marry one man and continue to think of another.

The baby was heavy and she moved it from her right arm to her left. Her life which, a few hours ago, had seemed so uncomplicated, now seemed fraught with difficulties. She wished that there was someone that she could talk to, but the truth of her feelings would shock her aunt indescribably. She felt a surge of longing for her dead mother. Perhaps she would have been able to give her guidance. Certainly no one else could. The problems awaiting her in Peking could be solved by no one but herself.

There was a cry of alarm from behind them and Olivia spun around, half-expecting to see red-sashed figures bearing down on them. Instead, a young woman, dusty and dishevelled, was standing beside an old man who had collapsed and was lying insensible on the ground. Instinctively Olivia began to run back towards them, the baby so heavy that she thought she would faint with weariness.

The peasants hurrying past on either side ignored the old man and his distraught companion. As she knelt at his side, Olivia saw the familiar bleached wood of the gnarled birch staff and recognized the old Chinese as the man Lewis had first spoken to when they had joined the highway south.

Lewis was there, even before she was. As the girl wailed and wrung her hands, they knelt in the dust at either side of the inert body. Lewis lifted a wrinkled eyelid, pressed his ear to the old man's chest, and then said tersely, 'There's a leather case in my saddle-bag. Bring it quickly.'

She rose obediently to her feet, hoisting the baby higher on her shoulder, swaying with tiredness.

'Give the baby to Lan Kuei for a while,' he said, his eyes dark with concern, but whether for her or the old man she had no way of knowing. 'She is more rested than you are now.'

She did as he told her, ignoring the panic-stricken comments of her aunt that Doctor Sinclair was once more unnecessarily delaying them.

As she ran back to him she saw that he was supporting the old man against his knee. She felt her throat tighten. No one else in the throng milling around them, not his fellow countrymen nor her aunt or Lady Glencarty, cared whether the old man lived or died. Only Lewis Sinclair cared. Sister Angelique had said that he was a man of integrity and honour, and watching him flip open the leather case and take a phial from it, Olivia understood only too well what she had meant. The drawing-rooms of polite society had been closed to him because he had married the Chinese girl, yet Olivia knew that there were many men, socially acceptable, who had Chinese mistresses tucked away in little-visited parts of the city. It was they, she thought fiercely, who should be ostracized, not Lewis Sinclair.

As she knelt beside him, he broke the phial against the old man's slack, parted lips.

'What is it?' she asked curiously.

'Digitalis. A heart stimulant.'

'Will it save him?'

Lewis shook his head. 'No,' he said as the old man's eyes fluttered feebly open, 'but it may enable him to reach Peking and die with a measure of decency. If he dies here, his body will simply be food for carrion. The manner of death is important to the Chinese.' He began to talk again to the still weeping girl and Olivia could tell that he was giving her instructions for the care of her aged relative.

At last he turned to Olivia. 'He needs shade. The sun will be high within an hour and he can't possibly continue the journey in his present condition.'

'But the horse? The pony? Couldn't we use one of those?' Olivia asked, distressed.

He shook his head. 'Peking may be in sight, but it is still a good two hours away and neither Sister Angelique or your aunt would be able to manage the walk in the heat of morning.' He bent down, scooping the frail figure up in his arms. 'There's a tree a little to the right. I'll leave him and his granddaughter in its shade with our remaining water.'

'But he's going to die out here for lack of a pony!' Olivia cried, stumbling to her feet and following him. 'We can *see* Peking! Surely help will be on its way? There will be horses and ponies soon, lots of them. Let me stay with him until they arrive.'

Lewis looked down at her, the old man inert in his arms, his face granite hard. 'And who do you think will send the horses and ponies, Olivia? From where is this help that you are expecting going to come?'

It was the first time he had used her Christian name. She stifled the quickening of her pulsebeats and said, 'Now it is daylight, they will be able to see the refugees making their way to the city. Even if the Empress does not send troops to their aid, Sir Claude or Mr Conger of the American legation will do so.'

There was a measure of pity in Lewis Sinclair's near black eyes as her regarded her. The delicate oval of her face was smudged with dust. There were blue shadows beneath her thick-lashed eyes. Her slender figure was swaying with weariness.

In the past few hours, she had experienced for herself the horrors of a Boxer attack. She had heard Sister Angelique's story and Lan Kuei's. She had seen the long, unending trail of refugees stumbling wearily towards Peking, and still she believed that the plight of those around her was unknown to the authorities; that at any moment diplomats and officers would come riding out to give aid to the sick and weary.

He said gently, 'Refugees have been streaming into the city for days now, Olivia. If the authorities had any intention of organizing any relief for them, they would already have done so.'

'But they *can't* know! When they see this ...' She stretched out her arm to indicate the highway packed with mules and carts and women and children, 'then they will send transport for the old and sick.'

'For old and sick Chinese?' Lewis asked wryly, the savagery he felt at the authorities' disinterest in the fate of the Chinese Christians firmly under control.

She stared at him, not wanting to believe that what he said was true, and yet knowing that he would never lie to her.

'Phillippe would organize an expedition if he knew,' she said, lifting her chin slightly.

'Phillippe?'

Her mouth was suddenly dry. 'My fiancé,' she said, wondering why the words were so difficult to form. 'He is a junior diplomat at the French Legation.'

Lewis merely nodded and began to carry the old man towards the shade of a tree. If Olivia Harland's fiancé was anything like the diplomat who had so insulted the memory of Pearl Moon, he doubted very much that he would have given more than a passing thought to the endless streams of peasants crowding into the city.

Olivia stood at the side of the dust-blown road and waited for him. She had told him now. He knew that she was engaged to be married. He had shown no disappointment, no distress. She tilted her chin still higher. Why should he? He was not in love with her. He was in love with his wife. With the woman who had changed the pattern of his life.

Bleakly she watched as, with touching tenderness, he laid the old man beneath the shade of the tree. His body was powerfully masculine, strong, hard and lean. The planes of his face were harsh, the nose strong. The jutting jawline showed no hint of weakness. He was speaking to the girl again, and she knew that his voice would have nothing of the abrasiveness that it so often held. His tenderness to the old and the vulnerable came from his strength. She wondered why she had not seen it before. Why she had thought him overbearing and arrogant.

He strode back towards her, his mouth a tight, compressed line. 'There's no more I can do for him. Once we reach Peking it may be possible to round up some volunteers and ride back with spare horses. If not ...' He shrugged his shoulders in a manner that left no doubt what would happen to the old man and those like him if he was unable to bring them help.

Olivia felt determination flood through her, vanquishing her fatigue. Before, she had thought only of reaching Peking; of ensuring that her aunt and uncle were safe. Now there was another reason for reaching the city quickly. To organize aid that had so far been unforthcoming.

'It won't only be the people on the highway who will need assistance, will it?' she asked as they rejoined their small, anxiously waiting party and Lewis once more lifted Ch'un on to his back. 'There will be the missionaries that you spoke of in the outlying missions around Peking. Missionaries who might not yet know that the Boxers have come so far south? They will have to be warned; have to be escorted into the city.'

He nodded, his face grim. 'Unfortunately, there are very few people in Peking who are likely to put themselves at such risk. There's Morrison, Peking correspondent to *The Times*. He's the first person I shall speak to when we reach the city. He once led an expedition to New Guinea and was left for dead with two spears in his body. He's also walked alone and unarmed across Australia and from Shanghai to the Burma frontier. There will be no delay on his part in riding out to outlying missions.'

Olivia remembered seeing *The Times* correspondent at

one of Lady MacDonald's soirees. He was a handsome man in his mid-thirties and she could well believe that he would fall in unhesitatingly with Lewis's plans. She remembered that he had been introduced to her as Dr Morrison and that he had a slight Scottish burr to his voice. Obviously, Dr Morrison and Lewis Sinclair had more than fearlessness in common.

'And who else?' she asked as he strode past the horse and the pony and Sir William and Lan Kuei and once again began to lead them south.

He frowned. 'There's young Chamot, the Swiss proprietor of the Hôtel de Pekin.'

'And is that all?' she asked, aghast.

'There may be one or two drifters and adventurers who will be willing to leave the safety of the city and ride out into the countryside, but I doubt if I will be able to raise a party of more than half a dozen.'

A hard knot of determination settled deep inside her. She would go directly to Phillippe and he would speak to his minister and official rescue parties would then be sent out.

A little way behind her Lan Kuei faltered, gasping for breath. Olivia turned quickly. The short respite while her baby had been carried for her had not been long enough. Olivia's arms ached, her legs felt like leaden weights and she yearned for rest, yet she quietly took the whimpering baby from Lan Kuei's arms and hoisted it once more against her shoulder. He looked across at her, the expression in his eyes one of admiration, warm and flattering. Her pulse leapt and she looked away from him quickly, terrified that he should see the emotion she was trying so desperately to hide.

As the sun rose, the way became more arduous. Peking shimmered before them in the heat haze like a mirage, a dream city of high crenellated walls, constantly before them and yet seeming as if it would never be attained. Clouds of dust gouged up by the wheels of carts choked them. The heat stifled them. They were pushed and jostled and there were times when Olivia wondered how she would manage to continue to put one foot in front of the other. Her exhaustion was obvious and Lewis said quietly, 'Give the baby back to Lan Kuei.'

Olivia looked behind her at Lan Kuei's half-closed eyes and swaying walk and shook her head. He did not argue with her, simply moving closer, bridging the narrow gap between them and taking a firm hold of her arm. She did not protest or try to pull away. She had neither the strength or the inclination. Cheng-yu still clasped Lewis's neck with his tired arms, his small black eyes dull and uncomprehending. Even Lady Glencarty's back had lost its ramrod straightness as she rode the pony, Sister Angelique behind her. It was her uncle that Olivia felt most sorry for. The experiences of the last few hours had left its mark on him and his austere, autocratic features had taken on the lines of unmistakable age. He was not accustomed to exercise and the long walk with the constant fear of attack was taking its toll.

Overcome with concern for him, she did not look where she was going and stumbled. Lewis's grip on her arm tightened as he steadied her and then, ignoring her protests, took the baby from her, adjusting Cheng-yu slightly so that he could both carry the toddler on his back and the baby in his arms.

Relieved of her burden, she continued to walk at his side. The dust stung her eyes and she had to shield them from the sun as she looked ahead and at Peking. To her dazed gaze it did not seem as if the walls were any nearer or if they would ever, ever, become any nearer. And though she knew by now that their pathetic procession must be clearly visible no riders surged out of the Tien An Men Gate, hastening to their aid.

'It will only take another hour,' Lewis Sinclair said, his smoke-dark voice piercing through her tiredness.

She pushed a tendril of hair away from her face and gave him an unsteady smile. It was unknowingly gentle and soft, full of such innocent sensuality that the breath caught in his throat.

She was beautiful and she was brave and she affected him in a way that he had not thought any woman ever would again. He remembered the fiancé awaiting her at the French Legation and hoped that he bore no similarity to the obnoxious young diplomat he had punched so squarely on the jaw.

'I can see the yellow eaves of the Tartar City,' her aunt said, almost senseless with relief.

Olivia blinked again into the sunlight. The massive forty-foot high walls no longer shimmered insubstantially but rose solidly from the sun-baked plain, the yellow glazed eaves of the gatehouses rising above them and higher still, the unmistakable shape of the White Dagoba. Nothing higher pierced the cloudless skyline and for the first time Olivia realized why. Anything higher would have offended the *feng-shui*. Their journey was nearly over, but her feelings were far too confused for her to share her aunt's wholehearted relief. Once inside the city, Sister Angelique and Cheng-yu and Ch'un would no doubt make for the Anglican mission, perhaps taking Lan Kuei and her baby with them. Her aunt and uncle and Lady Glencarty would make immediately for the British Legation and she would be obliged to accompany them. And Lewis Sinclair would seek out Dr Morrison and Monsieur Chamot. In all probability, she would never see him again. She looked across at him, at the strong assertive outline of his features, at the thick black hair, springy as heather, and her throat felt painfully tight.

Wearily they entered the south gate of the Outer City, moving slowly with the crowds along the raised causeway that in winter offered a dry thoroughfare over mud-swamped ground. The Chien Men Gate leading into the Tartar City lay ahead of them and Lady Glencarty and her aunt gazed at it with hungry eyes. Eventually, after being pushed and jostled on all sides, they left the Outer City behind and entered the tumultuous chaos of the Tartar City.

The raised causeway was now a street sixty feet wide and on either side were mat-shed booths and shops huddling three rows deep. This was the city of rope-dancers and jugglers, fortune-tellers and pedlars, that had so entranced her. It did so no longer.

The smell of unwashed and diseased humanity nearly overpowered her. She no longer could see anything exotic in the sight of the ragged story-tellers and scribes. She was aware only of the poverty. Of the half-naked children; the squalid, fetid hovels that were their homes.

'Oh thank God,' Letitia Harland sobbed in weariness as the roofs and walls of the legation quarter came into view. 'Oh, William, I am so tired. So very tired.'

William Harland's face was grey with fatigue but he patted his wife's hand reassuringly, knowing that he would have to forgo the luxury of a bath and a rest until after he had made a report of what had occurred, to Sir Claude MacDonald.

The Anglican Mission was on the opposite side of the city to the legation quarter and Sister Angelique asked Lady Glencarty to rein in the pony.

'This is where we must part,' she said gently. 'Doctor Sinclair, would you help me to dismount please.'

Lewis handed the baby once more to Olivia, swung Cheng-yu to his feet and lifted Sister Angelique lightly to the ground.

'Just one moment!' Lady Glencarty said sharply. 'This will not do, Doctor Sinclair. The Anglican Mission will be crowded to the doors with refugees. Goodness only knows what facilities will be there. Sister Angelique must accompany us to the legation quarter.'

'And the children?' Lewis asked, quirking an eyebrow.

Lady Glencarty glared at him. '*And* the children,' she said unflinchingly.

Sister Angelique shook her head. 'Thank you, Lady

Glencarty, but I shall be of more use at the Mission than I would be in the legation quarter.'

'Poppycock!' Lady Glencarty said fiercely. 'The streets are so crowded it will be impossible for you to make your way there on foot.'

'Doctor Sinclair will escort me,' Sister Angelique said composedly. 'But perhaps, as conditions at the Mission will be so crowded, you could take Ch'un and Cheng-yu to the legation quarter? I am sure they will be much more comfortable there for the time being.'

The prospect of entering the legation district with two Chinese orphans visibly shook Lady Glencarty but she said briskly, 'Kindly mount, Cheng-yu behind me, Doctor Sinclair.'

Lewis swung the tired and bewildered toddler up behind Lady Glencarty and Lady Glencarty transferred her attention to Lan Kuei. 'Would you like me to take the baby?' she asked majestically.

Lan Kuei shook her head. Lady Glencarty terrified her even more than did the Boxers.

'That's it, then,' Lady Glencarty said with a resurgence of vigour. 'I shall look after Ch'un and Cheng-yu until this commotion is over. Goodbye, Doctor Sinclair. I doubt that we shall meet again.'

'Your horse ...' Letitia Harland said nervously to him, wondering if she was going to be asked to dismount and make the last few yards of the journey on foot.

'I shall be back to attend to him after I have escorted Sister Angelique and Lan Kuei to the Mission,' Lewis said briefly. 'Goodbye, Sir William. Impress on Sir Claude the gravity of the situation, and the need for immediate reinforcements for the city.'

'I shall,' Sir William said vehemently.

The two men shook hands and then he was looking down at her and though she could not be sure, she thought that there was regret in the depths of his dark eyes. He was saying goodbye to her. She could scarcely hear his voice above the tumult of the crowds seething around them. His hand touched hers. She wanted to cling to it and instead released it with impeccable formality. There were tiny flecks of gold near the pupils of his eyes. A small scar above one eyebrow. The hard line of his mouth had softened slightly and for a moment she thought that he was going to smile at her in the same devastating, down-slanting way that he had when they found the pony at the Hoggett-Smythes', but she was disappointed. Only the briefest of smiles touched his lips and then he was striding away from her, shouldering a way through the dense crowds, Sister Angelique and Lan Kuei in his wake.

'Come along, my dear,' her uncle said to her wearily, 'another few minutes and we will be safely indoors.'

The constriction in her chest grew tighter and tighter. Once behind the high walls surrounding their home in the legation quarter, she knew that she would not be able to leave. She would not be able to go to the French Legation and speak to Phillippe. She would not be able to do anything to organize help for those still on the highway and in the outlying missions.

'No,' she said suddenly, 'There are things I have to do first, Uncle William. I'm sorry!'

'*Olivia!*'

She did not wait to hear his protests. She turned quickly, pushing her way through the teeming crowds, heading blindly, not in the direction of the French Legation, but towards the west side of the city and the Anglican Mission. She needed to know what conditions were like there. To see for herself. One thing she was now sure of, no one from the legations would have bothered to make the journey for themselves.

A Peking cart drawn by a running Chinaman nearly ran her down. Donkeys and mules tangled with each other. Chinese women with bound feet hobbled, pedlars shouted their wares, refugees from distant villages thronged aimlessly. There were loud cries from behind her as a sedan chair was carried ponderously through the throng, attendants clearing the way with flicks of bamboo rods.

She tried to move out of the way quickly but was not quick enough. The smarting lash of bamboo fell across her shoulders, making her cry out with pain and shock. Instinctively, she pressed herself back once more into the crowd as the sedan chair and its occupant and attendants continued on their imperious way. Her legs were shaking. Vainly she looked around for a wall upon which to lean and could see none. A pannier of rice cakes and tea was jammed hard into her back, and there was no apology forthcoming from the offending pedlar. For the first time she realized the colossal difference between being dressed as a European and being dressed as a Chinese.

She took in a deep, steadying breath, searching the crowd ahead of her, straining for a glimpse of Lewis Sinclair's glossy dark hair and powerful shoulders. He was nowhere to be seen. The smells of ginseng, garlic, tobacco and roasting meat assailed her on all sides. Doggedly she continued in the direction of the Anglican Mission, wondering how she could ever have thought this part of the city intriguing and exotic.

She avoided a turning to the south. The Mission was in the west of the city nearly parallel with the British Legation, but on the other side of the broad thoroughfare, leading from the Chien Men Gate. She fought back a wave of faintness, perspiration breaking out on her forehead. If she fainted here, in the street, she would very likely be trampled to near death. Suddenly, ahead of her, she saw an unmistakable head of black hair and a pair of strong shoulders forging a way through the crush.

'Doctor Sinclair!' she called, but her voice was drowned in the pandemonium around her.

From behind came the cries of another set of outriders accompanying a sedan chair. She was directly in its path and she tried feverishly to push herself out of its way. No one would give way for her. Those around her were too accustomed to the painful flicks of the bamboo whips that cleared a way for the sedans of officials and ministers to grant an inch of ground.

'*Doi mm jue!*' a voice barked raucously. Once more she tried to press herself out of the sedan's way.

'Doctor Sinclair,' she cried again. '*Doctor Sinclair!*' and then, desperately, '*Lewis!*'

He spun round, searching the crowds for a glimpse of her. With a sob of relief, she raised her arm, waving and then the vicious flick of a bamboo rod sent her stumbling to her knees. She was lost beneath a mêlée of feet and cantering hooves. Instinctively, she covered her face with her hands, rolling over on the ground with her knees hugged tight against her chest. The dust gouged up from the horse's hooves was choking her. Something hard hit her in the centre of her back, but she couldn't tell if it was a foot or a hoof or the corner of the sedan chair. She was gasping, choking for air, and then out of the nightmare a strong hand seized her, hauling her upright. She could barely see him, she was so dazed and stunned. He grasped her shoulders, shaking her as if she were a puppet.

'What the *hell*,' he demanded, his face white with rage and fear, '*are you doing?*'

'I ...' She gulped for air, trying to speak, aware that the sedan chair had halted and that the occupant was demanding to know why his passage was being delayed. She wondered vaguely, through a sea of pain, if she had unseated one of the accompanying riders.

'I was trying to find my way to the Anglican Mission,' she explained at last and then halted as the curtain of the sedan chair was flung angrily aside, her face so ashen that Lewis Sinclair swung her up into his arms, convinced that she was about to faint.

'Of all the idiotic, stupid, senseless things to do ...' he was saying savagely, but she was no longer listening to him. The occupant of the sedan chair was Phillippe.

Five

Her head was on his shoulder. His arms were around her, strong and secure. With savage intensity he stormed through the ragged and panic-stricken crowds, Sister Angelique and Lan Kuei in his wake. Not even at the door of the Anglican Mission did he set her once again upon her feet.

She did not try to free herself. Shock and exhaustion had taken their toll. The fanatical hatred on the faces of the Boxers who had attacked the villa seemed to have merged crazily into the furious anger which Phillippe had displayed to the crowds when his sedan chair had been momentarily halted. She was tired. She was hungry, and she was confused.

'Lay her down here, Doctor Sinclair,' Sister Angelique was saying in gentle tones.

Lewis looked round the cramped, noisy confines of the Mission massed with weary peasant women and wailing babies, and shook his head. 'They need every inch of space there is. She isn't hurt. Only exhausted. The best place for her is the legation quarter.'

'But surely you must see Bishop Favier?' Sister Angelique was saying, a new expressioin in her voice. 'If things are as bad at the North Cathedral as they are here …'

Olivia fought through a wave of all encompassing tiredness. Why was Sister Angelique, who was always so serene and calm, sounding so anxious? And why, now that he had delivered Sister Angelique and Lan Kuei to the Anglican Mission, should it be important that Lewis also see Bishop Favier, the Roman Catholic Vicar-Apostolic of Peking?

'I shall go there first,' he said grimly, 'and then I will make sure that Miss Harland reaches the legation quarter safely.'

She knew that she should be demanding to be set upon her feet but it was pleasingly comfortable in his arms. A tiny rivulet of perspiration ran down the olive skin of his neck. She wondered what it would taste like if she were to lick it away. The male scent of him was as heady as frangipani flowers. His sweat. The faint odour of horseflesh. The still perceptible tang of his cologne. She could feel the slam of his heart against her chest and as he held her, the warmth of his touch spread through her, soothing and easing her. She felt her eyelids droop and lightly close.

They flew open again as he moved suddenly, swinging purposefully on his heel, striding from the dim interior of the Mission and out into sun-bright streets.

'Where are we going?' He was not heading eastwards towards Legation Street, but towards the high, blind, purple-stained walls of the Imperial City.

'To the Peitang.'

His voice was crisp and curt and she knew that he was furiously angry with her. The feeling of comfort and ease fled. 'What is the Peitang?' she asked, as he stormed a way through the crowd.

'The Northern Cathedral,' he replied brusquely.

She wanted to ask why they were going there, but his sunbronzed face was hard and uncompromising and she fell silent, acutely aware of the indecent ease with which he was carrying her and the feeling of near nakedness as her breasts in their light covering of linen were pressed firmly against the lean, strong muscles of his chest.

Lewis had no need of outriders with bamboo rods to make a way for him. He forged his way through the crowd with ease, not hesitating as he approached the Tien An Men Gate, the Gate of Heavenly Peace, that led into the Imperial City. Olivia's arms tightened involuntarily around his neck. She had entered the Imperial City only rarely and was well aware of what lay at its heart. The bright enamelled roofs of the Forbidden City and the Summer Palace where Empress Dowager Tzu-hsi held court.

The city reminded her of a delicately carved box that her father had given her when she was a child. When it was opened another smaller box lay within and when that was opened there was another box, and then another. In Peking there was first the Chinese City and then the Tartar City which housed the legations, and the Anglican Mission. Then, through the Tien An Men Gate lay the Imperial City and within that the pink and yellow walls of the Forbidden City and Empress Tzu-hsi's palace, the Empress ruling like a spider at the centre of a magnificent web.

'Do you think the Empress is encouraging the Boxers?' she asked as he shouldered his way towards the Peitang.

'Yes.' His voice was clipped and unforthcoming. Bitter tears stung the back of her eyes. She had helped no one by her impulsive dash through the streets. She had barely seen the inside of the Anglican Mission and certainly would not be able to give a coherent account of conditions to Phillippe. Phillippe. Her heart contracted painfully. Where could he possibly have been going in such haste? His outriders had lain about them with their bamboo rods with vicious indiscrimination. His journey must have been vitally urgent.

She looked up into Lewis Sinclair's grim, impassive face and realized for the first time that he did not know who the occupant of the sedan chair had been. Something of great importance had obviously happened in the city and he was still, so far, unaware of it.

'Lewis. The man in the sedan chair. It was Phillippe.'

For an instant she felt the arms around her stiffen into rigidity. He halted, staring down at her, his eyes incredulous. 'Phillippe? Philippe who?'

'Phillippe Casanaeve, my fiancé.'

His breath hissed between his teeth and for a second she thought that he was going to let her fall.

'Something must have happened in the city of great importance,' she said nervously, aware that his anger was no longer that of being merely inconvenienced by her presence, but went far deeper. 'He was in a dreadful hurry. He wouldn't have allowed his outriders to behave like that unless it was a matter of life and death.'

'*Casanaeve!*' He uttered the name as if it were a blasphemy. It had been Monsieur Casanaeve that he had left spread-eagled on the floor of the French Legation after he had made his insulting remark about Pearl Moon.

She nodded, filled with sudden disquiet. There was a savagery in his handsome features that she had never seen before. 'It wasn't his fault that I was knocked to the ground,' she said hurriedly. 'He wouldn't have known about it. If he had known that someone had been injured, he would have stopped, no matter how important his mission.'

The ferocious expression in his narrow black eyes sent a shiver of fear down her spine.

'You think *that*?' he spat at her, letting her go so suddenly that she fell with an alarmed cry into a heap at his feet. 'You think a man like Casanaeve would *care* if he hurt anybody on his way from one soirée to another?'

Furiously she stumbled to her feet. 'Of course he would care!' she shouted, forgetting all about politeness, propriety, good manners. Not caring that they were in the middle of the street. That she looked like a street urchin and was behaving like one. 'Phillippe is a gentleman! He wouldn't have allowed his outriders to behave as they did unless he was on his way from the Summer Palace with vital information for his minister!'

For a second his eyes widened in disbelief, and then he began to laugh but there was no mirth in his laughter.

'My God! You really believe that, don't you? You believe

that what happened to you a half-hour ago was a rare occurrence. That your precious Phillippe was not even aware that his sedan chair had knocked anyone to the ground?'

Her hair fell around her shoulders, tumbled and dishevelled. There were smuts of dirt on her nose and cheeks and her Chinese garments were covered in layers of dust. 'Of course he didn't know!' she shouted in rage. 'If he had known, he would have stopped, no matter how important his mission!'

'Your *gentlemanly* Phillippe was on no mission!' Lewis yelled back at her. 'He's a junior diplomat, not a minister! The only reason for his "life and death" hurry would be to ensure that he wasn't late for his next social engagement.'

'*Liar!*' she hissed, drawing back her hand to deliver a stinging blow to his cheek.

'*Idiot!*' he shouted back, catching her wrist in a steel-like grip. 'You nearly died back there! You could have been trampled to death by the horses. By the crowds. And if you had been, Casanaeve wouldn't even have stopped!'

'He *would*!' she hurled back at him fiercely, trying to free herself from his hold and failing.

For a long second he stared down at her, his anger diminishing and dying. 'He wouldn't,' he said at last, and this time his voice was oddly flat. 'He knew that someone had been pushed into the path of his sedan chair. That was why it momentarily halted. He didn't ask if anyone was hurt. His only concern was in urging his bearers to continue as quickly as possible.'

Olivia knew that there was noise all around her. That pedlars were hawking their wares. That children were crying. That donkeys and mules were vying with camels for space on the beaten earth of the street. The uproar and tumult and clamour of the city was deafening. Yet in that moment, as she stared up at him and saw the pity in his eyes, it seemed as if she was entombed in silence. She could hear nothing but the beating of her own heart, the slight catch in her throat as she tried to breathe normally.

What he said was true. Somewhere, deep down, she had known it all along. The charming, exquisitely mannered companion that she had said she would marry was the same man who had so furiously yanked back the curtain of his sedan chair and demanded that his bearers continue without hesitation on their way. He had known that someone had been hurt, and he had not even asked after their welfare.

She looked up at him and he felt his heart throb and jar beneath his breastbone. 'Why?' she asked simply.

The world seemed to have spiralled down so that it held only the two of them. The blood surged through his body like a hot tide and he knew that he was ablaze with what had previously only smouldered. He wanted to take her in his arms and comfort her. To stroke her hair; to wipe the smuts of dust from her face; to kiss the soft, vulnerable mouth; to make love to her. He passed his hand briefly across his eyes. He had loved once and he had not thought to love again.

A wry smile touched the corners of his lips. His fellow Europeans had been united in their opinion that his choice of Pearl Moon as a wife had been deplorably unsuitable. Yet Olivia Harland would make an even more unsuitable wife. She would not be happy to live, as Pearl Moon had, in the distant province where his work took him. In Chihli and Shansi. The mere idea was madness and when he lowered his hand his eyes revealed nothing of the fierce emotion that held him in its grip.

'Because he is a European,' he said dispassionately in reply, 'and he thought that you were a Chinese.'

She nodded, and knew that in the noisy, crowd-packed street, her life had changed its course. She would not marry Phillippe Casanaeve. She would remain a spinster if need be, but she would never marry a man who had not the strength to show good manners and kindness to those weaker than himself. A man like Lewis Sinclair.

'Shall we continue towards the Cathedral?' she asked, her throat so tight that it was a physical pain.

He nodded. 'Can you manage?'

Maturity settled on her as tangibly as a cloak. 'I can manage,' she said steadily. She would manage today and tomorrow and all the other days for the rest of her life. She would manage on her own and without him because she had no alternative.

'Why do you need to see Bishop Favier?' she asked, trying to still her trembling as he took hold of her arm, steering her once more through the crowds.

'Because my son is in his charge,' Lewis said as they side-stepped a street barber touting for custom. 'That was my main reason for riding south to Peking. To leave Rory in the relative safety of Peking with Bishop Favier who is an old family friend, and to try and convince Sir Claude and his fellow ministers of the seriousness of the rapidly deteriorating situation outside Peking and the urgent need for troops.'

'I see.' She had thought that she had experienced pain but now she knew that she had never known the meaning of the word. It sliced through her like a knife. His son. It was foolish of her, but she had never thought that there might be a child.

The giant grey stone façade of the cathedral towered above them. In the compound surrounding it was an orphanage, a convent, a dispensary, and a school, all jammed to the doors with frightened-faced refugees.

'Where can I find Bishop Favier?' Lewis shouted across to one of the black-robed Sisters of Charity.

'He's in the dispensary, Doctor Sinclair,' the nun replied, barely hesitating in her swift trot towards the storeroom, a couple of Chinese boys in her wake.

As they pressed and pushed their way forward, Olivia gasped. 'The other refugees, the thousands that are still trying to reach the city, where will they go? Who can possibly look after them? There's less room here than there was at the Mission.'

'The legations are going to have to open their doors,' Lewis said as the imposing figure of Bishop Favier strode to meet them, grasping his hand warmly.

Olivia thought of the beautifully tended grounds surrounding the British Legation, the French Legation, the American Legation. It was impossible to imagine them swarming with children, but Lewis was right. There was nowhere else in Peking for them to go. There were eleven legations in the legation quarter, and all were spacious. Lady Glencarty had already set an example by inviting Ch'un and Cheng-yu into her home. Where Lady Glencarty led, surely others would follow.

The mêlée of children around them were so noisy that Lewis had to shout as he introduced her to the Bishop. Olivia was not quite sure how she should greet the Vicar-Apostolic of Peking and then was suddenly relieved to discover that under the present circumstances protocol no longer mattered. There were more important things to think about than the right way of addressing the head of Peking's Roman Catholic community.

'It must have been a dreadful journey for you,' Bishop Favier was saying to her. 'Let's go inside. I can't offer you rest or refreshment I'm afraid, but at least the noise level will be a little lower.'

'How many refugees are sheltering here?' Olivia asked him and then, just as Bishop Favier shook his head in despair, saying 'thousands', a little boy detached himself from the throng and threw himself upon Lewis.

'*Papa! Papa!* You said it would be weeks, months, before I should see you again!' His skin was no darker than that of his father; his hair was thick and black, tumbling over his eyebrows in a way so reminiscent of Lewis's that Olivia felt her heart catch in her throat. His eyes were grey and almond-shaped, and as Lewis caught him up in his arms and swung him around, they were alight with such naked joy that Olivia had to look swiftly away, terrified that her tight control would break at any moment.

'I have told our Minister repeatedly,' Bishop Favier was saying to her as they entered a minuscule room at the rear of the dispensary that, by some miracle, was strewn with books and paperwork and not refugees, 'that the religious persecution being waged against both Catholic and Anglican missionaries would lead to persecution against all Europeans. The Boxers will attack the city, I know it. The local community know it. But nothing I say will convince our Minister, Monsieur Pichon, that an attack is imminent.'

Olivia tried to give the Bishop her full attention but it was difficult when she was so acutely aware of Lewis's joyous reunion with his son. She kept her head firmly averted from them, determining to leave at the first opportunity. Bishop Favier could probably procure a Peking cart for her. She felt Lewis touch her arm lightly and then he was saying, 'Rory, I would like to introduce you to Miss Olivia Harland.'

Reluctantly she turned and held out her hand to Lewis Sinclair's son. He took it confidently and without shyness.

'Papa says you are very brave.'

Olivia felt her heart leap and her voice trembled slightly as she said, 'It was very kind of your father to say that about me, Rory.'

'He says you are his friend,' Rory continued, his eyes shining. 'Will you be my friend too?'

Remembering that hideous moment when she had declared so vehemently to Lan Kuei that Lewis Sinclair was no friend of hers, Olivia felt her cheeks heighten with colour as she said steadily, 'Yes, Rory. I would like to be your friend.'

Rory beamed happily and though she strove to return her glance directly to Bishop Favier, her willpower failed her. Instead, she raised her eyes from Rory's shock of dark hair and met those of his father. His eyes were alight with amusement and she knew that he was remembering the incident as clearly as she was. A smile lurked at the corners of his mouth and her discomfort fled. There was a bond between them now. Unspoken and intangible, yet there nonetheless. Not even his violent anger over her defence of Phillippe had dispelled it.

A smile tugged at the corners of her own mouth and he grinned, white teeth flashing a gleam of pure devilment in the depths of his dark eyes. Her own smile widened and it seemed to Lewis as if a shaft of bright sunlight had suddenly pierced the shadow of Bishop Favier's tiny room.

'And so we must contact Monsieur Chamot and Doctor George Morrison and Sir Claude,' Bishop Favier was saying urgently.

Lewis took his son's hand in his and reluctantly removed his attention from Olivia Harland and returned it to the Bishop.

'There must be a council meeting of the Corps Diplomatique,' Bishop Favier was saying, pacing the room, his hands clasped behind his back. 'Sir Claude MacDonald is the man we need to convince of the seriousness of the situation. Once the heads of all the eleven legations have met in council, a naval detachment can be sent for from Tientsin.'

'I am going directly to the legation quarter now,' Lewis said, squeezing Rory's hand comfortingly as he heard his gasp of disappointment. 'It may be that Sir William Harland has already had the opportunity to speak to Sir Claude. If not, then I will go immediately and then seek out Morrison and Chamot.'

'Good, good.' Bishop Favier nodded his head vigorously. 'You must leave now, Lewis. There is not a moment to be lost.'

Olivia turned her head away as Lewis hugged his son tightly and kissed him goodbye. As they left Rory behind with Bishop Favier and walked out once more into the crowded compound encircling the Cathedral, Olivia said tentatively, 'Can I come with you when you go to speak to Monsieur Chamot and Doctor Morrison?'

'No,' he said, and his voice was adamant. 'You need rest.'

'I am not really so tired,' she lied as he once more took her arm.

He looked down at her with a wry smile. 'You're exhausted. You have done all that you can, Olivia. You can do nothing more.'

She didn't protest. She knew that it would be useless. Even now she was slowing him down. She was a hindrance to him, not a help.

They struggled once more through the Wu Men Gate, vying with hurtling Peking carts and hurrying street traders. There was so much that she had been going to do, and now there was nothing. She knew, beyond a shadow of doubt, that it would be futile to approach Phillippe. He would be indifferent to the fate of the Chinese Christian converts trying to reach Peking before the next Boxer attack. And she knew instinctively that he certainly would not risk his own life by riding to the outlying missions and escorting the inhabitants to safety. The most she could do was try and speak to Lady MacDonald and urge her to make arrangements at the legation for the many women and children who would need shelter.

The broad, straight thoroughfare of Legation Street seemed blessedly empty after the teeming throngs in the west part of the city. She had hoped that she would be able to say goodbye to him in private, but as they approached the high walls surrounding the lush gardens of the Harland residence, there were exclamations of incredulity and relief and over a dozen household employees came surging down the pathway to meet them.

'It looks as if your uncle was just about to despatch a search party,' Lewis said dryly as maids and gardeners, cooks and houseboys surrounded them, and Sir William himself came hurrying in their wake.

'Thank God,' he said fervently, clasping Olivia tightly. 'I feared the worst, child. There are rumours that Boxers have already infiltrated the city and even that a date has been set for attacks upon the cathedrals and missions.'

'*No!*' Olivia cried out, remembering Sister Angelique and Lan Kuei at the Anglican Mission and Rory with his impish smile and shock of thick, dark hair.

'Come inside. You need food. Rest.' He was shaking Lewis's hand gratefully. 'I am to see Sir Claude in half an hour. Where can I contact you with news?'

'The Hôtel de Pekin,' Lewis said briefly.

Restrained by her uncle's arm, Olivia looked across at him in anguish. 'Lewis, the Boxers couldn't possibly infiltrate the city could they? The Mission. The Cathedral. The people there will be safe, won't they?' and then, like a cry torn from her heart, 'Rory will be safe, won't he?'

His eyes were black pits in the white grimness of his face. 'Unless the ministers send for troops, no one is safe,' he said and then, ignoring the watching circle of Chinese and European servants, ignoring Sir William who still had a protective hand on Olivia, he crossed the distance between them in one stride and hooked a finger under her chin, tilting her face upwards.

The moment was a pulsebeat in the stretch of time, but Olivia knew that it would last in her mind forever. In that moment she became his unreservedly. Dark eyes met blue and then his mouth came down on hers in swift, unfumbled contact. Joy rose up in her so wild and free that she thought she would die of it. From another world she heard her uncle's outraged protest, the gasps of shock and horror, and then he raised his head from hers, held her eyes steadily for a long moment and turned on his heel, striding swiftly out of the garden.

He was going to the Chamots. To Dr Morrison. He was going and she loved him and would always love him.

'Disgraceful. Unpardonable ...' her uncle was saying in agitation as he escorted her towards the house. 'The fellow should be horsewhipped.'

Olivia paid him no attention. He had kissed her. It was a

moment that she would remember always. A moment that no one could take away from her.

Her aunt was not there to greet her when they entered the house. She was still lying down, fortified by sal volatile and a little medicinal brandy. Olivia made her way straight to her room and as she wearily climbed the stairs she could still hear her uncle announcing that Sinclair was born to be hanged.

A small smile touched her lips. She didn't care if he was born to be hanged or not. He had altered her life irrevocably. She now knew what love was and she would never settle for second best. As her maid poured jugfuls of hot, steaming water into her bath, she lay down on the bed, her joy merging into despair. There was only one Lewis Sinclair. It was impossible to imagine that there could be another man with all his qualities. With his fearlessness and daring. His strength and his courage and his remarkable capacity for kindness. No other smile could be so devastating; no other eyes so dark and gleaming. Against her closed lids she saw again the commanding profile, the hard-boned face and strong, assertive jawline; the blue-black hair, thick and glossy, curling low over the collar of his shirt. Heat surged through her body and she clenched her fists tightly. He was married, married, married, and she could not have what she most desired.

Savagely she rose from the bed, dismissing her maid, wrenching herself free of the dust-clouded Chinese garments that she had worn ever since they had fled the villa. He had shown her what love could be like, but he could not give her his love and she could not take it. She stepped into the fragrant water of the bath, envying with all her heart an unknown Chinese girl that no European lady would deign to speak to.

When she finally returned to her bed, she slept for eighteen hours. It was seven o'clock the following evening when she finally awoke.

'I've ordered a supper tray to be sent up to you,' her aunt

said, sitting down by the side of her bed.

For a moment Olivia stared at her and then recollection returned in full.

'What did Sir Claude say when Uncle William spoke to him?' she asked urgently.

'Sir Claude has put all our fears to rest,' her aunt replied with terrifying complacency. 'He has had an audience with the Empress Dowager who has assured him that none of us will come to harm.'

Olivia stared at her aunt aghast. 'But surely he cannot *believe* her!' Hastily she pushed the bedclothes away and swung her feet to the floor. 'Has the Empress publicly condemned the Boxers?'

'I'm sure that she must have,' her aunt said serenely. 'Please get back into bed, Olivia. Your tray will be here in a moment.'

'I don't need a tray, Aunt Letitia. I'm not an invalid. I want to speak to Uncle William.'

'In that case, you will have to dress becomingly. He is at present entertaining Phillippe who has been *most* concerned about your welfare.'

Both of them looked simultaneously at the large emerald sparkling on the fourth finger of Olivia's left hand. Her aunt smiled happily. Olivia was going to make the most beautiful bride and Phillippe Casanaeve was without doubt the most handsome of all the diplomats in Peking. Olivia's mouth hardened into a tight line. She couldn't imagine why she hadn't removed the engagement ring before. Now, when it could be returned, was the moment to do so.

'Please tell Uncle William and Phillippe that I shall be down directly,' she said, ringing for her maid and opening her closet door wide to select a dress.

Her aunt rose with an indulgent smile, certain that Olivia was merely impatient to be reunited with her fiancé.

'The French,' she murmured to herself, as she left the bedroom, 'so charming, so courteous, so ... *continental*.'

Olivia pulled the ring from her finger and dropped it

unceremoniously into one of the cut glass dishes gracing her dressing-table. Phillippe Casanaeve had been most concerned about her health, had he? He certainly had not been when he had thought her a Chinese peasant girl lying in the dust and the dirt in the wake of his sedan chair.

By the time her maid arrived she had almost finished dressing. She had selected a gown of watered green silk and when her maid asked how she would like her hair to be dressed, asked simply that it be knotted in a simple chignon in the nape of her neck. Her maid did as she was bid, aware that since her ordeal there was a subtle change in her mistress's manner. A new sureness and certainty about her. It was as if, overnight, she had changed from being an extraordinarily pretty girl and grown into a stunningly beautiful woman.

Olivia surveyed herself in the full-length mirror and was pleased with what she saw. Then, picking up the emerald ring and cupping it in the palm of her hand, she made her way calmly downstairs to where her uncle and Phillippe Casanaeve waited.

Six

The chandeliers cast a brilliant light over the mahogany and silk and silver furnishings of the drawing-room. Her uncle and Phillippe rose simultaneously to their feet as she entered and she was pleased to see that the white, gaunt look that had strained her uncle's face was now receding. The web of lines around his eyes had deepened, but other than that, he looked no worse for his ordeal. She kissed him affectionately as he took her hands.

'I'm glad to see you looking so much better, dear child. You had us quite worried, but Doctor Fitzpatrick said all you needed was rest.'

'And he was right,' Olivia said reassuringly, stepping away from him and turning towards Phillippe.

'Olivia!' His voice was tender, his eyes full of concern. 'I vow, upon my life, that the fiends who caused you such distress will be caught and hanged.'

Dispassionately she allowed her hand to be taken and pressed against his lips. 'Your task may be a little difficult, Phillippe,' she said, and there was an undercurrent in her voice that startled her uncle and made him look at her with fresh concern. 'One Boxer is very much like another.'

'Your aunt tells me that you were injured in the streets yesterday afternoon,' Phillippe continued, unaware of the coolness in her voice. 'What happened? Are you quite recovered?' Solicitously he led her towards a chair.

'Quite, thank you,' she said, seating herself and looking up at him as if seeing him for the first time.

His blond hair shone. His blue eyes gleamed. No harshness or strong-boned aggression marred the classical purity of his features. His moustache was elegant. His sartorial elegance splendid. They were so close that she could smell the clean, starched linen of his elegant lace-trimmed evening shirt. The sweet aroma of the eau de Cologne that he favoured. He was handsome, charming, debonair. And she knew that never again would she want to be in the same room with him, or speak to him, or even acknowledge his presence if their carriages should pass in the street.

His handsomeness and charm were all on the surface; beneath was another Phillippe. A Phillippe that she had no desire to associate with, much less to marry.

'I wish I had been there,' Phillippe said fervently, as he sank on one knee beside her. 'If anyone had touched so much as a hair of your head, I would have whipped them to within an inch of their lives!'

Strangely enough she believed him, yet he had shown not the slightest concern for the Chinese girl his sedan had knocked to the ground beneath the trampling hooves of his outriders' horses.

The hand that held hers was beautifully manicured. Soft and white. She thought of Lewis's hands, large and strong, and a tremor ran through her.

Phillippe felt a surge of heat to his loins. In some way that he could not understand, she had changed. She had always been lovely. Now she was beautiful. There was a new quality about her. A new poise and self-assurance.

Her soft, dark hair shone glossily beneath the light of the chandeliers, held in a loose knot at the back of her neck by Chinese ivory combs in a manner he found unbearably sensual. In the delicate oval of her face, her eyes were smoke-blue, thick-lashed and wide-spaced. Before she had left Peking for the Western Hills, they had always gazed up at him with adoration: now there was something new in their depths. Something that he did not understand and that caused him a flicker of unease. With growing desire he noted the swell of her breasts beneath the aquamarine silk of her bodice and the curve of her hips beneath the fall of her skirt.

'Thank God that you are safe,' he murmured, wishing heartily that Sir William and Lady Harland were not in the room and that he could circle the enticing narrowness of her waist with his arms and kiss the smooth creaminess of her skin, the rosy softness of her mouth.

The emerald ring dug deep into the palm of her free hand. She could not return it to him with her aunt and uncle present. Perhaps, when it was time for him to leave, she would be able to spend a few minutes alone with him. Not minutes, she corrected herself as she remembered his furious face as he had exhorted his whip-bearing outriders onwards. A moment. One moment was all that she needed. One moment in which to tell him that she did not love him and that she could not marry him.

'You have no idea of the ordeal that we suffered,' Letitia Harland was saying. 'To be almost killed at the hands of the Boxers and then to be almost crushed to death on entering the city! It was terrible. Truly terrible.'

'Something will have to be done about the refugees,' Sir William said with a worried frown. 'The overcrowding is appalling.'

Phillippe, misunderstanding the cause of his concern, said in a voice touched by only the merest of accents, 'I quite agree with you, Sir William. The streets are so crowded there is barely room to move. I, myself, was nearly killed yesterday afternoon when a stupid Chinese threw herself beneath the feet of one of my bearers. It is high time the city gates were closed and all further entry barred.'

Sir William, who did not agree with him at all, cleared his throat, looking distinctly uncomfortable.

'And where do you propose that the refugees should go?' Olivia asked tightly, wondering how she could have ever imagined herself in love with a man so uncaring of others.

Phillippe shrugged. 'Tientsin,' he said indifferently. 'They will find somewhere. People like that always do.'

A chill ran down Olivia's spine. People like that. People like Sister Angelique and Ch'un and Cheng-yu and Lan Kuei. Her eyes sparked dangerously and before she could speak again her uncle said hastily, 'Tientsin is eighty miles away, Phillippe. Most of the refugees are on foot. It would be totally impracticable. Provision must be found for them here. I intend to speak to Sir Claude about it first thing tomorrow morning.'

Phillippe, skilled in the art of smoothly changing his opinions whenever it was politic to do so, nodded. 'Perhaps you would like it if I, too, approached my minister?'

Sir William was unable to suppress a sigh of relief. He had seen the flare of anger in Olivia's eyes and for one hideous moment he thought she was going to tell young Casanaeve exactly what her opinion was of his suggestion that the travel-weary refugees be barred entry to the city. He would have to talk to her when Casanaeve had taken his leave. It was obvious that as yet, he had no full understanding of the situation. It would never do if the engagement were broken off. He was highly eligible. Young, rich, and with a brilliant career ahead of him. To lose him as a future husband for Olivia over a few carelessly spoken words would break Letitia's heart.

'Was the Chinese girl hurt?' Olivia was asking Phillippe, and her uncle was aware again of the new and disturbing undercurrent in her voice.

Phillippe gave a slight, gallic shrug of the shoulders. 'I have no idea, my dearest Olivia. The horses were badly shaken. Such attacks are becoming commoner and commoner.'

Olivia's smoke-blue eyes widened. 'Attacks?' she asked queryingly. 'I am sorry, Phillippe. I had not realized that you had come under attack.'

White, even teeth flashed in a reassuring smile. 'Do not worry, Olivia. I am more than a match for any Chinese street gang.'

She was filled with a sudden desire to laugh. Street gangs, indeed! He had been safe in his sedan, surrounded by outriders clearing a way for him with their flailing bamboo rods and all that had happened was that she, in her inexperience, had not managed to dodge the cruel blows. She had been hit across the shoulders; had fallen and had temporarily halted his sedan. The crowd had been far too cowed to have attacked him. Her desire to laugh faded. They would not be cowed when the Boxers arrived. Lewis had told her that many Chinese were in sympathy with the Boxers. Chinese already safe within Peking's walls. She shivered. Chinese non-Christians would massacre Chinese Christians. Peking was not the safe haven the refugees believed it to be.

The emerald scorched her palm. Phillippe had risen to his feet and was standing at her side. She looked up at him and, uncaring of the presence of her aunt and uncle, said quietly, 'Phillippe, I would like to talk to you alone for a moment.'

His blue eyes gleamed. 'Of course, *chérie*,' he whispered huskily and then, turning to her aunt and uncle, said, 'Please forgive me. I have a meeting with the Minister at nine.'

'And will you speak to him about the refugees?' Sir William asked urgently.

Phillippe nodded. 'But of course, and tomorrow night, at dinner, Olivia will be able to tell him of your experiences herself.'

'Dinner?' Olivia asked questioningly as she rose and walked to his side. 'What dinner, Phillippe?'

'Monsieur Pichon would like us to join him for dinner tomorrow evening. Your uncle has already given permission for you to accept the invitation, providing you are feeling well enough to do so.'

Her heart began to slam painfully against her chest. Dinner with the French Minister? She would be able to tell him exactly what the conditions were on the highways leading to the city. She would be able to ask him to organize relief parties. To plead the cause of Bishop Favier in person.

'I am quite well enough to accept the French Minister's kind invitation,' she said steadily.

They had moved into the hall. The houseboy was handing Phillippe his top hat and walking cane, adjusting his silk-lined even cloak about his shoulders.

'Phillippe ...' Her fingers tightened around the ring. If she gave it back to him now, there would be no dinner with the French Minister the following evening. She would have thrown away her only chance of helping the missionaries and converts.

'Yes, *chérie*?' Phillippe said, taking her hand and kissing the tips of her fingers, his eyes burning into hers. He wanted to press her against him, feel her supple body moulded willingly against his. Kiss her until she lost her breath in the passion of his mouth and he could not do so. Sir William was still present and showed no signs of being discreet and leaving them alone for even the briefest of moments.

'I am looking forward to tomorrow night,' she said, and that at least was true, she thought, as she wriggled the ring once more on to the fourth finger of her left hand.

'*Je t'aime,*' Phillippe whispered and then, raising her hand once more to his lips, he bade her goodbye.

'A fine young man,' her uncle said as the servants closed the doors.

Olivia said nothing. There was nothing that she could say. Her uncle had suffered enough in the past forty-eight hours without having to know that it was Phillippe's outriders that had knocked her to the ground. She would never tell him. Telling him would achieve nothing.

She sighed as she kissed him goodnight. He would be bewildered when he learned that she had broken off her engagement to Phillippe, but better that he was bewildered rather than that he should be hurt by discovering that the young man he thought so honourable was not quite so honourable after all.

She went to her room but she did not go to bed. She stood at her window, staring out over the starlit roofs of Peking, wondering where Lewis was. What he was doing and who he was with.

In a bedroom several doors further down the corridor, Letitia Harland was saying anxiously, 'I think it most unsuitable that Olivia should attend a dinner at the French Embassy when we ourselves will not be present, William.'

'Please don't worry, Letitia,' Sir William said with a touch of weariness. 'We were invited, but I shall be seeing Sir Claude again tomorrow evening and that is of far more importance. Olivia will be escorted by her fiancé. The McClouds will be there and the Lejeunes.'

'But *we* will not be there,' Letitia Harland repeated obstinately, the lines of worry on her face deepening. 'I do not want anyone to think that Olivia is *fast*!'

'No one will think that, Letitia. Their thoughts will be on other things.'

'What other things, William?' Letitia asked as he settled himself down on the far side of the bed and blew out the lamp, plunging the room into darkness.

'Boxers,' Sir William said, and closed his eyes, wondering what fresh approach he could use to stir the Corps Diplomatique into action.

The next morning Olivia announced at the breakfast table that she was going to go over to the Peitang to help Bishop Favier and the Sisters of Charity care for the refugees.

'I'm sorry, Olivia,' her uncle said, and his voice was firm, 'You are not to leave this house again unescorted.'

'Then I shall take one of the houseboys with me,' she said steadily.

'No.'

Their eyes met over toast and marmalade and lightly poached eggs.

'The conditions there are dreadful, Uncle William. Please ...'

'No.'

Their eyes held and Olivia's heart sank. He meant what he said. Seeing her despair, he reached out and covered her hand with his, the expression in his eyes softening. 'I know how much you care, Olivia, and I know how much you want to help, but you cannot do so. Not without causing your aunt great anxiety.'

'The English Mission then?' she pleaded. 'It is much nearer and Sister Angelique is there ...'

He shook his head. 'I have given your aunt my word that you will not leave this house today until Phillippe calls for you this evening.' He rose wearily to his feet. 'I would be very grateful, Olivia, if you would enable me to keep my word to her.'

'Yes, Uncle William,' Olivia said, knowing that she was defeated.

The hot morning sun streamed through the windows, motes of dust dancing in the light. The day stretched ahead of her unendurably. In the Peitang Bishop Favier would be working tirelessly. In the English Mission, Sister Angelique would be caring for the babies and the old and the sick. And she ... She was doing nothing. In a gesture of futile impatience she screwed her table napkin into a tight ball and flung it down beside her empty plate. There was nothing to do but wait for the evening and then be instrumental in persuading the French Minister to organize immediate relief parties.

Restlessly she climbed the stairs past her own room and on and up to the top of the house, hoping that from one of the windows she would be able to see the streets of the City. She sighed with disappointment. The high walls surrounding the house and legations made it impossible. Only the roofs of the great Chien Men Gate were visible, but she could not see the crowds scurrying to and fro beneath its rose-red, tip-tilted eaves.

She wondered where Lewis was, and her heart hurt her. Had he made contact with Dr Morrison and Monsieur Chamot? Were they already riding far out into the Boxer riddle countryside to escort frightened missionaries and converts to the city in safety? She pressed a hand to her side as if in doing so she could ease the pain. It was two days since they had parted. Since he had kissed her so passionately in full view of her uncle and all the household staff. In two days he could have left the city and returned several times. By this evening her uncle might have news of him. Her pain increased. If he had, he would not tell her. She doubted if Lewis Sinclair's name would ever pass her uncle's lips again.

Descending the stairs, she heard the sound of female voices rising from the morning room. Her aunt had visitors.

'My dear, I cannot imagine *what* possessed her!' she heard one of her aunt's friends saying, 'to be actually *seen* riding astride a *Mongol* pony with two *filthy* peasant children!'

Olivia's eyes sparked angrily, and her hand tightened on the banister rail.

'They had nowhere to go,' she heard her aunt saying defensively.

There came a mirthless laugh. 'Of *course* they had somewhere to go, Letitia. There are *orphanages* for destitutes, are there not? To have brought such children into the legation quarter was an act of unprecedented folly. Just think of the *disease* that could be spread.'

'And then for Doctor Sinclair to *slam* into Sir Claude's study in such a manner!' another voice said, sounding awestruck.

'And to *order* him to send for more troops!' the first voice said, high on a note of disbelief. 'Why, the man must be mad!'

'But more troops *are* needed,' Olivia heard her aunt say timidly.

'If they are, Letitia, it is for the ministers to decide. Not a lunatic. He rode out yesterday to Hosfang with Doctor Morrison, *The Times* correspondent, and they brought back over *forty* missionaries and children! Into a city as overcrowded as this! It is sheer folly! Why could they not stay where they were?'

Olivia had heard enough. She marched across to the door of the morning room and entered it without even the briefest of knocks. 'Because they would have been burned to death,' she said, her eyes flashing, and in a voice so unlike her own that her aunt turned pale. 'They would have died at the hands of the Boxers just as my aunt and uncle and Lady Glencarty would have died if it had not been for Doctor Sinclair!'

Her aunt's distinguished guests stared at her open-mouthed.

'As for the children now living with Lady Glencarty,' Olivia continued, her whole body blazing with anger, 'You had better get used to them for where they came from there are thousands more and they are going to have to be sheltered here! In the only part of the city that still has room!'

'Olivia, please,' her aunt protested weakly.

'And Doctor Sinclair is *not* a lunatic!' Olivia continued undeterred. 'He is splendidly courageous and the only sane man in the city!' and before they could draw breath to answer her, she spun on her heel, her skirts whipping about her ankles, slamming the door behind her.

'Well, really …' she heard faintly from her aunt's guests. 'Such behaviour …' and when the bell rang for the maid, Olivia knew that it was to request some sal volatile.

She marched out into the garden, still furiously angry. How could they be so blind as to what was happening around them? No wonder Lewis had lost his temper and gone storming into Sir Claude's inner sanctum. A smile touched the corners of her mouth. She would have given a great deal to have seen the expression on Sir Claude's face when Lewis had burst into his room.

As she neared the miniature pagoda that decorated the lawns, she disturbed a flock of white pigeons. They fluttered out from beneath the eaves, spreading their wings and circling high above the pines that screened the garden from that of its neighbours. She watched them and her smile faded. In all likelihood she would never see Lewis again. It seemed a thing too monstrous to be true, but then so did the reality of his marriage.

She sat down on a wooden seat in the pagoda's shade, remembering the joy on Rory's face as he had rushed up to his father, flinging his arms around his neck.

Walking with Lewis across the dust-blown plain towards Peking she had been able to forget the existence of his Chinese wife. Rory's exuberant, undeniable existence made it impossible to do so any longer. And yet, she thought, watching the birds as they wheeled and soared, he had kissed her. He had looked at her with such naked desire that his face had been transfigured.

Her hands clenched tightly in her lap. Had it been only desire? Had there been love there too? She did not know and she would never know. Bleakly she rose to her feet. She must stop thinking about him. Thinking about him would not bring him back to her. Would not alter the fact that he had fallen in love and married years ago. How old had Rory been? Four, probably five. Five years ago she had been only thirteen. They had missed each other in time and in place and there was nothing that she, or anyone else, could do about it.

Her knuckles white, she forced herself to think about the coming evening. It would not be easy to talk to the French Minister in the impassioned way that she intended. A dinner table was not the place for serious conversation, especially when there were ladies present. A frown furrowed her brow. She needed to talk to him in private, but how and where? The problem occupied her thoughts all morning and even when she joined her aunt for lunch, no infallible solution had presented itself to her.

Phillippe's carriage arrived promptly at seven. She had dressed with care. Not in order to please Phillippe but so that the French Minister would be unable to ignore her. Her gown was of midnight blue silk, cut as low as propriety and her aunt would allow. Clusters of tiny seed-pearls decorated the bodice and emphasized the narrowness of her waist. The skirt fell gently over her hips, swirling out in a sudden flare around her ankles to reveal dainty satin evening pumps. Despite her aunt's protests, she had again dressed her hair with stunning simplicity, coiling it softly in the nape of her neck and securing it with a freshly plucked gardenia.

As Phillippe handed her into the carriage, he knew with pride that she would outshine every other woman in the room. He took her hand immediately the carriage doors closed behind them, about to take full advantage of the unprecedented privacy that the unchaperoned journey afforded.

His lips pressed heatedly against her temple and she froze with distaste, saying quickly, 'No, Phillippe, please! My aunt has given me her utter trust and ...'

'*Olivia!*' His voice was low and urgent, his hands hot about her waist as he pulled her towards him.

'Phillippe!' Her protests were silenced as his mouth came down on hers, his lips hard and insistent. She tried to pull away from him but he was too strong for her. How could one man's kiss be so different from another's, she thought wildly as she tried to free herself from his embrace. His hand was on her breast, his tongue deep in her mouth. With all the strength that she could muster, she drew back her hand and slapped him full across the face.

His head shot back, his blue eyes wide, first with astonishment and then with anger.

'*Qu'est-ce que'ne va pas avec toi?*'

The carriage continued on its way, swaying gently from

side to side. Olivia's distaste was replaced by panic. One word from Phillippe and the carriage would turn round and she would never set foot in the French Embassy.

She grasped his hands, knowing that the next few seconds were vital. 'I am sorry, Phillippe,' she said, her voice trembling vulnerably as she simulated remorse and distress, 'but to be alone with you like this ... it is so disturbing ... I am so frightened that I shall forget myself completely, and ...' Her words trailed away, her eyes eloquent.

For one long, endless second she was not sure if her ruse had worked and then his fingers tightened on hers and he was kissing her hands, murmuring endearments, telling her that she was a goddess, a witch, an angel.

With overwhelming relief, Olivia felt the carriage shudder to a halt. The journey was over and on the return journey there would be no need for pretence. Her engagement ring would be returned to him. She would never have to suffer his embrace again.

Monsieur Pichon was small and intense with a heavy black moustache. Madame Pichon was heavy-bosomed and draped in ruby-red velvet. Her first words as she greeted them, were 'How *relieved* I am that you have arrived in safety! There are rumours that the railway station at Fengtai has been burned to the ground by the Boxers.'

Olivia drew in her breath sharply. If the rumour were true, it would make her task of persuading Monsieur Pichon to take immediate action far easier.

As she entered the dining-room on Phillippe's arm, she was immediately aware of the air of suppressed anxiety. Their fellow guests were Mr and Mrs McCloud. Mr McCloud was a businessman and Monsieur and Madame Lejeune were friends of the Chamots and visiting the city as part of a long, leisurely trip to the East.

Only minutes after they were seated, Monsieur Pichon was called from the room and the guests toyed with their Terrine of Duckling, not liking to voice the fear that was uppermost in their minds. Only Phillippe seemed totally undisturbed by the rumours of an attack on Fengtai. Looking across the table at him, Olivia had the distinct feeling that the city would have to be overrun before Phillippe would accept that the Boxers were a danger.

When the Minister returned, his guests looked towards him anxiously. He sat down, obviously agitated, and after drinking deeply from his wineglass, said, 'The rumours are true. The railway station and locomotive sheds at Fengtai have been burned. So, too, have the houses of the Belgian engineers who were working there.'

There were gasps of horror from all the ladies apart from Olivia. She felt only a cold, hard knot deep inside her, able to visualize all too easily the scene that must have taken place.

'The steel bridge at Fengtai has been blown up,' Monsieur Pichon continued, pushing his plate away from him. 'Observers say that the smoke darkened the sky for miles around.'

'Was Fengtai a very important station?' Madame Lejeune asked hesitantly.

Monsieur Pichon nodded his head gravely. 'Yes, Madame. I am afraid that it was. It stood at the junction of the Peking to Tientsin line.'

'And the Belgians?' Olivia asked, her eyes holding Monsieur Pichon's steadily.

The maid came in. The plates were removed. Tarte aux Pommes à la Suisse replaced the duckling.

'The line to Tientsin is still in working order,' Monsieur Pichon replied. 'I am glad to say that the workers at Fengtai managed to escape to Tientsin by train.'

There were exclamations of relief from the McClouds and Lejeunes. Phillippe allowed his wineglass to be refilled and smiled across at Olivia as if to say that the panic had been over nothing.

Olivia did not return his smile. Instead she said tightly, 'Were all the construction engineers at Fengtai there when the attack took place, Monsieur Pichon?'

Monsieur Pichon was about to say yes, but something in the expression in Olivia's eyes prevented him from doing so. They smouldered at him from the pale whiteness of her face, demanding the truth.

His shoulders sagged visibly. 'No, Miss Harland. I am afraid that they were not. The engineers' main headquarters is a little distance away at Ch'anghsintien.'

'And ...?' Olivia demanded, every line of her body taut as she waited for his answer.

Monsieur Pichon cleared his throat uncomfortably. 'The damage done by the Boxers at the junction means that Ch'anghsintien is completely cut off. Withdrawal by rail to either Peking or Tientsin is now impossible.'

'Then they are trapped?' Madame Lejeune asked, her voice high, her dessert untouched on her plate.

Monsieur Pichon's face was grave. 'I am afraid so, Madame. There can be no help for them.'

'They *can* be helped,' Olivia said vehemently, leaning across the table towards him, her gentian-blue eyes brilliant. 'There are enough Europeans in the city to form a rescue party!'

Madame Lejeune, Madame Pichon and Mrs McCloud gasped at her effrontery. Monsieur Lejeune observed her high, rounded breasts as they pressed tightly against the silk of her bodice and tried to remember when he had last seen a more spirited and fiery creature. Mr McCloud listened to her with interest, impressed by the certainty in her voice. Phillippe regarded her with horror. Since the Minister had returned to the room she had subjected him to a virtual interrogation. Now she was behaving like a madwoman. She would never be invited to the embassy again. With every word that she uttered, she was ruining his career.

'Olivia! Restrain yourself!' he said angrily, his hand shooting out and grasping hers. She shook it away without even deigning to look at him.

'It is not possible,' Monsieur Pichon was saying. 'The

countryside is rife with Boxers. No small party could survive.'

'They *could*!' Olivia insisted passionately. 'Doctor Sinclair left the city two days ago accompanied by Doctor Morrison of *The Times*. Together they brought back to the city over forty missionaries and children!'

Phillippe had already risen to his feet, his face flushed, his lips tight. 'If you will excuse me,' he was saying to the wide-eyed guests, 'my fiancée has recently undergone a most horrendous ordeal at the hands of the Boxers. She is not quite recovered. She is emotionally distressed and ...'

He walked quickly to her side and tried to lead her from the room.

'Let go of me, Phillippe,' she said, her eyes sparking dangerously. 'I am *not* emotionally distressed. Not in the sense that you are implying. I am simply trying to convince the Minister that relief parties *can* be sent into the countryside! That now, right at this very moment, they *are* being sent!'

'*Olivia*!' Phillippe seized her arm, his voice ugly.

Both Olivia and the Minister ignored him.

'I heard about the Sinclair party,' Monsieur Pichon said, the dinner and his other guests forgotten. 'A very brave young man. It was Doctor Sinclair, I believe, who escorted yourself and your aunt and uncle and Lady Glencarty to safety?'

'Yes, and a nun, Sister Angelique, and a Chinese girl and three children.' Her eyes burned fiercely into his. 'Monsieur Pichon, the Chinese converts struggling to reach the city are *our* responsibility. It is we who converted them to Christianity. We cannot allow them to be slaughtered for their faith, without lifting even a finger to help them.'

Phillippe's fingers dug cruelly into her arm and his Minister said sharply, '*Laissez! Ecoutez!*'

Phillippe obeyed, knowing that he would never forgive her for the humiliation of the evening; for the dashing of all his hopes.

'Large numbers of troops must be sent for,' Olivia continued, aware that she now had the attention not only of the Minister but of the entire table. 'Very soon it will be too late. Peking will be cut off from all outside help.'

'But surely *Peking* is not in danger?' Mrs McCloud said waveringly. 'The Boxers would never dare to attack the city.'

Olivia turned to her briefly. 'They would, Mrs McCloud. That is their avowed intention. Bishop Favier says that already there are many Boxers inside the city only waiting for the signal to be given to don their red sashes and to rise against Chinese Christians and Europeans.'

'And who is Bishop Favier?' Mrs McCloud asked, her face white.

'The Vicar-Apostolic of Peking. His cathedral, the Peitang, stands in the west part of the Imperial City and is already crammed to the doors with refugees.' She turned her attention once more to the intently listening Minister. 'He is caring for hundreds of hungry and sick Chinese, aided only by the Sisters. He says he has tried time and time again to awaken the Corps Diplomatique to the severity of the situation. It is just as bad at the English Mission. There is barely room to breathe. They need organized help. Food and medicine.'

'How can you be so sure of the situation in the west of the city, Miss Harland?' the Minister asked, intrigued.

'Because I have been there,' Olivia said crisply. 'I have seen for myself.'

Monsieur Pichon nodded slightly. Yes, she would have. She was a most extraordinary young woman.

'I congratulate you, Phillippe, on your choice of a fiancée,' he said to his white-faced and furious subordinate. 'She is both brave and intelligent.' He clasped his hands beneath his chin, speaking to her as if they were alone in the room. As if she were his equal and a man.

'I, alone of all my colleagues, have shared your fears from the very first. At a meeting of the Corps Diplomatique four days prior to the party given by Sir Claude in honour of your Queen's eightieth birthday, I advocated that a naval detachment be sent for from Tientsin.'

Olivia remembered Lady Glencarty's spirited wish that his suggestion be vetoed.

'Today, after the attack on Fengtai, we again met in council and it was decided unanimously that guards must be sent for. If all goes well, they should be leaving Tientsin for Peking in two days' time.'

Two days. Olivia's relief was short-lived. The Corps Diplomatique had left it too late. In two days' time the Boxers could very well be at the city's gates.

'When you say guards, will they be soldiers or sailors and how many will there be?'

Monsieur Pichon's eyes gleamed. The enchanting Miss Harland should have been born a boy. She would have made a splendid asset at any conference table.

'Sailors and marines, Miss Harland. There are several warships lying off the coast at Taku. From Taku the railway runs the thirty miles inland to Tientsin and then continues the sixty-eight miles to Peking.' He paused and then added, 'The first detachment is, I fear, dangerously small in number.'

'How small?' Olivia asked.

The eyes of everyone in the room flicked from Olivia's head of soft, dark hair with the gardenia nestling in its depths, to the Minister's head, grey and bowed.

'Three hundred officers and men,' he said at last.

Mr McCloud, now fully convinced of the danger in which they stood, paled. 'Three hundred?' he whispered. 'Against Boxers?'

The Minister nodded unhappily.

Olivia's face was grave. 'The railway terminus for Peking is outside the city walls,' she said slowly. 'It will be very easy for them to be trapped and killed even before they reach the gates of the city.'

No one spoke. Maids cleared the untouched plates of

dessert away and Olivia realized, for the first time, that she had the attention, not only of the Minister, but of every other person in the room.

'What do you suggest, Mis Harland?' the Minister asked, and there was no mockery or condescension in his voice. It was a simple question, simply asked.

'That more troops be sent for before the railway link with Tientsin is broken and that relief parties be organized immediately and sent to Ch'anghsintien. The construction workers have their families with them. There will be women and children there, unprotected against Boxer attack.'

The Minister shook his head. 'Ch'anghsintien is too far,' he said, his eyes bleak. 'For the Belgians, nothing can be done.'

'I believe it can,' she said, her cheeks flushed, the set of her chin wilful. 'Will you form part of a rescue party, Mr McCloud?'

Mr McCloud felt his face staining an ugly, embarrassed red. He shook his head. 'No, I cannot ride very well. I would be a handicap to any rescue party.'

Olivia's eyes flicked contemptuously away from him and towards Monsieur Lejeune. 'And you, Monsieur Lejeune?' she asked. 'Do you not ride very well either?'

Monsieur Lejeune lowered his eyes and shook his head. 'No,' he said, his voice muffled. 'I am sorry, Miss Harland, but such a project would be suicide.'

Briefly her eyes meet Phillippe's. 'And you, Phillippe?'

'Of course not,' he said without hesitation. 'The very idea is lunacy.'

'Very well.' She turned once more to the Minister. 'Monsieur Pichon, would you call a sedan chair for me, please?'

'Our carriage is outside and waiting,' Phillippe said brusquely.

She stood for a second, her head high, the light from the chandeliers casting a nimbus of gold around the silky darkness of her hair. 'I shall not be riding in it,' she said, the tilt of her head emphasizing the long, lovely line of her throat.

'But where are you going, Miss Harland?' Monsieur Pichon asked in consternation.

Olivia smiled at him, a dazzling, defiant smile that took his breath away. 'To Ch'anghsintien,' she said, and spun on a satin heel, leaving the Minister and his guests staring after her in open-mouthed disbelief.

Seven

The night air was hot and humid. With her heart beating fast and light, she ran across to where the McClouds' and Lejeunes' sedan chairs were waiting. She had only seconds to form a plan; to think. She could not go to Ch'anghsintien unescorted. She needed companions. Assistance. Bishop Favier could not leave his cathedral. Her uncle, even if he had been willing, was too old and infirm. She had no idea where Lewis was, and no means of contacting him.

The sedan bearers were waiting for directions. 'The Hôtel de Pekin,' she said impulsively, sitting back and letting the curtain fall. She had promised her uncle that she would not leave the house unescorted until Phillippe had called for her. She had kept her promise. Now her duty was to herself, and to the Belgians trapped in Ch'anghsintien.

Her bearers trotted swiftly through the straight, dark streets. Monsieur Chamot, the proprietor of the hotel, had ridden with Lewis to bring the missionaries to safety. When he heard of the plight of the Belgian engineers and their families, he would surely accompany her with spare ponies. Her mind raced furiously. How many ponies would they need? How many people would be trapped in Ch'anghsintien?

The sedan chair rocked and swayed and finally halted outside the golden lantern-lit façade of the Hôtel de Pekin. Picking up her skirts, Olivia ran to the door, beating on it with her fists.

The clean-shaven gentleman who opened it displayed

remarkable aplomb at confronting an unescorted young woman, her cheeks flushed, her eyes bright.

'Monsieur Chamot, I must speak to you!' Olivia said urgently. 'The railway line at Fengtai has been attacked and the Belgian engineers and their families are trapped at Ch'anghsintien!'

Dr George Morrison's eyes sharpened. 'You had better come in, Miss ...'

'Harland,' Olivia said, stepping past him and into the spacious hall. 'Miss Olivia Harland.'

George Morrison's brows rose slightly. So this was the young lady that Lewis had escorted into the city. When Madame Chamot had asked for a description of her, Lewis had said merely that she was brave and intelligent, but there had been something in the tone of his voice that had attracted the journalist's attention. He had wondered then if Miss Harland had possessed other qualities. Now he wondered no longer. The beauty in her oval face was bone deep and there was sensitivity as well as purity in the delicate lines of her cheekbones and jaw. He was not surprised that she had made such a deep impression on his friend.

'The French Minister thinks it impossible to send out a rescue party for them. I thought that perhaps you would help me ...'

'Help you?' Dr Morrison asked queryingly.

'To ride to Ch'anghsintien with spare ponies,' Olivia said succinctly.

George Morrison regarded the determined tilt of her chin and reflected that Lewis Sinclair had not been wrong about her courage.

'Please, Monsieur Chamot. There is no time to be lost.'

George Morrison reached for his jacket. 'First of all, Miss Harland, I am not Monsieur Chamot. He is not here at present. Both he and his wife have already set off to Ch'anghsintien. We received the news a little over an hour ago. Allow me to introduce myself. I am Doctor George Ernest Morrison, Peking correspondent for *The Times*'

Olivia swayed slightly. Of course. She had seen him before at one of Sir Claude MacDonald's soirées but in her urgency she had not recognized him. In her disappointment, she leaned against the gold embossed papered wall for support. She had been too late with her news. They had heard already and a rescue party had been formed and despatched. Once again she could do nothing constructive but must remain passively in the Legation Quarter whilst others gave assistance.

'Are you all right, Miss Harland?' George Morrison asked, a small frown of worry puckering his brow. 'Perhaps you would like a glass of lemonade?'

Olivia shook her head, a tendril of dark hair springing loose and curling provocatively at the side of her face.

'No thank you, Doctor Morrison. It was just that I had hoped to be able to help. So many people are suffering and it seems that there is nothing that I can do. I had hoped that my coming here tonight would have helped the Belgians in Ch'angsintien. It had not occurred to me that you would already have had the news.'

'I am a journalist,' George Morrison said gently. 'It is my job to know what is happening.'

Olivia managed a small smile. 'Yes. And I am glad that you received the news so quickly. Will the Chamots be able to save the people who are trapped?'

'If they can reach them,' George Morrison replied, his frown returning. 'The countryside is in turmoil.'

Despite the airless heat, Olivia shivered. If Lewis had heard news of the Belgians trapped at Ch'angsintien he would have been one of the first to ride out to their aid. Had he ridden with the Chamots? She ran the tip of her tongue nervously along her lower lip, longing to ask and yet afraid that if she should mention his name, her voice would betray emotions that no one, least of all the perceptive Dr Morrison, must guess.

'How many people rode with Monsieur Chamot?' she asked, her heart beating fast and light.

'His wife, four Frenchmen, and a young Australian.'

She tried to speak but could not. He hadn't been with them. She still did not know where he was, or if he was safe. At last she managed to say, her voice trembling slightly, 'Madam Chamot must be an extremely courageous lady.'

'She is,' George Morrison replied, eyeing her curiously. Despite her attempts at composure, she was still deeply distressed and he had a shrewd idea that her concern was not entirely for the stranded Belgians. 'Madam Chamot is young and American, and as gallant as Doctor Sinclair assures me that you yourself are.'

He saw the sudden rush of colour to her cheeks and was just congratulating himself on having once again made a correct deduction when an upper bedroom door slammed and Lewis strode swiftly to the head of the stairs.

'I've taken your revolver, Morrison, as well as my rifle, and ...' He halted in mid-sentence, staring down at Olivia in stunned disbelief. The midnight-blue silk of her evening gown was cut low, revealing high, creamy breasts. Her hair shimmered, soft and dark and her eyes stared up at him, wide and incredulous. His hand tightened on the banister and he could hear his breath coming in harsh rasps.

'What the devil are you doing here?' he asked, shock and fear for her safety making his voice curt. 'The streets are unsafe. There could be an attack at any moment!'

The blood drummed in her ears. 'I was at the French Legation. The Minister received news of the attack at Fengtai and told us that some of the engineers and their families were trapped at Ch'anghsintien and I came to tell Monsieur Chamot. I thought that he would organize a rescue party and that I ...'

'He has done so already,' Lewis said, buckling his holster and running lightly down the remaining stairs.

'I wanted to ride with him,' Olivia finished, a dangerous spark in the depths of her blue eyes.

Dr Morrison folded his arms, leaned against the wall and watched with interest as Lewis sucked in his breath and said vehemently, 'Are you actively trying to get yourself killed? Have you any idea of the situation that now exists in the countryside?' He slung his rifle over his shoulder and headed for the door. 'Morrison, see to it that Miss Harland reaches home safely.'

'*No*!' The passion in her voice shocked even herself. It rooted Lewis and his companion to the spot. 'I will *not* be left behind! Madame Chamot has ridden to Ch'anghsintien with her husband and *I* am going to ride to Ch'anghsintien!'

His brow quirked upwards but there was no amusement in the depths of his night-black eyes. 'In that?' he asked, surveying the midnight blue silk in a way that flooded her body with heat.

'Yes.' Swiftly she crossed the Chinese tiled hall, standing between him and the open doorway. 'That is where you are going now, isn't it? You are going to try and catch up with the Chamots.'

His silence was her answer. She lifted her head high and this time there was no tremble of emotion in her voice, no trace of uncertainty. 'Then I either go with you, or I ride there alone.'

Something hot flickered at the back of his eyes and George Morrison wondered if it was merely admiration or more. Much more. The silence stretched out between them, so charged with emotion that George Morrison felt like an interloper. Then, swinging his rifle up on to his shoulder in a quick, decisive movement, Lewis said, 'The ponies are already saddled. There are no other clothes for you to change into. You will have to manage as best you can.'

Her smile was so sudden, so dazzling, that George Morrison caught his breath audibly.

'Of course,' she said, and without a second's hesitation bent down and lifted the hem of her gown, ripping wide the yards of shimmering silk. George Morrison had an amazing glimpse of remarkably narrow ankles and devastatingly well-shaped white-stockinged legs and then she was running out into the night in Lewis's wake. He saw Lewis help her up into the saddle, saw them both freeze momentarily at the brief physical contact, saw the two Chinese who were to accompany them pick up the leading reins of the spare ponies, and then Lewis raised his hand high in farewell, and they were gone.

The narrow grid of streets, usually so deserted apart from night-soil collectors, were now massed with refugees. Dull eyes stared at them as they galloped past. No one tried to apprehend them. Olivia felt exultant. The tearing of her skirt allowed her to ride astride in a manner that was amazingly comfortable and felt not at all strange after the first few minutes. The familiar dark shape of Lewis's body riding alongside her gave her a feeling of such completeness that she knew she would brave his wrath time and time again, if only she could have the joy of being with him.

They galloped headlong for the gate that led from the crowded Tartar City on to the outer Chinese City. As they passed beneath the dark silhouette of its upturned eaves, she called across to him, 'Will the Empress Dowager's troops stop us or help us?'

'Neither,' Lewis replied, urging on his horse as they gained the raised causeway of the Chinese City. 'She is still officially denouncing the Boxers, but is doing nothing to deter them. At the Diplomatique Corps' request, she sent a small contingent of troops to protect the missionaries west of the city. When we arrived there, the mission was under attack by Boxers and the troops had fled without firing a shot. When the Boxers reach the city gates, she will drop all pretence and the army will fight alongside the Boxers. Until then, it is my guess that she will not irrevocably commit herself. I doubt that we will find the army a hazard tonight.'

'But we will the Boxers?'

Her pony and his horse were racing neck and neck, the servants hard on their heels. In the darkness, his white teeth flashed in a sudden smile. The same smile that he had given her when they had been alone at the Hoggett-Smythes'.

'Yes,' he called back as they rode out of the main South Gate and into the dark countryside beyond, 'But I think they will have more to fear from us than we will have to fear from them!'

She laughed, her eyes bright, her heart so full that she thought it would burst. There could be no future for them together, but for now she needed no future. There was only the present and it was enough. She felt alive in a way she had never dreamed of before.

She closed her eyes, wishing with passionate ferocity that she could capture the fleeting moment forever. That it would never end. That never again would she have to return to the sedateness and stultifying boredom of life with her aunt and uncle. To a life without Lewis. Her fingers tightened on the reins. Her aunt had declared her intention of leaving China at the first opportunity and settling in Bath. A shaft of pain so intense it made her cry out seared through her heart. After China and its great open plains, she would not be able to breathe in the polite confines of Bath.

'Are you all right?' His smile had gone. His eyes were urgent, anxious.

'Yes,' she replied, thrusting away all thoughts of the future, racing with him, neck and neck, as they galloped over the parched earth. In the pale moonlight the long, weary trail of Chinese Christians could be seen making their pathetic way towards the city, their meagre possessions on their backs, their faces gaunt with fatigue.

They rode past them and then almost immediately struck out across country. Olivia felt a flash of fear and immediately suppressed it. She was a good horsewoman and the pony she was riding was strong and sure-footed. She had known of the dangers ahead of her when she had first determined to help the Belgians. Now she had to confront those dangers as bravely as the redoubtable Madame Chamot.

Lewis rode unerringly over country that to Olivia seemed

bereft of landmarks. In the far distance, where the black density of the hills rose to meet the night sky, she could see fires burning and could smell the faint but unmistakable acrid aroma of smoke.

'Villas,' Lewis called across to her briefly. She nodded, wondering if one of them was the Hoggett-Smythe villa. The ground underfoot became rocky and hard and soon they were scrambling down the side of a gulley. Lewis wheeled his horse around, at her side constantly at her pony slithered and pebbles tumbled. When at last the pony had safely negotiated the bank of the dried-out river-bed she raised her head to his and at the look of ferocious concern on his face, felt a thrill of pleasure so deep that it nearly robbed her of coherent thought. In that moment, if she had fallen, if he had taken her in his arms, she would have been his without reservation. No wife, no wedding vows, no sense of honour, would have restrained her. She trembled, overwhelmed by her shamelessness, by the depth of her need for him.

'There's a wood a little way ahead,' he said suddenly. 'We'll need to be careful.'

She nodded, not trusting herself to speak. Disturbed crows flapped noisily from the tress, cawing raucously. They had to slow their mounts to a canter and then to a walk. They were riding abreast, so near that she had only to reach out her hand to be able to touch him. Beneath the white linen of his shirt she could see the muscles of his back flex and tense as he pushed first one low-hanging branch aside and then another. Even in the darkness she could see where the blue-black hair curled low in the nape of his neck. She wanted to say his name, with love, just once. Behind them the Chinese servants followed stoically, the riderless ponies on leading reins in their wake. There would be no opportunity once they reached Ch'anghsintien and after ... After, they would no longer be alone.

The woods were at an end. He turned in his saddle, white teeth flashing in a smile that made her reckless. She leaned towards him, the love she felt for him flooding through her so that she could hardly bear it.

'Lewis …' she said, and his name sounded as if it had been torn from her heart.

He reined in sharply, every muscle and sinew of his body taut. She couldn't see the expression is his eyes. The moon had scudded behind a bank of cloud and she could only see his broad-shouldered silhouette. The hair tumbling low over his forehead. The whitening of his knuckles on the reins.

'Lewis, I …' She never did know what she had been going to say. The blood had thundered in her ears, her heart had drummed so painfully against her chest that she could hardly breathe and then had come the shouts and Lewis had immediately slapped her pony's rump and dug his heels in the flanks of his horse.

'*Boxers!*' he had shouted tersely as they broke free of the last of the trees, the servants crying out in terrified alarm behind them.

In one swift glance over her shoulder Olivia saw horsemen bearing down on them, flaming brands carried high. The frenzied shouts she had heard when her aunt and uncle had been trapped inside their burning villa once more filled the air, but this time she knew their meaning. '*Sha! Sha! Kill! Kill!*'

She sucked in her breath and spurred on her pony. '*Faster!*' she urged, bending low over its mane. '*Faster!*' She had not known it was possible to ride at such speed and in darkness. At any moment she expected her mount to stumble and fall, but its hooves pounded over the dried earth as sure-footed as if it had been enjoying an afternoon gallop on the English Downs.

'They've no gunshot!' Lewis shouted. 'When I rein in, keep on riding! Don't stop, no matter what you hear. *Don't stop!*'

There was no time to argue with him. To yell back that she had no intention of riding on while he attacked them singly and with his rifle.

In a flurry of dried earth he reined in, wheeling his horse around, slithering from its back as his servants rode on, the terrified ponies on the leading reins galloping in their wake, their haunches wet with sweat and fear.

The first shot had rung out before she could even begin to bring her pony under control. She slewed it round, sick with fear. Because no shots had been fired at them did not necessarily mean that the Boxers in pursuit were without arms. They had perhaps only been waiting until they had been nearer. Perhaps even now Lewis was lying dead or wounded.

There was another shot, and another. The flaming brands weaved in panic-stricken confusion. She saw the gleam of a massive sword wielded high, swirling round and round the head of its possessor, about to lunge down in deadly triumph.

The revolver, she thought desperately, as she scrambled from the saddle, running, stumbling in the darkness to where Lewis lay prone on the ground taking careful aim. Why had he not given her the revolver? The obscene sword hung high over his body. She saw him roll away, reposition the rifle and fire.

The noise was deafening. All around her nightmare figures shouted and surged. She was aware that Lewis was once more taking aim. She fell down beside him, half falling over his saddlepack, her fingers scrabbling for the revolver.

'*I told you to ride, goddamn it!*' she heard him shout, saw the vicious sword slicing down through the air towards her and then felt his body as it rolled on top of hers. For the next few seconds there was nothing in the world but noise. The firing of the rifle, the throbbing of hooves, the yells of the attacking Boxers. And then, terribly and unmistakably, the hot stickiness of blood as it soaked into her shoulder and trickled down her arm.

The ground reverberated beneath her and the noise receded. She wondered if it was because she was losing consciousness and then Lewis rolled free of her, grasping her shoulders, and she was dimly aware that the night was as silent and as still as it had been only minutes before.

'*Are you injured?*' In the moonlight his face looked as demented as the torchlit faces of the Boxers had done minutes before.

'I don't know. I'm bleeding, but it doesn't hurt.' Tentatively she raised her hand to her blood-soaked shoulder and then halted. The blood was not hers. It was Lewis's. She could see the gouged flesh of his upper arm, the linen of his shirt hanging loose, the blood flowing freely.

'It isn't me,' she said chokingly, 'it's you.'

He glanced down at his arm and winced. 'Can you tear off my sleeve and bind it?'

'It won't be enough.' The blood was running freely. Even in the darkness the wound looked ugly, wide and deep. 'Can you take off the rest of your shirt?'

'Not without help,' he said, and though she could not be sure she thought that the corner of his mouth had crooked into a smile.

The blood was running down his arm and she wondered how much he had lost already. How much it would take before he started to feel faint.

'Let me,' she said urgently, tearing off the mutilated sleeve, undoing his shirt and gently freeing his good arm and shoulder from the encasing linen. She had no experience of nursing but common sense told her that a pad was needed to staunch the flow of blood and she made one speedily, binding his arm deftly and surely.

At last she leaned back on her heels. Her hair was no longer pulled securely back away from her face. Short tendrils had escaped and clung damply to her cheeks and temples as she regarded him anxiously. 'Will that bandage be enough?'

'I couldn't have made a better one myself.'

She felt her cheeks flush. Incredibly she had forgotten that he was a doctor. 'Will you be able to ride?' she asked, sure that the flippancy in his voice was a mere disguise for pain.

'I will if we can find a horse,' he said wryly.

She rose to her feet, looking around in fresh anxiety. There was no sign of the horse and pony or the servants. The revolver that had been in her lap fell to the ground.

Lewis picked it up and stood beside her, only the barest intake of breath betraying the effort the movement cost him.

'And just what,' he asked, arching an eyebrow queryingly, 'were you going to do with this?'

'Shoot,' she replied, her eyes holding his steadily.

'Then next time,' he said, an odd expression in his voice, 'please see to it that you remove the safety catch first.'

There came the faint sound of hoofbeats and both of them froze and then Lewis let out his breath with a sigh of relief. 'The servants,' he said, 'and the ponies.'

The moonlight gleamed on the strong muscles of his chest. For the first time she became acutely conscious of his near nakedness. Of the pelt of thickly curling dark hair that his shirt had previously concealed; of his lean waist and the snug fit of his breeches around his narrow hips. She turned away from him quickly, trying to think only of the ponies. Of the fact that, temporarily at least, they were safe.

'We thought you were dead, *Tai Pan*,' the servants were saying to Lewis, prostrating themselves in their relief at finding him alive and themselves not deserted.

'I'm alive, but some Boxers are dead,' Lewis said dryly.

'No!' they both declared emphatically, 'No Boxers dead. Boxers cannot be killed, *Tai Pan*.'

'Those have been,' Lewis said, nodding his head in the direction of the inert bodies.

Olivia shuddered and looked away, but the Chinese stared and then shook their heads.

'Those not *real* Boxers, *Tai Pan*. Real Boxers not die. Those bandits, not Boxers.'

Lewis shook his head in despair at their gullibility and mounted his horse with a wince of pain.

'Will it take us long to get back to the city?' Olivia asked, already seeing an ominous dark stain seeping through the makeshift bandage.

'We're not going back to the city,' Lewis said with a swift kick of heel to flank. 'We're going to Ch'anghsintien.'

Olivia opened her mouth to protest but it was too late. He was already cantering away from her, his bandaged arm hanging limply at his side. She stared after him in dismay and then goaded her own pony into movement. His arm urgently needed expert medical attention but she knew that no amount of arguing would deflect him from his purpose. He had set out for Ch'anghsintien and he intended to reach Ch'anghsintien. The slight inconvenience of a sword-slashed arm would not, in Lewis's eyes, be any reason for turning back.

As she approached him he looked across at her and suppressed a grin. Her lips were pursed and the disapproval on her face would have done credit to Lady Glencarty.

They rode on in silence, saying nothing as the flames from far-off fires lit the sky with a lurid glow. Occasionally they could hear the distant clamour of fighting but no Boxers rode down on them. Olivia wondered if the sound of fighting was coming from Ch'anghsintien and her fingers tightened on the reins. Perhaps it was the Chamots' party that was being attacked. Perhaps even now they were riding into an ambush.

She glanced covertly across at Lewis, drawing strength from the sight of his hard-boned face and strong, assertive jawline. There was no glimmer of a smile around his mouth now. As the cries and shouts floated down to them from the surrounding hills, his face had become once again grim and forbidding. She felt a surge of despair. Even if they managed to save the Belgians, other Europeans were dying. Dying because no one in Peking was prepared to ride from the safety of its walls and offer assistance. By the light of the ever nearing flames she could see the dark silhouette of buildings.

'Ch'anghsintien,' Lewis said briefly.

Olivia felt her spirits soar. 'It isn't burning!'

'No,' Lewis agreed, his eyes flicking over the surrounding countryside, 'not yet.'

Olivia's heart began to beat fast and light as she saw lanterns and heard the sound of European voices raised in urgency. Within minutes they had ridden into the centre of the small outpost. Men, women and children were crowded into a small square, their faces anxious, their possessions scattered around them. At the centre, a tall, assertive Frenchman was trying to create order out of chaos.

'*Vous ne pouvez pas faire cela,*' he shouted, waving his arms emphatically as a woman tried to load a pony with a cot and a collection of cooking utensils.

At the sound of the approaching hoofbeats there were screams and the Frenchman seized his revolver and then his face split into a wide grin and he stretched his arms wide.

'Welcome, *mon brave!* You have ponies? We need them. There are over twenty men and nine women and nearly as many children needing transport.' His eyes widened as Olivia cantered up and reined in at Lewis's side. '*Mon dieu!*' he cried, leaping down from the crate that had served as his rostrum. 'Introduce me at once, my friend.'

Lewis grinned. The Boxers could be within hailing distance but Auguste Chamot was a Frenchman to his fingertips and a pretty woman would always have first claim on his attention.

'Auguste, Miss Olivia Harland. Olivia, allow me to introduce you to Monsieur Auguste Chamot of the Hôtel de Pekin.'

Olivia inclined her head and allowed her hand to be taken and kissed as if she were meeting the ebullient Monsieur Chamot at an elegant soirée in the Legation Quarter and not in the middle of an abandoned huddle of houses about, at any moment, to be attacked by Boxers.

'We have seven ponies,' Lewis said as Auguste reluctantly returned his attention to him. 'There are fires only one or two miles away. We ourselves were attacked by a small party and I doubt if we have more than minutes in which to save our own lives and those of the Belgians.'

Auguste Chamot nodded. 'There are carts for the children. Help me to persuade those women that they cannot take all their wordly goods with them.'

Lewis swung himself down from his horse and within seconds the two men were bundling the frightened children in the horse-drawn carts, while Olivia helped Madame Chamot to calm the half-hysterical women.

Madame Chamot did not waste time on introducing herself. She cast a swift look at Lewis's bandaged arm and asked briefly, 'He is hurt?'

Olivia nodded.

'Badly?'

'I think so,' Olivia replied as she hustled a middle-aged woman into a cart with the children. 'It was too dark to see clearly.'

Madame Chamot despatched a party of seven women behind the leadership of the young Australian who had ridden out with them.

'He should not have come,' she said tersely as the cries of '*Sha! Sha!*' grew louder and nearer. 'He has not slept for forty-eight hours.'

The men were mounted and under Auguste Chamot's orders were galloping down the street of beaten earth behind their wives and children. 'He will kill himself and it will still not help his pain.'

They were both running back to their ponies.

'His pain?' Olivia asked breathlessly as Madame Chamot swung herself expertly into her saddle.

'His wife,' Madame Chamot called over her shoulder as Lewis shouted at them to hurry. 'He misses her so much that it is destroying him.'

A burning brand was thrown on to a nearby rooftop and immediately gushed into flame. There was no time for further speech. There was only the urgent, desperate necessity of gaining open country before the Boxers should surround them and trap them within the burning buildings.

Olivia dug her heels into the sweating flanks of her pony, galloping out of Ch'anghsintien only yards behind Madame Chamot. She could see Lewis wheeling his horse around to protect their rear as the Boxers surged into the deserted streets. His face was white and taut with pain. She could see the blood oozing through the bandaging of his shirt.

'Dear God, don't let him die!' she prayed aloud as she galloped free of the last of the buildings. 'Don't let him faint! Don't let him fall!'

He was galloping abreast of her. She could smell the sweat and heat of his horse; see its mane flying; its neck outstretched, glistening with sweat.

The noise of hoofbeats and the rattle of the carts filled the air. Her gown had slipped from her shoulder and her hair had fallen from its pins but she was uncaring. She could not fall behind. Could not fail him. Fresh flames shot skywards behind them. One rifle shot and then another whipped past them in the darkness, and both Auguste Chamot and Lewis wheeled their horses round, firing back.

'*No, please no!*' she cried aloud, trying to rein in and failing. He had only one arm. He could not ride and handle a revolver at the same time. It was crazy. Suicidal. To fire his revolver meant that he had reined his horse to a standstill; that he was being left further and further behind them.

She turned her head, the desperate tears wet on her cheeks and then sobbed with relief. He was only yards behind her, his white teeth flashing reassuringly.

'They've dropped back,' he shouted. 'This time they're going to satisfy themselves with burning and looting.'

As he spoke there came a great whoosh of flame and building after building caved inwards. Olivia looked away. Ch'anghsintien was being destroyed, but its European inhabitants were safe.

Dawn was breaking as their exhausted mounts trotted wearily through the great South Gate. They were greeted with wide-eyed disbelief and Madame Chamot looked across at Olivia and laughed. 'I think it would be best if you came with me to the hotel before you are seen by your fellow countrymen. You do not look at all as a respectable young lady should.'

With sudden realization, Olivia looked down at herself. The midnight-blue silk gown was scarcely recognizable. Her white-stockinged legs and ankles were showing indecently. Her bosom, its exposure acceptable at the dinner table, was attracting blatant and appreciative stares from the crowds who had heard of their arrival and had come running to see if the story of the Belgian rescue was true. The gardenia that had pinned back her hair had long since fallen free and she was aware that she must look more like a gypsy than the well-brought-up niece of Sir William and Lady Harland.

'That arm needs seeing to immediately, *mon brave*,' Auguste Chamot was saying to a bone-weary Lewis.

Olivia turned to Madame Chamot. 'If I could borrow a dress, I would be grateful.'

'I have a golf skirt and shirtwaist that you might find suitable wear over the next few days,' Madame Chamot said practically. 'The sooner a doctor looks at Lewis's arm, the better.'

Olivia agreed fervently. In the pale light of early morning his fatigue could be clearly seen. The bones of his face seemed to have sharpened, the lines running from nose to mouth, white and deeply etched. He looked like a man on the edge of collapse and even as Olivia watched, he swayed in his saddle. Auguste Chamot tried to urge him towards the hotel but he would not do so until the last of the Belgians had left under safe escort for the safety of their legation.

'Will you have a storm to face when you return home?' Madame Chamot asked her as they wearily entered the hotel.

Olivia thought of the fury she would be met with and

nodded. Madame Chamot smiled. 'If the storm is very bad, remember that we could not have managed without the extra ponies that you and Lewis brought to us. And Lewis would not be alive now if it were not for your expert bandaging.'

Dr Poole from the British Legation was already assisting Lewis up the curved ornate staircase. Olivia watched him, her eyes dull. It was over. Once again they were no longer together.

'Could I send a message to my uncle?' she asked as Madame Chamot ordered baths to be run and clean clothes laid out.

Madame Chamot nodded, and when the bearer came, Olivia handed him a note saying merely that she had returned from Ch'anghsintien and was at present at the Hôtel de Pekin, but would be returning home during the course of the morning.

Once the note was despatched, she accepted the tea that had been prepared for her and then allowed herself to be led upstairs to a comfortable bedroom and a steaming hot bath.

Her muscles ached but she was too aware of Lewis only rooms away to be able to linger in the scented heat of the water.

When she had dried herself and dressed in Madame Chamot's exquisitely cut golf skirt and shirtwaist, she hesitated outside the door behind which she could hear Dr Poole talking to Auguste Chamot.

She jumped guiltily when the door opened suddenly and she found herself face to face with her fellow countryman.

'So this is the gallant Miss Harland?' Dr Poole said, beaming. 'Delighted to meet you, my dear. Your uncle will be proud of you. Monsieur Chamot tells me that you helped to save not only the lives of the Belgians trapped at Ch'anghsintien, but also the life of my colleague, Doctor Sinclair.'

Olivia tried to look into the room over Dr Poole's shoulder and failed.

'Monsieur Chamot is very kind, but I did very little.'

'You were magnificent, my dear. Magnificent,' Dr Poole said admiringly.

'Is it possible ... Could I speak to Doctor Sinclair?' she asked, wishing that Dr Poole would move. That she could see into the room.

'Doctor Sinclair is asleep,' Dr Poole said kindly.

Foolishly she wanted to cry. 'And his arm?' she asked anxiously. 'Will it heal?'

'If he gives it the chance. The tendons were not sliced through. What he needs now is rest.'

Genially he bade her goodbye and Monsieur Chamot escorted him along the corridors and down the stairs.

Olivia remained at the open door of the room. He was lying in the centre of a vast, brass-headed bed, his eyes closed, his hair tousled, his breathing deep and rhythmic.

Tentatively she crossed the thickly carpeted room and gazed down at him. His chest was still naked, but the remnants of his shirt were no longer around his injured arm. Instead, a fresh and expertly applied dressing held the wound together.

She had bathed and changed. She no longer had any excuse for remaining at the hotel. Again, as before, she would have to leave him. Hardly daring to breathe, she leaned over him, lowering her head, her lips lightly touching his brow.

At the touch he turned in his sleep, murmuring a word that could not catch, and then it came again, clear and full of love.

'Pearl Moon ... Pearl Moon ...'

The tears spilled down her cheeks. She loved him but he did not love her. He had never told her that he did so and he had never led her to believe that he did so. She wondered if the pain that she felt would ever ease or if it would remain with her forever. Despairingly she turned away from him and ran from the room, along the landing and down the curving flight of stairs, her heart so heavy that she thought it would break.

Eight

'Phillippe informed us of what you had done,' her uncle
said, clasping and unclasping his hands behind his back as
his anger at her behaviour was overcome by relief at her
safety. 'It was utterly irresponsible. Totally reckless. It has
prostrated your aunt. Doctor Poole has had to attend her.'
He paced the floor of his study, his distress obvious. 'In all
the years that you have been in our care, Olivia, you have
never once displayed the slightest disobedience ... And now
this! To ride off at night with a man who has already shown
you the grossest disrespect ...' William Harland removed a
silk handkerchief from his pocket and mopped his brow.
'The entire Legation Quarter will know of it before the
morning is out. The gossip will devastate your aunt. It will
be more than she will be able to bear.'

Olivia's heart went out to him, but she could not
apologize for her actions, only for the distress that they had
caused.

'I'm sorry that I have hurt and disappointed you and
Aunt Letitia,' she said with such depth of feeling that her
uncle halted in his pacing. 'But I *had* to do something to
help. I knew that there would be no official rescue party.'
Her eyes were urgent. '*Why* are no official rescue parties
being organized, Uncle William? There are others beside
the Belgians who need help. Is nothing to be done for
them?'

William Harland forgot that he was in the middle of
castigating her and took hold of her hands.

'Dear child, there is nothing anyone *can* do. The Boxers are now in complete control of the countryside. Troops have been sent for and we must simply await their arrival.'

The expression in her eyes told him exactly what she thought of such passivity and in his heart of hearts, William Harland agreed with her.

Horrific stories were circulating in the city of the atrocities perpetrated by the Boxers whenever Europeans fell into their hands. Atrocities which would have been perpetrated against his own family if Lewis Sinclair had not saved them. Lewis Sinclair who had refused to wait for the promised troops and had ridden out twice from the city and brought others to safety. If he himself had been younger, he would, like his niece, have most certainly insisted on riding with him. The knowledge dispelled the last of his anger.

'What you did was foolish, Olivia, but brave. I am proud of you, dear child. Very proud.' He blew his nose vigorously. 'And now you must go upstairs and make your peace with your aunt. The last twelve hours have been a great strain on her nerves.'

He waited until she had left the room and then sighed deeply. Letitia's constitution was not suited to stress. She needed constant comfort and reassurance and in the present situation there was none that he could give. The Boxers would attack, of that he was sure. And the small number of troops that had been sent for would not be enough to deter them. He sighed again and though he could not forgive Sinclair for the scandalously intimate way he had taken his leave of Olivia, only days ago, he wished heartily that there were more men like him in the city. They would be needed. Every last one of them.

Olivia was greeted by her aunt with open arms and copious tears. 'Olivia! I thought I would never see you again! Are you safe? Are you hurt?' and then, before Olivia could reply, 'How could you *do* such a thing to me, Olivia? To ride out alone with *that man*! When I think of what people will say. Never, *never* will I be able to attend a public function again. The shame of it has almost killed me! Doctor Poole has said that my nerves are so delicate they astound even him. Your poor uncle did not know how to explain your behaviour to Phillippe. He will abandon you, Olivia. You cannot expect a man and especially a *Frenchman*, to countenance you riding out at night with a man of Doctor Sinclair's reputation! A man who is married to a *Chinese*! Oh dear, I feel quite faint again. Your uncle says that Lady MacDonald has invited us to stay at the Legation. All British residents in the city are removing themselves there, but how can we go now? How can I possibly face people after what has happened?' She began to cry again and Olivia slipped her arm around her shoulders.

'It is not half as bad as you think, Aunt Letitia,' she said comfortingly. 'The talk in the city is of the coming troops and whether or not the Boxers will attack. No one is interested in whether I rode out with Doctor Sinclair or not. They have far more important things to worry about.

Letitia Harland shook her head vehemently, refusing to believe it. 'I'm sure I can hear Lady MacDonald's voice now! She must be downstairs talking to your uncle. She will be asking that we do not embarrass her by accepting her invitation. Oh, I can't bear it! I wish we had never come to this horrid country. I wish that we were in Bath and that none of this was happening.'

The bedroom door opened and her husband stepped into the room. 'That was Lady MacDonald,' he said, crossing to the bed and taking her hand as she wailed in anguish. 'She wishes me to inform Olivia that Sir Claude is very proud of the part she took in saving the lives of the Belgian engineers and their families.'

Letitia Harland's wailing ceased. She looked at her husband as if she could not believe what he was saying.

'The Belgian Minister has also called to express his gratitude and has asked that, when Olivia has rested, he be allowed to thank her personally.'

'Oh!' Letitia Harland's hand fluttered to her hair and her husband knew that she was already thinking of her wardrobe.

'Lady Glencarty, Madame Pichon and Mrs Conger have also called and expressed their admiration for Olivia's part in the Belgians' rescue.'

Letitia Harland wiped the last of her tears away with a lace-trimmed handkerchief and leaned back against her pillows. 'Then everything is all right!' she said with relief. 'Phillippe will not be angry any more. Olivia will not be thought fast and we shall be able to accept Lady MacDonald's invitation and move into the Legation until the troops arrive and the Boxers are chased back to wherever they came from.'

Sir William gazed down at her in fond exasperation. It would be cruel to disillusion her and tell her that the troops would barely be sufficient to protect the Legation Quarter. He merely patted her hand and said, 'Olivia has not rested since she returned to the city. She needs sleep, Letitia.'

For the first time Letitia noticed the paleness of Olivia's complexion and the blue shadows beneath her eyes. 'Rosewater,' she said, thinking ahead to the Belgian Minister's visit. 'You must put pads soaked in rosewater on your eyelids when you sleep, Olivia.'

'Yes, Aunt Letitia,' Olivia said, knowing that she was far too tried to do any such thing. She kissed her aunt on the cheek and as she turned wearily to make her way to her own room, she heard her aunt say musingly, 'Do you not think it odd, William, that Doctor Sinclair's wife is not with him in Peking?'

'No,' her husband replied with an abruptness that was unusual in him. 'Sinclair had no intention of remaining in the city. He was riding north when he came to our aid. If it were not for us, no doubt he would be with his wife at this very moment.'

'Oh dear,' Letitia Harland said helplessly. 'No wonder he looks so fierce at times. He must be most dreadfully worried about her.'

Olivia closed the door with an unsteady hand, her heart shrinking and tightening in the depths of her chest. Lewis Sinclair *was* most dreadfully worried about his wife. His concern for her was the reason for the deep frown that so often pulled his brows together when he thought himself unobserved.

She remembered the first time that she had seen him clearly. When she had looked across at him after recovering from her foolish faint, her head on his jacket, the evening sky stained crimson as the villa burned. She had been awed by his fearlessness and then he had turned his head and his gaze had inadvertently met hers and she had been shocked at the expression she had surprised in their dark depths.

There had been no exhilaration that the danger was over. No relief that the Boxers had fled. Instead there had been only pain. Inner pain, shattering in its intensity. It had confused and shaken her and she had told herself that she had been mistaken, but now she knew quite well for whom he had felt such anguish. It had been for Pearl Moon. In that moment, as her aunt and uncle and Lady Glencarty had stood helplessly by in the gathering dusk, he had known that his own brand of honour demanded that he escort them back to Peking and delay his return to his wife. And circumstances had dictated that his return be delayed indefinitely.

A shudder ran through her and she hugged her arms, stifling it with difficulty. How he must have resented them. Yet, apart, from the curtness that her aunt found so disconcerting, he had given no sign of it. And there had been the other times. The times when he had looked across at her and smiled and her spine had tingled. The time in the garden, when he had kised her.

On the ride to Ch'anghsintien she had known that she loved him and had dared to hope that her love was returned. She knew now that she had mistaken the comradeship of danger for something more. Something she could never have. It was his wife's name he had uttered in his sleep. His wife that he yearned for. His wife, who held his heart.

Wearily she lay down on the bed. She would not see him again. There was a limit to the hurt that her heart could bear and if she were to see him again, she might very well find that the limit had been exceeded. She pressed a hand to her aching temples. Perhaps her aunt was right after all. Bath would be a much simpler place to live than Peking. Simple, and safe – and unutterably dull.

That evening, for her meeting with the Belgian Minister, she dressed in a gown of pale lemon silk and the pride in her aunt's eyes told her that she had been forgiven for her reckless behaviour. The Minister was charming; the interview was pleasant; and her aunt was radiant at the honour she felt was being shown to them.

As the evening came to a close and the Belgian Minister courteously took his leave of them, she whispered to Olivia, 'Phillippe has sent a bearer to say that he will be calling in the morning.'

'Phillippe?' She had not spared Phillippe one single thought since she had left him at Monsieur Pichon's dinner table.

'Yes.' Letitia Harland's eyes glowed as she thought how happy the two young people would be to be reunited. 'No doubt your uncle told him how very fatigued you were after your ... your *expedition*.' Despite the fact that she was assured the European community viewed Olivia's escapade as admirable and not scandalous, she was still unable to mention it without a shiver of alarm. 'I am sure that he would have been to see you hours ago if your uncle had allowed him to.'

Olivia was aware that once again she was going to cause her aunt distress. 'I'm sorry, Aunt Letitia,' she said as the maid closed the door behind the Minister and his sedan bearers carried him home through the straight, dark streets, 'But I have no desire to see Phillippe again.'

'Not see Phillippe?' her aunt asked, wondering if she was hearing properly. 'But my dear child, you *must* see Phillippe! He is your fiancé.'

Incredibly Olivia realized that, in the eyes of the world, her aunt was correct.

'So *that* is why you have been looking so pale and drawn?' her aunt said, believing that she at last understood what it was that was so patently disturbing her niece. 'You believe that Phillippe will not understand about your ... your *journey* to Ch'anghsintien?' Her plump arm hugged Olivia's waist comfortingly. 'Of *course* he will understand, my dear. Why, he will be as proud of you as your uncle is!'

Olivia doubted that very much. And whether he was or not, it made very little difference to her. She was most certainly not going to marry him.

With something like disbelief she saw that she was still wearing his ring. Had been wearing it ever since she had slipped it back on her finger for the dinner party at the French Legation. As her aunt gasped in horror she removed it and held it lightly in the palm of her hand. When Phillippe called in the morning she would see him. But only to return his ring and officially break off an engagement that she knew she should never have entered.

When Phillippe entered the Harland residence the next day, it was with much more thoughtfulness than he usually displayed. He had discovered to his amazement that his fiancée was being hailed as a heroine.

'She is *très gallante*, your fiancée,' the Dutch Minister had said to him in undisguised admiration the morning that the Belgians had entered the city safely.

He had accepted the compliment with tight-lipped hauteur, determined that at the earliest opportunity Miss Olivia Harland would be his fiancée no longer. And then other callers at the French Legation had sought him out.

'Very plucky,' had been his counterpart's opinion at the British Legation.

'A remarkably brave young lady,' Mr Conger had said to him. 'You must be very proud of her.'

Phillippe, who had never before been addressed personally by the head of the American Legation, concurred that he was.

The compliments did not stop there. M. de Giers, the Russian Minister, also deigned to speak to him in person. 'A magnificent act of derring-do,' he said with a stiff inclination of his head. 'I congratulate you on having such a courageous fiancée, Monsieur Casanaeve.'

Far from Olivia's behaviour wrecking his career, it seemed that she was adding it lustre. Despite the consternation at the Boxers' advance, he was inundated with dinner invitations. Everyone, Sir Claude MacDonald, the Belgians, the Germans, even the Russians, wanted to meet Olivia. All in all, it was a very satisfactory state of affairs and he was astute enough to know that all good will towards him would be instantly lost if it were discovered that he was no longer her fiancé.

He tweaked an imaginary speck of dust from the perfection of his dove-grey suit and adjusted his silk tie, reflecting that the new, high-waxed shirt collars suited him admirably. No, he could not terminate his engagement at the present moment, but terminate it eventually he most certainly would. Miss Olivia Harland was far too wilful to make a suitable wife.

He had believed her to be charmingly shy, demurely biddable. Never had he believed her capable of speaking and behaving as she had at Monsieur Pichon's dinner table. And the way that she had looked at him. Him. Phillippe Casanaeve! The eyes that had once gazed at him so adoringly had flashed with defiance and something else. Had it been contempt? Scorn? No. That was impossible. She had simply been histrionic. Determined to be the centre of attention at all costs. Well, she had succeeded. And she had succeeded in wrecking forever her hope of becoming Madame Phillippe Casanaeve.

He wondered if she would be aware of it yet. Lady Harland was greeting him with undisguised nervousness and the thin smile he was bestowing on her tightened with satisfaction. She, at least, was well aware of the possible calamitous consequences of her niece's foolish escapade. No doubt Olivia was equally nervous and apprehensive. A moment's passing glory was little compensation for the loss of a husband as eligible as himself. Well, it would amuse him to forgive her. To enjoy her relief and gratitude. Later, when her name was no longer on everyone's lips, he would take great pleasure in exacting his revenge for the humiliation he had suffered at his Minister's dining-table.

'Oh, Olivia, there you are, my dear,' her aunt was saying flusteredly as Olivia entered the room.

For a second his resolution wavered. She was wearing a blouse of white lace, boned high at the throat, the sleeves long and full and fastened tightly at the wrists by rows of pearl buttons. Her skirt was of deep lavender and instead of sweeping the ground, merely skimmed her neatly booted feet. Instead of being freezingly prim, the stark severity emphasized her softly rounded breasts and the curve of her hips and was stunningly and unknowingly sensual.

As he fought down his first, instinctive surge of desire, he noticed with annoyance that she was betraying neither nervousness nor apprehension. He crossed the room quickly towards her, taking her hand in his and pressing it warmly against his lips.

'Olivia! How could you behave so recklessly? I have been beside myself with worry!'

'Have you, Phillippe?'

He looked up sharply, believing for one incredible moment that there was mockery in the low, measured tones.

She was looking infuriatingly beyond him to her aunt. 'Would you excuse us for a few moments, Aunt Letitia? I would like to speak to Phillippe alone.'

Letitia Harland gasped in agitation. She *could* not leave

them alone. If she did so, then Olivia would hand Phillippe back his ring and the engagement would be broken. There would be no splendid marriage service in the cathedral. No envy amongst her friends at the excellent match that Olivia had made.

'No ...' she began to say and then wavered. Never before had she realized how *firm* Olivia could look. Cornflower-blue eyes held hers steadily and instead of continuing with her refusal, Letitia found herself saying weakly, 'Very well, dear. But only for a *few* moments. Remember that you have had a very trying experience and are not ... are not quite *yourself* as yet.'

With this last despairing indication that nothing Olivia said was to be taken seriously, she unhappily left them together and went in search of a darkened room and sal volatile.

Phillippe waited expectantly for his fiancée's apology. Her coolness, when he was certain that she was inwardly trembling in fear of his disapprobation, both irritated and aroused him. Her behaviour had shown that she would not make a compliant wife, but he was becoming increasingly aware that she would be a damnably exciting mistress.

'I'm sorry, Phillippe,' she said at last, her voice low and with the faint trace of huskiness that he had always found so entrancing, 'But I cannot marry you.' She held out her hand and the emerald sparkled in her cupped palm. 'I hope you will understand and ...'

'*Pardon?*' he said incredulously, wondering if his command of English had temporarily deserted him and he had misunderstood what she was saying.

'I cannot marry you, Phillippe,' she repeated with sincerity but without regret.

He stared into the beautifully etched, pale oval of her face and felt suddenly cold. She was not pretending. She was not waiting for him to contradict her. For him to forgive her for her rash and reckless behaviour. He had been about to circle the enticing narrowness of her waist with his arm and press her close against him. To murmur that of course he forgave her. To take advantage of their being alone and slide his hand down over the erotically pristine lace and caress the small breasts that were rising and falling so tantalizingly. Thwarted desire choked him and then hard on its heels came anger. How dare she release *him* from their engagement! *Mon Dieu!* The news would spread like wildfire. There would be speculation. Perhaps even ridicule.

'*No!*' he said explosively, his nostrils pinched and white. 'I will not have my name on the lips of every gossip monger in Peking!'

'I'm sorry, Phillippe,' she repeated, and as she turned slightly the morning sun fell through the window full on her face. With something of a shock he saw that her eyes were bruised with grief and lack of sleep. For him? Was she releasing him because she knew of the embarrassment that she had caused him?

His breath caught in his throat and he stepped towards her, closing her fingers over the ring, inhaling the fragrance of her hair and skin. She froze instantly and he knew that her grief and lack of sleep was not for him. His pale eyes hardened.

Then for whom? The answer came instantly, almost robbing him of speech. *Sinclair!* It was Sinclair who had accompanied her from the Western Hills to Peking. Sinclair she had ridden to Ch'anghsintien with. His breath hissed between his teeth. He had still not exacted his revenge for the humiliating way Sinclair had struck him to the ground in the portals of the legation. And now he was to be the cause of further, public humiliation.

'*Sinclair!*' he spat, his face so contorted by rage and hate that it was scarcely recognizable. 'When did he take your virginity? On the way to Peking? In the fields around Ch'anghsintien? Is that how he took you? On the earth like a Chinese? Like his wife?'

Her hand caught him full across the cheek. 'How *dare* you

speak of him like that?' she gasped, her eyes feral as he stumbled under the force of her blow. 'You're not fit to wipe his shoes!'

He seized her so savagely that she cried out in pain. '*Harlot!*' he hissed, digging his fingers brutally into her shoulders. '*Whore!*' With a vicious thrust, he sent her sprawling on the floor.

She didn't give him the pleasure of knowing how much he had hurt her. Instead, she lay at his feet, regarding him with contempt. 'Why do you hate him so much? Is it because he is all the things that you are not? Brave and honourable and kind?'

Swiftly he knelt down and as she shrank away from him, he seized her wrist, holding her fast. His eyes were mere slits and the expression of elation in them terrified her more than all his previous fury. 'And dead!' he said with relish, scooping up the emerald ring that had fallen to the floor and thrusting it into his pocket. 'When the Boxers attack, Sinclair will be the first to fall!'

'You can't know that,' she said, and her voice was no longer steady but naked with fear.

He began to laugh, rising to his feet and smoothing an imaginary crease from the sleeve of his jacket. 'Oh, but I can, *chérie*. When the Boxers attack, no one will query from which direction the bullets are fired. And one will be fired at Sinclair, I give you my word.'

'You couldn't,' she said unbelievingly, scrambling to her feet, here face ashen. 'It would be murder!'

He paused at the door, smoothing his sleekly clipped moustaches with an elegantly manicured forefinger. 'If it is, *chérie*, only you and I will know.'

'Phillippe!' The door slammed in her face as she ran towards it. 'Phillippe, no!' Her fingers slid helplessly around the onyx knob and then she heard the outer door close. He had gone. It was too late.

She leaned against the door, pressing her face against the cool smoothness of the wood. He had not meant what he said. He couldn't have. It was too monstrous. He had simply been trying to frighten her. Distantly she could hear the singing birds as they twittered in their cages and the faint tinkle of windbells and then there was a nervous tap on the other side of the wood and her aunt called out anxiously, 'Olivia? Olivia, are you all right?'

'Yes, Aunt Letitia,' she lied, and with a deep, steadying breath, turned and opened the door.

The troops arrived that evening and as Monsieur Pichon had predicted were pathetically few in number. 'A detachment of United States marines on shore leave, and an assortment of officers and men to guard the Legation,' her uncle said, pacing his study in agitation. 'What are the authorities thinking of? We need a fighting force. An army!'

'The marines did march up Legation Street with fixed bayonets, dear,' his wife said, her mind not on the troops but on Phillippe Casanaeve. Perhaps all was not lost. He and Olivia had had a lovers' tiff, that was all. She would invite him to dinner and in a few days' time all would be well again.

'The streets were massed with hostile Chinese,' Sir William continued, ignoring his wife and speaking directly to Olivia. 'Perhaps now the ministers will realize how great our danger is. It is impossible to tell who is a friend or an enemy. I'm sure I recognized one of Mr Conger's servants among the crowd but one Chinese looks so like another that it was impossible to be certain.'

'I think we can be sure of our own servants,' Olivia said quietly from the depths of a high-winged leather chair, 'and I think that we should insist that they accompany us when we move into the British Legation.'

'But good heavens, Olivia, Lady MacDonald will have plenty of servants to see to our needs,' her aunt cried. 'And who will look after the house in our absence if they do not? I am sorry, my dear, but that is a very foolish idea. Very foolish indeed.'

Sir William shook his head. 'No, Letitia. Olivia is right. The servants are Christians and will be gravely at risk if an attack takes place.'

Letitia looked up at her husband's grim face and her lower lip trembled. She had thought that when the troops arrived there would be no more talk of an attack. How could Olivia remain so calm? She looked so petite and vulnerable as she sat curled up in William's chair, the lights from the chandelier dancing in the smoke-dark depths of her hair and emphasizing the soft, captivating tilt of her brows. It seemed impossible to Letitia that anyone so prettily feminine should have ridden hard through the night over rough country with only the intimidating Dr Sinclair for company.

As if reading her aunt's thoughts, Olivia raised her eyes to her uncle's. 'Has there been any news of Doctor Sinclair?' she asked, her clasped hands tightening in her lap.

William Harland frowned. He did not wish to speak of Lewis Sinclair. He found it devilish difficult disapproving of a man he in so many respects admired, but his flagrant kissing of Olivia had been unforgivable. In Sir William's eyes, it deserved a horse-whipping.

'I understand that the Chamots have had to keep him under lock and key in order that he comply with Doctor Poole's instructions and rest,' he said tersely.

'Lady MacDonald says that she has it on very good authority that Doctor Sinclair is proving to be a very bad-tempered patient,' Letitia said with an air of satisfaction at being able to contribute to the conversation. 'Monsieur Chamot has had to remove his boots and breeches in order to prevent him leaving his room.' She faltered as her husband subjected her to a quelling glance. 'I am only repeating what Lady MacDonald herself said, William.'

'Quite so,' Sir William said, 'and did she speak of our removal to the Legation.?'

'She has asked that we make arrangements quickly. Sir Claude has said that very soon everyone will be converging on the British Legation as it is situated in the safest position, well away from the Chien Men Gate, and is commodious enough to shelter a large number of people. Our rooms are to be at the rear, overlooking the grounds which I think will be very pleasant, don't you, Olivia?'

Olivia did not answer. Her thoughts were far away from the British Legation. They were centred on the Hôtel de Pekin and the unruly patient she longed with all her heart to nurse.

The next morning, one sleeve of his jacket hanging loose, his left arm in a sling, the patient in question rapped impatiently on the Harlands' door, demanding to speak to her.

She had been walking from one bedroom to another with a pile of clothes that were to be taken to the British Legation when she heard the unmistakable deep rich tone of his voice. She froze, her heart hammering so wildly that she thought it would choke her.

'No, I do not wish to see Lady Harland,' he was saying firmly to the houseboy who had opened the door. 'I wish to see Miss Harland,' and without any more preamble he stepped inside.

The landing on which she was standing looked down on to the central, marble tiled hall and she could see him clearly. His hair still curled glossily in the nape of his neck. Despite his injured arm, he still carried himself with cool assurance. But something about him had changed. The strong-boned face was no longer harsh in repose. The hard line of his mouth had softened and once again she was aware that once he must have laughed easily and often.

The blood pounded in her ears. He had come to see her as she had known that he would. She clutched the bundle of clothing tightly. She would not see him. Nothing could be gained by it. Nothing.

There was a rustle of taffeta and her aunt stepped into

view. 'Good morning, Doctor Sinclair, how nice to see you,' she said unconvincingly. 'Sir William is not here at the moment and ...'

'It was not Sir William that I wished to see,' Lewis said pleasantly.

'Oh!' Her aunt gazed round helplessly for aid and then, as none was forthcoming, said feebly, 'Perhaps you would like to come into the drawing-room, Doctor Sinclair?'

'I would like to see Olivia.'

'Oh dear! I do not think ... Sir William would not be pleased ...'

Olivia knew now what it was that was different about him. He was no longer unhappy. The dark inner pain had been eased. She closed her eyes, digging her nails deep into her palm. There could be only one reason for the new lightness of spirit that sat so easily on him. Pearl Moon must have made her own way to Peking. In the hours that he had been confined at the Hôtel, they must have been reunited.

He was frowning slightly. 'Perhaps if I explain my reasons for calling ...'

She couldn't bear to hear any more. Swiftly she turned and entered the nearest bedroom. The arrangements for their removal to the British Legation were nearly complete. Her aunt would soon have the constant companionship of Lady MacDonald. Knowing that if she paused even for a moment she would be unable to hold back the tears that stung her eyes, she dropped the clothes she was carrying and searched hastily on the dressing-table for a pen and paper. She would go to the Anglican Mission and work with Sister Angelique. She needed activity. Work so hard that it would push all other thoughts from her mind.

'I have gone to the Anglican Mission,' she wrote hastily. 'I shall join you later at the British Legation. Love, Olivia.'

From the bottom of a wardrobe she retrieved a capacious straw bag and hurriedly stuffed it with a change of clothing, then she paused, her heart beating light and fast.

There had been no sound of a door opening and closing. The wind bells were silent. Lewis was still in the house. She tiptoed back out on to the landing and then, as the hall remained deserted, hurried swiftly towards the back staircase. Five minutes later, panting for breath, her straw bag clutched beneath her arm, she was pushing her way through the crowds of the Tartar City.

Nine

'*Marry* Olivia?' Letitia Harland gasped incredulously. 'Whatever can you mean, Doctor Sinclair? You cannot possibly marry Olivia.'

Lewis looked down into her plump, agitated face and suppressed a flicker of impatience. He should have waited until Sir William had returned before declaring his intentions. It was only natural that Lady Harland had other, more grandiose plans for Olivia's future.

'I can, and I am going to,' he said with a certainty that terrified her.

She stumbled backwards, jarring a small table and sending a jade figureen toppling. The man was a monster. Did he think, because his wife was Chinese, that his wedding vows were not binding? She remembered the talk that had swept the Legations at the time of his marriage. The head-shaking and the condemnation. The prediction that no good would come of it. And now ... Now he wanted to put the past behind him and marry suitably. Marry Olivia. Letitia grasped the back of William's high-winged chair, determined that he would not do so. She had never been brave but now she was filled with primitive courage. It was her cub that was being threatened. Her fledgling.

'No!' she declared vehemently. 'Never!'

Lewis's brows shot upwards. He had not expected to meet with such violent opposition from so mild a source.

'I think,' he said gently, 'that it would be best if I spoke to Olivia, don't you?'

Letitia held on firmly to the chair. 'Olivia is not at home,' she said, crossing her fingers so that the lie should not stain her immortal soul. 'She is visiting with her fiancé.'

She heard him take in his breath sharply and was suffused with a sense of triumph. It was not really so terrible a lie. Phillippe *was* Olivia's fiancé. The little tiff of yesterday morning would soon be made up and she was sure that William would applaud her for her ingenuity.

'Then I shall wait,' he said, and this time there was a new edge to his voice. A steely determination that sent fresh flutters of apprehension down her spine.

'The wedding is to take place very soon, Doctor Sinclair. A proposal of marriage to my niece at such a time could only cause embarrassment.'

Disbelief flared in the dark depths of his eyes and the muscles along his jawline tensed and hardened.

'I don't believe you,' he said tightly.

'I spoke to Monsieur Casanaeve in this very room only yesterday morning,' Letitia said, glad that at least that much was true. 'There can be no prospect of you marrying my niece. None at all.'

'You will forgive me if I prefer to hear that statement from Olivia herself,' he said, his eyes holding hers so unrelentingly that she began to tremble.

'You forget yourself, Doctor Sinclair,' she retorted, holding on gallantly to the last remnants of her courage. 'There is one insuperable obstacle to you even *talking* to my niece on such a subject.'

'And that is?' His voice was cold and hard and his eyes had narrowed as if he knew very well what it was she was about to say.

Letitia wished vainly that William would come. That Dr Sinclair would apologize for his unforgivable behaviour and leave. He did not do so. Instead he waited, his eyes never leaving hers until she said at last, her voice quivering with outrage, 'Your *wife*, Doctor Sinclair!'

The silence that followed was the most dreadful that

Letitia had ever experienced. At the cold contempt in his eyes she shrank back against the chair, no longer brave but extremely frightened. A nerve had begun to tic at the corner of his jaw and his mouth was etched by thin, white lines.

'I am sorry you think so,' he said chillingly. 'It is not a view that I had expected to meet in this house. Good day, Lady Harland.'

He strode past her, not trusting himself to remain another minute in the room. Dear Lord. Would it never end? Was Pearl Moon not to be forgiven her nationality even in death? If he married Olivia, would she, too, have to endure ostracism because her predecessor had been Chinese? He slammed out into Legation Street, his fists clenched, his face ashen. It was a future he could never subject her to. She would be better off marrying Casanaeve.

'William? William, is that you?' Letitia Harland called, running from the drawing-room and into the hall as her husband returned from his meeting with Sir Claude. 'Oh, William!' She threw herself into his arms, the tears coursing down her cheeks. 'That dreadful man came while you were out! I do not think that he can be very well, William, for he said that he wanted to marry Olivia!'

'Marry Olivia? Young Casanaeve? Of course he does. I told you not to worry about the tiff they had,' Sir William said, disentangling himself gently from his wife's unexpected embrace.

'Not Phillippe,' Letitia said, clinging to his arm. 'Doctor Sinclair!'

Sir William stared down at her, a curious expression in his eyes. 'Did he, indeed?'

'Yes he did, William, and I told him that he could not do so. I told him that Olivia was to marry Monsieur Casanaeve and he looked most terribly angry and said that he didn't believe me!'

'But Olivia is no longer engaged to Monsieur Casanaeve,' Sir William said, a frown marring his brow.

'I know, but what else was I to say to deter him? He was so very, *very* determined. Do you think that he did not marry his wife in a Christian church, William? Perhaps he is allowed to take more than one wife.'

'Where is Olivia now?'

'Upstairs, packing clothes ready for our removal to the Legation. I was so frightened that she would hear him. Just imagine how offended she would have been.'

Sir William was silent. He did not think that Olivia would have been offended at all.

'Are you not proud of me, William? I told Doctor Sinclair that Olivia was not in the house, but with Monsieur Casanaeve! Why are you frowning so? It was only a little lie and cannot possibly cause harm.'

Sir William's face was grave. 'I think, my dear, that it might very well cause harm.'

Letitia stared at him uncomprehendingly. 'But how could it? Olivia cannot marry Doctor Sinclair. He already has a wife.'

Sir William passed his hand over his eyes and then said sombrely, 'Mrs Sinclair was murdered in a Boxer attack five months ago. Lewis Sinclair is a widower.'

Letitia was momentarily robbed of speech. At last she said with difficulty, 'But ... how dreadful. I did not know.'

'It is apparently a well-established fact. Sir Claude was most surprised that I was not aware of it.'

'Oh dear. And do you think that ... would Olivia have wanted ...' she faltered. The expression on her husband's face told her only too well what the answer to her unspoken question was. 'I only acted for the best, William. Truly I did.'

He patted her hand. 'I know my dear,' he said reassuringly. 'And now let us speak to Olivia.'

As he climbed the stairs he felt weary. Sir Claude's news had not been optimistic. There was now no doubt that the Empress Dowager was in league with the Boxers and that the Boxers had the support of Imperial troops. Railway and telegraphic communications had been disrupted and even the most optimistic believed that a Boxer attack on the city was inevitable. The situation was grave and he had worries enough without Letitia well-meaningly making things worse. He knocked on Olivia's door and then, when there was no reply, entered with a deep feeling of foreboding.

The note was placed prominently on the dressing-table. He crossed the room swiftly, his hand shaking slightly as he picked it up.

'What is the matter, William? Where is Olivia? Oh, what is happening?' his wife cried, pressing her hands against her chest, wondering how many more shocks she could sustain.

'Olivia has gone to the Mission to help the nuns,' her husband said briefly, tucking the note in a pocket of his waistcoat and striding past her and out of the room.

'But she cannot!' Letitia shrieked in anguish. 'We are not safe here! She must come with us to the British Legation!' She ran after him, along the landing and down the stairs. 'We must get her back, William.'

'I intend to,' he retorted, seizing his walking cane, cramming his homburg on his head, 'But it's useless my trying to cross the city to the Mission. The streets are in chaos.'

'Then where are you going?' she asked, clinging on to his arm, her face ashen.

'The Hôtel de Pekin. Lewis will know what to do. He'll get her back.'

Without any of his usual aplomb he hurried outside, calling impatiently for his sedan. Great heavens, what a mess it all was. He should have known that Olivia would not remain idly in the house once arrangements for the move to the Legation had been completed. He should have guessed her intentions. He mopped his brow in a fever of agitation. There would be no protection for the Mission when the Boxers attacked and he knew with dreadful certainty that they would attack soon. Very soon.

At the hotel Madame Chamot greeted him, her face pale, her eyes heavily shadowed. 'Lewis is not here,' she said, her voice taut with strain. 'He went out this morning, against Doctor Poole's orders. When he returned he was like a man possessed. He ordered that his horse be saddled and he has ridden out of the city, intent on another rescue mission.'

'But he is injured!' Sir William protested, aghast.

Madame Chamot shrugged wearily. 'I know, but he would listen to no-one. Not even my husband.'

Sir William leaned heavily on his cane. 'The countryside is alive with Boxers,' he said defeatedly. 'He will not return alive,' and with stooping shoulders he turned and made his way slowly back to his sedan.

In the west of the Tartar City the noise and clamour was deafening. Shopkeepers were boarding up their shops, hastily throwing their goods into handcarts. No one was walking. Even the Chinese women with their bound feet were scurrying through the streets in undisguised agitation. Olivia clutched her straw bag closer to her chest and tried not to be swamped by the panic stricken crowd around her. She was nearly at the Mission. Once there, surely she would be far too busy to think about Lewis? She dodged between a string of dirty camels and a shabby and overloaded donkey, a pain seizing her chest as if a dagger had been driven between her shoulder blades. Would she still hear of him at the Mission? Would she know where he was? What he was doing? If he was safe? Despite all her good intentions, the tears ran freely down her face.

'Oh Lewis,' she whispered, standing suddenly still amid the tumult around her. 'I love you so much!'

A small, wiry Chinese with a heavy pannier bumped into her and a Peking cart rattled past. She began to move again, wiping away her tears, knowing they were a luxury she dare not indulge in.

The sisters at the Mission greeted her with open arms. Every inch of space was taken up by the paliasses of refugees. Children cried, weary and hungry. The sick lay, hollow-eyed, exhausted by their long trek to what they hoped was safety.

'What is happening?' Sister Angelique asked her as they stepped over a pile of meagre possessions. A pot and a pan and a few precious bags of rice. 'We have heard nothing for two days now.'

'Some troops have arrived, but not enough.'

'How many?' The skin was tight over her bones, so translucent that Olivia could see the blue of her veins clearly.

'A little over three hundred.'

The small, bird-like figure at her side shook her head in consternation. 'You are right. It is not enough. Will there be more?'

'I don't know,' Olivia said truthfully. 'The Boxers are severing all our communications with the outside world. Telegraph lines have been cut down. Railway tracks torn up.'

'And now they are at the city gates,' Sister Angelique finished for her. 'Well, so be it. We must simply put our trust in God.' She led Olivia into a small, windowless room that had once been a pantry. 'I'm afraid that this is all I can offer you,' she said, indicating a small mattress. 'Lan Kuei sleeps next to you. She will be pleased to see you again.'

Olivia put her straw bag down. 'What would you like me to do first, Sister Angelique?'

'Help with the children. Most of them are sick and all of them are frightened.' She put a frail hand on Olivia's arm. 'And thank you for coming, dear child. We need all the help that we can get.'

In the days that followed, Olivia marvelled at the sisters' strength. They were nearly all elderly. All were tired. Yet they carried on stoically accepting everyone who came in search of shelter, rationing and re-rationing their small supply of food.

She was cutting up sheets and rolling them into bandages

when one of the Chinese converts brought news that the grandstand on the European racecourse had been burned to the ground.

'It cannot be long now before the Boxers flood through the gates,' Sister Angelique said, regarding the huddled refugees with troubled eyes. 'I had hoped that by now we would have been sent some protection. A handful of guards, however small.'

Olivia put another bandage to one side. 'If they have not come now, I doubt they will come at all,' she said quietly. 'The troops who arrived were detailed to guard the legations.'

'Then if they will not come to us, we must go to them,' Sister Angelique said calmly. 'The children must be escorted across the city before it is too late.'

'It may already be too late,' Lan Kuei said, joining them and speaking low so that she should not be overheard and create even more alarm. 'It is not only the grandstand that is burning. There are fires in the commercial quarter. All shops selling foreign goods have been pillaged and many people have been killed.'

Sister Angelique, who had worked till two in the morning, had slept late. 'I did not know,' she said, her softly wrinkled face grave. She turned to Olivia. 'There is no time to be lost, Olivia. The protection we have waited for has not come. We must try and take as many of the children as possible to the British legation.'

As she spoke a panic-stricken ripple ran round the crowded rooms and corridors and they could hear, quite distinctly, the roar of flames and the crash of rafters and masonry.

'We'll take them in groups of twenty,' Olivia said swiftly. 'Sister Agatha and Sister Louise are fit enough to help. Hurry, Lan Kuei, tell the sisters that they are needed and organize the children.'

Lan Kuei's skin had taken on a waxen tinge and her eyes were large and frightened. 'But if the Boxers are in the streets we shall all be killed!'

'We shall all be killed if we remain here,' Sister Angelique said succinctly. 'Hurry, child. Do as Olivia says.'

Olivia was already pressing through the crush, Sister Angelique at her side. 'The legations may already be barricaded,' she said as she hastily began to assemble a group of bewildered children around her.

'I pray not. If only they had sent soldiers to protect us! If only Doctor Sinclair was here.'

Olivia grasped the hands of two of the children. If Lewis had been there she would not have been afraid. Lewis would have seen that she and all the refugees were safe.

'Don't cry,' she said to the childen with outward calm. 'Keep close to me.'

Inwardly she felt as if a bucket of iced water had been poured down her spine. At any moment the legations would be under full-scale attack and Phillippe had boasted to her that when they were, Lewis would be the first to fall.

'He couldn't have meant it,' she whispered feverishly as she herded the children towards the door, but as she remembered the crazed exultation on Phillippe's face her fear increased. She had not warned Lewis. He had no idea that danger lay within the legation compound as well as without. If he died, she would be partly to blame.

'Lan Kuei will follow you,' Sister Angelique was saying, a small island of calm amid a crowd of consternation. 'When you reach the legation do not attempt to come back. There is nothing further that can be done here.'

'And you?' Olivia asked, suppressing the urge to grip the frail wrists and drag Sister Angelique bodily in her wake.

'I will stay,' Sister Angelique said. 'Goodbye, my child. God go with you.'

Olivia held her tightly and then turned, ushering her small charges out of the Mission and into the dust-filled street. Determination overcame fear. She had to reach the legation in safety because she had to get a message to Lewis. She had to tell him of Phillippe's threats.

The street was choked with fleeing Chinese. Peking carts thundered over the parched earth. Cries of fear merged with the ever-nearing orgiastic howls of '*Sha! Sha!*'

'Keep together!' she shouted over the din. 'And hurry! Don't stop for anything!'

The pig-tailed child gripping her hand screamed in terror as a huge tongue of fire surged skywards only yards away from them. 'Run!' Olivia shouted. '*Run!*'

She stayed in the rear, terrified that a child should fall and be left behind. Her heart was slamming violently against her breastbone as she urged them onwards, hardly able to keep upright as the panic-stricken Chinese swept past her. She could not see the Boxers but she could hear them and hear the screams of those who got in their way as they rampaged the nearby streets. A child fell and Olivia breathlessly hauled it to its feet, running, running as the roar of flames grew louder and rafters and masonry crashed into the heart of the burning buildings.

They fled down one street and then another, carried on by a tide of distraught peasants and furiously driven carts and charging animals. Smoke stung their eyes and dust choked them and then, just as Olivia glimpsed the main thoroughfare bisecting the city, and could almost see the walls and trees of the Legation Quarter, the terrified cries around her shrieked in intensity.

'Boxers! Boxers!' the children screamed and Olivia whipped round to see red-sashed, blood-crazed figures bearing down on them, slashing and stabbing indiscriminately.

'Run!' she cried again, her throat hoarse, '*Run!*', and then stood in their wake, standing full square in the path of the demented horde as if her slender body alone would halt their frenzied charge.

A sea of swords and spears sliced the air. They were so near that she could see the fanatical expression on their faces, the glazed madness in their eyes, and then, over and above the demented shouts of '*Burn! Burn! Kill! Kill!*' she heard the unmistakable clatter of galloping hooves and a posse of cavalry charged into the street. She saw the uniforms. The European faces. The black stallion, its nostrils dilated, its mouth foam-flecked, and flung herself out of their way.

'*Missy! Missy!*' the children shrieked, clutching her hands, her dress.

She pressed a hand against the knife-like pain in her side, struggling for breath. 'It's all right,' she gasped, 'Stay with me. Don't get lost.'

She didn't look back. Didn't wait to see what was happening. She could hear the clash of steel and a volley of rifle shots and as the smell of cordite hung heavy in the air she hurried the children feverishly towards Legation Street. They raced down it as if the devil were at their heels and then, as they swerved left, running breathlessly past the Mongol Market and towards the British Legation, galloping hooves bore down on them. It was only one horse. She had seen it and recognized it the instant the patrol had charged into the street. Now, knowing only too well whose dark, forbidding face she would look up into, she stumbled to a halt, leaning breathlessly against a smoke-grimed wall.

'I thought you were enjoying the safe protection of Monsieur Casanaeve!' he said savagely, wheeling his horse round, one arm still in a sling, the hand holding the reins clenched, the knuckles white.

She could see the rivulets of sweat running down his neck. The flecks of gold in the dark iris of his eyes. The spring of his hair as it tumbled low over the black bars of his brows.

Anger at the shamelessness of her need and desire for him flared through her. 'I don't know what you mean,' she snapped, her head high, her eyes flashing as they met his.

'Like hell you don't!' His voice sliced across her nerve ends like a whiplash. 'Why aren't you in the legation? The Japanese Chancellor has been murdered. The entire commercial quarter has been fired. Chinese Christians have been speared and burnt to death and you're strolling through the streets with a score of children as though it's Sunday in St James's Park!'

'I was *not* strolling!' she hissed, her eyes brilliant with rage. 'I was taking the children from the Anglican Mission where they will almost certainly be killed, and escorting them to the British Legation!'

The satanically winged brows flew together in a fierce frown. 'How many children are still there?' he rasped.

She shook her head, a stray tendril of hair clinging damply against her heat-flushed cheeks and temples. 'I don't know, hundreds.'

He swore blasphemously and she forgot the torment of seeing him in the overwhelming relief of knowing that here, at last, was help. She moved swiftly, crossing the distance between them, pressing herself against the hot flank of his horse as she looked up into his dark-visaged face, her eyes urgent. 'They have no protection, Lewis. No guards. Nothing. Lan Kuei and two sisters are escorting children as well. They need help.'

'And you?' His voice had lost its rasp of fury. It was smoke-dark. Throbbing with undertones that robbed her of breath and made her limbs shake.

'I can manage,' she said unsteadily, her voice barely audible as the horse moved restlessly and his booted leg brushed against her breast. 'The Legation is only yards away.'

'Cut past the Bell Tower,' he said brusquely, 'I'll see to it that the children are brought safely through the streets.'

Her throat was tight with desire and longing as she said hoarsely, 'Rory, is he safe?'

He nodded, his eyes so dark that she felt as though she were drowning in their bottomless depths. 'Sir Claude sent a small force out yesterday to bring him and other children from the Cathedral to the Legation.'

From the far side of Legation Street a great arc of flame spat skywards and there were shouts and terrified cries. In a swift, purposeful movement he leaned down, seizing her chin between his fingers, tilting her face so that it was only inches away from his. 'When you reach the legation, don't leave it,' he rasped, and then his head swooped low and his mouth was on hers, his kiss searing and savage, robbing her of every last vestige of self-control. She heard herself moan, knew that she was swaying in near insensibility and then he was looking down at her, breathing harshly, his eyes burning like live coals.

'I'll be back,' he said thickly, digging his heels into the stallion's flanks, wheeling round and away from her.

'Lewis, please!' She flung herself after him, catching hold of the reins, panting for breath. 'Listen to me! Just for a moment.'

She could see his muscles tense; see the whipcord hardness of his shoulders and chest as he looked down at her, his eyes dark with expectancy.

'Phillippe has threatened to kill you,' she gasped, her voice catching in her throat, ragged and torn.

She heard his swift intake of breath and then the heat in his eyes was crushed and he was regarding her with an expression that made her drop her hand falteringly from the reins. 'I'm glad that you reminded me of Monsieur Casanaeve,' he said at last and his voice was ice-cold. 'I was in danger of forgetting about him. Goodbye, Miss Harland.' And without a backward glance, he spurred his horse, galloping away from her and towards Legation Street to the west of the city and the Mission.

She stared after him in stunned disbelief and then pressed the back of her hand to her mouth, shaking uncontrollably.

'*Missy? Are you all right, Missy?*'

The children were staring at her with large eyes. Lewis's arrival had scattered them but now they edged towards her, frightened and uncomprehending.

'Yes,' she replied with difficulty. 'I'm all right. Look, you can see the legation walls from here. We have only a little way to go now. Hold each other's hands tightly.'

She was shaking, lost in a miasma of pain and bewilderment. For one brief, earth-shattering moment she had forgotten everything but her need of him. Had capitulated utterly. And he had spurned her. Icy indifference had replaced the heat of desire with such devastating speed that even now she could not quite believe it.

She pressed a hand to her burning lips. It would have been better if she had not seen him. If she had never seen him. If her heart had remained dormant and had not been awakened to the savagery of a passion that could never be fulfilled. The dust gouged up by the hooves of his horse settled. He was gone and she was left once again with only the memory of him. Sick at heart she turned and shepherded her small charges to safety.

There were so many people milling about the legation grounds that she was momentarily disconcerted. The spacious front pavilions were piled high with the luggage of those taking refuge. Swarms of Chinese servants hurried backwards and forwards, unloading handcarts piled high with furniture and household items. A heavy-bosomed Belgian lady was agitatedly supervising a dozen coolies as they carried her mahogany wardrobe and dressing-table into the legation and the room so kindly assigned to her by Lady MacDonald.

The cases of provisions littering the lawns were in stark contrast to the preciously hoarded bags of rice in the Anglican Mission. Imbeck's and Kierrulff's, the two shops in the Legation Quarter, had been rifled and stocks of tinned salmon and caviar and chicken in aspic were piled high. A cow wandered incongruously past a dozen cases of champagne and a small flock of sheep grazed where once only garden parties had taken place.

She forced her way through the crush, the children pressing close behind her, French, Russian and Belgian voices assaulting her ears on all sides.

'Olivia! Thank goodness! Letitia was most dreadfully

worried about you,' Lady Glencarty boomed, bearing down on her, majestic in purple silk. She flicked an eye over the children and then said peremptorily, 'Where is Sister Angelique?'

'She would not leave the Mission,' Olivia said, realizing with amazement that she was actually glad to see Lady Glencarty again.

Lady Glencarty's rocking-horse nostrils flared and her lips compressed into a tight line. 'Foolish woman,' she said gruffly. 'Are those children hungry?'

'Yes.'

'Then let's feed them.' She swept an elderly Russian aside, sent a knot of harassed looking diplomats scattering and with regal aplomb led Olivia and the children through the crowds and towards the legation with the ease of a Moses parting the Red Sea.

'What on earth is happening?' Olivia asked. 'Is the entire legation quarter taking shelter here?'

'Very nearly,' Lady Glencarty said tightly, 'It is the largest of the legations and isn't overlooked by the Tartar Wall. That means, of course, that it isn't immediately exposed to attack. The other legations will hold out for as long as possible but the plan is that they will be able to fall back here if it is necessary.'

As they shepherded the children indoors they were jostled and pushed by teams of coolies carrying provisions. 'Everything is chaotic,' she said bad-temperedly. 'Lady MacDonald has tried to ensure that different nationalities are quartered together. The stable house is full of Norwegians. The Russians have another of the outbuildings and the missionaries and the children evacuated from the American Mission are camping in the Legation's chapel. I think the chapel would be the best place to quarter your little band, though they're grossly overcrowded as it is.'

'There are more children on their way,' Olivia said as they squeezed into a crowded corridor. 'Doctor Sinclair is escorting them across the city at this very moment.'

'He'll have to be quick,' Lady Glencarty said grimly. 'Our ultimatum runs out at four this afternoon.'

Olivia caught her arm, halting her brisk stride. 'What ultimatum?' she asked, her heart beginning to slam in slow, thick strokes.

Lady Glencarty stared at her. 'I thought you had heard. I thought that was why you had left the Mission?'

'We've received no news, apart from the burning of the grandstand, for days. I came because it was obvious no troops were going to be sent to us and the burning and pillaging was only streets away.'

Lady Glencarty's heavily boned face was rigid with suppressed emotion. 'The Empress sent the ultimatum yesterday. It said that China could no longer protect us and that we must protect ourselves by leaving the city by four this afternoon.'

'But she has never had the slightest intention of protecting us!' Olivia cried, scandalized. 'And how can we possibly leave the city when the countryside is swarming with Boxers whose avowed intention is to kill us?'

'We can't,' Lady Glencarty said briefly. 'Though at the time the ultimatum arrived there were those who were foolish enough to believe that she would grant us safe conduct.'

'There are so many missionaries and converts in the city that the number of Peking carts needed to transport them would be over a mile long,' Olivia said sharply. 'It would be impossible. They would be slow-moving and unprotected. What answer did the diplomatic corps give the Empress?'

'It was decided that the German minister, Baron von Ketteler, would speak with the Empress's ministers this morning.' She paused, and Olivia could see that under her lavish dusting of powder, her face had taken on a sickly tinge.

'What happened?' she asked, filled with foreboding.

'He left the legation quarter in a sedan chair, indicating his official status and with two Chinese outriders. Fifteen minutes later the outriders galloped back, with the news that he had been killed. His assassin was a Manchu, a soldier in full uniform. Since then there has been no further talk of flight. Only of defending the legation quarter until help should arrive.'

'Are more troops on their way?' Olivia asked, appalled.

'They've been sent for, but no one knows when they will arrive. Telegraph and rail communications have been severed. Sir Claude has told us to prepare for a siege that could last for weeks, maybe months.'

They began to force their way once more down the noisy, crowded passageway. Olivia thought of the hundreds of converts milling the grounds. The scores of missionaries who had converged on the city. The diplomats and their families and their servants. 'Does anyone know how long the food and water supplies will last?'

Lady Glencarty shook her head. 'It's impossible to tell. We don't even know how many people are taking shelter here. Every last tin of food from Imbeck's and Kierrulff's has been purloined and the Hôtel de Pekin has provided us with what appears to be unlimited cases of champagne. If the water supply runs out we'll be able to have a fine party.'

She stopped at the entrance of what had previously been a games room and was now a makeshift and crowded dining-room. 'I'll see that the children are fed and taken to the chapel. Your uncle and aunt have been given rooms at the rear of the Legation.' She paused and then said gruffly, 'Sister Angelique should have come with you. She will stand no chance of survival in the west of the city. None at all.' Her eyes suspiciously bright, she turned and swept into the dining-room, the children following in her wake.

Olivia circumnavigated a group of soldiers, marvelling at the way adversity had altered Lady Glencarty for the better. Even Lewis would have been impressed by the concern she was showing for Sister Angelique. Her hands clenched, the nails digging deep into her palms.

Lewis. How was it possible not to think of him? He was

in her blood and her bones and she knew with a surge of despair that she would never be free of him. As she hurried up a flight of stairs and along the passageway leading to the rear of the building, she wondered if Pearl Moon and Rory were in the chapel with the American missionaries and their Christian converts. She determined that as soon as she had seen her aunt and uncle she would make enquiries to ascertain exactly where they were and ensure that they had enough food and adequate sleeping accommodation.

An empty chill seeped through her veins. Fate was indeed cruel. She had no desire to make the acquaintance of the woman she was so envious of, yet she had no choice. Ensuring that his wife and child were well cared for was the least she could do for the man she loved.

The door of her aunt's room was ajar and she could hear her asking plaintively how long it would be before they could leave the city. She sighed with impatience. Adversity had not had the same effect on Aunt Letitia as it had had on Lady Glencarty.

She stepped into the room and her aunt whirled round, crying out in surprise and relief.

'Olivia, oh Olivia! How could you *do* such a thing? My poor nerves have suffered most terribly. William, come quickly, Olivia has returned!'

She was hugged and kissed and then her uncle asked, his voice grave, 'What is the situation in the Tartar City?'

'It is very bad,' Olivia replied, a shiver running down her spine. 'The whole of the commercial quarter has been burnt to the ground, bands of Boxers are pillaging and looting and nowhere is safe.'

'Have you heard about the ultimatum?'

She nodded. 'Lady Glencarty told me.'

'The situation couldn't be worse. We have no way of knowing if troops are on their way to us, or what opposition they are meeting with. We have no heavy artillery and are dangerously low on ammunition.'

'And the refugees,' Letitia cried in consternation. 'Have

you seen how many of them there are, Olivia? They will all have to be fed and how we will manage, I don't know. It's my belief that we shall be reduced to eating the horses.'

'Hush, Letitia,' her husband remonstrated. 'Let Olivia tell us what is happening at the Mission.'

'Sister Angelique would not leave,' she said briefly. 'Doctor Sinclair is bringing the remaining children across the city and into the Legation.'

'Lewis Sinclair?' Letitia's plump face was ashen. 'Oh, dear, how terrible. He cannot know ...'

'Know what?' Olivia asked tightly, the blood beginning to pound in her temples.

Letitia's hands fluttered nervously. 'Sir Claude despatched a small group of men to the Peitang. They were to bring back Doctor Sinclair's son and other children. Only ...' She faltered at the terrifying expression on Olivia's face. 'Only it was not possible to reach the Peitang. Instead, the American Mission was relieved.'

'Bishop Favier is completely cut off,' Sir William said, his lean face gaunt. 'It was decided that lives could not be risked in trying to reach him'

A swirling blackness threatend to suck Olivia into its vortex. She fought to remain conscious. To remain upright.

'Do you mean that Lewis is bringing other children to safety when his own son is still in danger?' she asked, aghast.

'Conditions are chaotic,' her uncle said, unable to meet her eyes. 'It has not been possible to tell Sinclair.'

She stared at him for one long, unbelieving second and then spun on her heel, running for the door.

'Olivia!' her aunt shrieked, 'Come back! No one can reach the Peitang! Not even the troops!'

Olivia grasped the door, turning to look at her aunt. 'I can!' she said, her eyes feral.

'Olivia, wait!' Her uncle was crossing the room towards her. 'Letitia is right. What you are intending to do is madness. It's nothing short of suicide.'

'Does Mrs Sinclair know that Rory is still in the Peitang?' she asked, already determining her quickest route.

Her uncle looked at her blankly and then recollection filled his eyes. 'Mrs Sinclair is dead,' he said heavily. 'It happened some months ago in a Boxer attack on the village they were living in.'

The floor seemed to shelve up to meet her. She clung tightly to the doorknob.

'And we didn't know,' her aunt was saying, her words spilling over one another in her eagerness to impart the news. 'Sir Claude knew and everyone else seemed to know, but we didn't, not until after Doctor Sinclair came here and ... and ...' She faltered, seeing too late where her chatter was leading her.

'Why did he come to the house?' Olivia asked, her voice beating against her ears, high and brittle.

Letitia looked helplessly at her husband and then, as he remained silent, said nervously, 'He wished to speak to you Olivia. He wished to ask for your hand in marriage.'

Olivia gave a small cry that sounded as if it had been torn from her heart and her uncle said awkwardly, 'Your aunt told him that you were soon to marry Phillippe. She did it for the best. She thought that Doctor Sinclair's wife was alive and ...'

Olivia did not wait to hear any more. She had heard all that she needed. At last she understood. Everything was clear. Only one more thing was necessary. To rescue Rory and bring him to the safety of the Legation.

Ten

The corridor was crammed with nervous, hysterical ladies searching for suitable material with which to make sandbags. Doors opened on to rooms where sewing machines whirred frantically. She caught a glimpse of Lady MacDonald, her best curtains clutched against her bosom as she hurried with them into one of the hastily converted sewing-rooms. Other ladies were scurrying back and forth with monogrammed pillowcases and silk pyjamas and bales and bales of exquisite Chinese brocade.

She darted between them, running feverishly towards the head of the stairs. A score of Chinese schoolgirls, their meagre belongings clasped in their arms, were struggling upwards against a tide of coolies pushing their way down to retrieve more of the diplomatic ladies' possessions. It was nearly impossible to move and Olivia had to push and squeeze her way between the throng, her heart pounding.

There were only four hours before the ultimatum expired. When it did so, not only Boxers would descend in full force. They would be augmented by the Empress's troops. By Manchu Bannermen with modern weapons. By General Tung Fu-hsiang's Kansu warriors. As she struggled through the crowds massing the entrance hall she knew that if she found herself on the streets at four o'clock she would have to remain there. The walls surrounding the Legation compound would be barricaded, the gates so heavily defended that no one would be able to pass through.

Even now, as she hurried out into the gardens, she knew

with a flare of panic that leaving the Legation would not be easy. The lawn was crowded with soldiers and civilians. The hectic activity that had been taking place when she had entered had now been stepped up to a pitch of frantic turmoil. Sandbags were being hauled up on to walls; trenches were being dug; fire buckets replenished. And the gates were under heavy guard.

She hovered twenty or thirty yards away, knowing full well that she would be refused permission to pass. From the west side of the city came the noise of firecrackers and a cacophony of horns and bugles. She wondered if it were the Boxers celebrating their destruction of the missions and shops and homes of the Christian Chinese and dug her nails into her palms.

She *had* to leave the compound. There were no soldiers to help defend the Peitang. Rory could not be left to die, while his father, believing him to be in the legation, saved the lives of others.

She moved forward determinedly and then caught her breath. The soldiers were hastily unbarring the gate. She saw an overloaded cart approach creakily, heard the firing from beyond, and did not hesitate. Her heart pounding, she raced to the gate and as the soldiers struggled with the heavy wooden bars defending it, squeezed past the cart and out into the street.

She could hear them shouting furiously after her, but she did not pause. Her heart hammering crazily, she ran furiously in the direction of Legation Street. The heat was no longer heavy and still; a north wind from the Gobi Desert was blowing sand down into the city and she longed for a scarf to cover her nose and mouth. More fiercely still, as she battled her way through the crowds, she longed for Lewis's pistol.

The smell of fear was everywhere. Chinese, fleeing from the destruction in the west of the city, could find no shelter in the east. No one knew where the roaming bands of Boxers were. Where they would strike next. Olivia pushed onwards down Legation Street, her aunt's words singing in her ears. Lewis loved her! He had come to the house to ask for her hand in marriage! She had only to see him again for all the misunderstandings to be over. The future stretched before her, clear and shining. She would be Lewis's wife, a mother to Rory. They would be a family and would never be separated again. Never.

In the great wide thoroughfare bisecting the city she halted abruptly. The Chien Men, the huge, one-hundred-feet high, triple-tiered central gate was nothing but a smoking, blackened husk. The whole city was being destroyed, not just the Christian quarter and she wondered if the Empress Dowager, immured in the heart of her Summer Palace, either knew or cared.

The Peitang was over two miles away and unlike the other cathedrals and missions, was not in the Tartar City but within the blind, purple-stained walls of the Imperial City. Peking carts veered wildly past, their dark blue hoods flapping, their drivers exhorting the horses to even greater speeds.

She stepped hastily out of the way, forging relentlessly through the crush towards the massive, castellated Tien An Men Gate. Tien An Men meant the Gate of Heavenly Peace, but there was nothing heavenly or peaceful about the ragged, squalid and diseased crowds surging beneath its ornate wooden eaves.

The sound of horns and bugles that she had heard earlier now became louder and the Chinese scrambled frantically out of the way as a squadron of cavalry burst into the street. For a second Olivia's heart leapt and she almost expected to see Lewis's black stallion at their head, but then she, too, pressed herself into the throng so that she should not be noticed.

The cavalry were not European. They were white-turbanned, their waving banners scarlet and black and the weapons that they flaunted were modern Mausers. Olivia saw their weather-beaten, hardened faces as they rode past and guessed that they were General Tung Fu-hsiang's famous Kansu warriors.

Were they riding out towards the legations? Were they going to attack before the stated hour of four o'clock? Determination hardened within her. There could be no going back now. She could only go onward, to the Peitang and to Rory.

Mat-shed booths clustered three deep in the shadow of the high and purple walls and she ran past them, gasping for breath. She was nearly there. Already she could see the soaring stone façade of the Cathedral as it dwarfed the low, surrounding buildings. She wondered how effectively Bishop Favier and his priests had barricaded themselves and just how difficult it would be to gain entry, refusing to even think that she might not be able to do so.

The hot, dry wind carried with it the smell of smoke and her thoughts turned to the Anglican Mission and Sister Angelique, and then there were cries of terror and the crowd in front of her began to surge backwards, stampeding in terror.

She caught a glimpse of scarlet. Of lethal swords brandished high; orgiastic howls of '*Sha! Sha!*' thundered in her ears and then she was knocked to the ground as the fleeing peasants sought to escape the wave after wave of Boxers, leaping and charging down on them.

Her hands were splayed on the dust-beaten earth. She was trodden on, kicked. Vainly she tried to struggle to her feet and was knocked once more to the ground.

A Chinese ran past her, blood streaming copiously from a cut on his head. A sob rose in her throat. She didn't want to die in the street. To die before she had been able to tell Lewis that she loved him. She clenched her fists, her eyes bright. She would *not* do so! The mat-shed booths and shops were only yards away. She scrambled to her hands and knees and then ran determinedly for the nearest, cavernous door.

Seconds later she was imprisoned in stinking,

claustrophobic darkness. The pounding, running feet outside shook the makeshift walls and roof. She was aware of other people in close proximity, their breathing harsh and heavy. She closed her eyes as the sounds from outside became more hideous and the smell of blood fouled the air.

It would take only one lighted brand to be tossed on the roof and she would be burned alive with people she could not even see. She pressed her hands on the rough wood behind her, praying for the horror to be over. The door rattled and the dark, heavy shape of a body slid sickeningly down against it. After what seemed an eternity the shouts and cries grew fainter until at last there was silence.

She looked around, her eyes adjusting to the darkness. An old man was crouched in one corner, a woman at his side. They were gazing at her with wide-eyed horror, as if she were responsible for the massacre on their doorstep.

'I think they've gone,' she said at last, unsteadily.

The old man muttered unintelligibly, showing no desire to leave his corner. The woman stood up nervously.

'Do you speak English?' Olivia asked, wondering how she was going to open the door with the weight of the body against it. Her question was met by a look of blankness. She sighed. 'The door,' she said, tapping the wood behind her. 'Please help me to open it.'

She had to get outside. She could not stay like a cornered rat, hiding in the gloom until the roof above her head was ignited by cinders. For a little while only the dead and the dying would be in the streets outside. It would take her ten minutes, perhaps less, to reach the Cathedral. If she did not go now, she might not have another chance.

She put her shoulder to the door and pushed. It opened a little way and more light penetrated the darkness, but the body slumped across it prevented it from opening enough to allow her to step outside.

'The door,' she repeated impatiently to the watching peasant woman. Hesitantly the dark-clad figure stepped forward. Olivia leaned her shoulder against the wood. 'I need you to push,' she said, 'like this.'

The woman nodded and as the old man continued to mutter incoherently, she leaned her weight against the door.

'That's right,' said Olivia gratefully. 'Now push!' This time the door opened wider. The disturbed body toppled sideways and with a shiver of distaste Olivia lifted up her skirt and stepped over it and into the street.

At the sight that met her eyes she pressed her hands against her mouth. The dead lay with the dying, the parched earth saturated with blood. Survivors were edging from darkened doorways, searching for friends and relatives and a low keening noise filled the air, so terrible that she knew she would never be able to forget it. Despairingly she began to stumble once more in the direction of the Cathedral, filled with terror at the thought of what she might find there.

More horsemen galloped into the street, this time not General Tung Fu-hsiang's warriors but barbarically splendid Manchu Bannermen. They rode uncaringly over the dead and injured, banners waving high. They were ready for war, loaded with rifles and carbines, and heading towards the Legation Quarter. Hardly daring to breathe, she watched them as they clattered by. The Boxers were now the least of their troubles. The Empress Dowager had come out in open support of the rebels, as Lewis had said she would, and now it was not only swords and lances they had to fight, but trained soldiers and modern weapons as well.

Wave after wave of them surged down the street, the vivid colours of their jackets and the emblems depicted on them searing the eye. Their trousers were scarlet, embroidered with huge black dragons. The banners they carried were gold and crimson, blue and yellow, triangular and square, a blazing jumble of colours and shapes. In their wake ran foot soldiers, their swords contrasting sharply with the modern carbines slung across the backs of the cavalry. There were hundreds of them. A whole army riding out to attack a compound three-quarters of a mile square, defended only by pyjama silk and damask-curtained sandbags.

The minutes ticked by and still they came and Olivia knew with dreadful certainty that she would not be able to enter the Legation Quarter again. It would be completely circled by General Tung Fu-hsiang's warriors and Manchu Bannermen. If the Peitang doors were closed against her, there would be nowhere she could go. Nowhere she could hide.

The last of the soldiery rode by and she was grateful for the concealing clouds of dust gouged up by the horses' hooves. As the crowd surged once more into the street she merged with them but for every inch of headway she made, she was knocked back a yard. The Peitang's ornate Gothic façade soared before her but she could not reach the walls surrounding it, much less its doors.

The air was now thick with smoke as fresh fires broke out and ash rained down on her hair and shoulders. Again and again she tried to push her way forward, only to be jostled further and further back. Panic began to well up in her. There was only an hour or so before the ultimatum ran out. Before not only the Boxers, but the troops began a full-scale attack. The milling peasants in the streets and squares around the Peitang would be replaced by Manchu Bannermen and she would either be killed in the crush or shot by a Chinese bullet. If only she could see another European face! But the Peitang's doors and gates were closed as the crowd surrounding it became increasingly hostile, blaming its occupants for the carnage they were suffering.

The pressure of bodies on all sides was stifling. She tried with fresh determination to force her way through the eddying mass and a pig-tailed Chinese turned on her savagely.

'*Kuie-tzu*!' he hissed, 'Foreign devil!' From all around her the cry was taken up and suddenly she was no longer part of the crowd but a creature apart. An object for their hatred.

'*Kuie-tzu! Kuie-tzu!*' A sea of ferocious faces chanted, and then her hair was seized and a nightmare forest of hands grabbed her. Her hair tumbled from its pins; pearl buttons were torn from her blouse, and she screamed loud and high.

She didn't see the Peking cart being driven savagely through the crowds towards the Cathedral. Didn't see its driver rein in sharply as the cries of '*Foreign devil!*' filled the air. She was fighting for her life – kicking, scratching, biting, as the hate-crazed crowd tried to tear her limb from limb.

She could no longer see clearly. Everything was a blood-red haze. She could feel herself being pressed down, down, and then, as she lashed out vainly with her small booted feet, she was aware that the baying yells of those attacking her had changed into cries of pain and outrage. A human whirlwind had descended on them, parting them like a scythe in a sea of corn. She could see the black tumble of his hair, the raging blaze in his eyes, his white-hot fury as he hurled first one pig-tailed Chinese over the heads of the crowd, and then another.

'*Lewis!*' She could barely breathe, scarcely stand. His arm was around her waist, she could hear the slam of his heart, feel the heat of his body.

'*What the devil,*' he asked savagely as he forced a way through the still frantically shouting Chinese, '*do you think you are doing?*'

She half fell against the Peking cart. 'Rory isn't in the British Legation. He's still in the Peitang,' she gasped as he picked her up in his uninjured arm and threw her bodily into the rear of the blue cloth-covered cart.

'I know,' he hurled back at her. 'Hold tight.'

The cart lurched into movement. The shouts intensified and she could smell the hatred and sweat of the Chinese hemming them in on all sides. She gripped the low wooden sides as Lewis drove roughshod through their midst. She

could hear him shouting in English. Hear a heavily
accented, European voice bellowing in reply and then they
were hurtling into the Cathedral's compound and Lewis
was swinging her down from the cart. As they raced
towards the Cathedral's great doors they were flung open
by a young French naval officer. '*Hurry!*' he yelled at them.
'*Vite! Vite!*' and then bullets whizzed over their heads,
ploughing into the ground and ricocheting off the
Cathedral's stone-grey façade.

With a savage expletive Lewis seized hold of her, his arm
so tight around her waist that she was almost lifted off her
feet. Bullets spat around them, cannon fire thundered
deafeningly and then the Cathedral's massive door
slammed shut behind them and as Olivia half fell against
him, gasping for breath, Lewis said tersely to the
Frenchman.

'How many men have you?'

'Two officers and forty-one French and Italian sailors.'

'And refugees?'

'Somewhere between three and four thousand. Less than
a hundred are European. There are twenty-two Sisters of
Charity, a handful of priests ... and ourselves.'

Lewis swore softly beneath his breath. She wanted to
take him in her arms. To tell him then and there that she
loved him. That she had no intention of marrying Phillippe
Casanaeve. That it was him that she wanted to marry. His
jaw was granite-hard, his eyes narrow, and she remained
silent, knowing that now was not the time nor the place to
speak to him.

There was another volley of gunfire, loud and sustained
and he turned to her, his face grim.

'Tell Bishop Favier that I am here. And Rory,' and then
he spun on his heel, running to a vantage point, his pistol in
his hand, the young Frenchman in his wake.

Rory. She had to find him. Had to reassure him that his
father was safe. And she had to discover what food and
medical supplies there were. How long they could survive

under siege.

'Not very long,' Bishop Favier said to her gravely. 'I laid in a substantial store of supplies, fearing that this was what would happen, but I did not foresee the very great number of refugees who would seek shelter here. We have rice, beans and millet, but little else.'

Olivia thought wryly of the vast cornucopia ransacked from Imbeck's and Kierrulff's; of the champagne and tinned salmon, and reflected that the siege at the Cathedral was going to be far different from the siege at the Legation.

'Where is Rory?' she asked, picking up a crying toddler and soothing it.

'In the dispensary, helping the Sisters.' He hesitated for a moment and then said, 'Poor child. You know, of course, that he lost his mother some months ago? It was a terrible tragedy. His father's life and his own have been very bleak since she died.'

A nun hurried towards him, seeking his advice, and Olivia turned and made her way quickly to the chapel. Lewis's life had indeed been bleak when she had first met him, but when the siege they were living under was over, she was determined that it would be bleak no more. A man who had loved once steadfastly and truly was capable of loving just as deeply again. And of having that love returned in full measure.

She entered the crowded dispensary and did not have to ask for Rory. His curly black hair was as distinctive as his father's. He was rolling bandages with great zest and when he saw her, his eyes widened in surprise and pleasure.

'What are you doing here?' he asked in a tone much like his father's.

Olivia smiled. It seemed as if she was going to be answerable in the future to not just one forceful male, but two.

'I came here to see you. Your father is here as well.'

Rory pushed the bandages to one side and scrambled to

his feet. 'Where is he? Can I see him?'

'Not just now,' Olivia replied, picking up one of the linen strips he had discarded, and rolling it neatly. 'The Empress Dowager has sent her soldiers to help the Boxers and they are attacking both the Legation Quarter and the Cathedral. Your father is going to be very busy until the siege ends.'

'I wish I could fight!' the small figure at her side said passionately. 'It's boring staying here rolling bandages.'

'Then come with me,' Olivia said, holding out her hand. 'I'm going to help the sisters nurse the sick and I could do with a good assistant.'

'There'll be injured people too,' Rory said, his hand slipping easily into hers. 'I don't mind the sight of blood ...' He faltered and then said a little tremulously, 'As long as it isn't Papa's blood, that is.'

'It won't be,' Olivia said fiercely. 'We won't let it be.'

His hand squeezed hers. 'You're awfully nice,' he said warmly. 'I'm glad that you've come.'

Olivia's throat tightened as she gazed down at the head of rumpled curls. 'So am I, Rory,' she said, aware that he had captured her heart just as surely and irrevocably as his father had done.

From that point on the days and nights merged into one. The firing from outside was incessant, a constant barrage that set the nerves on edge and made all but the most exhausted sleep impossible.

'If only it would rain,' a Sister of Mercy said to her at the end of the first, long week. 'It's so hot. Perhaps rain would calm the Boxers.'

'And calm us,' Olivia agreed wholeheartedly, her blouse and skirt damp with sweat as she helped bind up a deep sword slash that one of the Italian sailors had sustained.

The previous night he had been a member of a sortie led by Paul Henry, the young French officer, and Lewis, which had successfully and very daringly captured one of the enemy's cannons. Now she could hear it blasting in retaliation against the artillery fire raining down on them.

The soldier groaned, his brow hot, and Olivia prayed that he would not develop a fever.

There had been no news from outside. It was impossible to tell what was happening at the legations. A messenger that had been sent out had been decapitated and his head displayed triumphantly before the main gate. Since then there had been no further attempts to make contact with the outside world.

Everyone worked: the sisters, the Chinese converts, the children. Ammunition was limited and carefully rationed, and the Chinese converts had been armed with pikes and trained as lookouts. The only time she saw Lewis was when he snatched a few hours' sleep, throwing himself on to a pallet on the floor, his face grim, the smell of cordite on his hands and clothes.

The lack of food was causing almost as much concern as the savage and combined onslaughts of Manchu Bannermen and Boxers. The daily food ration for each adult was a pound of rice, beans or millet, and it was obvious that as the siege continued it would have to be reduced drastically.

Rory refused to be separated from her. He acted as her auxiliary, at her side constantly in the hospital and the children's crèche. At night his pallet was next to hers and he would pray solemnly for his father and wish again and again that he was old enough to fight.

Bishop Favier's serenity was unassailable and Olivia drew deep strength from it as one hideous day followed another. Occasionally, when tiredness and hunger and revulsion at the sight of the injuries she had to tend nearly overcame her, she would close her eyes and remember the sight of the hoopoe swooping down low over the serried ranks of pines. It was possible, if she kept very still, to recapture the feel of the sun on her face and the pleasure she had felt at being in China. She wondered if that pleasure would ever be recaptured or if it would be tainted for good by the sights she was now witnessing.

'What are you thinking of?' Rory asked her curiously one day as she closed her eyes in search of inner strength.

She smiled. 'Of a hoopoe. It's the last thing I can remember of peace and tranquillity. I thought it very beautiful, and China beautiful as well.'

Rory's face was wistful. 'China *is* beautiful. In Shansi there are great high mountains and huge sweeping rivers, and wild ponies and crested pheasants.'

'Then we must remember those things and not begin thinking that this is all there is of China,' Olivia said as cannon fire battered the Peitang's stone walls.

'I keep thinking of my father,' Rory said unhappily. 'I'm sure he isn't careful. I heard him discussing the possibility of capturing another cannon.'

Olivia felt her blood chill. She, too, was certain that Lewis was far from careful. She looked wearily around her at the sick. They lay on mattresses packed close together on the floor. The windows had been sandbagged and the heat was unbearable. They had no anaesthetic, very little antiseptic, and had been reduced to using sawdust as a dressing for the wounds. Three or four shells burst deafeningly overhead but there was no answering fire. Ammunition was so short that not a round was fired unless it was certain to find a mark.

She wondered what would happen when the last of their ammunition was gone. How would they hold off the Boxers then? With pikes and with their bare hands? The children's faces had become sad and wizened, waxen through lack of food. One of the converts had shown her how to make a soup out of the roots of dahlias and lilies and she dug in the compound grounds for them daily, braving rifle and shellfire to do so.

Her glimpses of Lewis were precious and fleeting. His face had become leaner, the strong-boned nose even more hawklike. The fearlessness and daring she had first sensed in him was now given full rein.

Together with the courageous Paul Henry, he fought

tirelessly, scorning to remain behind the barricades when recklessness would inflict punishment on their attackers. When she could be spared from the sick-beds she would dart across the open compound between the outbuildings, the dispensary, the chapel, the stores and stables, and take him his precious rations. Too often she was beaten back by the intensity of the firing and she would know that somewhere in the smoke and dust he was striving to knock out one of the cannons that were trained on the Peitang. That he was doing so hungry and tired and without water. Occasionally, when he slithered down from the walls, his eyes would meet hers, burning with fury at the helplessness of their position and with concern for her as her cheekbones became more hollow, the shadows beneath her eyes darker.

Once, when she had handed him his precious allowance of water, their hands had touched and she had gasped aloud. He had sucked in his breath, the air between them throbbing with tension as he said her name thickly, and then a shell burst terrifyingly close and he had yelled at her to take cover.

She had not seen him again for forty-eight hours. Now, as she thought of him leading a sortie to capture another of the enemy's cannons, she knew that she had to speak to him.

'I'm going to take some rations to the wall,' she said to a nearby Sister of Mercy. 'The young sailor in the far corner needs a new dressing on his leg. Bishop Favier suggested we use powdered peat this time instead of sawdust.'

As she turned to leave the stifling, fly-filled room, one of the Italians charged in on them, sweat pouring down his face. 'The Boxers have blasted a way through the perimeter wall! They're pouring over in hundreds! Get sticks, knives, anything!'

The gentle-faced Sister of Mercy to whom Olivia had been talking, seized a cane and began to run. Olivia raced behind her, a hastily snatched knife in her hand.

'The children!' she prayed aloud. 'Please, Lord, don't let them kill the children!'

The tumult and confusion in the compound was deafening. The Chinese converts armed only with their rudely made pikes, were charging in their hundreds to halt the swarming, red-robed figures leaping over the breached wall. She could see the distinctive figure of Paul Henry fighting furiously against the invading mob, and as a cloud of cannon smoke cleared, she could see Lewis too.

Bullets rained over her head, spitting into the ground. With every able-bodied man defending the breach the rest of the perimeter walls were dangerously open to attack and to her horror she saw a crazed Boxer leap down on to the roof of the stable, a burning brand in his hand. She cried out, calling to the sailors who were feverishly rolling the captured cannon into a firing position. As she did so, a small, dark figure ran furiously forward, running and bounding across the compound and its fury of bullets, charging head-first towards the stable.

'*Rory!*' she shrieked, her voice drowned by the pandemonium around her.

He didn't halt. Didn't waver. The burning brand was thrust deep in the roof of the stable, and then the Boxer prepared to leap and Rory raced onwards, fists clenched, face set.

She didn't know that she could move so fast. She streaked towards the stable, the blood pounding in her ears, her heartbeat slamming high in her throat. The Boxer leapt from the roof with a triumphant howl, knocking Rory flat on his back, rolling over and over with him amid clouds of choking dust. She could see the tiny hands pummelling the red-garbed shoulders, see the curved blade of the Boxer's knife as he drew it from his sash and raised it high over Rory's throat. She knew she was shouting, screaming dementedly, and then her own knife plunged deep between the Boxer's shoulders and Rory was scrambling free. She snatched up his hand, pulling him from under the ghastly weight, and then a bullet whined through the air, hitting her shoulder, spinning her backwards.

She saw Rory's mouth widen in horror, felt the dark, sticky heat of her own blood, and then colour and sounds zigzagged hideously and she spiralled down into darkness, unable even to say Lewis's name.

Eleven

Someone was holding her, carrying her in strong arms. Consciousness fluttered near and fled in a sea of pain. She could hear his voice, raw with urgency. She fought her way up through clinging darkness and her eyelids flickered open.

'Olivia! Olivia, can you hear me?'

She tried to smile reassuringly and his hand tightened on hers, filling her with warmth.

'Thank God,' he said, his voice cracking with relief.

She was lying on a mattress on the floor of the chapel. There was a dull roar in her ears and over and above it the sound of shouting and rifle fire.

'The wall,' she whispered, her eyes widening in alarm.

'It's safe. We fought them back and the wall has been barricaded.' He leaned towards her, 'Olivia, listen to me. You have a bullet deep in your shoulder.' His eyes held hers steadily. 'You've lost a lot of blood, Olivia. It has to come out.'

She nodded. She knew what he was saying. That he had no anaesthetic, no antiseptic. She could feel the darkness rolling over her in waves, and this time she welcomed it. She was so tired. So very tired.

There was a moment of vivid, searing pain that tore her cruelly into consciousness. Her back arched and she cried aloud, aware of restraining hands holding her down; of Sisters' white coifs as they stood over her; of Lewis's dark hair and of his fingers working swiftly and deftly. Pain zigzagged through her and she clenched her teeth, fixing her eyes on the ceiling, concentrating with fierce intensity on a hoopoe swooping low into a distant valley.

She knew that he had finished, that he was talking to her and she knew the words that she wanted to say but they would not come. There was only the merciful darkness and she floated down into it, her mind and her heart whispering his name, her lips silent.

Sometimes, when she woke, he was not there. There was noise and gunfire and stifling heat, and Rory, his small hand holding hers tightly. She would sink back into oblivion, believing that she was high in the hills, riding her horse through the pine woods, Lewis beside her, his dark eyes alight with laughter and love.

'Lewis ...' she whispered longingly, 'Lewis ...'

'I'm here.' His voice was gentle. He was sponging her forehead and as she looked up into his face, so dearly familiar, so strong and so kind, she knew that she might be dying and that she had still not told him that she loved him.

Weakly she raised her hand and touched his arm. 'Lewis, I want to talk to you.'

'Later Olivia. You are very weak. Try and drink some water.'

She sipped at the warm, unpalatable liquid that he held to her mouth and then motioned for him to take it away. The darkness would come back and then it would be too late.

He was kneeling beside her on one knee and she covered his hand with both of hers.

'Do you remember when you visited me at my uncle's and Aunt Letitia would not let you see me? She told you that I was out with Phillippe.'

A shadow crossed his eyes and his jaw tightened imperceptibly. He nodded.

A smile touched the corners of her mouth. 'You wanted to ask me a question,' she said softly, all the love she felt for him in her voice and in her eyes.

In the distance she could hear the incessant rattle of gunfire and the explosion of shells but it seemed very quiet in the chapel. It was as if there were no one else in the world. Only herself and Lewis.

'The answer would have been yes,' she said, joy flooding through her as she saw his face change. Saw it become brilliant with an expression of such fierce love that it was transfigured.

He groaned, bending his head to hers, his lips touching her temples, her eyelids, her mouth. 'I love you,' he whispered hoarsely. 'You are my heart, my body, my soul.' He pressed her hand to his mouth and she could feel the dizzying blackness surging up to claim her. But only for a little while. Only until her body had recovered its strength. For when it did, she was marrying Lewis.

'I love you,' she whispered, her eyes closing. 'I shall always love you, Lewis.'

The bombardment on the Cathedral continued. The meagre daily food ration was reduced by a third and leaves from the trees were added to the dahlia and lily soup. On the eighteenth of July, a week after she had been shot, the Boxers exploded a mine under one of the compound buildings, killing over fifty, and injuring hundreds more. She barely saw Lewis. She doubted if he slept at all. There were limbs to amputate. Dead to be buried. Rory remained steadfastly at her side, swatting away the tormenting flies, his small face lean from hunger and fatigue.

Three weeks later the buoyant Paul Henry was killed, a bullet through his throat. Olivia was no longer in the chapel. Despite Lewis's protests, she had dragged herself to her feet and was once more in the crèche, helping nurse the children.

She had known the instant that he entered the crèche that something terrible had happened. 'Paul is dead,' he had said, his voice hard and bitter, perspiration soaking the tattered remnants of his shirt. She had held him close, sharing his grief. Paul Henry had been a heroic figure. His zest had sustained them. His contempt for danger had communicated itself to his men and it was unthinkable that he would no longer be harrying them to not only defend the Peitang but to attack fearlessly at every possible opportunity.

When he was buried she had wept, and it was that night that Lewis spoke to her for the first time about Pearl Moon.

'My parents found her abandoned outside the walls of the village they were proselytizing,' he said, his arm around her shoulders as the fighting lulled and they sat on the ground in the darkness, their backs resting against the hard heat of the dispensary wall. 'She was brought up as my sister and I suppose, when I was a child, that was how I loved her.' He paused, saying gently, 'Later that changed. I loved her and I married her, and despite the narrow-minded attitude of my fellow Europeans, we were very happy.' He turned slightly, tilting her chin with his fingers so that he could see the pale oval of her face. 'It was a happiness that I shall never forget and shall never want to forget. I thought when she died that I would never be happy again.'

He was silent for a little while and then he said quietly, 'It was Pearl Moon who taught me how to love and she taught me well. She taught me to cherish it and care for it and she taught me to recognize it. Our life together will be richer for what she bequeathed to me, Olivia.' He kissed her and her eyes were wet with tears. Pearl Moon's gift to them was one without price and one she would cherish always.

The siege dragged horrendously on into its seventh week. Funerals now took place every day and Bishop Favier was emaciated and hollow-eyed. As Olivia prepared yet another body for burial, she wondered if her aunt and uncle were still alive. If Sister Angelique had survived and Lan Kuei and her baby. She pressed a hand into her aching back. The not knowing was the worst part. They could hear artillery fire taking place in other parts of the city, but could see nothing. The world outside the compound walls had ceased to exist. Somewhere, presumably, were governments anxious for their safety. Troops who could relieve them. But where they were and what they were doing, no one had even the strength to conjecture.

On the tenth of August the last of the rice was set aside for the fighting men. It seemed that the end could be only days or hours away, yet when the Boxers triumphantly detonated a bomb beneath the Peitang's crèche, everyone, converts, children, the sick, were galvanized into furious action. There was no thought of capitulation, only of frenzied rescue-work and the grim determination that they would never give in. Never.

The next day, as they searched for dahlia roots in the grounds of the compound, Rory said suddenly, 'Can you hear gunfire, Olivia?'

'I've heard nothing else for eight weeks,' Olivia said wryly, wishing that the pain behind her eyes would ease.

'I know, but this is different. Listen.'

She leaned back on her heels and listened. The noise was like dull thunder, heavy and merciless, and then, very faintly, a bugle sounded *La Casquette du Père Bugeaud*.

'It's the relief force!' she gasped, scrambling to her feet. 'They must be at the gates!'

Others too had heard the bugle. The Boxers' standards had vanished from the walls of the Imperial City. For the first time in eight weeks they were no longer under fire.

'It's over!' The shout went up. 'The relief forces are coming! It's *over*!'

She grabbed Rory's hand, running to find Lewis, her eyes shining, her pain and hunger forgotten.

'He's there!' Rory cried as a hard-muscled figure leapt agilely down from the perimeter wall. 'Papa! Papa! It's over!'

He hurtled towards Lewis who caught him and swung him high in his arms, hugging him tight. She ran towards them and he set Rory down, opening his arms wide, white teeth flashing in his lean, sun-burned face.

'For us, it's the beginning,' he said, his dark eyes gleaming as his arms closed around her, his mouth coming down on hers hard and long as cheers and hurrahs rang out for the advancing troops.

Epilogue

It was September. Rain had cooled the dust-parched earth. The savage red-garbed hordes had melted away with the same rapidity with which they had appeared. In the countryside life went on, grim and feudal, as it had for centuries. The gossip in the small villages dotted about North China's great plain no longer revolved around Boxers, but speculated on the whereabouts of the Empress Dowager.

In Peking, the streets, houses and shops were devastated, but trees flowered amidst broken walls, sunlight filled empty courtyards and the silence, after the weeks of barbaric howling, was sweet. The great city gates were open, guarded only by international troops, and the palace in the Forbidden City was empty, for Empress Tzu-hsi had fled.

'Queen Victoria would never have done such a thing,' Lady Glencarty said to Letitia Harland as they strolled the Legation lawns amidst a throng of elegantly dressed wedding guests.

'I should think not!' Letitia said, deeply shocked. 'Queen Victoria would never have allowed the siege to take place in the first place!'

Lady Glencarty smiled maliciously. 'How she must have hated it. Changing out of those splendid robes of hers and dressing in coarse blue cotton like a peasant.'

'And cutting those long, long fingernails short and riding out of the city, hidden in a Peking cart. I wonder where she is now. Do you think that she will return?'

'Oh, she'll return,' Lady Glencarty said darkly. 'But I shall not be here when she does, thank goodness. I leave for England in ten days' time.'

'Does Sister Angelique travel with you?' Letitia asked, thinking how pretty the parasols looked and how charming Lady MacDonald's peach silk dress was with its tiers of ruffles at the hem.

Lady Glencarty frowned slightly. 'Yes, and of necessity we shall have to travel slowly. She is still terribly emaciated. It is a miracle that she is alive at all.'

'It is a miracle that *any* of us are alive,' Letitia said with a shudder. 'I cannot understand why Olivia should be so thrilled at the prospect of remaining in China. I am sure that she and Lewis could have settled most happily in Bath.'

Lady Glencarty shook her head. 'No,' she said firmly. 'Never. They have both succumbed to the strange fascination that China so often exerts over the European mind. Lewis did so long ago.' She paused as Lewis and Olivia approached, their arms lovingly linked as they greeted their guests. Lowering her voice she continued, 'Perhaps Olivia did so when she met him, perhaps before. Who is to say? It is enough that she has succumbed totally now and that her future lies here, in China, with the man she loves.'

Letitia sighed and gazed tenderly at the bridal pair. Olivia's cloud of soft dark hair was swept high, held in place by ivory combs etched in gold. Her gown was of beige Chantilly lace, her elbow-length gloves of matching silk. Lewis had bent his dark head close to hers and she was laughing up at him, her gentian-blue eyes alight with love.

'It was a beautiful wedding,' Letitia said, dabbing her eyes with a lace-edged handkerchief. 'And Bishop Favier was right in wanting to perform it in his half-destroyed cathedral. It was a wonderful way to reaffirm faith in the future.'

Lewis and Olivia neared them and Letitia felt her throat tighten and wondered how she could ever have thought Lewis unapproachable and forbidding. He was smiling down at her, his dark eyes affectionate.

'No tears, Letitia, please.'

'No Lewis, of course not,' she said, her eyes still overly bright. 'It's just that I'm so happy and Olivia looks so beautiful and ... Oh dear. I *am* going to cry. I can't help it.'

'What you need, Letitia,' Lady Glencarty said bracingly, 'Is more champagne.'

Letitia nodded and Olivia said mischievously, 'It's a wonder there's any left. Uncle William tells me that you drank nothing else all through the siege.'

'I couldn't, Olivia.' Her aunt said defensively, 'There was not enough water and I was *obliged* to drink champagne.'

Olivia hugged her tight, kissing her cheek. 'Darling Aunt Letitia, may you *always* drink champagne!'

Beyond the trees, in the clear blue sky, a bird swooped low and Olivia caught her breath, her hand tightening in her husband's. 'Look Lewis,' she whispered, moving away from her aunt and Lady Glencarty, 'Can you see?'

The September sun gleamed on the gaudily coloured wings, the proud defiant crest and long, curved beak.

'A hoopoe,' Lewis said softly, his arms closing around her.

The bird flew high once more, wheeling in a graceful circle above their heads.

She lifted her face to his, her eyes radiant. 'It's promising us happiness, Lewis.'

Tenderly he traced the delicate outline of her face with the tip of his finger. The high, pure cheekbone; the straight, perfect nose; the soft, sensuous curve of her lips.

'We shall always be happy, my love,' he said, his rich, smoke-dark voice deep with the love he felt for her.

Her body curved yieldingly against his. 'Always,' she murmured, a low sigh in her throat, her heart filled with joy as she raised her face for his kiss.